THE GREAT AWAKENING

Fig. 1. Hieronymus Bosch, *Ship of Fools* (1490–1500)

First published in 2020 by punctum books, Earth, Milky Way.
https://punctumbooks.com

ISBN-13: 978-1-953035-08-0 (print)
ISBN-13: 978-1-953035-09-7 (ePDF)

DOI: 10.21983/P3.0285.1.00

LCCN: 2020945724
Library of Congress Cataloging Data is available from the Library of Congress

Copy Editing: Lucy Barnes
Book Design: Vincent W.J. van Gerven Oei

spontaneous acts of scholarly combustion

HIC SVNT MONSTRA

The Great Awakening

New Modes of Life amidst Capitalist Ruins

Edited by Anna Grear & David Bollier

p.

Contents

Acknowledgments

This book has its origins in our collaborations with Professor Burns H. Weston, a distinguished law scholar specializing in human rights and international law at the University of Iowa. The three of us shared a keen sense of the productive synergies that could be developed by bringing together the emerging practices of the commons with human rights and law. Much of Burns's thinking on this topic found expression in the 2013 book that he co-authored with David Bollier, *Green Governance: Ecological Survival, Human Rights and the Law of the Commons.*

Burns and David sought to follow up this work — drawing in Anna Grear, a legal theorist and radical human rights scholar with whom Burns had been collaborating — to further explore how the commons, law, and social transformation could be re-imagined. However, as the project began to take shape, Burns tragically and suddenly passed away in October 2015.

We miss our spirited, fiery, passionate, and optimistic friend and colleague. We are thrilled to see the seeds he helped to plant for this project yield such a rich harvest of ideas. This anthology is dedicated to him.

We also wish to thank the Open Society Foundations for its generous grant, which enabled us to convene two workshops that brought many of the ideas in this volume to the surface in new configurations. Our appreciation also extends to the University of Iowa, and especially Jonathan Carlson, for their stellar administrative support, and to the Charles Léopold Mayer

Foundation, which graciously hosted a group of scholars, activists and others involved in the project at *La Bergerie,* its lovely retreat center north of Paris. The intense, far-ranging discussions in those workshops helped us to clarify the framing of this book and to identify which strategic themes to develop.

Finally, we wish to thank the twenty-seven scholars and activists who participated in our two workshops in 2016 and 2018, respectively, and the twelve contributors to this book, who have all helped bring such depth and clarity to emerging topics that remain very much on the frontier of new modes of living amidst capitalist ruins.

Introduction

Anna Grear and David Bollier

The catastrophic, slow-motion decline of neoliberal capitalism and its accomplice, the nation-state, presents a disturbing picture. The symptoms of pressure are everywhere: stranded polar bears on shrinking ice floes; desperate refugees washing up on the shores of Europe; angry white supremacists threatening adversaries with violence and committing violent terrorist crimes; authoritarian leaders — including a US President — flouting the rule of law; a surge of "deaths of despair" from suicide, drugs, and alcohol; and much more.

Basic structures of contemporary life seem to be falling apart, no longer able to contain the chaotic energies unleashed by global capitalism, digital technologies, libertarian market culture, and modernity. One might call it a Great Unraveling. Yet, paradoxically, this period of history might also be called, accurately, the Great Awakening.

There is a growing awareness of the need for a fundamental shift in mindset and culture, as suggested by the youth climate protests of recent times; the rise of progressive politics; and a general sense that the system is broken and needs to be replaced. Amidst the messy unwinding of obsolete paradigms, many sturdy, fresh, and green sprouts of change — marginal, as yet, to the public consciousness — are emerging. A growing cohort of self-identified commoners, working largely outside the circles of respectable opinion, is developing important new frameworks of thought and innovative tech platforms. Such commoners bring an almost dizzying array of creative approaches to central challenges of human social organization. They are pioneering, for example, creative hacks of law and new sorts of currencies. They are re-imagining regional food systems and systems for keeping agricultural seeds shareable. They are developing new models of peer production such as "cosmo-local production," which lets people share knowledge and design globally, open-source-style, while building physical things locally.

Notwithstanding pervasive crises and traumas, it turns out that this is a fertile time to reinvent the world with collaborative initiatives. This book explores some of the more promising ones, with special attention paid to tracing out the new consciousness and worldviews they reflect. It quickly becomes clear that commons are not just inert, unowned resources (such as oceans, space, and the atmosphere) as economists would have us believe. They are living eco-social systems that are incubating alternative rationalities. Through commoning, groups of people — some at very large scales — are demonstrating some profoundly new ways of being, knowing and acting in the world.

In exploring the many ingenious ways in which people are healing themselves and the world from the ravages of modernity and capitalism, we take considerable inspiration from the title and central project of Anna Lowenhaupt Tsing's landmark book, *Mushroom at the End of the World: On the Possibility of Life in Capitalist Ruins*.[1] She describes her book as "an original examination into the relation between capitalist destruction and collaborative survival within multispecies landscapes, the prerequisite for continuing life on earth."[2] By exploring how a prized and hardy mushroom, matsutake, flourishes in neglected, disrupted landscapes — and how collaborative human

---

1   Anna Lowenhaupt Tsing, *Mushroom at the End of the World: On the Possibility of Life in Capitalist Ruins* (Princeton: Princeton University Press, 2015).
2   Ibid., dust jacket.

efforts are needed to harvest matsutake — Tsing sheds light on what she calls "third nature," or "what manages to live despite capitalism."[3] We share Tsing's conviction about the importance of collaborative labors as essential for continuing life on Earth. Collaborative survival will require some serious experimentation and creativity. This means messy beginnings, a willingness to improvise, new types of collaborative institutions, and, ultimately, an awareness that we must act and live within a re-storied ontological-epistemological reality.

Despite the alienation produced by capitalist plunder and the conditions of precarity characterizing contemporary life, Tsing suggests that we need to do more than resist and critique our condition. We need to

> look around to notice this strange new world, and [....] stretch our imaginations to grasp its contours. This is where mushrooms help. Matsutake's willingness to emerge in blasted landscapes allows us to explore the ruin that has become our collective home.[4]

The commons, we suggest, is also an archetypal form of bio-material intelligence that emerges from within the blasted landscapes of capitalist ruins. Commons, like fungi, take root in unexpected places forged by networked connections, and express sometimes-unlikely, but promising, modes of evolution. Commons can be a rich and hopeful contribution to the quest for collaborative survival, and the contributors to this book show how the social imagination in its varied forms is inventing necessary new modes of living.

While commoning manifests in many different ways, it usually challenges, with varying degrees of self-awareness, some fundamental frameworks for understanding human consciousness and behavior, social organization, and political economy. Attempts to re-imagine the city as a commons, to use blockchain

---

3   Ibid, viii.
4   Ibid, 3.

software to enable cooperation on open networks, and to integrate commercial agriculture with natural ecosystems — such ventures demonstrate that the ontology and epistemology of standard economics are hopelessly crude and reductionist. As the reader moves through the ten chapters below, it will become clear that the philosophical paradigms outlined by Adam Smith, John Locke, Thomas Hobbes, and René Descartes — among others — resemble fading suits of vintage thinking. The garments may still be wearable as far as mainstream socio-political, legal, and economic thinking and practice are concerned, but they no longer really fit, nor are they apt for the unprecedented circumstances facing all life on Earth.

Our ambition in this volume is to deconstruct some of the fraying frameworks of thought that still govern public debate and, as importantly, to sketch out the rudiments of a new, hopeful world story and life-way now emerging. If a Great Awakening is underway (as we believe it is), it is time for us to look more closely at some of its cutting-edge initiatives and their provocative philosophical and legal implications. It is time to consider how commoning will change politics, governance, and indeed, the nation-state. In ten essays with diverse perspectives, this book explores many epochal shifts in social practice, law, economics, and political philosophy that have not yet been adequately explored.

The book opens with three essays that deconstruct the present global predicament and its multiple crises, especially the structural crisis that climate change poses for modern life. Sam Adelman describes the emergence of the grand narrative of the Anthropocene (the so-called "Age of Humans"), locating it in relation to the grand narratives and dominant tropes of modernity concerning science, reason, and progress, and the intersection between modernity and capitalism. The chapter exposes the myth of progress that drives the hubris of economic growth, ecomodernism, and neoliberalism. It also reflects on the narratives that undergird the Anthropocene, such as accounts of the world as naturalist, post-nature, eco-catastrophist, and eco-

Marxist (Capitalocene). It is essential, argues Adelman, to reach beyond the "age of unreason" and pursue "a great awakening."

In his essay, Richard Falk addresses the fast-approaching horizon of planetary crisis and the fundamental uncertainties and dilemmas it poses. He argues that the world and its populations currently inhabit a confusing "twilight zone" in which it is far from clear where power, formerly dominated by states, will migrate in the times ahead. Like Adelman, who addresses the problem of "Holocene rationality" — the mindset of our current geological era — Falk notes the problematic character of problem-solving when it is entangled in the structures, practices, and procedures of the Holocene. Climate change, nuclear weaponry, loss of biodiversity, the persistence of poverty, hunger and malnutrition, and the threat of pandemic disease lurk behind the horizon of twilight, becoming more dire as the nation-state wanes. Human rights and global interests also suffer for the lack of effective mechanisms to protect them, and yet no clear alternative to the state-centric world order is near — a dilemma that points to the need for radical change.

Transitionality is also a core theme for Andreas Karitzis, particularly transitionality of the liberal political system. Karitzis, though, moves beyond the narrow remit of politics to argue that there is a pressing need for people to embrace a transformative "personal stance, collective mentality, and tools of political and social mobilization." This is indeed a time of confusion because everything seems to be in flux: "Transformations that are radically shaking established institutional architectures and changing the rules and methods of political practice at the very same moment that new actors are emerging, thus complicating things even more." One challenge in the necessary re-storying of the system involves developing a new ontology for political life and new forms of everyday practices — a set of cultural capacities that are mutable, nuanced, and creative enough to thrive in the transitionality of the contemporary period.

Where, then, might such forms of life and a new ontology be found? This is where commoning holds out so much hope and creativity. In this book, some authors offer a mere handful of examples drawn from a far wider, burgeoning field of life-form creativity — in digital spaces, agriculture, and urban life, for example — while others link such practices to vigorous new ontological foundations, including new ontological foundations for commons themselves.

Michel Bauwens and Jose Ramos frame the commons as a much-needed "mutualization for the Anthropocene." While individuals predominantly register the contemporary moment as being one of crisis, the reality is that a global transition is underway, nothing short of the "birth of the 'planetary' as an element of human experience, and [...] the transition from social orders based on exploitation to social orders based on generative mutuality." This is a historical juncture, argue Bauwens and Ramos, in which the urgent need to reduce the human footprint on the planet combines with commons-based approaches that can mitigate the systemic crises of the political economy. The authors urge a collective re-imagination of the way in which human beings live together — as urban dwellers, Internet users, and political actors — pointing out that commons and commoning are "globally distributed, networked, and highly visible." The central challenge, argue Bauwens and Ramos, is to facilitate, at various levels, the emergent systemic shift to a new planetary political economy.

A pivotal aspect of this shift, and central to commons-based praxis, is the need to resist enclosure. The commodification, privatization, and financialization of shared wealth are the leitmotif of our time, facilitated by the relentless prioritization of traditional legal forms of property and contract that tend to serve the exclusionary interests of individuals and corporations. Commoners are no strangers to the problematics presented by such dynamics. In the face of such fierce pressures, Maywa Montenegro offers a finely drawn, sensitive, and intimate account of the struggle to protect open source seed. This struggle centers on new forms of "seed freedom" that emerge from the idea of the commons. In the face of the corporate market power and its propagation of GMO crops, pesticides, and herbicides, and patents that privatize the "common wealth," social movements seek to reclaim what has been appropriated. Montenegro's chapter, exploring the practice of commoning as a biocultural form located within a nascent, emerging politico-economic order, traces the "origins and early development of the Open Source Seed Initiative (OSSI), which seeks to 'free the seed.'" OSSI, suggests Montenegro, is one example of a growing transnational commoning movement aimed at "un-enclosing" intellectual property.

Primavera De Filippi and Xavier Lavayssiere explore analogous tensions in relation to peer-to-peer production on the internet. The internet was once an open ecosystem for permissionless innovation and a fertile virtual ground for the "emergence of commons-based communities relying on alternative legal regimes and new participatory models to promote openness and distributed collaboration." In recent years, however, the internet has increasingly become dominated by large corporate players using centralized platforms and proprietary applications to control, in effect, essential online infrastructures. More recently, the authors note, a new software technology, blockchain, has emerged, combining peer-to-peer technologies, game theory, and low-level cryptographic algorithms ("cryptographic primitives"). This technology, for all its promise of decentralization and disintermediation, however, ultimately relies — at least in its present form — on market dynamics and economic incentives, resulting, along with other factors, in governance by the infrastructure. De Filippi and Lavayssiere address these shortcomings, arguing that a "more comprehensive governance model must be elaborated — one that extends beyond the realm of pure algorithmically verifiable actions, and that supports or facilitates the governance of the infrastructure." A new governance model is also needed to establish a collaborative economy that is hospitable to direct interactions among a network of peers, without the need for an external authority or for an intermediary.

These familiar tensions — between centralization and control; and distributed, networked and innovative commoning practices — come to view again in David Bollier's chapter. Noting the power and diversity of commoning in contemporary life, Bollier points to the difficulties facing commoning as a "legal activity." Commons, he notes, are alien to many aspects of the dominant market/state system, and "the state is predisposed to ignore the commons, criminalize its activities, or exploit its resources in alliance with the business class." In response, as the "Commonsverse" develops, "a major challenge is imagining how law might affirmatively support commoning." Bollier explores a range of creative "legal hacks" — adaptations of existing law that attempt to make the relationship between commoning and modern state law more functionally compatible. Legal hacks, argues Bollier, "have been proliferating in recent years as commoners discover that state legal institutions — legislatures, courts, regulatory bodies — are simply too closely aligned with corporate interests to offer genuine support to commons."

The resistance from law to commoning is unsurprising in the light of the deep commitments of the legal system — and particularly, the legal system as it inhabits the grand narratives of modernity and capital, as set forth by Adelman in the opening chapter of the book. In his chapter, Vito De Lucia engages critically with the deep foundations of law, characterizing the commons as "a rich and hopeful horizon of practices attempting to resist the increasing encroachment of capitalist modernity on natural ecosystems and communities." De Lucia brings this characterization of commoning as resistance into direct, critical conversation with the commons itself, by offering an analysis of the conceptual intersection of the commons, ecology, and law, which he sees as "a space of productive theoretical engagement for rethinking law with and through ecology." For De Lucia, commoners reconceive "Nature" by responding to the living world as "co-participant[s] in a set of collaborative *relations*" in which humans retain a crucial role while striving to integrate the natural and the artificial in "an organic whole." A central aim of De Lucia's analysis is to offer a "thinking of law beyond Law, where Law with a capital L is set to represent legal modernity." Against the universalistic aspirations and totalizing closures of

Law, De Lucia positions the commons as a loosely-conjoined set of open-ended, complex assemblages from which a more responsive, responsible type of living law can emerge.

Picking up the theme of complexity, Paul Hartzog offers a rigorous account of a new reality that is both dynamic and non-linear. Hartzog argues that commons, cooperation, and complex systems synergize in ways that leverage diversity into an effect that he calls "The Difference Engine." This expresses a dynamic, adaptive cluster of new forms of social, political, and economic space in which new modes of being, "diverse and evolving, fluid and anarchical," are currently emerging. This new space, argues Hartzog, is "ontologically generative in the sense that it continually creates and activates new forms of difference, resulting in a 'perpetual revolution.'" Ultimately, he argues, this new situation demands that we embrace horizontal collaboration and diversity as functional necessities, rather than continuing to enforce regimes of conformity, hierarchy, and similarity. Descriptively, Hartzog's aim is to produce an understanding of complex adaptive systems and patterns. Normatively, his aim is to sketch the practical possibility of harnessing complexity to "create a more harmonious, mindful, and just civilization."

In the final chapter, Anna Grear weaves together themes that appear in various ways in the earlier chapters. Locating her analysis firmly against the neoliberalization of nature, Grear turns towards a politically aware, critical New Materialism as the basis for commons ontology. In terms convergent with De Lucia's suggestion that commoners see "Nature" as "a co-participant in a set of collaborative *relations,*" Grear explores what it might mean to think of non-human actants as *commoners*. She pushes this line of thought still further, embracing the "agency" of inorganic matter and considering the potential insights for a political ecology of the commons. Ultimately, argues Grear,

> the trans-corporeal nature of climate risk and the toxic flows marking all planetary existence suggests the vital importance of a highly politicized and critical commons onto-epistemology, one alive to the potentially oppressive implications of

'nature' as a construct, and alert to its pattern of historical injustices and their links with contemporary mal-distributions of risk, hazard, life and death.

For Grear, feminist New Materialist accounts hold out hope for a vocabulary and an approach re-grounding commoning as a form of human-nonhuman onto-*insurgency.*

Taken together, the chapters of this volume offer a richly textured encounter with a range of vibrant, commons-centered reflections. In different ways, they address the planetary tensions caused by neoliberal enclosure and eco-destructiveness, while illustrating the power of complex, adaptive commoning in cultivating a new paradigm. If the lineaments of this new world remain only dimly perceptible by the terms of the current order — and worse, stoutly resisted by the market/state system when it is understood at all — one is tempted to invoke Galileo's alleged riposte when forced to recant his claim that the Earth moved around the sun: "... And yet it moves."

Systems that rely on distributed intelligence, community collaboration, ecological stewardship, and an ethos of sharing are remarkably generative. They are structurally capable of meeting needs in flexible, earth-respecting ways. They are socially constructive and responsive to the people who live within them. Their great promise, while still embryonic, draws upon a deep onto-epistemological shift in how one approaches the world. This is precisely why new/old systems of commoning offer such a rich solution-space and why they represent something of a Great Awakening for the modern mind. Forms of commoning do not look to magic blueprints for change, but rather to demonstrated patterns and norms that allow people to build new sorts of institutions grounded in their actual needs and where they actually live in a human-nonhuman knot of connections. In short: commoning offers a compelling evolutionary strategy for escaping some structural dead-ends in which humanity now finds itself entrapped.

2

Modernity, Anthropocene, Capitalocene, and the Climate Crisis

Sam Adelman

This chapter discusses grand narratives, myths and discourses in the Anthropocene during and beyond modernity. The two main protagonists are abstractions to which responsibility has been ascribed for the climate and ecological crisis confronting humanity, other species, and the Earth system: Anthropos, the telluric super-agent who has produced a new geological epoch, and capital. The first section of this chapter discusses the emergence of the grand narrative of the Anthropocene. In section two, I discuss the Anthropocene in relation to the dominant tropes of modernity on science, reason and progress, and the intersection between modernity and capitalism. I pay particular attention to the idea of progress as and through economic growth, ecomodernism, and neoliberalism. Section three examines some of the grand narratives of the Anthropocene, the Age of Humans. These include: naturalist, post-nature, eco-catastrophist, and eco-Marxist (Capitalocene) narratives. The penultimate section considers problems created by the persistence of what I call Holocene rationality. In the concluding section, I argue that the Anthropocene is an age of unreason that we must transcend in pursuit of a great awakening.

1. The Emergence of the Anthropocene Narrative

Natural scientists use the concept of the Anthropocene to high-light the rupture of the Earth System.[1] In 2002, Nobel chemistry laureate, Paul Crutzen, popularized the concept when arguing that "[i]t seems appropriate to assign the term 'Anthropocene' to the present, in many ways human-dominated, geological epoch."[2] Crutzen contended that the Anthropocene was argu-ably inaugurated by James Watt's refinement of the steam en-gine between 1763 and 1775, which enabled the widespread use of coal as a source of energy and launched the Industrial Revo-lution.[3] Others suggest that humankind became a full-fledged Promethean, telluric force during the Great Acceleration:

> The second half of the twentieth century is unique in the entire history of human existence on Earth. Many human activities reached take-off points sometime in the twentieth century and have accelerated sharply towards the end of the century. The last 50 years have without doubt seen the most rapid transformation of the human relationship with the nat-ural world in the history of humankind.[4]

---

1   Clive Hamilton, "The Anthropocene as Rupture," *The Anthropocene Review* 3, no. 2 (2016): 93–106, at 94. Hamilton describes Earth System as an "integrative meta-science of the whole planet as a unified, complex, evolving system beyond the sum of its parts."

2   Paul Crutzen, "Geology of Mankind" *Nature* 415, no. 4687 (2002): 23. In 2000, Crutzen and Eugene Stoermer had introduced the concept in the newsletter for the International Geosphere-Biosphere Programme in which they described the ways in which mankind had become a "signifi-cant geological, morphological force": Paul Crutzen and Eugene Stoermer, "The 'Anthropocene,'" *Global Change Newsletter* 41 (2000): 17–18.

3   Watt improved the steam engine invented by Thomas Newcomen in 1712.

4   W. Steffen et al., *Global Change and the Earth System: A Planet under Pressure* (Berlin: Springer, 2005), 131. See also Will Steffen et al., "The Tra-jectory of the Anthropocene: The Great Acceleration," *The Anthropocene Review* 2, no. 1 (2015): 81–98.

Whichever periodization is favoured, it is widely accepted that *Homo sapiens* is altering the geo-history of the Earth.[5] Future geologists will find evidence in the planet's stratigraphy of radio-nuclides from nuclear weapons testing, greenhouse gas emissions, the 300 metric tonnes of plastic produced annually, and enough concrete to cover the surface of the planet — more than half of which has been produced in the past two decades.[6] In addition to anthropogenic climate change, seven other planetary boundaries have been breached or are under threat.[7] Nearly half the Earth's land surface has been transformed by human activity during the Great Acceleration, with significant impacts on nutrient cycling, biodiversity, ecosystems, and soil structure. More than half of accessible freshwater is utilized directly or indirectly by human beings, and underground water resources are being rapidly depleted.[8]

The idea of the Anthropocene is gaining increasing purchase in the academy and public discourse as a shorthand for the power of human agency in the Age of Humans. It is a powerful trope — indeed, an overarching grand narrative — about the climatic harms caused by overweening arrogance, hubris and

---

5 The International Commission on Stratigraphy has yet to decide whether to accept the Anthropocene as a new geological epoch as proposed by the Working Group on the Anthropocene that began its work in 2009. Periodizations are inevitably contested. Proponents of the Capitalocene, such as Moore, argue that it can be traced back as far as the emergence of mercantile capitalism in the sixteenth century: Jason W. Moore, "The Capitalocene, Part I: On the Nature and Origins of Our Ecological Crisis," *The Journal of Peasant Studies* 44, no .3 (2017): 594–630.

6 The total amount of concrete produced by humanity is about 1 kg/m² across the whole surface of the Earth. Enough plastic wrap has been manufactured since 1950 to cover the whole Earth, and enough aluminium foil to cover Australia: Will Steffen, "Welcome to the Anthropocene," *Australasian Science* 37, no. 2 (2016): 28–29. More than 8 million tonnes of plastic are dumped into the oceans annually, see *Plastic Oceans,* http://www.plasticoceans.org/the-facts/. Stratigraphy is both a branch of geology and an archeological record of human activity.

7 Johan Rockström et al., "Planetary Boundaries: Exploring the Safe Operating Space for Humanity," *Ecology and Society* 14, no. 2 (2009): 32–65.

8 Ian Angus, *Facing the Anthropocene: Fossil Capitalism and Crisis of the Earth System* (New York: Monthly Review Press, 2016), ch. 2.

greed, and the onto-epistemological challenges that climate change poses to our understandings of what it means to be human in geo-human history.[9] Like Donna Haraway, I use the concept despite deep reservations. I use Anthropocene because, in Haraway's words, "the word is already well entrenched and seems less controversial to many important players compared to the Capitalocene."[10] (Haraway argues that both narratives "lend themselves too readily to cynicism, defeatism, and self-certain and self-fulfilling predictions.")[11] For a start, the idea that an undifferentiated humanity is responsible for the rupture in the Earth System is historically inaccurate. Most of the individuals historically responsible for carbon dioxide emissions — the super-agents of the Anthropocene — are from developed, industrialized, Western countries.[12] Bonneuil and Fressoz note that "Great Britain and the United States made up 60% of cumulative total emissions to date in 1900, 57% in 1950, and almost 50% in 1980. From the standpoint of climate, the Anthropocene should rather be called the 'Anglocene.'"[13] According to Malm and Hornborg, "In the early 21st century, the poorest 45% of the human population accounted for 7% of emissions, while the richest 7%

---

9   Some writers are already discussing the possibility that the Anthropocene may be an interlude that will be succeeded by yet to be named epoch. See for example, Luc Semal, "Anthropocene, Catastrophism and Green Political Theory," in *The Anthropocene and the Global Environmental Crisis: Rethinking Modernity in a New Epoch,* eds. Clive Hamilton, Christophe Bonneuil, and François Gemenne (London: Routledge, 2015), 87–99.

10   Donna Haraway, "Tentacular Thinking: Anthropocene, Capitalocene, Chthulucene," *e-flux* 75 (2016), http://www.e-flux.com/journal/75/67125/tentacular-thinking-anthropocene-capitalocene-chthulucene/.

11   Donna J. Haraway, "Staying with the Trouble: Anthropocene, Capitalocene, Chthulucene," in *Anthropocene or Capitalocene? Nature, History, and the Crisis of Capitalism,* ed. Jason W. Moore (Oakland: PM Press, 2016), 34–76, at 59.

12   The idea of super-agency is borrowed from Clive Hamilton, *Defiant Earth: The Fate of Humans in the Anthropocene* (Cambridge: Polity Press, 2017).

13   Christophe Bonneuil and Jean-Baptiste Fressoz, *The Shock of the Anthropocene: The Earth, History and Us* (London: Verso, 2016), 132.

produced 50%.'"[14] From the start of the Industrial Revolution to the last quarter of the twentieth century, the climate catastrophe was overwhelmingly the responsibility of white, bourgeois and predominantly Christian men.[15] Anna Grear argues that Anthropos is a narrow, self-interested figure that excludes most of humanity and all of nature. For this reason, the Anthropocene is also a crisis of hierarchies. Grear maintains that:

> any ethically responsible future engagement with "anthropocentrism" and/or with the "Anthropocene" must explicitly engage with the oppressive hierarchical structure of the anthropos itself — and should directly address its apotheosis in the corporate juridical subject that dominates the entire globalised order of the Anthropocene age.[16]

In an influential essay, Dipesh Chakrabarty argues that human history and geological history have converged as an unintended consequence of individual greenhouse gas emissions undifferentiated by class, gender, race or historical context. "Species," he writes, "may indeed be the name of a placeholder for an emergent, new universal history of humans that flashes up in the moment of the danger that is climate change."[17] Chakrabarty's "speciesism" disconnects the Anthropocene from the underlying structures of social and environmental exploitation such as colonialism and capitalism.

---

14 Andreas Malm and Alf Hornborg, "The Geology of Mankind?" *The Anthropocene Review* 1, no. 1 (2014): 62–69, at 64.

15 Rapidly industrializing countries in the global South are responsible for a growing proportion of greenhouse gas emissions but their historical responsibility is far lower than that of OECD member states.

16 Anna Grear, "Deconstructing Anthropos: A Critical Legal Reflection on 'Anthropocentric' Law and Anthropocene 'Humanity'," *Law and Critique* 26, no. 3 (2015): 225–49.

17 Dipesh Chakrabarty, "The Climate of History: Four Theses," *Critical Inquiry* 5, no. 2 (2009): 197–222, at 221. See Malm and Hornborg, "Geology of Mankind" and Grear, "Deconstructing Anthropos" for critiques of Chakrabarty's argument.

This gives rise to a second reservation, namely a tendency amongst many theorists of the Anthropocene to obscure or subordinate the contributions of capitalism and colonialism to the climate crisis. Jason Moore argues that the concept of the Anthropocene is problematic because it does not give sufficient weight to the ways in which a particular mode of production reinforced the anthropocentric epistemologies at the heart of modernity. For this reason, he argues that the term "Capitalocene" more accurately captures the historical processes that have brought us to this conjuncture.[18] Neither modernity nor the Anthropocene are comprehensible in the absence of the histories of (carbon) colonialism and capitalism. As Bonneuil and Fressoz argue:

> [The] industrial development model and its metabolism in terms of matter and energy, which altered the geopolitical trajectory of our Earth, is inseparable from the history of capitalist world-systems, of unequal ecological exchange, of colonialism and imperialism, of exploitation and underdevelopment.[19]

2. The Grand Narratives of Modernity

Bruno Latour contends that the Anthropocene is "the most decisive philosophical, religious, anthropological and [...] political concept yet produced as an alternative to the very notions of 'Modern' and 'modernity.'"[20] This may be true if the Anthropocene is understood as an intellectual era after and beyond mo-

---

18 Jason W. Moore, "Introduction" to *Anthropocene or Capitalocene? Nature, History, and the Crisis of Capitalism* (Oakland: PM Press, 2016).

19 Bonneuil and Fressoz, *Shock of the Anthropocene*, 228. See also Alf Hornborg, "Zero-Sum World: Challenges in Conceptualizing Environmental Load Displacement and Ecologically Unequal Exchange in the World-System," *International Journal of Comparative Sociology* 50, nos. 3–4 (2009): 237–62.

20 Bruno Latour, "Facing Gaia: Six Lectures on the Political Theology of Nature," Gifford Lectures on Natural Religion, 2013, http://www.bruno-latour.fr/sites/default/files/downloads/GIFFORD-BROCHURE-1.pdf.

dernity. However, it is chronologically untrue if we accept that the Anthropocene began around the turn of the nineteenth century and thus overlapped with, and was indeed largely impelled by, modernity's faith in science and particular forms of rationality and progress that we might term "Holocene epistemologies". Ecological devastation has clearly intensified during the Great Acceleration, the beginning of which is often traced back to the 1950s, but whose foundations were laid two centuries earlier.[21]

The concept generally described as modernity had its origins in the eighteenth-century Enlightenment. A central component of modernity is the idea that Europe had launched humanity on an irreversible linear, progressive, and teleological trajectory towards the future through a radical *rupture* — an onto-epistemological rupture with the past impelled by equally radical previous ruptures, most notably the Cartesian rupture between nature and society and that between feudalism and capitalism. In Latour's words:

> Modernity comes in as many versions as there are thinkers or journalists, yet all its definitions point, in one way or another, to the passage of time. The adjective "modern" designates a new regime, an acceleration, a rupture, a revolution in time. When the word "modern", "modernization", or "modernity" appears, we are defining, by contrast, an archaic and stable past.[22]

In addition to progress, modernity's defining tropes include rationalism, secularism, technocentrism, and assertions of the discovery of absolute universal truths.[23] The moderns' Age of

---

21 There is a danger of infinite regress in identifying the origins of the Anthropocene as a geological epoch that has induced some writers to argue that it was initiated by agriculture.

22 Bruno Latour, *We Have Never Been Modern,* trans. Catherine Porter (Cambridge: Harvard University Press, 1993), 10 (emphasis added).

23 Ellen Meiksins Wood writes: "The so-called Enlightenment project is supposed to represent rationalism, technocentrism, the standardization of knowledge and production, a belief in linear progress and universal, abso-

Reason was also the age of humanism that celebrated individual agency and autonomy as well as the cognitive faculties of Europeans. In the Holocene, modernity was also an apotheosis of human exceptionalism based upon a series of myths, to which we now turn.[24]

2.1 Reason and Science

The first of these myths celebrates the (reductive) modern faith in reason and science. The transition to Western modernity was driven by the conviction that the world could be shaped by human agency and reason rather than by the vicissitudes of nature or supernatural forces. Scientific method and Enlightenment rationality shaped Western socio-cultural norms and practices. In the seventeenth century, the Scientific Revolution gave rise to the perception of nature as inert and passive — a perception that infused the law and facilitated the mechanistic materialism that underpinned the Eurocentric Promethean impulse towards domination over alien others.[25] Machines became structural models for Western epistemology and law.[26] Separation, exclusion and domination became persistent economic, legal, and political leitmotifs.

The rupture between humanity and nature was foundational to modernity. Francis Bacon argued that nature was an inanimate machine whose secrets could be extracted through technologies that would enable men to transform it "from a teacher

---

lute truths": "Modernity, Postmodernity, or Capitalism?" *Monthly Review* 48, no. 3 (1996): 21–39, at 23.

24 The Holocene is the second and most recent epoch of the Quaternary period. It began approximately 11,700 years ago and is characterized by a stable climate that facilitated agriculture and the development of human civilizations.

25 Sam Adelman, "Epistemologies of Mastery," in *Research Handbook on Human Rights and the Environment,* eds. A. Grear and L. Kotzé (Cheltenham: Edward Elgar Publishing, 2015), 9–27.

26 Fritjof Capra and Ugo Mattei, *The Ecology of Law: Toward a Legal System in Tune with Nature and Community* (Oakland: Berrett-Koehler, 2015).

to a slave."[27] In 1641, Descartes introduced the idea of a division between the realm of the mind (*res cogitans*) and that of matter (*res extensa*), setting in play a dualism that continues to shape much of humanity's engagement with the environment through a praxis of domination and alienation.[28] Val Plumwood argues that such dualisms are relations of separation, domination, and exclusion, which generate hierarchies in which highly-valued constructs (men, humans) are contrasted with subordinate ones (women, nature). Identity is formed in a process "which distorts both sides of what it splits apart, the master and the slave, the coloniser and the colonised […] the masculine and the feminine, human and nature."[29] Plumwood argues that the occidental relationship between people and nature:

> explains many of the problematic features of the west's treatment of nature which underlie the environmental crisis, especially the western construction of human identity as 'outside' nature.[30]

In a similar vein, Lorraine Code maintains that:

> The imperialism of overdeveloped countries imposing their knowledge, social orderings, customs, economics, and other values, with scant concern for local sensitivities of land or of people, is one of the most visible wide-ranging — anti-ecological — products of the excesses of scientism, reductionism, and the instrumental-utilitarian moral and political theories that sustain an ethos of dominance and mastery.[31]

---

27 Carolyn Merchant, *The Death of Nature: Women, Ecology, and the Scientific Revolution* (New York: Harper & Row, 1980), 169.

28 René Descartes, *Discourse on Method and the Meditations* (London: Penguin, 1968).

29 Val Plumwood, *Feminism and the Mastery of Nature* (London and New York: Routledge, 1993), 32.

30 Ibid., 2.

31 Lorraine Code, *Ecological Thinking: The Politics of Epistemic Location* (Oxford: Oxford University Press, 2006), 8. Alf Hornborg describes an alternative narrative to the Anthropocene in "The Political Ecology of the

Latour has argued that science, technology, and society are co-produced through reciprocal changes in the relationships between facts, theories, machines, human actors, and social relations.[32] In his view, there has never been a complete separation between human and non-human or nature and society. In *We Have Never Been Modern,* Latour contends that the "modern constitution" bequeathed to us by the likes of Robert Boyle and Thomas Hobbes was a programme for purifying the discourses of nature and society by purging all traces of each in the other. This process of modernity was intensified by secularisation and the construction of boundaries between academic disciplines — a project that failed because such a radical separation has never been possible: we could never be modern so long as we denied that nature and culture/society are inextricably entangled.[33] Latour argues that science cannot exist without the contamination of its "pure space" by economics, law, and politics. His solution is a non-modern constitution for a "Parliament of Things", in which natural and social phenomena are comprehended as hybrids that emerge through the interaction of concepts, people, practices, and objects.[34] Hybridization is the diametric opposite of purification: everything of historical significance occurs in a "middle kingdom" in which nature and society are intermingled and includes such hybrids as genetically modified organisms, cybernetics and robotics.[35] The nature-culture divide must therefore be reconceptualized as an assemblage of "nature-cultures," which existed in premodernity and persist beyond modernity.[36] Latour's concern is that modernity cannot acknowledge the unavoidability of hybridization without col-

Technocene: Uncovering Ecologically Unequal Exchange in the World-System," in *The Anthropocene and the Global Environmental Crisis,* eds. Hamilton, Bonneuil, and Gemenne, 1–13.

32 Latour, *We Have Never Been Modern.*

33 Ibid.; Bruno Latour, *Science in Action: How to Follow Scientists and Engineers through Society* (Cambridge: Harvard University Press 1987).

34 Latour, *We Have Never Been Modern.*

35 Ibid.

36 Ibid, 96ff.

lapsing back into premodern undifferentiation, which is why modernity must vigilantly maintain the myth of purification at all costs.[37]

Hybridity and fluidity are central aspects of Donna Haraway's Chthulucene thinking about the onto-epistemological challenges of the Anthropocene. "What happens," she asks:

[W]hen human exceptionalism and bounded individualism become unthinkable in the best sciences across the disciplines and interdisciplines? Seriously unthinkable: not available to think with. Why is it that the epochal name of the Anthropos imposed itself at just the time when understandings and knowledge practices about and within symbiogenesis and sympoetics are wildly and wonderfully available and generative [...]?[38]

Much of the literature on the Anthropocene is framed by the implications of the central illusion of Holocene rationality, but this framing does not necessarily translate into humble intellectual acceptance of the consequences of what was always self-evident to those with eyes to see. Modernist rationalism persists in its blind war, effectively denying ecological limits while enacting an accumulative logic of plunder and control.

While the rise of secularism destabilized religious and philosophical orthodoxies and led to demands for greater individual autonomy and liberty which culminated in the American and

---

37 Ibid.
38 Haraway in Moore, *Anthropocene or Capitalocene?*, 60–61. See also Damian White, Alan Rudy, and Brian Gareau, *Environments, Natures and Social Theory: Towards a Critical Hybridity* (London: Palgrave Macmillan, 2015). Symbiogenesis is an evolution term that refers to cooperation between species to increase their chances of survival. Sympoetic evolutionary systems are collectively produced but do not have self-defined spatial or temporal boundaries. Information and control are distributed among their components. They have intrinsic potential for surprising change. On the latter, see Haraway's description at KIASualberta, "Donna Haraway - SF: String Figures, Multispecies Muddles, Staying with the Trouble," *YouTube*, June 27, 2014, https://www.youtube.com/watch?v=Z1uTVnhIHS8.

French revolutions), it also opened the way to possessive individualism, overturning centuries of commons land governance — a sea change that extended private property by legitimating the conquest of nature. Legally and politically, modernity
was marked by the consolidation of land ownership — by the
Westphalian state through sovereignty and patrimony over
natural resources, and for individuals as private property. John
Locke, for example, grounded his theory of individual property
rights in the biblical injunction that commanded industrious
and rational men to subdue the Earth, while John Stuart Mill
argued that individual freedom and autonomy depended upon
"a high degree of success in their struggle with Nature."[39] State
sovereignty — for Hobbes, the basis of security and protection
in the "war of all against all" in the state of nature[40] — became
the foremost facilitator of the sustained and unsustainable war
against nature that today produces ecological instability everywhere.

Max Horkheimer argued that mastery of nature is a pyrrhic
victory that leads to disillusionment. The "disease of reason," he
declared, "is that reason was born from man's urge to dominate
nature."[41] With Theodor Adorno, he famously argued that the
"dialectic of enlightenment" turns reason into an iron cage; attempts by human beings to arrange nature for subjugation have
the unintended consequence that the power of nature over people "increases with every step they take away from the power
of nature."[42] Reason produced wilful ignorance in the form of
the quintessential delusion of modernity — the idea that nature

---

39 Respectively, John Locke, *Two Treatises of Government* (Cambridge: Cambridge University Press, 1988), II.v.32, 290 and John Stuart Mill, *Considerations on Representative Government* (1861; Lahore: Serenity Publishers,
2008), 40.

40 Thomas Hobbes, *Leviathan* (London: Penguin, 1985), 186.

41 Max Horkheimer, *Dawn and Decline: Notes 1926–1931 and 1950–1969*
(New York: Seabury, 1978); Max Horkheimer, *Eclipse of Reason* (Columbia:
Columbia University Press, 1947), 176.

42 Max Horkheimer and Theodor Adorno, *Dialectic of Enlightenment* (Stanford: Stanford University Press, 2002), 30–31.

could be tamed, once considered to be the yardstick by which human freedom is measured — signified nothing so much as the constraints of fetishized science and reason.[43] The underlying paradox of technologically-impelled progress is this: the expansion of human powers, driven by hubristic delusions of mastery, progressively circumscribes those very powers due to increasingly intense climate-related weather events.[44] The Anthropocene calls for humility in the face of existential threats such as global heating and pandemics but encounters the hubris of technological modernizers and the masters of the universe who annually gather in Davos. Modernity's destructive delusions persist despite, or possibly because of the freedoms it brought.

Modernity provided a mixed legacy of real freedoms and Promethean delusions of mastery. While the natural rights of some were acknowledged but nowhere permanently guaranteed, capitalism generated technological innovations such as the steam engine that unleashed unconstrained economic growth and extractive industrialization. From the start of the Industrial Revolution, the prosperity on both sides of the Atlantic Europe brought by rising standards of living was accompanied by widespread ecological destruction. By the middle of the nineteenth century, Europeans were increasingly aware of rapid deforestation throughout the continent,[45] while ecocide and genocide were prominent features of the "white man's burden" of spreading colonialism, imperialism, Christianity and modernity to the ends of the earth.[46]

The contradictions of modernity have not gone unaddressed. Boaventura de Sousa Santos contends that modernity is charac-

---

43 David Harvey, "The Fetish of Technology: Causes and Consequences," *Macalester International* 13, no. 1 (2003): 3–30.

44 Caroline C. Ummenhofer and Gerald A. Meeh, "Extreme Weather and Climate Events with Ecological Relevance: A Review," *Philosophical Transactions of the Royal Society B* 372, no. 1723 (2017): 20160135.

45 Bonneuil and Fressoz, *The Shock of the Anthropocene*, ch. 9.

46 In his 1899 poem "The White Man's Burden: The United States and the Philippine Islands," published in the *New York Sun*, Rudyard Kipling invites the United States to assume colonial control over the Philippines.

terized by the tension between two pillars: regulation (exemplified by science and law) and emancipation — and that regulation persistently overwhelms emancipation.[47] These contradictions are exemplified by science. Science underpins material progress, not least through continuous innovations that enable nature to be "tamed," giving rise to a particular way of knowing, but also, paradoxically, to the quintessentially modern faith in technoscience as progress. Science, for example, provides rigorous and incontrovertible evidence of ecological devastation and frightening, reductionist, "solutions" such as geoengineering. We rely on climate science in formulating demands for climate justice *despite* our awareness that scientific objectivity and neutrality promote technocratic and undemocratic responses which tend to ignore socio-economic and political factors.

Philippe Descola argues that "[t]he exaltation of Science as the archetype of valid knowledge and the transcendent source of truth inhibits any reflexive thought on this bizarre cosmology that the Moderns have created."[48] The Age of Enlightenment was simultaneously an age of unreason. The Anthropocene is also an Agnotocene, a period of wilful ignorance.[49] It was hubristic agnotology that greeted the fall of the Berlin Wall in 1989, exemplified by Fukuyama's assertion that history had ended with its culmination in the form of capitalism and liberal democracy.[50] Such ignorance matters — decisive outcomes hang upon it. The implications for justice are serious. Santos et al. argue that there is no ignorance or knowledge *in general* and

---

47 Boaventura de Sousa Santos, *Toward a New Legal Common Sense: Law, Globalization and Emancipation* (Cambridge: Cambridge University Press, 2002).

48 Philippe Descola, *The Ecology of Others* (Chicago: Prickly Paradigm Press, 2013), 61.

49 From agnotology, the study of the production of zones of ignorance: Bonneuil and Fressoz, *The Shock of the Anthropocene*, 198. In the Age of Unreason, moderns did not understand nature, misconstrued it, or chose wilful ignorance about their place in it.

50 Francis Fukuyama, *The End of History and the Last Man* (New York: The Free Press, 1992).

that no complete knowledges exist.[51] Because knowledges operate in constellations, global social justice is not possible without
a global cognitive justice that accords equal respect to different
epistemologies. Global social justice is thus made possible only
by "substituting a monoculture of scientific knowledge by an
ecology of knowledges."[52]

2.2 Growth as Progress

We turn now to the second great myth of modernity.
Donna Haraway writes that:

A kind of dark bewitched commitment to the lure of Progress lashes us to endless infernal alternatives, as if we had no
other ways to reworld, reimagine, relive, and reconnect with
each other, in multispecies wellbeing.[53]

Progress is a central ideological pillar of modernity, capitalism,
and the Enlightenment, which has buttressed Western epistemologies since the Scientific Revolution (not least in the idea of
development as modernization and economic growth).[54] An associated aspect of this belief in progress is the notion that Western rationalism has grasped and refined universal principles
that govern everything. Likewise, the development of Europe
was promoted as a universal pathway for humanity to follow
on the basis that Europe's individualistic credo was a globally
applicable transcultural truth. The influence of such universaliz-
ing logics, especially of liberalism and capitalism, reached their

---

51 Boaventura de Sousa Santos, João Arriscado Nunes, and Maria Paula
Meneses, "Opening Up the Canon of Knowledge and Recognition of Difference," in *Another Knowledge is Possible: Beyond Northern Epistemologies*,
ed. Boaventura de Sousa Santos (London: Verso, 2007), xx–lxii, at xlviii.

52 Ibid.

53 Donna Haraway, "Staying with the Trouble," in Moore, *Anthropocene or
Capitalocene?*, 54.

54 See Jorge Larrain, *Theories of Development: Capitalism, Colonialism and
Dependency* (Malden: Polity, 2013); Richard Peet and Elaine Hartwick,
Theories of Development: Contentions, Arguments, Alternatives (New York:
Guilford Publications, 2015).

apogee with the advent of neoliberalism in the last quarter of the twentieth century.

Progress narratives have, and always had, a dark side. Modern liberal notions of universal justice were developed through the construction of otherness and accompanied by the resultant exploitation, expropriation, and dispossession of such others — including indigenous peoples, women, and nature. In short, the West's development was contingent upon the underdevelopment of the rest of the world through political, economic and carbon colonialism, and ecologically unequal exchange.[55] As Malm and Hornborg argue, historical inequalities based upon the use of specific technologies made the Anthropocene possible, both as a mind-set and an epoch.[56] Jeremy Baskin argues that the term Anthropocene:

> reveals the power of humans, but it conceals who and what is powerful, and how that power is enacted. It draws "the human" into "nature" but not the multiple and unequal social values, relations and practices of power that accompany actual humans.[57]

In an analogous vein, Peter Fitzpatrick writes that:

> Enlightenment creates the very monsters against which it so assiduously sets itself. These monsters of race and nature mark the outer limits, the intractable "other" against which Enlightenment pits the vacuity of the universal and in this opposition gives its own project a palpable content. Enlight-

---

55 See, for example, Walter Rodney, *How Europe Underdeveloped Africa* (London: Bogle-L'Ouverture Publications, 1972). On carbon colonialism, see Andreas Malm and Alf Hornborg, "The Geology of Mankind?"

56 Andreas Malm and Alf Hornborg, "The Geology of Mankind?"

57 Jeremy Baskin, "Paradigm Dressed as Epoch: The Ideology of the Anthropocene," *Environmental Values* 24, no. 1 (2015): 9–29, at 16.

ened being is what the other is not. Modern law is created in this disjunction.[58]

In exposing the mythology of modern law, Fitzpatrick describes how property becomes

> the foundation of civilization, the very motor-force of the origin and development of society, the provocation to self-consciousness and the modality of appropriating nature [...]. What is being universalized here is a particular form of Occidental property. Where it is absent there can only be its precursors or savagery.[59][...]
>
> By 1800 the West already controlled over a third of the earth's surface. With its expansive claim to exclusive rationality, with its arrogation of a universal and uniform knowledge of the world, and with its affirmation of universal freedom and equality, the Enlightenment sets a fateful dimension.[60]

Richard Norgaard argues that the belief in progress is so deeply entrenched in modernism that questioning it risks accusations of backwardness. It contains

> several aspects which have already terminated the future for many humanities and is likely to result in an early demise for its perpetrators as well [...] [T]he modern belief in progress was so strong during the nineteenth century that Western and westernized peoples lost much of their sense of responsibility for the earth and for future generations. We believed that progress through Western science would solve everything and thus that responsibility entailed accelerating the advance of science.[61]

---

58 Peter Fitzpatrick, *The Mythology of Modern Law* (London: Routledge, 2002), 45.
59 Ibid, 33.
60 Ibid, 65.
61 Richard Norgaard, *Development Betrayed: The End of Progress and a Co-evolutionary Revisioning of the Future* (London: Routledge, 1994), 44.

Furthermore, progress is closely linked to the wilful pursuit of endless economic growth despite clear evidence that breaching biophysical limits and planetary boundaries threatens all forms of economic activity.[62] At least since the so-called Great Recession, the climate crisis and low growth have combined to undermine the belief that future generations would always be materially better off than their ancestors, the Western idea of progress is increasingly questioned, but still holds a powerful level of mythic force in the global legal order.

2.3 Capitalism and Development

We turn now to the mythic status of the relationship between capitalism and development, which is the driving factor for so many contemporary social and ecological ills. Marx wrote that money that does not expand is not capital.[63] Growth is thus the *sine qua non* of capitalism and the driving force behind ecological rifts and the rupture to the Earth system.[64] Capitalism can be traced back to sixteenth-century mercantilism and Europe's colonial expansion through the appropriation of slaves, land and natural resources. However, the advent of the Industrial Revolution and the emergence of the Anthropocene inaugurated 250 years of carbon-based industrialization, urbanization, proletarianization, and technological transformation. By the end of the eighteenth century, capitalism had become the dominant global mode of production. And, as Horkheimer and Adorno argue, capitalism's control fetish arises from the foundational Enlight-

---

62 There is a 5 per cent chance of staying within the 2°C target in the Paris Agreement by the end of the century with current economic, emissions and population trends, and just a 1 per cent chance that temperatures will rise by less than 1.5°C: Adrian E. Raftery et al., "Less Than 2°C Warming by 2100 Unlikely," *Nature Climate Change* 7 (2017): 637–41. On the growth fetish, see Clive Hamilton, *Growth Fetish* (Crow's Nest: Pluto Press, 2011). Richard Norgaard, *Development Betrayed,* 32 argues that modernity is the key driver of ecologically unsustainable practices.

63 Karl Marx, *Capital Volume 1* (Moscow: Progress Publishers, 1887), ch. 4.

64 John Bellamy Foster, Brett Clark, and Richard York, *The Ecological Rift: Capitalism's War on the Earth* (New York: Monthly Review Press, 2011).

enment narrative of mastery over nature through instrumental reason.[65]

The "discovery" by the West of the Third World after the Second World War led to the emergence of developmentalism — an ideology rooted in progress measured by economic growth, industrialization and modernization.[66] GDP — rather than justice or wellbeing — became the dominant measure of national virility. The West sought to universalize its model of development through capitalism — which has embedded within it Cartesianism, utilitarianism, anthropocentric axiology, and history, understood as linear and teleological progress from backwardness to modernity. Arturo Escobar observes that questioning development leads to accusations of implicitly calling modernity itself into question.[67] The dominant contemporary narrative of development is sustainable development — a vague and capacious concept that appeals to states and transnational capital by fostering the illusion that endless economic growth, environmental protection, and the delivery of social justice through poverty reduction can be simultaneously achieved.[68] At the center of this hegemonic conception of development is the ecomodernist dream of deriving profits from a green economy.[69] The solution to the ecological depradations of capitalism, it seems, is more of the same.

65 Horkheimer and Adorno, *Dialectic of Enlightenment*; Adelman, "Episte-mologies of Mastery".

66 Peet and Hartwick, *Theories of Development*, 3.

67 Arturo Escobar, "El post-desarrollo como concepto y práctica social," in *Políticas de Economía, ambiente y sociedad en tiempos de globalización,* ed. Daniel Mato (Venezuela: Facultad de Ciencias Económicas y Sociales, Universidad Central de Venezuela, 2005), 17–31.

68 Sam Adelman, "The Sustainable Development Goals, Anthropocentrism and Neoliberalism," in *Global Goals: Law, Theory and Implementation,* eds. Duncan French and Louis Kotzé (Cheltenham: Edward Elgar, 2018), 15–40.

69 Michael Shellenberger and Ted Nordhaus, "An Ecomodernist Manifesto: From the Death of Environmentalism to the Birth of Ecomodernism," *The Breakthrough Institute,* April 15, 2015, https://thebreakthrough.org/articles/an-ecomodernist-manifesto.

2.3.1 Ecomodernism

Ecomodernism reprises the main tropes of modernity, on growth and progress, by transmuting classic liberalism into neoliberalism.[70] It is a market-obsessed discourse that sits comfortably alongside developmentalist narratives such as sustainable development due to the substantial overlaps between modernisation theory and ecological modernisation.[71] To ecomodernists, we have not been modern enough. Having learned nothing and forgotten nothing, they advocate market solutions to climate change and ecological destruction according to the perverse logic that the only way to save nature from the depredations of the market is to commodify and monetize it.[72] For ecomodernists, the end of nature is inconsequential because the end of nature constitutes an opportunity to remake it in Man's image — in a good, profitable Anthropocene form. Technology is seen as a tool to save humanity from the harms wrought by technology during the Holocene experiment with the Earth system — unrestrained technological interventions can be made to yield unending profits using unproven technologies.[73] From this perspective, the Anthropocene is the continuation of the Enlightenment story of domination and progress. Ecomodernists celebrate the prospects of a "good" Anthropocene in which unreason, faith, and technological fetishism combine to perpetuate the illusion that planetary catastrophe will be averted with

70 Erik Swyngedouw, "CO2 as Neoliberal Fetish: The Love of Crisis and the Depoliticized Immuno-Biopolitics of Climate Change Governance," in *The SAGE Handbook of Neoliberalism,* eds. Damien Cahill, Melinda Cooper, Martijn Konings, and David Primrose (London: Sage, 2018), 295–307.

71 Adelman, "The Sustainable Development Goals"; Ariel Salleh, "Neoliberalism, Scientism and Earth System Governance," in *The International Handbook of Political Ecology,* ed. Raymond L. Bryant (Cheltenham: Edward Elgar, 2015), 432–46.

72 Ryan Gunderson, "Commodification of Nature," in *The International Encyclopedia of Geography: People, the Earth, Environment and Technology,* ed. Douglas Richardson (Chichester: John Wiley & Sons, 2016), 1–20.

73 Shellenberger and Nordhaus, "An Ecomodernist Manifesto." See also Clive Hamilton, "The Theodicy of the 'Good Anthropocene'," *Environmental Humanities* 7, no. 1 (2016): 233–38.

the discovery of a technological silver bullet (which is doubtless already patented).[74]

There is thus a chronological disjuncture between the tenacious persistence of the rationality of Holocene modernity and of Anthropocene "post"-modernity. We live in a period in which zombie categories — neoliberalism and Holocene onto-epistemologies — continue to dominate despite being incommensurate with the scale and urgency of the climate and environmental crises. The contradictions of the Holocene metamorphose in the Anthropocene because, in Antonio Gramsci's words, "[t]he crisis consists precisely in the fact that the old is dying and the new cannot be born; in this interregnum a great variety of morbid symptoms appear."[75]

2.3.2 Neoliberalism

The latent contradictions at the heart of capitalist modernity, between science and reason, between the laws of nature and individual autonomy and freedom, and between economic growth and ecological sustainability, erupted with the spread of market fundamentalism and neoliberal globalisation. Whereas mainstream neoclassical economists regarded markets as means of achieving ends such as social justice or individual wellbeing, neoclassical economics conflated markets and society and views competition as an iron rule of nature.[76] This dismal economics reduced *Homo sapiens* to feral competitors, market actors, bloodless profit-and-loss calculators, and efficiency maximizers — the economic counterparts to abstract legal personality. Unreason elevated (or reduced) neoliberalism to an article of faith, a quasi-religion at odds with the precepts of Enlighten-

---

74 Calls to geoengineer the Earth's climate will increase as average global temperature increases. See Sam Adelman, "Geoengineering: Rights, Risks and Ethics," *Journal of Human Rights and the Environment* 8, no. 1 (2017): 119–38.

75 Antonio Gramsci, *Selections from the Prison Notebooks* (London: Lawrence & Wishart, 1971), 276.

76 Jason Read, "A Genealogy of Homo-Economicus: Neoliberalism and the Production of Subjectivity," *Foucault Studies* 6 (2009): 25–36.

ment, a triumph whose hollowness is measured by the Great Recession, Brexit, Trump, the climate crisis, and the shambolic responses of the US and UK to the coronavirus pandemic. Unreason dressed up as ineluctable logic led to deregulation, free trade, and to the privatization of the planet.[77]

Against reason, Friedrich von Hayek argued that only markets can deliver social justice because, unlike human beings, they do not discriminate.[78] Hayek's grandiose epistemological claim is that the market — an abstraction — is omniscient, and therefore the only legitimate form of knowledge because human values are merely subjective opinions.[79] Inequality is inevitable but not unjust, and poverty is nobody's fault.[80] Neoliberalism is, of course, a deeply ideological project. As Hayek's disciple Margaret Thatcher bluntly stated in her inimical way, "Economics are the method, the object is to change the heart and soul."[81]

Hayek believed he was solving the central problem of modernity, that of objective knowledge. Markets revealed truth and delivered justice. Self-interest was pseudo-scientifically

---

77 See for example, Timothy Luke, "Eco-Managerialism: Environmental Studies as a Power/Knowledge Formation," in *Living With Nature: Environmental Politics as Cultural Discourse,* eds. Frank Fischer and Maarten A. Hajer (Oxford: Oxford University Press, 1999), 103–20.

78 Friedrich A. von Hayek, *Law, Legislation and Liberty, Volume 2: The Mirage of Social Justice* (Chicago: University of Chicago Press, 2012). See also Friedrich A. von Hayek, *The Road to Serfdom* (London: Routledge, 1997). Targeting totalitarianism, his philippic served as a generalized libertarian assault on regulation, and his ersatz "scientific" economics attacked both the epistemological and material foundations of the Enlightenment. See Kasper Støvring, "The Conservative Critique of the Enlightenment: The Limits of Social Engineering," *The European Legacy* 19, no. 3 (2014): 335–46.

79 Friedrich A. von Hayek, "Economics and Knowledge," *Economica* 4, no. 13 (1937): 33–54, at 33, 52, et passim.

80 Raymond Plant, "Hayek on Social Justice: A Critique," in *Hayek, Co-ordination and Evolution: His Legacy in Philosophy, Politics, Economics and the History of Ideas,* eds. Jack Birner and Rudy van Zijp (London: Routledge, 1994), 164–77, at 165.

81 Ronald Butt, "Mrs Thatcher: The First Two Years," *Sunday Times,* May 3, 1981. http://www.margaretthatcher.org/document/104475. Another of Hayek's apostles who wrought untold damage was Milton Friedman.

made axiomatic, and value was reduced to individual preference, opinion or, most often, to price. Today we are governed
by big data, algorithms, and artificial intelligence that reduce
what is most human — volition, freedom to reason, to feel, and
to choose — and subordinate these to market consumerism enacted by mouse clicks.

3. Beyond (Post-)Modernity: The Grand Narratives of the Anthropocene

Jean-François Lyotard famously defined postmodernity as "incredulity towards metanarratives."[82] As we have seen, modernity has been replete with metanarratives and myths such as
the insidious idea of progress as the engine of history, driving
humanity onwards and upwards towards the final unfolding of
Hegel's Spirit, Marx's communist vision, or America's manifest
destiny.

It was perhaps inevitable but nonetheless ironic that the Anthropocene — the Age of Humans — has emerged as the grand-
est of all metanarratives in which *Homo sapiens* is apotheosized
as the telluric super-agent capable of transcending the mixed
legacy of modernity, either by reflexively abjuring its excesses
or completing the unfinished project of the moderns.[83] Beck argued that the problem does not lie in modernity but in our failure to reflect upon its lessons. The essential lesson of the climate
crisis is that reflexive modernization has failed:

---

82 Jean-François Lyotard, *The Postmodern Condition: A Report on Knowledge,* trans. Geoff Bennington (Minnesota: University of Minnesota Press,
1984), x, xxiv. Fredric Jameson argued that postmodernity emerged in
conjunction with neoliberal globalisation. Fredric Jameson, "Notes on
Globalization as a Philosophical Issue," in *The Cultures of Globalization,*
eds. Fredric Jameson and Masao Miyoshi (Durham and London: Duke
University Press, 1998), 54–77.

83 Hamilton, *Defiant Earth,* 110, argues that "turbo-charged agency was the
essence of modernity, combining freedom of oppression with power over
nature, using science and technology and the institutions that mobilized
them."

> Western modernity's belief in linear progression contradicts the ongoing self-disenchantment of Western modernity [...] in the light of climate change, the apparently independent and autonomous system of industrial modernization has begun a process of self-dissolution and self-transformation. This radical turn marks the current phase in which modernization is becoming reflexive, which means: we have to open up to global dialogues and conflicts about redefining modernity.[84]

It seems we must decide with Latour whether we have never been modern; with Ulrich Beck, whether to reflexively embrace the opportunities of ecomodernism; or with Clive Hamilton, whether we are not yet modern enough.[85]

Christophe Bonneuil discerns four grand Anthropocene narratives: (1) the mainstream naturalist narrative, in which the human species is "is elevated to a causal explanatory category in the understanding of human history", and simple modernity gives way to the reflexive modernity advocated by Beck and Giddens; (2) a post-nature narrative promoted by ecomodernists; (3) an eco-catastrophist narrative; and (4) an eco-Marxist narrative.[86]

In the *naturalist* grand narrative, science is the "*deus ex machina* that was not part of the cultural–political–economical

---

84 Ulrich Beck, "Climate for Change, or How to Create a Green Modernity?" *Theory, Culture & Society* 27, nos. 2–3 (2010): 254–66, at 264.

85 Latour, *We Have Never Been Modern*; Beck "Climate for Change;" Hamilton, *Defiant Earth*. Haraway argues that we have never been human: Donna Haraway, "When We Have Never Been Human, What Is to Be Done?" *Theory, Culture & Society* 23, nos. 7–8 (2006): 135–58.

86 Christophe Bonneuil, "The Geological Turn: Narratives of the Anthropocene," in *The Anthropocene and the Global Environmental Crisis,* eds. Hamilton et al., 19. On reflexive modernity, see Ulrich Beck, Anthony Giddens, and Scott Lash, *Reflexive Modernization: Politics, Tradition and Aesthetics in the Modern Social Order* (Stanford: Stanford University Press, 1994). Bonneuil and Fressoz, *The Shock of the Anthropocene,* cogently demonstrate that past societies were not unknowing, unreflexive, nor ignorant of risks to the global environment of their activities.

nexus that made the Anthropocene, but which will now guide humankind and save the planet."[87] This is a discourse that reproduces the dominant tropes of modernity, of Man's progress "from environmental obliviousness to environmental consciousness, of Man equaling Nature's power, of Man repairing Nature."[88] The naturalist narrative "abolishes the break between culture and nature, between human history and the history of life and Earth" so that the "entire functioning of the Earth becomes a matter of human political choices." [89] Bonneuil observes that crisis normally denotes a transitionary state, but that in the Anthropocene, we have passed the point of no return.[90]

The *post-nature narrative* entails a great inversion. Whereas modernity promised emancipation from nature's determinism, in the Anthropocene, humanity is inescapably reinserted into an engineered environment in which it is no longer dominant. The rift between nature and society is closed but not healed. The post-nature narrative "shares — and even radicalizes — the Promethean tropes of the first grand narrative as well as the belief that environmental awareness or reflexivity is very recent", but departs from the naturalist narrative "in viewing the Anthropocene as a story of feedback loops, connections, networks and hybridity that cut across most of modernity's boundaries."[91] Beck discerned emancipatory effects in the epochal changes of the Anthropocene that make possible new ways of being and

---

87 Bonneuil, "The Geological Turn," 23. Baskin ("Paradigm Dressed as Epoch: The Ideology of the Anthropocene," *Environmental Values* 24, no. 1 (2015): 9–29, at 16) writes that "We know, too, that the terms 'Nature' and 'Culture' are not universal categories, nor is there only one understanding of how they are connected. A range of alternative 'ontological routes' exist, including those fundamentally incommensurable with the dominant perspective of the contemporary West and modernity, the 'Naturalist' approach, as Descola labels it. Thinking through 'nature' is not straightforward, but it is essential to any coherent concept of the Anthropocene."

88 Ibid.

89 Bonneuil, "The Geological Turn," 33, 39.

90 Ibid, 35.

91 Ibid, 24.

thinking by extending and deepening modernisation.[92] Other authors have proclaimed the "end of modernity" in simpler, non-reflexive forms. For example, in contrast to modernizers who postulate a premodern natural world distinct from society, Latour suggests that we need to "ecologize" rather than modernize, and that political ecology can transform by transcending the division between nature and society.[93]

The *eco-catastrophist narrative* is one of limits and finitude, in which endless growth and inevitable progress crash into the biophysical limits of the Earth system. It is characterized by "a non-linear and non-progressivist conceptualisation of time and history", in which the climate crisis offers opportunities for alternative forms of economics such as degrowth and *buen vivir,* as well as a new egalitarian, participatory politics in resilient post-growth societies.[94] This narrative is either fatalistic or realistic, depending on one's interpretations of reason and progress.

The "Capitalocene" is an *eco-Marxist narrative* in which the main driver of the Anthropocene is not undifferentiated *Homo sapiens* but capital.[95] This account is theoretically and empirically plausible in light of abundant evidence of the myriad ways in which the logic of capital (that compels growth), the exploitation of fossil fuels, faith in technoscience, and tropes about progress and developmentalism impel the rupture in the Earth system. Capitalism emerged long before the Industrial Revolution but there is little doubt that capitalist relations were deepened and spread through the use of fossil fuels. The Capitalocene describes the "geology not of mankind, but of capital accu-

92 Ulrich Beck, "Emancipatory Catastrophism: What Does It Mean to Climate Change and Risk Society?" *Current Sociology* 63, no. 1 (2015): 75–88.

93 Bruno Latour, *Politics of Nature: How to Bring the Sciences into Democracy,* trans. Catherine Porter (Cambridge: Harvard University Press, 2009), and *An Inquiry into Modes of Existence: An Anthropology of the Moderns* (Cambridge: Harvard University Press, 2013).

94 Bonneuil, "The Geological Turn," 27.

95 As Moore (*Anthropocene or Capitalocene?,* 50) argues, it is "an ugly word for an ugly system."

mulation" through specific sets of social relations.[96] It explains neoliberalism, green economy, ecomodernism, and sustainable development in ways that the construct of the Anthropocene cannot, because the latter ignores or masks the structural violence of capitalism. The Capitalocene, by contrast, explains carbon colonialism and unequal ecological exchange. For Moore, it "signifies capitalism as a way of organizing nature — as a multispecies, situated, capitalist world-ecology."[97]

4. Beyond the Holocene

We await the official verdict on whether the Anthropocene is a new geological epoch. This is important but not decisive because the term is now widely used in the humanities, social sciences, and other disciplines. What is striking, however, is the disjuncture signalled by the scientific implications of the Anthropocene and the limitations of Holocene epistemological responses, many of which fit comfortably within the main tropes of modernity — albeit as variations on a theme. Modernity perdures because moderns are trapped in the iron cage of Holocene onto-epistemologies. Modernity is the last gasp of Holocene rationality in a period in which Kantian individuals still hubristically believe they are masters of their own fates as well as that of the Earth and, as such, are the point of departure for thinking in and about the Anthropocene.

First, the impulse towards universalization, deployed to obliterate otherness through exclusion, now becomes a mechanism of inclusion. "We," an undifferentiated collective, are deemed to have acquired telluric super-agency and responsibility for the rupture to the Earth System, regardless of the vast differences in our historical contributions to climatic harms. Whereas the French and American revolutions sought to universalize the interests of white, bourgeois, Christian men during the Age of

---

96 Andreas Malm, *Fossil Capital: The Rise of Steam Power and the Roots of Global Warming* (London: Verso, 2016), 390–91.

97 Moore, *Anthropocene or Capitalocene?*, 6.

Enlightenment; the Anthropocene normalizes and universal-
izes the actions and interests of a small segment of humanity
in the Age of Humans. Second, whereas modernity celebrated
humanity's liberation from nature through technological domination, the Anthropocene veers between lamenting the realization that this freedom was illusory and reinserting "'man' into
nature only to re-elevate 'him' within and above it."[98] Third, as
Baskin argues, modernity's "use of 'instrumental reason' generates a largely uncritical embrace of technology" which, in the
hands of ecomodernists, "legitimises certain non-democratic
and technophilic approaches, including planetary management
and large-scale geoengineering, as necessary responses to the
ecological 'state of emergency.'"[99] Much writing on the Anthropocene criticizes the excesses of technologically-induced environmental degradation, but much of it retains modernity's faith
in techno-scientific solutions. Fourth, as its name implies, the
Anthropocene perpetuates modernity's thoroughgoing anthropocentrism.

Peter Fitzpatrick writes that "Towards the end of the period
of Enlightenment, the sovereign subject is dethroned and there
remains no one to do the work of the gods."[100] Nietzsche insisted
on the necessity of confronting the full implications of the death
of God[101] (and, by implication, accepting the death of nature);
in the Anthropocene, ecomodernists and geoengineers step forward to do the work of the gods.

The Anthropocene is a metanarrative about exploitation of
the environment, with a twist. Instead of abundance, "nature"
is now characterized by new leitmotifs about limits, thresholds,
and planetary boundaries. Too often, this results in a focus on
the ecological consequences of industrial capitalism rather than
on the underlying socio-economic, political, and legal structures that produce them. Despite this, a disconcerting faith

---

98 Baskin, "Paradigm Dressed as Epoch," 11.

99 Ibid.

100 Peter Fitzpatrick, *The Mythology of Modern Law* (London: Routledge,
2002), 92.

101 Hamilton, *Defiant Earth*, 117.

persists in humanity's technological capacity to overcome Anthropocene constraints. There is also discontinuity about history. Chronologically, the advent of geo-human history implies that we have moved beyond modernity. In this sense, the Anthropocene is tantamount to a new meta-historical concept that transcends the bounds of Holocene history, a story about the meaning of the past and the making of the future. A third, contradictory, discontinuity concerns the nature–society binary. The Cartesian rupture is reconceptualized but not reconciled. In Anthropocene literature, human and natural systems are entangled and shape each other, but are not reconciled. Nature now assumes a frightening otherness beyond humanity's control that breeds fear and feeds Promethean urges. The clearest continuity is anthropocentrism because, after all, what else distinguishes the Age of Humans?

The Anthropocene forces us to understand time and history anew because it is no longer possible to accept the modern conception of history flowing from the rupture that Jacob Burckhardt described as "the break with nature caused by the awakening of consciousness."[102] In the words of W.B. Yeats, history is "changed, utterly changed" by the geological super-agency of a section of humanity with demiurgical pretensions but limited power to decide geo-human history and much less. The superagency of some circumscribes the power of all. It is the power of the powerless. Postmodern theorists such as Fredric Jameson argued that neoliberalism had brought about fundamental changes in the way cultural and political history is experienced. From the nineteenth century onwards, the chronology of modern history was linear and teleological, with the past progressively unfolding into a future whose destination seemed predetermined. In contrast, postmodernity was a space-time in which this onward march of history disintegrated into a perpetually rehashed present. The end of history and the triumph of liberal democracy and capitalism was declared at the end of the Cold

---

102 Jacob Burckhardt, *Reflections on History* (1868; rpt. Indianapolis: Liberty Classics, 1979), 31.

War, even as Walter Benjamin's angel of history was stirring a storm that "drives [us]irresistibly into the future, to which [our backs are] turned, while the pile of debris before [us] grows toward the sky. What we call progress is *this* storm."[103]

A stark choice confronts us in the Age of Humans: whether to perpetuate the Age of Unreason or follow a different path. Marx wrote that "Reason has always existed, but not always in a reasonable form."[104] During the Anthropocene, the logic of capital has proved more powerful than autonomous, sovereign Kantian rationality. We might dispute Latour's conclusion that "modernity is a concept, not a thing that happened" on the basis that the Anthropocene is the materialization of modernity but, nonetheless, concur that "[w]e have never been modern in the very simple sense that while we emancipated ourselves, each day we also more tightly entangled ourselves in the fabric of nature" so that "the reality of this modernisation has been its opposite".[105]

For Clive Hamilton, "[m]odernity was not an illusion but the arrival of the time of greatest promise and greatest danger, each represented by real social forces that have fought out the great political and social battles."[106] Hamilton inveighs against the Kantian subject and post-humanist approaches — the latter because they tend to discount human agency and belittle humanity and its achievements:

> The Anthropocene shows up humans as super-agents, powerful even beyond the imaginings of the Moderns, the agent who broke the bounds of Cartesian subjectivity to enter into

---

103 Fukuyama, *The End of History and the Last Man*; Walter Benjamin, "On the Concept of History," in *Selected Writings, Volume 4, 1938–1940,* eds. Howard Eiland and Michael W. Jennings (Cambridge: Belknap Press of Harvard University Press, 2006), 392.

104 Karl Marx, "To Arnold Ruge in Kreuznach, September, 1843," in Karl Marx and Friedrich Engels, *Collected Works,* vol. 3 (London: Lawrence & Wishart, 2010), 133–45, 143.

105 Bruno Latour, "Fifty Shades of Green," *Environmental Humanities* 7, no. 1 (2015): 219–25, at 221.

106 Hamilton, *Defiant Earth,* 110–11.

the object only to find itself confronted by a power over which it can never prevail.[107]

Our response should be acceptance of our super-agency and the awesome responsibility that comes with it and the magnitude of the choice between preservation and destruction:

> Only when we accept the greatness of the human project and the extreme danger that goes with it can we pose the epoch-defining question: how are we to use our power to pacify and protect the Earth rather than destroy it?[108]

Hamilton believes that alternative cosmologies such as *buen vivir* do not have answers to the Anthropocene:

> To turn to them for answers shoulders them with an impossible burden. We made the mess and "going native" ontologically is no answer. Looking upon Indigenous cultures with awe and regarding them as having magical potency is to fetishize them, a tendency now taken so far by some as to attribute to them the power to fix the climate and reverse the geological destabilization of the planet. There is no need to reject the historical truth of modernity and go looking among premodern ontologies for an alternative. *The only way forward* is to begin from where we are, in modernity, and from there work toward a "beyond-modernity" way of being.[109]

Indigenous cosmovisions may not be the answer, but Hamilton's dismissive approach implies that there is no wisdom to gain from onto-epistemologies that value harmony, humility, and ecocentrism — not least because it is immensely difficult to discern answers by perpetuating the hubristic follies of modernity. As noted above, Santos et al. argue knowledges operate in

---

107 Ibid, 101. Emphasis in original.
108 Ibid, 111.
109 Ibid, 106. Emphasis in original.

constellations and that there is no monolithic, singular knowledge — modernist, or otherwise. Global social justice is only possible with global cognitive justice, which, itself, is possible only by "substituting a monoculture of scientific knowledge by an ecology of knowledges,"[110] and it is this "transition from a monoculture of scientific knowledge to an ecology of knowledges [that] will make possible the replacement of knowledge-as regulation with knowledge-as-emancipation."[111]

It appears that we are confronted with a stark choice between rejecting modernity, aiming to transcend it, or celebrating and deepening it. For Hamilton, this is Hobson's choice because "there is no going back to pre-modern ontologies for an understanding; we must look ahead to *the evolution of modernity* itself, driven by its own endogenous forces and contradictions within a larger order."[112] The Anthropocene, he writes, "finally allows a clear view of what humans are" — an assertion open to ambiguous interpretations.[113]

5. Conclusion

Karl Marx begins *The Eighteenth Brumaire of Louis Bonaparte* with the acerbic observation that history repeats itself first as tragedy and then as farce.[114] In the following paragraph, Marx writes that human beings "make their own history, but they do not make it as they please: they do not make it under self-selected circumstances, but under circumstances existing already, given and transmitted from the past. The tradition of all dead generations weighs like a nightmare on the brains of the living."[115] For the foreseeable future, humankind and the Earth will make geo-human history under circumstances created by

---

110 Santos et al., "Opening up the Canon of Knowledge," xlviii.

111 Ibid, li.

112 Hamilton, *Defiant Earth,* 110.

113 Ibid, 120.

114 Karl Marx, *The Eighteenth Brumaire of Louis Bonaparte* (Moscow: Progress Publishers 1972), 10.

115 Ibid.

a relatively small number of human beings whose works have circumscribed the agency and power of all beings in the Anthropocene.

Born in the age of reason, the Anthropocene epitomizes unreason, which, ironically, seems entirely appropriate in this post-rational, post-truth era. The Age of Enlightenment witnessed the apotheosis of human beings through humanism, but the Age of Humans too seems like an ironic misnomer. Whereas modernity was predicated upon the fallacy that humanity could free itself from the dictates of the realm of necessity, today human beings are (re-)immersed in the nature that cannot be tamed. Amitav Ghosh writes, "Quite possibly then, this era, which so congratulates itself on its self-awareness, will come to be known as the time of the Great Derangement."[116] Albert Einstein is reputed to have remarked that no problem can be solved at the same level of consciousness that created it.

It is time for a great awakening.

---

116 Amitav Ghosh, *The Great Derangement: Climate Change and the Unthinkable* (London: Penguin 2016), 11.

3

Twilight of the Nation-State (at a Time of Resurgent Nationalism)?

Richard Falk

1. Prelude

"Twilight" implies transition from light to dark — a temporary set of circumstances, neither light nor dark, but in between, albeit with a trajectory towards night, darkness, decline — even disappearance. This metaphoric understanding of twilight should not be taken too literally. In the setting of this chapter, the metaphor of twilight calls attention to the idea, with its plural interpretations, that the era in which sovereign states were the dominant political actors in the world is definitely coming to an end. However, this does not necessarily imply an emergent irrelevance of states as the locus of political community or of the state-based system as the foundation of world order.

Sovereign territorial states are highly likely to continue to assume responsibility for order and for defense of the national society enclosed within their internationally recognized boundaries. It is almost unimaginable for governments of states to give up the juridical nationalism exerting administrative control over the whole of a sovereign territory, the unchallenged authority to organize defensive arrangements, the power to raise revenue by imposing taxes of various kinds, or control over entry and exit from the state's territory. Even if the United Nations (UN) and other institutions were to be reformed to allow for the participation of various political actors other than states, it would still be expected that states would be the most important participants.

Despite the resilience of states and of a state-centric framework for international relations, there are some profound changes underway that do suggest a decline in the role of states in certain crucial respects. The world and its peoples currently inhabit a twilight zone that we struggle to interpret because the realities of the historical moment are unprecedented and beset by contradiction. To begin with, it would seem that the real levers of hard and soft power will increasingly elude statist control. At the same time, it remains far from clear "to *where?*" the power formerly dominated by states is expected to migrate in coming years. This kind of fundamental uncertainty is a distinctive feature of the present age.[1] This underlying issue of the redistribution of power and authority at a global level is one of the questions that must be addressed if the twilight characterization of the state's role is to be treated as descriptive and generally accepted as accurate.[2]

There is also a more ominous reading of twilight as an acknowledgment that the current global challenges associated with climate change and nuclear weaponry will not be met in

---

1   Emblematic of this zeitgeist was the first World Forum organized by TRT World (a Turkish English-language radio and TV channel similar in format and intent to CNN or to Al Jazeera English) around the theme of "Inspiring Change in an Age of Uncertainty," featuring several world leaders, prominent media personalities, government officials, and even a few academics, including myself. Hotel Conrad, Istanbul, October 18–19, 2017. No one took issue with this theme, which would never have been chosen in the last half of the twentieth century when the structure of international relations, at least, seemed stable, if not certain, and hardly worth problematizing.

2   The linearity of the metaphor can also be questioned and subjected to doubt in this chapter. The degree of certainty that night will follow twilight does not pertain in the political domain where reversibility and stagnancy could persist, that is, the state could recover its salience or at least achieve a new stasis.

a responsible manner. If this is so, such failure will produce not only a range of catastrophic consequences for modern civilization, but also quite possibly for the entire future of the human species and its habitat. In this regard, deploying twilight as a metaphor for the contemporary situation is a way of identifying the first biopolitical moment in human experience. This recognition entails an uncomfortable realization about the way the world is organized, as well as its trajectory: no adequate political mechanism is available to protect the *global* or *human* interest as distinct from the national interest or its aggregation.[3] When the stakes are relatively localized (as in responding to a natural disaster or to a human tragedy), national governments, international institutions, and civil society actors can often fill the institutional and normative gap, providing the resources and leadership required by the situation.[4] Even if these actors fail adequately to protect global public goods, the harmful consequences to human society and its habitats are sub-systemic rather than systemic.[5] Matters are more urgent in the face of climate change and nuclear catastrophe: this is the transformative rupture — namely, failure to address these challenges of global scope has systemic and biopolitical implications.[6]

When the systemic challenge involves fundamentals of production and consumption (as with climate change, or control over the ultimate weaponry of destruction), then the absence of effective mechanisms for upholding global and human interests leads to policy failure, the consequences of which are altogether more problematic. As a result of such present failure, strong sig-

---

3   This is the central argument of Richard Falk, *Power Shift: On the New Global Order* (London: Zed Books, 2016).

4   On the US providing a global leadership that achieves many of the positive goals associated with world government, see Michael Mandelbaum, *The Case for Goliath: How America Acts as a World's Government in the Twenty-First Century* (New York: Public Affairs, 2005).

5   For an understanding of the scale and scope of past catastrophic change see Jared Diamond, *Collapse: How Societies Choose to Fail or Succeed* (New York: Viking, 2005).

6   Falk, *Power Shift*, 253–62.

nals are currently being sent that appear to vindicate a dark view of what to expect in the future.[7]

2. Conceptual Clarifications

There is also a conceptual issue that affects how we think about the future of the nation-state. When considering the decline of the state, are we thinking primarily of the state as a unitary political actor on the global political and economic stage? Is the modern state being gradually displaced by regional and global institutions and by democratizing developments, such as the rise of transnational civil society actors, proposals for a directly elected global parliament, and increases in digital networking on a planetary scale? Or are we also considering the state as a fulcrum of psycho-political loyalty (patriotic, as distinct from juridical nationalism) that is losing support in relation to the territorial population who identify increasingly as regional or global citizens? Are citizens withdrawing support from central governments in favor of local, communal, and sub-state identification and participation? The frequency of internal strife and political polarization challenges belief in the capacity of current territorial states to establish order within territorial boundaries. Unresolvable civil strife is an emergent world order issue of increasing visibility and frustration, as well as the source of some of the most intense and enduring violent political conflicts throughout the non-Western world.[8]

---

7 We perceive the future "through a glass, darkly" if at all, which provides ample reason to rely on an epistemology of humility to sustain hope. That is, since we cannot know the future, we should strive for what is necessary and desirable. This view is elaborated upon by Falk, *Power Shift*, 101–28.

8 Among recent instances, Scotland, Iraqi Kurdistan, and Catalonia are of relevance. For an analysis of the international issues in the political and historical context of the 2017 encounter of Spain and Catalonia see John Dugard, Richard Falk, Ana Stanic, and Marc Weller, *The Will of the People and Statehood,* Report at the request of Esquerra Republicana de Catalunya, October 30, 2017. For a focus on the conflictual aspects of internal struggles to reshape the dynamics of self-determination see Mary Kaldor,

There is, finally, a geopolitical issue associated with the differentiated political, economic, and cultural roles of states that exert significant extra-territorial influence on global policy; such states differ significantly from what might be termed the "traditional Westphalian territorial state." The relevant range of examples encompasses micro-states at one end and superpowers at the other end of the spectrum. I have written about the United States in the past as the first "global state" in history — extending its presence and security role to the far corners of the planet by an unprecedented combination of hard-power militarism and soft-power dissemination of its popular culture and life style.[9]

The Westphalian model of the territorial sovereign state is of "a normal state," with of course many variations in: size; status; population; form of government; wealth; military capabilities; regional and extra-regional role; religious, cultural, and ethnic composition; and internationally-recognized boundaries. At the height of Westphalian state-centrism, plural ethnicities that claimed a distinct nationalism were frequently disregarded, despite grievances — or at most, such issues were viewed as questions pertaining to treatment of minorities. If sub-state nationalisms were strongly asserted in the form of a secessionist movement, they were either suppressed by the state as necessary, partially accommodated by grants of autonomy and self-government, or, in extreme cases, the prior state was fragmented violently or through negotiations by successful movements of secession. States were presumed to be multi-national, plural, and secular, while nationality was psycho-politically rather than

New and Old Wars, 3rd edn. (Cambridge: Cambridge University Press, 2012).

9   See Richard Falk, "Ordering the World: Hedley Bull After 40 Years," in *The Anarchical Society at 40: Contemporary Challenges and Prospects,* eds. Hidemi Suganami, Madeline Carr, and Adam Humphreys (Oxford: Oxford University Press, 2017), 41–55, in geopolitical sequel to role of "Great Powers." On role of Great Powers, see Hedley Bull, *The Anarchical Society: A Study of Order in World Politics* (New York: Columbia University Press, 1977).

juridically conceived. The well-governed Westphalian state was dominant internally and diplomatically, although there were always non-state actors of varying degrees of influence with competing agendas and extra-national roles and identities. A purely statist world order — in short — was always a fiction, or at best a conceptual convenience.[10]

The prevalence of the twilight metaphor was partly a reflection of the strong belief that at the end of the Cold War, economic globalization would weaken the territorial orientation of problem-solving and policy priorities. This belief gained currency, too, as global security concerns became briefly marginal with the disappearance of the kind of strategic rivalry that was so prominent during the Cold War epoch, and as transnational networking associated with the Digital Age made territorial boundaries less significant. An increasingly transnational and deterritorialized conception of trade, communications, and organization administration (as well as the efficiency of capital), created the practical foundations for advocacy of neoliberal capitalism as prefiguring a digitized and robotic future.[11] States would serve the world economy best if they allowed market forces and technological momentum, not the wellbeing of the national citizenry, to shape their conduct and viewpoint. This was one version of a statist twilight primarily generated by the globalization of capital and technology. This prospect has been

---

10 See Stephen Krasner, *Sovereignty: Organized Hypocrisy: Change and Persistence in International Relations* (Princeton: Princeton University Press, 1999); see also Joseph A. Camilleri and Jim Falk, *The End of Sovereignty: The Politics of a Shrinking and Fragmenting World* (Hants: Edward Elgar, 1992).

11 Most extravagantly expressed by Francis Fukuyama, *The End of History and the Last Man* (New York: The Free Press, 1992). Even Huntington's far more accurate anticipation of renewed conflict was based on a new era of inter-civilizational rather than inter-state warfare, see Samuel Huntington, *Clash of Civilizations and the Making of World Order* (New York: Simon and Schuster, 1997). Both of these influential formulations can be read as alternative expressions of the twilight hypothesis. For a negative assessment of economic globalization as shaped by neoliberal ideology see Richard Falk, *Predatory Globalization: A Critique* (Cambridge: Polity, 2000).

somewhat superseded by the resecuritization of world politics after the 9/11 attacks on the United States and the resultant choice to respond by way of "war" and military intervention rather than reliance on "criminal law enforcement."[12]

Also, the metaphor of twilight (as commonly deployed) was not at all in agreement that the sequel to state-centrism would be the darkness (conceived of as chaos and conflict) as the presumed aftermath of twilight.[13] Indeed, some hopeful commentators anticipated "a businessman's peace," as well as an indefinite series of technological breakthroughs, in which an integrated capitalist world economy would do away with wars, geopolitical rivalry, ecological challenges, and ideological tensions that were regular features of a state-centric world order.[14] Others — especially in the English-speaking West — worried about the dangers of nuclear conflagration also believed that, with the decline of the state as a political actor, the next stage of world order would be some kind of world government thought by true believers to be the only means to ensure a viable future.[15] So,

12 For discussion see unpublished paper, Richard Falk, "After 9/11: The Toxic Interplay of Counterterrorism, Geopolitics, and World Order," presented at a workshop on "Is there an After After 9/11?" Orfalea Center on Global and International Studies, University of California Santa Barbara, January 20–21, 2018.

13 There was some thinking along this line, most explicitly by Robert D. Kaplan, *Coming Anarchy: Shattering the Dreams of the Post Cold War* (New York: Random House, 2000); also, Huntington, *Clash of Civilizations,* but Fukuyama's twilight is followed by the presumed forever sunshine of globalized liberalism.

14 Perhaps the most graphic assertions along these lines were made by the American president, George W. Bush, shortly after the 9/11 attacks: "We have the best chance since the rise of the nation state in the seventeenth century to build a world where the great powers compete in peace instead of prepare for war." Further, "[m]ore and more civilized nations find themselves on the same side, united by common dangers of terrorist violence and chaos:" Address to the Graduating Class, West Point, June 2002; also, in the cover letter to National Security Strategy of the United States, White House, Washington, DC, September 2002.

15 Most significantly argued by Daniel Deudney, *Bounding Power: Republican Theory from the Polis to the Global Village* (Princeton: Princeton University Press, 2004).

after all, to designate the present period as a time of twilight for the state, even if it turns out to be a hypothesis borne out by history, tells us nothing about what kind of political future might emerge in the form of a new world order. In effect, there are many alternative post-Westphalian world order possibilities that can be evaluated from the perspective of likelihood, desirability, and functionality.

3. Climate Change

The presence of systemic challenges in a world order reality that is sub-system dominant (that is, shaped by sovereign states, especially those that are dominant) has yet to be sufficiently appreciated. True, there is attention given to the advent of the Anthropocene, in recognition of the extent to which human activities are now principal drivers of important changes in the quality and even sustainability of the global habitat.[16] Yet problem-solving is still caught up in the structures, practices, and procedures of the Holocene, which dealt with habitat and security challenges by way of sub-systemic responses and policies that assume that crises could be devastating, but not threatening to the system as a whole.[17] In different ways, climate change and nuclear weapons are illustrative of the global challenges facing humanity in the age of the Anthropocene, but there are others — the protection of biodiversity, eradication of poverty, the prevention of hunger and malnutrition, and the control of pandemic disease.

From a conceptual perspective, climate change is a clear instance of the limits of statist problem-solving in circumstances where the global scope of the problem is acknowledged. The

---

16 See Richard Falk's chapter, "The World Ahead: Entering the Anthropocene?" in *Exploring Emergent Thresholds: Toward 2030*, eds. Richard Falk, Manoranjan Mohanty, and Victor Faessel (Delhi: Orient Black Swan, 2017), 19–47.

17 These terms used to classify geological eras are here used metaphorically to identify the scope of problems and problem solving in the context of global governance.

unevenness of state responsibility for the buildup of greenhouse gases, which is aggravated by the difficulty of establishing causal connections between emissions and harm, creates controversy and tensions. With a strong consensus within the community of climate scientists and among civil society activists, the governments of the world came together to negotiate an historic agreement to control greenhouse gas emissions sufficiently to minimize increasing harm from global warming. The result was a notable achievement: 193 governments signed onto the Paris Climate Change Agreement in 2015, and there resulted a celebration among the participating diplomats. Yet the success of the Paris Agreement, as measured by maximizing the cooperative potential of a statist problem-solving procedure, was, from another point of view, an ominous failure. The Agreement, although impressive as an exercise in inter-state lawmaking, was disappointing if the measure of success was prudently addressing the challenge. The Paris Agreement was neither responsive enough to the dangers nor sufficiently obligatory to provide a credible and responsible addressal of the dangers of global warming if measured against the limits on CO_2 dissemination urged on governments by the overwhelming majority of climate specialists.

The Agreement did not go far enough in curtailing emissions and its compliance provisions were basically voluntary without even the pretension of enforcement.[18] Further, it did not account for the churlish nationalism of some governments, highlighted by the Trump refusal to adhere to its restrictions unless America was given a "better deal" in a revised agreement.[19] In other words, despite being one of the most impressive achievements

---

18 See the text of the Paris Agreement on Climate Change (2015) to discern its essentially voluntary compliance framework. "Paris Agreement," New York: United Nations, 2015.

19 At the time of this writing, Trump has not yet formally expressed objections to the Paris Agreement beyond suggesting, in vague generalities, that it is "a very bad deal for America" and hurts the competitiveness of American business by raising costs of production via constraints on carbon emissions.

of international problem-solving — known in international circles as either "multilateralism" or "a lawmaking treaty — " occurring under UN auspices, the outcome reached seems almost certain to expose future generations to the multiple ravages of global warming. In this crucial respect, the twilight we are now experiencing is most likely to be followed by a long night as there is no path visible to promote a solution consistent with the collective wellbeing of humanity. So long as problem-solving in the setting of climate change is predominantly state-centric, there is almost no realistic prospect of restricting greenhouse emissions to safe levels, leaving society caught between reigning attitudes of despair and denial. This assessment is not meant to belittle the relevance and local benefits of sub-state climate change initiatives motivated by self-interest and a commitment to promote public goods that is stronger than that of the current national government.[20]

4. Nuclear Weaponry

It may be most reasonable to connect the start of the Anthropocene with the dropping of the atomic bombs on two Japanese cities in August 1945, and the decision by the United States, followed by other governments, to develop their own capability to produce far more powerful and destructive nuclear weapons. Present nuclear arsenals combined with prevailing military doctrine create the potential to alter the human and natural habitat in fundamental ways that may not be reversible over long stretches of time.[21] In line with the analysis of this chapter,

---

20 The climate-change policies of California are a dramatic example, accentuated by the anti-environmental posture of the Trump presidency. Individuals and communities may voluntarily adopt climate-friendly behavioral patterns including vegan diets, electric cars, solar power.

21 See "nuclear famine" studies. There are also other indications of toxicity and disruption of ecological and social structures on a more or less permanent basis. For human impacts via food see the briefing paper by Ira Helfand, "Nuclear Famine: Two Billion People at Risk: Global Impacts of Limited Nuclear War on Agriculture, Food Supplies, and Human Nutri-

nuclear weapons pose a systemic challenge in several respects: there is no way to confine the zone of devastation to particular states engaged in warfare; after more than seventy years, it is apparent that states are unable to find a solution that is consistent with international law, international morality, and a sustainable world order. What has replaced a systemic solution is a legally, morally, and ecologically unsatisfactory structure that can be denominated as "nuclear apartheid," resting on a nonproliferation regime, to prevent unwanted additional countries from acquiring the weaponry, and on a managerial regime (known as arms control), in which nuclear weapons states seek to minimize risks of unintentional, accidental, and mistaken usage.[22]

A similarly critical assessment relating to climate change can be made with respect to nuclear weaponry, although more pointedly. From a global and human perspective, it has seemed obvious from the moment of the first use of an atomic bomb that it was in the human interest to get rid of the weaponry by way of an unconditional prohibition reinforced by verified and enforced disarmament. Yet the geopolitical temptations of this weaponry were too great to overcome and an alternative framework was developed that retains the weapons for some while trying to preclude acquisition by most others.[23] At present, the world is faced with a crisis involving the insistence by the United States that it will not tolerate the retention of the weaponry by North Korea, even though North Korea has a strong security argument that provides a justification for possessing a deterrent against hostile foreign forces, including the United States. In this context, state-centric world order has demonstrated its

---

tion," *Physicians for Social Responsibility,* December 10, 2013, https://www. psr.org/blog/resource/nuclear-famine-two-billion-people-at-risk/.

22 For elaboration see Richard Falk and David Krieger, *The Path to Nuclear Zero: Dialogues on Nuclear Danger* (Boulder: Paradigm, 2012).

23 Even when a cautious call for steps toward a world without nuclear weaponry is set forth, as by Barack Obama in his Prague Speech of 2009, nothing happens as the roots of nuclearism are too deep to challenge effectively.

inability to insulate the systemic reality from the potential catastrophe of nuclear war.

Here, the nature of the problem is better grasped by taking account of the *geopolitical* dimensions of world order rather than of the difficulties and limitations of aggregating national interests. There is ample documentation of the reluctance of the United States or Soviet Union to embark upon a disarmament process that would involve the elimination of the weaponry.[24] Additional countries either acquired the weaponry or accepted nuclear weapons as the foundation of their security via alliance assurances. That is, the state structure was incapable of protecting the global or human interest, or even the national interest of most or all states, and in this functional sense, it seems appropriate to regard the nation-state as in long-term normative decline. By splitting the world between nuclear (and nuclear dependent) and non-nuclear states, there is present a systemic crisis with no foreseeable means of overcoming it.

At least, after decades of passivity, the non-nuclear states singly and collectively — with strong transnational civil society support — are at least posing a political and moral challenge to nuclearism, though not yet as a geopolitical challenge. The Nobel Peace Prize in 2017 was given to a civil society group, ICAN, which promoted adherence to a UN Treaty of Prohibition (known as the BAN Treaty) with respect to nuclear weaponry. Endorsed by 122 countries, it was opposed by all of the existing nuclear states and by allies that have accepted protection by reliance on nuclear deterrence. In other words, unlike climate change, where despite a variety of differences in national circumstances, all governments were willing to agree on a common solution that reflected their interest; with regard to nuclear weapons, the leading nuclear powers altogether reject a multi-

---

24 See Richard J. Barnet, *Who Wants Disarmament?* (Boston: Beacon Press, 1960) for a strong early critique of disarmament diplomacy that publicly advocated disarmament while bureaucratically opposing it. Over the decades, nuclearism has become entrenched in the governmental structures of the main nuclear weapons states that have been identified as the "deep state" or "military-industrial-complex."

lateral approach. The United States, the United Kingdom and France even issued a statement declaring their conceptual and unrepentant opposition to the BAN Treaty.[25] Here, the world order deficiency associated with the lack of capability to protect human and global interests because of the primacy of the *geopolitical* is transparently evident. In this regard, the aggregation of national interests by way of multilateral agreement cannot even be attempted, as there is this fundamental split between those states accepting the ultimately Faustian bargain of nuclear weaponry and those seeking a world without nuclear weaponry.

5. From the Perspective of Global Governance

Until ten years ago, the idea of a statist twilight was seen mainly as a recognition that the state, as it had evolved in Europe since the seventeenth century, was being displaced transnationally by economic globalization and was newly threatened by transnational mega-terrorism and cyber attacks.[26] At the same time there was an emerging awareness that the most manifest threat to human wellbeing was being posed by the effects of global warming brought about by the accumulation of greenhouse gas emissions. The recent confrontation between North Korea and the United States, which has featured apocalyptic threats from the leaders of both countries, reawakened the world to the dangers of nuclear war and to the fragility of existing global security arrangements.

Overall, the increasingly global scope of policymaking and problem-solving was regarded as making it dysfunctional to

---

25 See Richard Falk. "Challenging Nuclearism: The Nuclear Ban Treaty Assessed," July 14, 2017, https://richardfalk.wordpress.com/2017/07/14/challenging-nuclearism-the-nuclear-ban-treaty-assessed/; "Nobel Peace Prize 2017: International Campaign to Abolish Nuclear Weapons (ICAN)", October 8, 2017, https://richardfalk.wordpress.com/2017/10/08/nobel-peace-prize-2017-international-campaign-to-abolish-nuclear-weapons-ican/.

26 For speculation along these lines, see Richard Falk, *The Great Terror War* (Northampton: Olive Branch Press, 2003).

rely on state-level governance and calculations of national interest. This is because the items on the political agenda most likely
affect the totality of lives and the collective destiny of humanity — especially future generations — regardless of where one is
situated on the planet.[27] Revealingly, these globalizing concerns
have not led governments to create stronger structures of global
governance. Despite the fact that the dangerous inability to protect at-risk global and human interests might have led more responsible governments and their citizens to work feverishly to
establish a more independent and adequately-resourced United
Nations, adequately addressing global challenges is impossible
without augmented institutional capabilities backed up by the
level of political will needed to generate and implement legal
norms that reflect human and global interests. How these will
be determined is a major adaptive challenge to a fundamental
realization that the Westphalian framework, even if responsibly
reinforced by geopolitical leadership — which is presently at low
ebb — cannot satisfy minimum requirements of world order. It
is a disappointing part of these dire circumstances that there is
such a weak popular mobilization around this twenty-first-century agenda of challenges. It is time to acknowledge that, despite
the seriousness of global challenges, states separately and aggre-
gately have shown little ability, and inadequate political will, to
respond in a manner that is adaptive.[28] In effect, the non-decline
of the state, or even its seeming resurgence as an exclusivist
nation-state, is accentuating the weakness of global governance
when it comes to global, systemic issues. In this respect, the state

---

27 For stimulating conjecture along these lines, see Robert W. Cox and
    Timothy J. Sinclair, *Approaches to World Order* (Cambridge: Cambridge
    University Press, 1996); Stephen Gill, ed., *Global Crises and the Crisis of
    Global Leadership* (Cambridge: Cambridge University Press, 2012).

28 See Falk, *Power Shift*, ch. 13 — raising the biopolitical question as to wheth-
    er there is a sufficient species will to survive as distinct from individual,
    communal, and national wills to survive that are robust, and actually, part
    of the distinctive problem of superseding and complementing responses
    at lower levels of social integration by reliance on species and global scale
    responses.

continues to bask in sunlight, as if awaiting twilight to subdue its anachronistic orientation and priorities.

Instead of a rational and convincing pattern of adaptation, this rendering of a radiant twilight has produced a series of institutional innovations that were supposed to serve as a vehicle for the pursuit of multilateral cooperative arrangements on world affairs. This gave rise to such diverse arenas as the G-7, G-8, G-20, annual gatherings of the IMF and World Bank, BRIC meetings, Shanghai Infrastructure Investment Bank, as well as to private sector initiatives such as the World Economic Forum, the Council on Foreign Relations, and the Trilateral Commission. Such constellations of institutional configurations contribute to the impression of organizational decline, as does the emergence of a variety of anti-capitalist initiatives associated with the World Social Forum, Non-Aligned Movement, including commoning in various forms.[29]

On a regional level, the European Union led the way in establishing economic markets, monetary integration and procedures, as well as providing the glimmerings of a political community that aspired to diminish the practical and psychological importance of statehood, national boundaries, and sovereign rights in the very geographic setting that gave rise in the first place to the European states system. The European Union also invented the rather dissonant idea that despite strong, diverse, and spatially-concentrated ethnicities and antagonistic religions within sovereign borders, the state was also the sole juridical source of national identity.[30] In effect, the architects of statism cleverly appropriated the national feelings of community felt by such ethnic groups, and made it into a statewide abstraction with varying degrees of existential validity usually only descrip-

---

29 See also the networked adaptation to the new era as depicted by Anne-Marie Slaughter, *The New World Order* (Princeton: Princeton University Press, 2004).

30 The idea of nationality is purely juridical, given practical relevance by passport and international identity papers. In some countries, for example Israel, the state draws a distinction between citizenship and nationality, privileging the latter on the basis of Jewish ethnicity.

tively representative of the dominant ethnicity. This ambiguity is at the root of confusions associated with the current nationalist discourse, in which statists try to overwhelm the identities of separate nationalities or regionalisms by stressing their version of "the nation" as encompassing all.[31]

When it came to security, for many states, twilight was superseded by nighttime conditions decades ago. During the Cold War Era, the main issues of war and peace were addressed by competing alliances, hierarchically organized under the leadership of two ideologically and geopolitically competing superpowers, the United States and the Soviet Union, with Europe regarded by these titanic opponents as the main theater of strategic confrontation. Wars and crises occurred in this period at the edges of the geopolitical orbits of effective control wielded by each superpower, and especially in Germany, Korea, and Vietnam, which were divided along such ideological and geopolitical lines. Korea alone continues to threaten world order in the post-Cold War Era because it remains divided in a context where dangerous tensions have induced the leadership of North Korea to carry deterrence logic to its ultimate extreme, which, in turn, has led the United States to respond over the past twenty-five years with coercive diplomacy, hegemonic pretensions, and hard power threats that, if actualized, would produce a horrendous catastrophe with the potential for many millions of casualties.

With the collapse of the Soviet Union in 1991, the United States chose to constitute itself as the first "global state" in history, relying on a network of hundreds of foreign bases, navies

---

31 The Trump presidency has illustrated the dynamic of the double coding of nationalism and love of country. For Trump's white political base, the acclamation accorded to America is understood in a non-plural white-supremacist manner, which terrifies and angers those Americans who are non-white or socially vulnerable. It raises the critical question as to what is "America" as state and nation. Such interrogation should be directed at many states that are trying to build various forms of exclusionary governing structures. These issues are well explored in Mazen Masri, *The Dynamics of Exclusionary Constitutionalism: Israel as a Jewish and Democratic State* (Oxford: Hart, 2017).

in every ocean, and the militarization of space and even cyber-space, aiming to establish a global state that eclipsed the sovereignty of all other states, which are unwilling to dilute the traditional scope of their sovereign rights when it comes to national security (except to some extent China and Russia).[32] This American global state relies on the consent of many, and on coercion toward a few, in pursuit of its goals. This is most clearly evident in relation to the conduct of counterterrorist warfare and counter-proliferation diplomacy, using non-territorial innovations such as drones, cyber sabotage, special ops elite covert forces, as well as relying on traditional territorial instruments of hard power such as military intervention. Such a heavy investment in achieving globalized military control is also seen as supportive of neoliberal capitalism, and also tends to downgrade the relevance of the Westphalian state to either of its prime roles — in relation to development and to internal and external security.[33]

These statist mutations may be better or at least alternatively understood as "eclipse," "partial eclipse," and even as "temporary eclipse," rather than as "twilight" — which seems too vague and seemingly irreversible in relation to present concerns, except to professional students of international relations, because of several mitigating factors. For one, the United States was widely valued for its role as a largely responsible global leader, helping to fill the gap created by the absence of mechanisms for protecting human and global interests, distinguishing this from seeking to achieve such goals by aggregating separate national interests in a variety of international arenas, often with the uni-

---

32 This sense of establishing a global security system administered by Washington was most clearly put forward during the presidency of George W. Bush in the National Security Doctrine of the United States of America (2002): see advice to China to concentrate on trade, and not waste resources competing with the US in the domain of security.

33 The "Westphalian state" should be contrasted with the "global state" constructed by the United States, as well as with the concept of "empire." See, generally, Richard Falk, *The Declining World Order: America's Imperial Geopolitics* (New York and London: Routledge, 2004), esp. 3–65; also Falk, "Does the Human Species Wish to Survive?" and Falk, *Power Shift,* 253–62.

versalizing imprimatur of the United Nations.[34] Put differently, the twilight of the state may be less descriptive of the changing reality of world order than what might be termed "the twilight of global leadership," which has important ideological and structural implications.[35]

Yet another shake of the geopolitical kaleidoscope yields a different fate for the nation-state, an outcome that seems plausible in light of the recent upsurge of right-wing populism and the related pushback against new waves of non-Westerners who seek to emigrate to the West. It is this re-intensification of nationalism at the state level in its most exclusionary forms that makes the idea of "twilight" particularly inappropriate as a present descriptor of the current international reality, although it might have seemed a more accurate descriptor a decade ago.[36]

In response to a series of disruptive transnational flows, including of people, money, goods, drugs, crime, and political extremism, the managers of governance structures of states are claiming increasing autocratic authority over domestic space. In other words, the mainstream prophesies of the twilight of the state got it wrong. Instead of twilight, there is an appearance of a second dawn — more Westphalian than the Westphalian image of the ideal sovereign state, yet continuing to be pushed and pulled in post-Westphalian directions.

6. War and Peace after 9/11

A momentous decision that diminished the sovereignty of many states was bound up with the American response to the 9/11 at-

---

34 For instance, overseeing the negotiation of several multinational agreements, including the Law of the Seas Treaty in 1982, and generally seeking to combine its national interests with sensitivity to the interests of others, but still largely within a state-centric imaginary.

35 See Gill, ed., *Global Crises and the Crisis of Global Leadership.*

36 See Mathew Horsman and Andrew Marshall, *After the Nation State: Citizens, Tribalism, and the New World Disorder* (London: HarperCollins, 1994) somewhat prophetically arguing that the future will witness the decline of the state due to the rise of anti-internationalist values and political movements.

tacks — in particular, the bipartisan decision to treat the events as "acts of war" rather than as "crimes against humanity" or as "international terrorism." Engaging in war rather than in cooperative transnational law enforcement meant that the issue was placed in the domain of statecraft, but with neither main actor in the conflict being a state in the original Westphalian sense. When this consideration was combined with a public discourse that demonized the adversary as "evil", there was no end game other than extermination. Negotiations previously underlay all past "wars", while the dynamics of demonization were understood to be for the purpose of mobilizing anger and support in one's own society and for creating war propaganda.

However, this war discourse was never meant to be conclusive, and so, there was always political space available for diplomacy and a negotiated end to the war that included political compromises, acknowledging the adversary as representative of a sovereign state and as being entitled to diplomatic status and privileges. The label of terrorism can be removed at will, and the legitimate grievances of the terrorist entity can be acknowledged, as was the case when the United Kingdom negotiated The Good Friday Agreement with the IRA or when the leaders of the Israel and the Palestine Liberation Organization shook hands on the White House lawn.

The public discourse from both sides in the War on Terror subverts the legitimacy of the other, demonizing its core identity, and makes diplomacy irrelevant because neither side is prepared to live with the other on any basis. Given the asymmetric nature of the conflict with respect to targets and technology, the world as a whole becomes, for the first time, a battlefield and the sovereign rights of states are not respected. Targets for the non-state actor, whether that actor is Al Qaeda or ISIS, can be anywhere and anyone: for the global state, the alleged terrorist or supporter of the terrorist campaign is treated as a legitimate drone or special ops target wherever located. In the process, international humanitarian law is negated, civilian innocence is sacrificed in different ways by both sides, and the security of territorial states is both subverted and upheld by extra-territorial political actions.

7. Conclusion

Despite the twilight metaphor, the truer reality of the present situation is a confused light that can be interpreted in different ways, and which embodies deeply contradictory trends.

On the one side, there is a backlash against economic globalization giving rise to populist support for economic nationalism which risks trade wars, protectionism, and depression. Such tendencies are furthered by the security concerns associated with transnational terrorism and migration flows arising from chaotic combat and climate refugees. The political expression of these concerns is reflected in the global rise of right-wing populism, autocratic governance, and declining support for democracy and human rights.

On the other side is the fraying of borders and territorial security by the tactics of both sides in asymmetric warfare, exposing the vulnerability of the modern state, however militarized, to low technology weaponry that creates societal shockwaves of fear and destroys symbols of power and invulnerability — as was the case with the attacks on the World Trade Center and Pentagon in 2001. Digital technology combined with advances in artificial intelligence and robotics creates a borderless world in which the tactics of drone warfare and cyber war are emblematic of the deterritorializing of combat and homeland security. This kind of deterritorializing of warfare can be traced back to the radiation effects of nuclear weaponry, such as from nuclear tests and accidents (Chernobyl, Fukushima).[37]

In addition to war, the dense causal complexity of global warming, in terms of the locus of greenhouse gas emissions being substantially disconnected from the locus of harm, offers

---

37 Not explicitly formulated in Robert J. Lifton and Richard Falk, *Indefensible Weapons: The Political and Psychological Case against Nuclearism,* rev. 3rd. edn. (New York: Basic Books, 1991).

another kind of deterritorializing in which ecological security depends on the behavior of the global whole as well as on that of certain national parts. Related issues of biodiversity pose analogous issues in relation to the global dependence on on diversity being out of sync with the territorial sovereignty relied upon to preserve the world's most biologically diverse rainforests.

How these contradictory tendencies will be mediated over time is, perhaps, the great unanswerable question that casts a shadow over the future of humanity. At present, there is no discernible alternative to state-centric world order, yet, as argued here, this type of problem solving is incapable of providing solutions for the fundamental global challenges that must be addressed to avoid a catastrophic future for humanity. It was also argued here that the central world order deficiency, overshadowing the others, is the absence of mechanisms for the effective and just protection of human and global interests. In this central functional and normative respect, the problems confronting all nation states can only be realistically and equitably addressed if governments assent to major transfers of sovereign authority from the national level to regional and global actors.

In effect, the viability of sovereign states depends on their paradoxical willingness to relinquish traditional sovereign rights, especially those associated with geopolitical roles. In the short run, the populist surge at the national level precludes such an adjustment and gives rise to precisely the opposite reaction. The "America First" ethos is concretized by the rejection of free/fair trade, by the withdrawal of the United States from the Paris Climate Change Agreement of 2015, and by a refusal to participate in a UN effort to address the challenges of global migration. This broad American retreat from global leadership is epitomized by the overall displacement of earlier liberal internationalist efforts to maximize international cooperation. The new approach features regressive moves favoring bilateralism and transactional interactions among states that privilege power disparities.

We can only hope that Trump and Global Trumpism are temporary phenomena, which, over time, prompt constructive responses from other political actors around the world, and give rise to a new populism that recognizes the urgency of implementing global and human interests for the sake of sustainability and of the future wellbeing of the human species and its habitat. I believe that if states are at the center of this re-energizing of world order in light of global challenges, their twilight will be prolonged, but if leading states do not promote global and human interests with a sense of urgency, then the sun may catastrophically set on their primacy as world-order actors rather abruptly.

4

The Decline of Liberal Politics

Andreas Karitzis

The claim that we live in a highly transitional period has become commonplace — one of the bromides we hear from journalists, analysts, and all manner of experts, who cite the tumult of war-zones, the collapse of state administrative systems, refugee waves, terrorist attacks, environmental destruction, and political and social upheavals. Momentous events provide explosive release of underlying tensions that are the result of multiple transformations that have evolved and accelerated over time. These transformations, taking place on many and varied levels of our societies — and which, by nature, do not go off with the "bang" of "big" events — determine which trajectories our societies will follow in the future.

At this moment of world history, a decisively important transitional period, it is essential to imagine the appropriate personal stance, collective mentality and tools of political and social mobilization that we must develop. But in order to do so, we must first determine the horizon and depth of the transition in motion. Second, we must identify the transformations in the fields in which social and political antagonism is taking place — transformations that are radically shaking established institutional architectures and changing the rules and methods of political practice at the very same moment that new actors are emerging. Third, there is a need to find a new ontology[1] as well as a new "life form — " that is to say, to develop and practice a functional set of subjective and collective capacities more compatible with the period's transitionality.

Below, I will attempt roughly to outline some of the aspects of these three "duties," placing emphasis on transformations in the political sphere.

1. The Horizon and Depth of the Transition

Leaving aside the "big" events, transitionality is characterized by the reduced momentum of entrenched institutionalizations and mentalities, and by their transcendence through the development of various processes that generate new questions and transform older ones.[2] In specifying the horizon and depth of the transition currently underway, the issue is to discern how deep these challenges reach. In the next sections, I review this question from the perspective of different historical "cycles."

Persistent Capitalist Crisis

One account of the transitionality structuring the present period looks to the capitalist system's historical periodicity: growth–crisis–creative destruction–restructuring–growth. According to this approach, transitionality is linked to the restructuring/renaissance of the capitalist growth machine, and to an accompanying destruction/destructuring.[3] The emergence of new policies, social upheavals, geopolitical tensions, new players, and so on can be explained as symptoms of the rebirth of the capitalist

---

1 David Bollier, "Commoning as a Transformative Social Paradigm," *The Next System Project,* April 28, 2016, http://thenextsystem.org/commoning-as-a-transformative-social-paradigm.

2 Andreas Karitzis, *The European Left in Times of Crises: Lessons from Greece* (Amsterdam, Quito and Buenos Aires: Transnational Institute [TNI], Instituto de Altos Estudios Nacionales [IAEN], Consejo Latinoamericano de Ciencias Sociales [CLACSO], 2017).

3 Most thinkers of Marxist origin tend to focus their attention on identifying aspects of capitalist dynamics in today's developments.

machine. This capitalist logic is surely an important parameter in contemporary developments, but, nonetheless, this explanatory model does not fully explain the nature of the unfolding transition.

Moreover, this type of explanation — if allowed to monopolize our understanding — tends to "normalize" or routinize the very idea of transition. It presupposes, explicitly or implicitly, that the capitalist rationale of organizing production and society can assume different forms while remaining essentially unchanged: "We may be experiencing the negative consequences of the alternating of capitalist phases, but the capitalist framework is not ruptured and we remain under the influence of its general principles." This kind of reasoning leads to a peculiar complacency, since it stems from a radical anti-capitalist argumentation. It is consoling to think that already-available cognitive maps and conceptual frameworks can explain current developments. However, this line of analysis also limits creativity in addressing the deep challenges of the present time, by promoting a narrow-minded understanding of movements' role as simply opposing the strategies of capitalist elites.[4]

This critique does not reduce the importance of developing social and political methodologies of mobilization that could help citizens without economic power to become a significant force in combating elite strategies. Indeed, incorporating strategies of mobilization into a broader and more robust framework for comprehending the transition could have catalytic implications.

Another "Peasant Uprising"

Another explanatory frame for our current transition looks to the deterioration of the power relationship between elites and people with no economic power.[5] According to this model, the

---

4   The term "elites" refers to various entities with economic power (individuals, corporations, foundations, administrations, etc.). I prefer to keep its reference vague due to transformations at this level as well.

5   Immanuel Wallerstein, *Utopistics: Or, Historical Choices of the Twenty-first Century* (New York: The New Press, 1998).

period from the French Revolution to the 1970s witnessed — with slumps and reversals — a broadening of the influence of people without economic power in critical decisions.[6] The consolidation of institutions of representative democracy and the hegemony of liberal ideas ultimately secured the passage to modernity, shaping a political framework where taking crucial decisions was no longer the exclusive privilege of the elite. After the 1970s, however, we see this momentum systematically wane. A new transition period that arrested modernity's liberatory qualities began as elites embraced the neoliberal school of thought. In combination with developments in technology and other fields, emancipatory movements could not preserve and expand their strategic momentum. In the light of this, we could say that transitionality is ultimately "conservative." It is organized around the return of a regime wherein crucial decisions remain the exclusive province of traditional elites — that is, transitionality is organized around the deprecation of the democratic ideal.[7]

Contemporary neoliberal elites now nourish their standing historical ambition to end the cycle that began with the people's entry into the social and political process two-and-a-half centuries ago. Their choices are focused on this goal: to demolish the belief that a new era for humanity began with the French Revolution — more democratic, open, pluralistic, and less authoritarian — and to recast modernity as a "moment" within a medieval era that was merely interrupted. The leap of liberation in modernity can thus be portrayed as just one more "peasant uprising" lasting for an unacceptably long time.[8]

---

6 I would like to clarify that I am using the French Revolution as an indicator for the beginning of modernity. Regarding the origin of modernity there are a lot of different and interesting approaches. For a very insightful example, see Giovanni Arrighi, *The Long Twentieth Century* (London and New York: Verso, 2010).

7 Wolfgang Streeck, *Buying Time* (London and New York: Verso, 2014); Wendy Brown, *Undoing the Demos* (New York: Zone Books, 2015).

8 Indicatively, it is worth mentioning the renewed interest from opinion leaders in the "cosmopolitan" character of the Ottoman Empire and the framing of people's involvement in decision-making as a disturbing factor that medieval meritocracy successfully contained.

The period spanning the French Revolution to the present can be viewed as an unstable, transitional condition that dismantled the traditional elites and formed the prerequisites for new, oligarchic structures to emerge in a new techno-economic environment. On this account, modernity, as well as capitalism's dynamic nature, do not inaugurate a new phase in human history. Modernity merely represents a turbulent passage from one despotic system to another. In any case, such despotic systems appear to be relatively stable, as their dominance throughout human history demonstrates.

Moreover, the economic and social patterns of such systems appear to be compatible with, and resilient in, a finite environment. Yet, the mentality of perpetual development that characterizes capitalist thinking — or rather the perpetual "progress" and change that are the face of modernity — are blatantly inappropriate for organizing life on a finite planet, even if they appear to be absolutely logical in periods when one institutional and social order declines and another is incubated. Our own transitional times suggest the beginning of the end of the intermediate phase and are characterized by the emergence of a new absolutism. We can easily imagine a combination of pre-modern and post-liberal traits that will eradicate the side effects of modernity that "annoy" the elites.[9]

Clearly, this explanatory model intensifies concern about the nature of future societies and allows us to consider the capitalist rationale as historical. Nonetheless, this approach, too, does not seem to exhaust the possible explanations for the current transition. It implies that the current transition is taking place in a relatively stable anthropological framework. We have reason to believe, however, that there are many other ways to conceptualize the transition and its possibilities.

---

9   Pierre Dardot and Christian Laval, *The New Way of the World: On Neoliberal Society* (London: Verso, 2013), 301–21.

Evolutionary Challenges and Deep Transformations on Steroids
A series of long-term trends are approaching critical limits. Technological advances and the universal character of problems, like the depletion of natural resources and accelerating environmental precarity, are creating unprecedented challenges. For the first time in our evolutionary history, humankind in its entirety has a planetary history and faces a shared (if unevenly and unfairly distributed) fate. Up until yesterday — in historical time, that is — each human civilization had its own distinct history; crossroads; and periods of rise and decline, savagery and liberation. Today, humankind is faced with dangers at the level of species survival, existential questions that go to the heart of what it means to be human, and challenges that ultimately require development of a sense of common humanity.[10]

Furthermore, and for the first time in our history as a species, we find ourselves constrained within the limits of an ecologically finite world. Few places on the planet remain outside the boundaries of human reach, and there is no longer a "frontier" that holds hope of a "new beginning" or a "new world" far away from the one rapidly deteriorating. This is creating asphyxiating cultural-material conditions for the overwhelming majority of Earth's population.

We are thus trapped in a world system that, with each passing day, shows signs of the dismantling and decline of existing

---

10 I refer to common fate and challenges of human civilizations, which are indeed totally new in our evolutionary history. Their implications are usually underestimated: by using the term "humankind" it seems that we put together the elites and the rest of us. In this case the "common fate" claim is refuted by the fact that the elites are gradually isolated by our societies and building their own protective environment, which seems to be more resilient in the face of existential challenges. However, at the level of human civilizations (all of which have divisions between elites and the rest), the claim holds water and, as I said, the implications are extremely important for the future. So, instead of dismissing the claim based on the perennial division between the elites and the rest, it will surely be more productive to start thinking about the respective implications and to take advantage of them. I would like to thank Anna Grear for the clarification of this point.

institutions and processes. As noted above, long-term trends are reaching their asymptote limits: environmental imbalance, food insecurity, and depletion of natural resources. These trends call into question deeply embedded evolutionary characteristics — mentalities, cultures, institutionalized architectures — that have shaped humanity for millennia but that now act as a brake on our own evolution. The period's transitionality seems to call for an evolutionary leap marked by both novel potentialities and by the danger of a deep regression.

For the first time in human evolutionary history, the connectivity between people, the transmission of information, technical expertise, and experience exceed anything that existing mentalities and institutional structures can conceive of and handle. We have the technological capability to record and process massive amounts of data (machine learning/artificial intelligence) about the world around us and within us, as well as about our own activity — again, an unprecedented development in our evolutionary history. These and other developments (automation, biotechnology etc.) are triggering cataclysmic changes in our relationship with the world, with ourselves, and with those around us. It is not easy to evaluate the impact or consequences of this at the moment, but these developments are radically expanding the horizon of contemporary challenges. And while the shock that these developments deliver heightens the risks, the self-same developments simultaneously offer the possibilities for a necessary evolutionary leap.[11]

The sketch above presents just some of the aspects of the transition underway. The obvious implication is that collective action must now and in the future orient itself in a totally different conceptual framework and imaginary. The quest for a new ontology and for a new lifeform requires directions that truly take account of the depth of the transition. Furthermore,

---

11   Geoff Mulgan, *Big Mind* (Princeton: Princeton University Press, 2018); Adam Greenfield, *Radical Technologies* (London: Verso, 2017); Paul Mason, *Postcapitalism* (London: Penguin, 2016); Moises Naim, *The End of Power* (New York: Basic Books, 2013); Alec Ross, *The Industries of the Future* (New York: Simon & Schuster, 2016).

we live in one of those rare historical moments when such quests — which may seem abstract, theoretical, and detached from real life — truly connect with existential concerns and practical questions emerging across the entire breadth of human life and activity.

The current global economic crisis is a symptom of a deeper decline that itself is mired in the multifaceted destabilization of societies. As noted above, the acceleration of developments on many levels (new technologies, environmental instability, depletion of natural resources, reordering of the geopolitical balance of power, and so on) transforms our traditional way of apprehending social and political antagonisms. A world order in a downward spiral is pulverizing the existing cognitive maps and established methodologies for managing social issues and securing basic functions.

All this is taking place with those most unfit to lead securely holding the levers of power. The elites are both a symptom of, and a catalyst for, the deteriorating situation. As they gradually disengage from the social order, they are shaping their own supralocal bio-world and developing a cynical, predatory mentality towards the larger societies in which they are embedded.[12]

When those control a society's means of survival and reproduction detach themselves from that society, the rest of the population is faced with unprecedented dangers. When the elite's primary concern is not the stable functioning of their own system of exploitation but the hyper-concentration of power, the private seizure of wealth, and the capture and control of resources (land, energy, infrastructure, water, etc.), then societies face the danger of disintegration. When the modern capitalist world is rapidly transformed into a medieval-type global oligarchy, then societies' basic functions are destabilized. The majority of people are multiply disenfranchized, the very meaning of

---

12 Peter Mair, *Ruling the Void* (London: Verso, 2013), 75: Christopher Lasch, *The Revolt of the Elites and the Betrayal of Democracy* (London and New York: Norton Paperback, 1995).

the "citizen" gradually recedes, and dignified living and access to basic good becomes the central object of struggle.

Evolutionary Threshold: The Sumerian Legacy
As noted earlier, effective political and social mobilization against the elites' choices requires a deep understanding of the disputes of our times. Are we in a historical mega-cycle? This may be the case if the current transition is related to the inadequacy of evolutionary characteristics that have organized human mentalities and institutional architectures for millennia — indeed, from the first appearance of the permanent, complex human settlements from which we descend.[13] From this perspective, we may be facing fundamental questions that have preoccupied human societies since Sumerian times.[14] This prompts us to ask what shifts in evolutionary strategies, dispositions, and mentalities were produced by permanent human settlement, the periodicity of agriculture, the emergence of the state, and the development of complex management systems.

Such questions are not solely of historical interest. They are urgently contemporary. Institutions, established practices, collective regulations, and social rules are governed by deep, ineffable norms with many layers of "historical sediment" that shape our semantic and imaginary horizon. And just as some of these layers were formed as human societies advanced to a radical transition and linked their fate to the cultivation of plants, so these "underlying" layers are related to the deeper qualities of our contemporary institutional and collective behavior. The external challenges to fundamental forms of institutional and col-

---

13 For the complexity and the prejudices related to this transition, see David Graeber and David Wengrow, "How to Change the Course of Human History (At Least, the Part That's Already Happened)", *Eurozine,* March 2, 2018, https://www.eurozine.com/change-course-human-history/.

14 The Mesopotamian civilizations are some of the first that emerged from the passage to agriculture and social complexity and are the civilizations from which the contemporary Western societies draw their origin. The term "Sumerian" is used as an indicator of the beginning of the respective mega-cycle.

lective human organization are so severe that, as we move even further into the new period, responses based solely on recent layers of "historical sediment" seem terribly inadequate.

If current elites draw inspiration from the accumulation of power, barbarity, and control of resources and people, then it is clear that they are not moving beyond the anthropological constants, power axes, and trends that have driven most cultural evolution within human societies since the Sumerians.[15] But if the transition is deeper than this, the depth of the changes taking place means that the elites' current strategies are not only unable to address the challenges, they are exacerbating their negative aspects and laying the ground for a radical regression. Such regression, we must emphasize, is not a rare phenomenon in human evolutionary history.

The conceptual and operational framework for dealing with the challenges facing the human species cannot be supplied by current institutional designs, narrow-minded elite strategies, and the prevailing neoliberal mentality. Real solutions must be based on sustainability, solidarity, and openness in order to counter the long-term tendency to exceed bio-social limits. Solutions must address the rise of inequality and barbarism, and the threat of military/financial authoritarianism — and now, digital authoritarianism.[16]

The neoliberal framework is fundamentally unable to offer real solutions. That is why it is now vital to explore ways of conceptualizing and administering complex societies based on values like democratic and decentralized decision-making, and to imagine new ways of managing basic social functions that could replace neoliberal governance. Seeking such a path forward is a broad responsibility, to be sure, but it can also unify people with different political and ideological origins.[17]

---

15   David Graeber, *Debt: The First 5000 Years* (New York: Melville House Publishing, 2012).

16   Vasilis Kostakis and Michel Bauwens, *Network Society and Future Scenarios for a Collaborative Economy* (Basingstoke: Palgrave Macmillan, 2014).

17   Andreas Karitzis, "Unleash the Kraken!" in *Supramarkt,* eds. Cecilia Wee and Olaf Arnt (Nössemark: Irene Publishing, 2015), 425–39.

The methodologies of mobilization we are looking for must communicate with the depth of the transition underway in order to be relevant to today's challenges. They are likely to have operational advantages over those adopted by the elites, since they will be developed within a broader semantic landscape and imaginary.

We have entered a period of great risk but also of tremendous possibilities unprecedented in human history. As underlined earlier, never before in our evolutionary course have populations had such access to information and knowledge; never before has the ability to fulfill social functions been so distributed. Never before have we had simultaneous access to centuries-old values from different cultural environments previously isolated from one another. Even though, for the first time in our evolutionary history, humans have a common fate, there is a danger of not activating and coordinating the many embodied capacities and values of so many different cultures. We need to find ways to utilize them creatively in the rise of a "new form of life" that are adapted to the new conditions and capable of decisively confronting the unprecedented challenges and dangers we face.

In the current phase, then, the critical challenge is not to find the definitive solutions to the impasses facing the species. It is mainly to identify which individual and collective mentalities and practices are in a position to address them — that is, to specify which qualities and capacities can provide the tools to develop effective solutions. The values, mentalities, ontologies, and life-forms that will mark the transition to, as well as determine the nature of, future human societies are precisely those with the potential to confront the challenges of the times.

2. The Decline of Liberal Politics

In an era of rapid change and fast-paced transitions on many levels, the field of politics — as the field of institutionalized power — reflects and consolidates the turbulent social environment, displaying its many shocks, destabilizations, and transformations. Of course, politics are very diverse phenomena that take place in many contexts, so we will not refer to all cases here but to the field of politics as it has developed in democratic, liberal societies. More specifically, we will base this stage of our analysis on the recent European and Greek political experience. This will help us identify how social and political antagonisms are transforming deep-rooted institutional architectures and the rules and methods of conventional political practice.

From Inclusion to Exclusion

In Europe, elites have successfully limited democracy (understood as the ability of people without economic power to influence crucial decisions regarding the course of their societies). Pervasive symptoms include the weakening of political institutions, serious shocks to powerful traditional political formations, the appearance of "odd" political formations,[18] the rise of far-right agenda and political forces, and the emergence of new forms of political organizing.[19]

A series of "reforms" on several levels over the course of decades have transferred critical decisions from the jurisdiction of the nation-state to private entities controlled by elites. This "vacating" of state power has taken many forms[20] — privatizations of public assets and civil infrastructure, the rise of various "independent" authorities,[21] and the development of the neoliberal European institutional architecture — fiscal, financial, numismatic, banking, and so on. Each of these shifts in institutional authority has transferred decisions from nation-states to struc-

---

18 The Five Star Movement (Italy) and En Marche, the fast-track victorious party of Emmanuel Macron (France) could be classified as two of the peculiar political formations that have popped up in Europe in recent years.

19 Podemos, political platforms in certain cities (Barcelona, Madrid, Naples, Zagreb, etc.), and networks of commons could be classified as new and informed ways of political organizing.

20 Alasdair Roberts, *The Logic of Discipline* (Oxford: Oxford University Press, 2010), 3–22.

21 Ibid., 23–45, 97–116.

tures that are designed to obstruct or even eliminate participation by citizens without economic power.[22]

The transfer of critical decisions — and thus powers — from the post-war liberal capitalist state to "places" and agents of power which are, by charter, anti-democratic is one of the basic blows against what we call the representative, liberal order. Even though the traditional liberal order centered upon the so-called capitalist state, its architecture secured a modicum of power for people without economic power.[23] The post-war state was the apex of the liberal democratic order. The robust institutions of representative democracy and the subordination of vital infrastructure and social services to their jurisdiction, in principle, rendered critical decisions accessible to citizens.[24] But the neoliberal state's evisceration of those powers has degraded the very nature of these representative institutions, the way in which politics is exercised, and the integrity of traditional political formations.[25] This is causing the weakening and decline of representative democratic institutions.

The way in which this has happened has a very characteristic pattern: instead of a head-on attack on democratic political structures to curtail citizen access to critical decisions, the preferred approach has been an indirect weakening of democracy instead, through a piecemeal shift of pivotal state authorities from their fields of jurisdiction. Let us look more closely at this process.

As noted above, at one time, citizens without economic power had the ability to intervene and to influence critical decisions through the democratic, inclusive nature of representative

---

22 Mair, *Ruling the Void,* 99–143.

23 The post-war liberal state in Western Europe was defined by the increased power of the people, which was one of the major outcomes of the Second World War.

24 Streeck provides a powerful explanation of how liberal democratic regimes balanced opposing interests after the Second World War, thus creating the conditions for today's landscape of power struggles. See Wolfgang Streeck, *Buying Time* (London and New York: Verso, 2014).

25 Mair, *Ruling the Void,* 17–44; 45–73.

institutions and the state's general commitment to addressing social needs. In principle, citizens could use social mobilization, political organizing, and other forms of civic participation to try to influence government decisions. These traditional democratic methodologies chiefly organized the *expression* of relevant needs and also *exercised moral and political pressure* on the government and the state. These efforts often yielded results, either in the form of the adoption of citizen demands or in the withdrawal (partial or total) of state initiatives seen as detrimental to large population segments. Elections provided citizens with a crude power to oppose governments that were not responsive to their needs.

The popular classes have had a more autonomous political presence by organizing more permanent movement structures and political parties with more radical orientations. Devising and implementing an independent political strategy has helped people without economic power have greater access to the decision-making that affected them. Indeed, the development of well-organized radical struggles activated a political process that resulted in shifting the whole political system towards a more progressive agenda.[26] It is obvious that these kinds of inclusive feints have been integral to the elites' strategy for maintaining their hegemony. Nevertheless, in such struggles, we can see a range of radical methodologies of political intervention that could, under given conditions, broaden the scope of citizen influence and curtail the elites' options.

Of course, the post-war liberal order was far from ideal for the popular classes across the board. The apex of liberal democracy was rife with coups. Coups occurred whenever a radical change in the balance of power was considered necessary to avert a serious questioning of the elites' dominance.[27]

---

26 The presence of radical left parties, strong labor unions and diverse movements in Western Europe after the war increased people's influence over crucial decisions. This condition put serious pressure on the elites. Their response would be the launch of the neoliberal project during the 1970s.

27 The Greek military coup in 1967 is an example of this sort of adjustment.

In summary, the strategic goal of the liberal democratic order was the reproduction of the elites' dominance through a formally inclusive institutional architecture and political mentality. The choice of an inclusive architecture was the result of a positive balance of power at the time. The political significance of this architecture for us today is that it has provided space for the development of radical political and social initiatives within a democratic public space (except in the case of coups, as noted).

Not surprisingly, entire generations of political and social activists who were raised and became active within such a framework developed a distinctive set of tactical skills and capabilities. These often entailed, for example: lists of demands, political programs and statements, and mobilization slogans that sought to express people's needs and aspirations. Movements organized themselves around demands in order to resist or apply pressure, and political fronts participated in elections and representative institutions. Indeed, the very meaning of involvement in politics gradually became identified with expressing needs or ideas through rhetorical or verbal confrontation.[28]

As we said earlier, the premise that allowed these traditional, expressive methodologies of doing politics to flourish was that the elites were more or less committed to accepting the democratic "game." They were notionally willing to listen to people's demands in shaping the strategic coordinates of societies (meanwhile tempering these demands through the soft power of the mainstream media and other means). Such a commitment made expressive skills pivotal in social and political antagonism (within a certain scope, of course).

The primary shift in the political environment today, and in the emerging transitional period, lie precisely in the shift from an inclusive strategy to an institutional and political architecture expressly organized around exclusion.[29] Aspects of this shift can be seen in the sweeping influence of neoliberal thinking in dominant political parties and in the forms of institutionalized

---

28 Karitzis, *The European Left in Times of Crises.*
29 Dardot and Laval, *The New Way of the World.*

neoliberalism seen in the EU architecture and financial bailout agreements.

This is a key reason why expressing demands to the state through movements, and by participating in elections, in order to change the balance of forces within the state, cannot deliver the change that the majority of the people need today. Once the political center of gravity is shifted from inclusion to exclusion, political expression becomes less effective (albeit still necessary). Meanwhile, the "neglected" qualities and skills of being able to implement different sets of ideas and values acquire greater importance, as we will see below.

A few decades after the fall of "actually existing socialism," we are experiencing the fall of "actually existing liberalism," so to speak. From a historical perspective, the two falls are nearly simultaneous and mark the beginning of a hard clash between the elites and the people.[30] The neoliberal project signifies an open, ambitious, and brutal strategy to radically change the basic coordinates of human societies and modes of subjectivity.[31] The elites — under the pressure of the ongoing capitalist crisis and the rest of the challenges described earlier — have launched an offensive to eradicate the emancipatory dynamic of modern societies. This neoliberal offensive seeks to exclude people from participating in crucial decisions, limit the satisfaction of vital needs, erode normal civility, and enclose shared resources, spaces, knowledge, information etc. The offensive waged by mainstream political parties also entails austerity measures, various types of privatization and structural reform, and bail-out agreements for favored industrial and service sectors.

The Greek Case

The EU–IMF bailout agreements for Greece offer a specific and clear picture of the broader ongoing political transformations identified here. The bailout agreements prefigure the institutionalization of the neoliberal order, i.e., the successful removal

30 Wallerstein, *Utopistics.*

31 Wendy Brown, *Undoing the Demos* (New York: Zone Books, 2015).

of key funding and liquidity functions from the state, and the shift and concentration of power into anti-democratic institutions that assume control over vital functions of Greek society. The bailout conditions have created a perplexing and hazardous socio-political conjuncture that now exposes the distinct limitations of traditional liberal politics.

The political system has crossed a critical threshold, entering a mode of functioning which could be described as the "Squeeze Effect:" the national spectrum of political activity has been squeezed and forced to function within a nearly non-existent space of freedom allowed by lenders in the bailout agreement. As the state loses control over crucial institutional, economic, and social issues, it gradually divests the political level of liberal democracy of its content, rendering its processes irrelevant and its geometry incoherent.

The deforming implications of the "Squeeze Effect" further erode the function of democratic political representation. After the right-wing and social-democratic parties adopted neoliberalism as their political program, they decisively downgraded their aspirations to be agents of political representation. Now, we are in the phase of institutionalized neoliberalism that takes the anti-democratic mode of neoliberal governmentality in Europe to new extremes.

Because of the "Squeeze Effect," the Greek political system has become utterly incoherent as a voice of the people, amplifying confusion and feelings of despair within Greek society. Moreover, the "Squeeze Effect" further alienates political functionaries from the real-life conditions of the population, making the political sphere impervious to the people's anxieties, frustrations, and wishes. The negative social consequences and psychological fallouts inflicted by austerity and social decline can no longer be expressed at the political level. Such consequences cannot be represented, democratically expressed, or positively transformed in ways that might contribute to social stability and cohesion. Without a minimally proper function of political representation in place, these social and psychological wounds — in the form of negative and (self-)destructive dispositions — spread across all social networks of interpersonal relations. The social alienation and disintegration can only deepen.

The basic coordinates of the political system in Greece are changing profoundly. The politicians and political parties are no longer accountable to the people through the mechanisms of representative democracy. Rather, they are accountable to market players and to their respective institutions (corporations, banks, investment firms) because they see that orientation as the only way to fund vital economic and social functions. In this context, the criteria for political success are significantly modified: being a successful politician no longer means that you are responsive to people's demands and needs, but rather, it amounts to being able to increase the competitiveness of the economy according to the profit analysis and investment criteria of capital owners. In other words, the greatest service that a politician can provide to his or her society is optimal compliance with the objectives of financial entities that can ensure the smooth running of society. We are thus witnessing a different codification of power relations in terms of accountability: political accountability towards citizens through democratic means is replaced by direct accountability to capital-owners and market mechanisms.

Specifications for an Updated Political Mentality and Methodology
If, indeed, the shift from inclusion to exclusion in the political field (and its related institutions) is at the core of the transformations and upheavals in contemporary liberal democracies, then we must reconsider the meaning of political action and organizing in these new conditions. How are we going to modify and enrich our methodology of political and social mobilization in order to respond to these profound challenges? How are we going to cope with growing levels of social exclusion and re-assert people's participation in crucial decision-making? What kind of methodology of politics will allow us to be more effective without presupposing the democratic rules we used to take for granted? What kind of political methodology will allow us to transform and restore democracy?

Priorities

The weakening of democratic, representative institutions and intensifying exclusion have resulted in an extremely harsh political environment, especially for people without economic power. The key question is how to develop autonomous strategies for collective survival and political power?

First of all, we must shift priorities from increasing the level of political representation to strategies for building popular power. Instead of trying to improve political representation in a European framework designed to ignore the popular classes and their needs, we must set up autonomous networks of production of economic and social power. These include ecosystems of resilient, dynamic, and interrelated circuits of co-operative productive units, alternative financial tools, and local cells of self-governance with community control over infrastructure facilities, digital data, energy systems, distribution networks, etc. The components of such an ecosystem can be found all around us: energy communities in Germany and other countries, social and solidarity economy activities almost everywhere, alternative financial tools and local self-governance experiments in the South, platform cooperativism in the digital world etc. What is lacking is the proper framework of connectivity, methodologies of institution-building, and large-scale coordination for decentralized decision-making and leadership. But this is exactly the *political* aim of our times. Figuring out the internal and external configuration of these crucial components is what shifting priorities will contribute to.

A network of this kind will check the attempt of the elites to control social and economic activity, reclaiming crucial decisions regarding basic social functions and infrastructure on behalf of the people without economic power. Organizing people's activities at a large scale, based on a set of values that is compatible with today's challenges would be the necessary components of a radically different political mentality. Such networks are ways of gaining the degree of autonomy necessary to defy the elites' despotic control over society. In other words, people must be able to reclaim control over the management of basic social functions. In order to create the popular power needed for the required degree of autonomy, we must shift our emphasis from representing people's demands to facilitating and organizing people's self-provisioning and governance.

A strategic shift from representing "opinions" to supporting and cultivating citizens' productive activity changes the metrics for success. A basic criterion should be the degree of participation of the people in developing a competitive ecosystem to produce social power, and its effectiveness in utilizing people's abilities and skills. This shift would also require the development of new interfaces between state and other institutions with the ecosystem. In this context, skills for a robust and effective democratic, collective operation, and social cooperation are needed. Democracy and cooperation are no longer something to be held as admirable abstractions or noble duties, but acquire vital operational significance: the production of the power we need emerges from the liberation of people's embodied capacities. This potential is released and activated only when people cooperate equally towards a shared goal. The value of their incorporated potential must be acknowledged by transferring decisions involving this potential to them.

We can, therefore, imagine hybrid socio-political organizations that — while uncategorizable according to traditional terms — bolster, connect, facilitate, and transfer technical expertise to various nodes of the network and integrate them to increase its sustainability. These political organizations can initiate the creation of innovative institutionalizations that reinforce the networks at hand, cultivate the relative mentalities, and so on. Such hybrid socio-political organizations that achieve balance between political representation and the production of power can act as a catalyst for a network generating popular power, which is necessary to respond to the current pressures.[32]

---

32 The political experience that is being created in Spain by municipality platforms and the authorities — exploring practical ways to activate people's robust participation in decision making, planning, and implementation — is an important site of experimentation in this direction. Nevertheless, useful ideas and tools can also be traced in unexpected places such

Leadership

Developing a new political methodology requires a new leadership model. We refer not only to conventional notions of leadership, but to leadership functions distributed at every level of a complex organization. Leadership is a real, structural consequence of complex organizations, produced by the need to connect multiple parts of a complex system. Contact among parts does not involve all of each part — and this is where leadership emerges as an essential function.[33]

The political orientation towards developing an ecosystem of producing popular power demands a different kind of leadership. A new species of collective, fluid and distributed leadership that does not show a propensity for detaching decisions. These leaders do not absorb decisions from the rest by virtue of their greater access to information and direct link to other network nodes.[34] This is because, if the ecosystem's strength is produced by the "extraction" of the incorporated potential of the many, and this "extraction" is possible only when these people have access to the decisions linked to this potential, then the main feature of the leadership model that corresponds to this rationale is the *coordination* of others in the decision-making. "Good leadership," therefore, creates the conditions for making sound decisions in collective and distributed ways and does not simply strive for "better" decisions. Such leadership's main concern is the continuous enhancement of this distributed de-

---

as mainstream institutions and the business world. Open innovation and distributed leadership models that are highly appraised in the corporate culture, and the notion of multi-level governance coined within the EU establishment, can be valuable sources of inspiration and provide orientation and guidelines for the productive reinvention of social and political mobilization.

33 Certainly leadership has other meanings, but we will not outline them here.

34 It is worth noting here that digital technologies, and specifically the speed at which information is disseminated in real time, as well as the easy access to data created by the processes occurring simultaneously at different places in the system, may facilitate the development of a different leadership model.

cision-making function, the integration of new methods and tools, the evaluation of the experience for optimizing the processes, and so on. In other words, if we detach decisions from people, we are weakened because we do not allow the maximum possible utilization of their potential — and this is tantamount to "bad" leadership.

Reinventing the Public Sphere and Political Practice

An innovative political organization in the twenty-first century should strive to align and mobilize creative social forces in order to develop sustainable and resilient survival strategies. As existing institutional architectures deteriorate, we need to conceive of a new type of public sphere and political practice. We need structures and institutionalizations to deliver decision-making processes that enable citizens, through their organizations and agents, to actively participate in shaping politics. The aim is for decisions to be taken democratically in order to be more effective — taking account of many viewpoints in the final outcome, guided by citizens' needs and potential, and seen as an open and trustworthy process. It is crucial, too, for the central state to decentralize power and transfer decisions (and responsibilities) to the social field.

Of course, there will always be the need to make decisions for strategic issues and to shape the legislative framework that determines the range of possibilities. So, it also seems important to reconfigure the tools of representation that create the bodies for this kind of decision-making towards a less rigid architecture. And, upgrade direct democracy to diversify the ways of making these decisions. In other words, the emphasis on more distributed forms of organization and on the decentralization of power, resources, and decisions does not eliminate the need for the radical modifications of representative structures.

The question of linking the general will and the will of individuals first arose when societies with high levels of social division of labor appeared. In such societies, different viewpoints and priorities inevitably emerge as a result of differentiated positions in the social division of labor. Every member of society is governed by a tension: on one hand, as a citizen, he or she can and must have an opinion on the society's general direction, and on the other, as an agent of a specific position in society, he or she is guided by an individual viewpoint within it. Managing this tension is the quintessential issue of politics today.

It would be a mistake to think that overthrowing the current capitalist elites automatically solves the problem of managing the relationship between the general will and individual wills, since power can accumulate in other forms. Through the mega-cycle inaugurated by permanent settlement in Sumeria, omnipotent elites have usually emerged to manage this need. Thus a paramount challenge today is to manage differences and different viewpoints in a manner that will not produce elites with exclusive control over decisions.

The typical elite strategy has been barbaric and exploitative subordination of the majority of society, and a monopoly over decision-making power. This is presented as the only valid way to distribute resources and direct society. Managing differences is "solved" through the hard exclusion of the majority of viewpoints and by identifying the general will with the narrow interests of the economically powerful. Nonetheless, as we have emphasized, this is not a credible response to today's challenges but a dangerous symptom of decline and regression. Furthermore, we have reasons to believe that the new conditions of intellectual production and technological knowledge are creating the possibilities for a qualitative leap forward.

A different strategy must, on the one hand, curb the barbaric, elitist response and, on the other, attempt to offer its own more transformative solutions. In this endeavor, it is critical to realize that the existence of disputes and differentiations should not be seen as a weakness. It is a product of the social structure itself, which should be accepted in a positive way. In any case, the very meanings of democracy and cooperation must be reinvented. Operationally, they are the best possible ways for effectively managing and combining diverse viewpoints.

The quest for a new type of public sphere and political practice also raises the issue of how decisions should be distributed between conventional, universal, and representative institutions as well as social institutions serving more specific needs. Broadly speaking, we would say that autonomy and decentralization should be paramount goals; they tend to strengthen the operational autonomy of particular social institutions with situational knowledge and experience, and trusted internal processes.

Nonetheless, in order to safeguard broader cooperation, the decentralization of power cannot allow network players to have absolute strategic autonomy. The individual wills of particular structures, agents, and productive units must engage with each other and find alignment. Strategy and general orientation are the purview of the structures of public policy in which representative institutions, autonomous public structures, and social subjects together delineate broad strategy.

The Fertility of the Notion of Commons

If we seek a new public sphere and political practice, the notion of commons can, under certain conditions, contribute to the emergence of valuable new institutions and processes. In general, the commons sector attempts to renew, enrich, and broaden the meaning of the term "public." Commons thinking provides an expanded conception of the meaning of "public" that transcends the meaning of "state" (albeit, without necessarily diminishing the state's significance in political strategy). It also emphasizes the creation of commons "cells," hubs, and federations, which together reconceptualizes the public space and could transcend the disintegration of existing democratic institutions. This turn towards commons could be seen as a citizens' response to the increasing authoritarianism of contemporary state systems and to their unwillingness to guarantee people's rights.

To avoid misunderstanding, it is worth underlining that emphasizing social organization — which, in a way, is suggested by the meaning of "commons" — does not imply the rejection of traditional political practice. Nor does it deny the importance of state institutions in brokering social and political antagonism. On the contrary, such a shift is necessary if citizens and liberation forces are to acquire the power to respond to the current assault on democracy. It is a way that traditional political practice can (re)acquire its essential functions.

Creating productive systems based on the commons can, in addition, provide ideas and tools for modifying traditional political thinking and methodology. By combining participation and representation in different ways, we can transcend the dysfunctional traditional framework of representative democracy. The real democratic practices that occur through commoning can enhance political participation and upgrade the level and intensity of participation in collective processes. Indeed, political participation can be understood differently and move from an emphasis on discrete moments of participation (elections, demonstrations, single-issue campaigns) towards far more substantive types of collaboration in attaining common goals. Participation could mean co-decision-making, co-management, and co-responsibility.

The meaning of commons helps expand our social imaginary as it "pushes" us to think, experiment, and explore new ways of improving collective administration. The creation of a space for institutionalizing collective existence, which transcends and reframes the existing state-market demarcation, can contribute to unlocking the socio-political imaginary on issues of vital importance. We can reconceive governance at the micro and macro scale and articulate functional "cells" of different logics at the local, regional, and inter-regional levels.

We can shape new and better ways of achieving various functions that are more effective than bureaucratic organization. Of course, we are not simply referring to a different culture of governance, but to something much broader. We are referring to the possibility of an evolutionary leap to a meta-Sumerian productive–institutional–organizational–cultural paradigm. We could develop an integrated articulation of production, governance, and mass participation in new types of institutions, as well as ways of managing/coordinating on a mega-scale. A vital infrastructure of networks and links for managing the commons could give rise to a new social and political economy that would increase the resilience of people without economic power, laying the groundwork for a political strategy with greatly expanded horizons.

Let us be honest: we will never be in a position to limit the power of the elites, halt the current course of decline, and face the unprecedented challenges to our societies, and humankind in its entirety, unless we develop a new governmentality. This new polity must be based on the logic of democracy, decentralization, autonomy, and cooperation applied to mega-scale issues such as the management of large populations, composite societies, and extended regions.

Hybrid Politics

Unfortunately, the traditional forms of liberation politics are not in a position to respond to the novel circumstances and social and political antagonisms of our time. Although there are some hopeful shifts, the traditional advocates of emancipation struggle to make progress in an increasingly toxic political environment, which itself is designed to be impenetrable to the needs of people without economic power. The liberation of societies cannot be based solely on traditional political practice because elites, no longer willing to be bound by the democratic will, are making the democratic institutions that control basic functions inaccessible to citizens. Not surprisingly, countless social initiatives and efforts appear weak, marginalized, isolated, and sporadic as they face the same difficulties repeatedly. They do not seem capable of achieving the "critical mass" needed to scale up and form comprehensive functional circuits to be effective.

It is time for the sectors struggling for emancipation to reassess the established methodologies, priorities, and inherited formations for mobilizing citizens. The goal should be to unleash citizens' capabilities in creative new ways and to operationalize integrated networks for producing economic and social power. Only under these circumstances can we truly hope to confront the aggression of the elites, who will resist all attempts to claim popular power over political decisions.

In the transitional period that we have entered, resistances are emerging almost everywhere around the world, but they are hobbled by having one foot in the past and another barely in the future. Obsolete forms of political imaginary, organizational principles, and mentalities coexist with more advanced ones relevant to the present and the future. It is clear that we must combine traditional and contemporary methodologies while recognizing their respective limitations. The former are directed at a declining political architecture while the latter, which are better-equipped to deal with future challenges, have not yet matured. Nonetheless, it is clear that any political initiatives will not make headway in current circumstances unless they try to combine both methodologies. The traditional political methodology allows a political presence in the existing political field, while more innovative processes can, under some conditions, offset the divesting of powers to some extent. In other words, no political platform or party that hopes to influence developments in the conventional political field will succeed if it does not leverage the untapped potential of connectivity, distributed knowledge and information, organizational innovations, and digital technologies. An emancipatory strategy of social change cannot overlook social changes that are underway, or be indifferent or hostile to the potential emanating from human activity in many fields today. Utilizing the embodied capacities of the people will allow it to swiftly change the broader negative political environment.

We are thus living in a period that requires a radical modification of the political imaginary as well as of the organizational principles of social and political mobilization. To make this possible, we must combine effectively the incredible current output of new ideas, practices, regulations, and rationales, that emerge almost everywhere. These are not often directly linked to the disputes of social and political struggle but, under certain conditions, could shape the ground for organizing social power to allow people without economic power to acquire the muscle to influence developments. This should be achieved with a detailed diagnostic process of the weaknesses and impasses of the traditional political practice without losing sight of the fact that the party *function* remains important.

We refer to the party's function here in order to differentiate it from its historical organizational structure and action methodology.[35] The party's traditional (post-war) structure and methodology cannot meet the demands of the current social and political struggle, and thus, cannot satisfy the respective party function. But the party's function is absolutely necessary since the collective organization towards common goals enables people without economic power to become a historical agent capable of influencing developments. The aim today should be to develop a new "operating system" for a party that fights for emancipation — that is to say, an operating system comprised of new organizational principles and methodologies for social and political activism. Thus, we seek those new forms and mentalities that can fulfill the party's function. It is worth noting that the party's key role does not necessarily lead to a "vanguard" rationale. In a methodology of real support for the development of a new competitive ecosystem, the party is a very important node among others whose interfaces are not based on fixed, hierarchical relationships.

But where will this "new synthesis" take place? Who will identify and take the practical steps towards a new form of activism? As usual, this "duty" falls to the struggling sectors of humankind. It falls to those who, in different ways, with different backgrounds and from different springboards, with different reasons and different causes, take on the responsibility of resisting their own elimination and their societies' decline. These people are already developing new forms, directions, methodologies, and practices. They already constitute an extensive section of humankind spanning the entire planet and different fields of labor.

---

35   Mair, *Ruling the Void,* 89.

Nonetheless, we must remain cognizant of the fact that we are living in a period where the fast pace of developments in various sectors "wrenches" apart societies, thus widening the distance between a) large segments that are multiply excluded and have scant access to knowledge and information; and b) between those strata that are oppressed and asphyxiated yet maintain some access to work, knowledge and information. The gap between the "excluded" and the "trapped" is widening. Closing this gap is an issue of cardinal importance, because only a composite political strategy that unifies these "tribes" of people without economic power could regain the power to a) effectively confront the elites and halt the current course; b) develop a survival strategy for large segments of the population left swinging in the wind; and c) develop an emancipation strategy capable of managing the current challenges of contemporary society and humankind as a whole.

3. Epilogue: A New "Life Form" for a Highly Transitional Era

A basic prerequisite for promoting innovative institutionalizations and, ultimately, the emergence of a new public sphere and political practice, is the cultivation of subjective qualities that creatively embody the characteristics of a transitional period.

We are accustomed to thinking and acting as if our actions must be well-organized tactical moves in a relatively stable environment in order to achieve a specific goal. If indeed we are at the dawn of a strongly transitional period, it is obvious that we must take into account the following:

- Traditional institutions and practices are disintegrating. Consequently, our framework of thought and action in this environment must consider whether or not it exacerbates the disintegration of the various parts of political functioning. More specifically, instead of thinking that our activity is an action taking place in a static environment, it is more fruitful to think of it as one set of dynamics that reinforce and weaken specific qualities.

- Our framework of thought and action will be intensely differentiated over time, thus nothing should be seen as a given nor should we project current conditions onto the future. Furthermore, we must not take current classifications for granted because the increased entropy, number of shocks and upheavals, and emergence of new elements could well alter the institutional architecture and socio-politico-cultural nature of future societies.

- If we assume that the transitional period we have already entered may lead to a relatively stable social and institutional order, it is worth keeping in mind that we are at the beginning of the transition whose semantic and imaginary horizon is governed more by the previous order of things and less by the one emerging. Thus, today's ideas, innovations, institutionalizations and processes are experimental efforts at an early stage. They must be evaluated on the basis of their fertility and not on their potential for finalizing solutions (although they must contribute to current survival strategies). The evaluation criteria and investment of resources and time in some of these must be based on whether they engender the qualities which we believe must characterize the emergent new order — even if they do not produce final, sustainable results.

Thus our subjective and collective mentalities must eschew metaphors and thinking that reference chess or the martial arts, which suggest confrontations between well-defined opponents on familiar battlefields with organized armies. The new mentalities required must cultivate other mental and imaginary formations. They must allow for osmosis and the utilization of connectivity, nurture the ability to identify key processes underway, and invigorate resourcefulness and the need to think and act in an entirely different way.

Furthermore, qualities and capabilities that simulate cellular dynamics (greater autonomy of action of different parts, distributed coordination, and so on) are critical for the emergence of new political subjects. We need flexible collective agents of so-cial and political mobilization able to respond to a high degree of volatility in the socio-political environment. A multicentric architecture can help unleash the embedded capabilities of people without economic power and counter the centuries-old trend of detaching decisions and consolidating power. This is a trend that unfortunately afflicts many social and political move-ments, limiting their emancipatory potential.

The new forms of life must also cultivate a more modest stance towards the "grandeur" of the modern West. The histori-cal, experienced modernity was not, as it turns out, a firm step towards emancipation. It has been an unstable and awkward se-ries of self-entrapments with massive costs: a not-so-successful encapsulation of the incredible capabilities and potential that opened up during this same period. Our capacity to shape a new life form in the future requires us to learn from nonmod-ern and premodern forms of collective existence and individual self-awareness.[36]

Let me reiterate that my point of reference in this essay is the European framework of struggles and the methodologies and mentalities that European movements should develop. Eman-cipatory forces and movements in other areas of the planet may need a substantially different set of social orientations and strat-egies.

In conclusion, it is worth underlining a dimension of the contemporary dilemma that is often overlooked. Our societies suffer from the "end of history" syndrome.[37] The prevailing life-motif promotes the idea that a good life is essentially an indi-vidual achievement. Society and nature are just backdrops, a wallpaper for our egos, the contingent context in which our soli-tary selves will evolve pursuing individual goals. The individual owes nothing to no one, lacks a sense of respect for the previous generations and responsibility towards future ones — and indif-

---

36 Alvaro Garcia Linera, *Plebeian Power* (Chicago: Haymarket Books, 2014).
37 The syndrome is named after the famous book by Francis Fukuyama, *The End of History and the Last Man* (New York: The Free Press, 1992).

ference is the proper attitude regarding present social problems and conditions.

Today, at the dawn of a new era of total threat, our societies — and political movements and parties as part of them — seem to seek quick and easy ways to restore the previous liberal configuration. They do not want to disturb the naïve and comforting "end of history" notion or to engage more deeply in collective practices. The only thing we are willing to give is singular moments of participation. But mobilizing people's energies to participate more intensively in traditional political processes will not yield the transformations we need. On the contrary, the whole point is to redefine political operations in such a way that will transfer decisions closer to people's everyday lives. People need to see that their political participation can be a crucial part in production and management at all levels.

So, in order to make politics meaningful again, we must abandon the tendency to believe and to act as if things will change easily and quickly through the revival of the previous institutional and political configuration of post-war liberal capitalism. We must finally confront the reality that neoliberalism is "burning the bridges" with the past. We can only move forward by accepting the fact that we are entering a long period of hard struggle in which we must drastically change the coordinates of our political imagination. We must escape from the fascination of the post-war ideals of social configuration.

Today, being politically active in a meaningful way goes hand in hand with the emergence of a new ideal for social and individual life. It means radically transforming the persistent desire for a status quo that is no longer available — an immature response to the existential threats around us. That requires fortitude and courage, which are crucial but forgotten political qualities.

5

Awakening to an Ecology of the Commons

Michel Bauwens and Jose Ramos

We live in a transformative moment in human history, at once on the precipice of crisis and simultaneously awakening into a new awareness of ourselves as commoners and planetary beings. For the individual, this transformative moment in human history feels more like a crisis than a transition — drawn out, full of dangers, obstacles, and growing pains. The moment, however, is the birth of the "planetary" as an element of human experience, and this transition is, according to our perspective, the transition from social orders based on exploitation to social orders based on generative mutuality. In this chapter, we explain the intertwined and integral emergence of the planetary and the commons as complementary fields of experience and their role in the reimagination of who we are.

1. The Commons as Mutualization for the Anthropocene

Much is now written about the so-called "Anthropocene," a new epoch that signifies humanity as more than just a passive traveller on planet Earth. The Anthropocene signals humanity as a transformer, or a terraformer, of our planet — producing effects comparable to grand geological shifts.[1] For the purpose of this discussion, we can distinguish three "movements" of the Anthropocene.

The first movement is, of course, the significance of humans as a species with planetary impacts. This is the popular definition of the Anthropocene — humanity has become such a powerful aggregate force that we can assign a geological era to ourselves! If this was the only dimension of the Anthropocene, however, we would be no different than the species that generated the first planetary crisis approximately 2.5 billion years ago, anaerobic cyanobacteria, which led to the Great Oxygenation Event where the planet was literally poisoned by excess oxygen, a waste product of cyanobacteria.[2]

Fortunately, the Anthropocene also signifies an *awareness* of ourselves as a planetary species with planetary impacts.[3] We are not just blindly having an impact on the planet, we are increasingly aware of our powerful and precarious effects. We have the power to reflect on who we are, to evaluate what it means to be human. While the first movement of the Anthropocene — human instrumental power — is far more advanced than the second movement — reflective planetary awareness —, this second movement is catching up with the first, for obvious reasons.

Finally, a third movement of the Anthropocene closes the loop on the first two — reflexive planetary responses.[4] Reflexive planetary responses signifies the capacity for humanity to leverage the second aspect (reflective planetary awareness) toward coordinated, intelligent responses to the challenges we collectively face. This third movement of the Anthropocene is by far the most embryonic, and yet ultimately the most crucial,

---

1   Noel Castree, "The Anthropocene: A Primer for Geographers," *Geography* 100, no. 2 (2015): 66–75.

2   Lynn Margulis and Dorion Sagan, *Microcosmos: Four Billion Years of Microbial Evolution* (Berkeley: University of California Press, 1997).

3   William I. Thompson, ed., *Gaia, A Way of Knowing: Political Implications of the New Biology* (Barrington: Lindisfarne Press, 1987).

4   Elena M. Bennett et al., "Bright Spots: Seeds of a Good Anthropocene," *Frontiers in Ecology and the Environment* 14, no. 8 (2016): 441–48.

without which we have little hope of any real long-term viability. These three aspects play out a classic action learning cycle: act — reflect — change, but at a grand scale that we have only begun to experience today.

The body of ideas and research on the commons is a critical part of the second movement of the Anthropocene — our capacity to interpret and understand ourselves in the current era; while the praxis of the commons, termed "commoning," is critical to the third movement of the Anthropocene — our reflexive planetary responses.

The stakes are high. The Anthropocene is a crucial time for humanity, in which our very survival is at stake. In this chapter, we want to argue for a crucial link between the necessity to reduce the human footprint on the planet and its natural resources, and the modality of the commons, i.e., the pooling and mutualization of resources.

This hypothesis was one of the key reasons for the creation of the P2P Foundation, as from the very beginning, we gave the following analysis of the global *problematique*:

1. Our current political economy proceeds from the point of view of permanent and unlimited growth, something which is both logically and physically impossible on a finite planet. We called this the "pseudo-abundance" of the material world.

2. Our current political economy proceeds from the point of view that marketization and commodification are the best way to manage and allocate immaterial resources as well, via intellectual property. This creates an artificial scarcity for what are objectively abundant resources, especially in the context of a digital society and its means of cheap reproduction and distribution of knowledge. We called this "artificial scarcity in the world of immaterial resources."

3. The two first mistakes are compounded by the fact that our economic organization produces more and more human inequality.

The solution to this state of affairs seems obvious. It must be possible to have a political economy that respects the carrying capacity of our planet, and it must be possible to share the knowledge necessary to do so. At the same time, these two conditions must be accompanied by economic forms that respect social justice.

But what is the link between this desire for societal and planetary transformation, and the specific modality of the commons?

Following Alan Page Fiske in *Structures of Social Life*,[5] and Karatani's[6] historical vision of the evolution in these modes of exchange, we can distinguish four modes for allocating resources:

1. Communal Shareholding or Pooling, i.e., provisioning systems are considered as a collective resource, collectively maintained and shared by a particular community of stakeholders according to their own rules and norms. This is the commons modality, which is both a shared set of resources, a joint activity, and a governance system.

2. Equality Matching, i.e., the gift economy as a system based on reciprocity, in which gifting and counter-gifting create social relations and maintain balance.

3. Authority Ranking, i.e., redistribution according to rank, which includes state-led redistribution. This modality becomes dominant with the emergence of class-based societies characterized by state formation.

5   Alan P. Fiske, *Structures of Social Life: The Four Elementary Forms of Human Relations: Communal Sharing, Authority Ranking, Equality Matching, Market Pricing* (New York: Free Press, 1991).

6   Kojin Karatani, *The Structure of World History: From Modes of Production to Modes of Exchange,* trans. Michael K. Bourdaghs (Durham: Duke University Press, 2014).

4. Market Pricing, i.e., the exchange of resources according to "equal value," which becomes dominant in the capitalist political economy.

Before creating the P2P Foundation in 2006, we had taken some time to study past societal transitions, and one of our findings was that mutualization had been an important element of the transition from the Roman system to the feudal system, which had a dramatically lower ecological footprint.[7]

Indeed, consider the mutualization of knowledge by the Catholic monastic communities, which were also the engineers of their time. According to Jean Gimpel in his book about the first medieval industrial revolution, Catholic communities were responsible for nearly all the technical innovations of that era.[8] They effectively functioned to create commons across three co-related aspects. Firstly, the creation of a global European sphere of collaboration within the Catholic Church and its monastic orders through the mutualization of knowledge. Secondly, the collective property and distribution formats of monastic life, through the mutualization of shelter and shared units of production, the provision of shelter, culture, and spirituality, as well as a dramatically lower use of resources than that of the Roman elite. Thirdly, the relocalization of the economy around a subsistence economy based on feudal domains.

The resemblance to our own circumstances is uncanny. Faced with ecological and social challenges, we see a re-emergence of knowledge commons in the form of free software and open design communities; we see a drive towards mutualization of productive infrastructure, for example, the emergence of

---

7   Mathis Wackernagel and William Rees, *Our Ecological Footprint: Reducing Human Impact on the Earth* (Philadelphia: New Society Publishers, 1998). See also Mark D. Whitaker, *Ecological Revolution: The Political Origins of Environmental Degradation and the Environmental Origins of Axial Religions: China, Japan, Europe* (Cologne: Lambert Academic Publishing, 2010).

8   Jean Gimpel, *The Medieval Machine: The Industrial Revolution of the Middle Ages* (New York: Penguin Books, 1977).

fablabs, makerspaces, coworking spaces and also the capitalist "sharing economy," which is focused on creating platforms for underutilized resources; finally, we see new technologies around distributed manufacturing, prototyped in makerspaces and fab-labs, which point to a re-organization of production under a "cosmo-local" model.[9]

We thus see strong resemblances between this and other historical patterns that correlate to our present-day situation. The importance of mutualization and commons-based strate-gies today is strengthened by our reading of long-term histori-cal change. Another example of this is provided by Whitaker, who offers a comparative review of 3,000 years of civilizational overshoots in Europe, Japan, and China.[10] His central thesis is that elites in class-based societies overshoot their resource base, not as an exception but as a rule, and that the classes closely tied to actual production periodically revolt and create transforma-tive social movements, which have historically taken a religious form.[11] Thus, what we thought we were seeing in the post-Ro-man European transition may not be an exception, and can also be found in Chinese and Japanese history. In each of these tran-sitions, the mutualization of infrastructure is a key element of the transformation.

Additionally, William Irwin Thompson earlier identified the civilizational tendency for overshoot across Babylonian, Greek, Roman, and European civilizations, where a civilization's core growth comes at the expense of its peripheries, and where the overshoot ultimately undermines the viability of the core civi-lization itself. Thompson pointed toward a commons frame-work as a solution, an arrangement he termed *enantiomorphic*.[12] Finally, Thomas Homer-Dixon's detailed analysis of energy use within the Roman civilization came to a convergent view: growth dynamics were earlier based on large "energy returns on

---

9   Vasilis Kostakis et al., "Design Global, Manufacture Local: Exploring the Contours of an Emerging Productive Model," *Futures* 73 (2015): 126–35.

10 Whitaker, *Ecological Revolution*.

11 Ibid.

12 William I. Thompson, *Pacific Shift* (New York: Random House, 1986).

investment" (the amount of energy needed to exploit new energy sources), but diminished over time as social and ecological externalities mounted up.[13]

As a civilizational crisis emerges, a number of related dynamics can also emerge: the image of the future that helped to animate the extant civilization may begin to lose power.[14] Images of the future may become dystopian, and narratives that are civilization-contradicting emerge and serve to unravel the core belief and logics that have wedded people to the old system. A creative minority from a variety of perspectives produce new seed visions that attempt to offer solutions amidst crisis.[15] Some of these may be "fantasy" visions and solutions that reiterate the core logic of empire without addressing its contradictions, giving people a false sense of hope. Some visions and solutions, however, are based on a square reading of their civilization's contradictions (e.g., in our context, growth) and invite new pathways that are outside of the epistemological orbit of empire.[16]

The merit of this comparative review is in providing an understanding of the non-exceptionality, or even regularity, of civilizational overshoot. For example, Whitaker's thesis and documentation argues that every class-based system founded on competition between elites creates a "degradative political economy" and an overuse of both internal and external resources.[17] Against this, in predictable fashion, eco-religious movements arise that stress the balance between the human and the human, the human and the totality (the divine), and the human

---

13   Thomas Homer-Dixon, *The Upside of Down: Catastrophe: Creativity, and the Renewal of Civilization* (Washington, DC: Island Press, 2010).

14   Fred L. Polak, *The Image of the Future: Enlightening the Past, Orientating the Present, Forecasting the Future* (New York: Sythoff, 1961).

15   Johan Galtung, "Arnold Toynbee: Challenge and Response," in *Macrohistory and Macrohistorians,* eds. Johan Galtung and Sohail Inayatullah (New York: Praeger, 1997), 120–27.

16   Elise Boulding, "Futuristics and the Imaging Capacity of the West," in *Cultures of the Future,* eds. Magoroh Maruyama and Arthur M. Harkins (The Hague: Mouton, 1978), 146–57.

17   Whitaker, *Ecological Revolution,* book abstract.

and the environment. These ideas, led by religious reformers but followed by people who directly face the challenges of production and survival, give rise to temporary re-organizations of society. It is these commons-based transformations that allow overshooting systems to find new ways to work within the biocapacity of their own regions. It is this dynamic — which until now has played out on local, regionally limited scales — that is now necessary on a planetary scale.

2. Thematic Arcs of Transformation

Based on such a reading of civilizational rise and fall, how then can we deepen our interpretation of the contemporary shift from an extractive and degradative political economy to a commons-based one? In other words, where are we in this second movement of the Anthropocene: our capacity to enact reflective planetary awareness? In this next section, we provide our reading of key thematic lines of transformation.

2.1 Capitalism

The first thematic arc we can draw is the growth trajectory of capitalism. From its inception in the fifteenth and sixteenth centuries, the core logic of capitalism followed the practice of the extraction of value and the externalization of costs. From the conquest of the Americas, to the East India Company, theft was at the heart of it. Early forms of primitive accumulation were superseded by more sophisticated forms — the invention of the modern corporation with its core entitlements: limited liability and legal personhood. While constrained for a time — following the post-war Keynesian shift, the New Deal, communism, and the construction of social democracies — the neoliberal turn from the 1970s onwards saw its resurgence. Today, the sheer scale of our ecological crisis, the perversity of legacy industries (e.g., fossil fuel and mining) with their retrograde influence on policy, and extreme inequality all combine to create a dead end. In short, any kind of decent future must, by definition, end current levels of extraction and externalization of costs.

A 500 year half-cycle saw the gradual and episodic emergence of modern-day capitalism from seed to dominant form. In its early period, amid conquest of "virgin" lands inhabited by hitherto unexploited peoples and ecosystems, its growth could continue. But when capitalism's dominance achieves totalizing influence, it reaches a point of radical contradiction. To continue to grow requires the exploitation of the very people and systems that have been integral to capitalism's functioning. Robinson discusses this shift as being a transition from extensive capitalism (planet-wide) to intensive capitalism, the commodification of life-worlds, and subjectivity. Capitalism has nowhere to go except to exploit the inner spaces of our relationships and personal mind-heart spaces, the "mental commons."[18] Meadows and colleagues, with the Club of Rome, discussed this early on as concerning the limits to economic growth on an ecologically-finite planet.[19] Finally, Beck has argued that the current capitalist-industrial system is typified by the continuous production of social risk that sits in fundamental contradiction to human welfare. As corporations innovate products and exploit markets, sheltering behind the protection of the legal convention of limited liability, the capitalist-industrial system intensifies social risk across issues as diverse as climate change, the impact of automation, artificial intelligence, GMOs, and gene editing, the impact of chemicals, weaponization, etc.[20]

The second half of this cycle is therefore a reversal of the logic of extraction and externalization and a shift towards generativity and internalization. Thus, an integral part of the mantra for commons solutions in the contemporary era is stewardship for future generations, building the value of shared commons, and relational integrity — an ethos of care within an awareness of deep interdependence. Hence — today — the almost endless mantra to create a circular economy. The emergence of the plan-

18 William I. Robinson, *A Theory of Global Capitalism* (Baltimore: John Hopkins University Press, 2004).
19 Donella H. Meadows et al., *The Limits to Growth* (New York: Pan Books, 1972).
20 Ulrich Beck, *World Risk Society* (Cambridge: Polity Press, 1999).

etary as a category of mutual survival and wellbeing fundamentally underlines the future impossibility of endless externalization of costs. As Thompson has argued, there is no longer any "other" place or persons to externalize onto:

> If we make such things as Agent Orange or plutonium, they are simply not going to go away, for there is no way in which to put them. If we force animals into concentration camps in feed lots, we will become sick from the antibiotics with which we inject them; if we force nature into mono-crop agribusiness, we will become sprayed by our own pesticides; if we move into genetic engineering, we'll have genetic pollution; if we develop genetic engineering into evolutionary engineering, we will have evolutionary pollution. Industrial civilization never seems to learn, from DDT or thalidomide, plutonium or dioxin; catastrophe is not an accidental by-product of an otherwise good system of progress and control; catastrophe is an ecology's response to being treated in an industrial manner.... Precisely because pollution cannot go away, we must generate only those kinds of pollution we can live with. Precisely because enemies won't go away, for the fundamentalists' process of inciting hate only creates enemies without end, we have no choice but to love our enemies. The enantiomorphic polity of the future must have capitalists and socialists, Israelis and Palestinians, Bahais and Shiites, evangelicals and Episcopalians.[21]

2.2 *The State*

The second thematic arc we can draw is the growth trajectory of the state. The Peace of Westphalia in 1648 marked the birth of the modern state, and a roughly 400-year half-cycle has seen the gradual and episodic evolution of the modern-day state to its dominant form. For sure, the invention of the modern state solved many problems of its time, helping to create shared identity and community beyond religious lines, stabilizing borders,

---

21 Thompson, *Pacific Shift*, 140–41.

and ensuring more effective administrations of welfare for citizens. Major contradictions, however, have today emerged in the status of states.

The first contradiction concerns ultimate authority. Over the last century the nation state has assigned to itself the status of ultimate authority. Today, the nation state is in crisis in part because it lacks the capacity to address many global/interstate challenges, and also because, importantly, its design often prevents it from acting beyond national interests.[22] Meanwhile, a variety of citizens' groups — some local and others transnational — have assumed moral stances that are transnational/global in character. This process is seeing the transfer of ultimate authority from the state to transnational citizen groups.[23]

The second contradiction concerns the crisis in the democratic process or in structures of legitimate governance. It concerns the power of lobby groups, corporations and oligarchs, much of which is transnational in character, to influence and direct state policy in contradiction to the values and desires of national citizens.[24] Increasing citizen engagement and desire for devolved localized governance or direct/participatory democracy runs counter to the increasing closure of the political process.

These two contradictions give rise to the state's limitations in the governance and management of shared commons. The state's role in protecting ecological commons (oceans, rivers, beaches, groundwater, etc.) and building social commons (roads, services, libraries, etc.) is perpetually constrained. Firstly, the state's role is constrained by virtue of its own limitations within an interstate system where national interest is positioned above participation in a global community — creating a zero-sum dynamic in which global common concerns are merely add-ons or

---

22 John Keane, "Cosmocracy and Global Civil Society," in *Global Civil Society: Contested Futures,* eds. Gideon Baker and David Chandler (New York: Routledge, 2005), 149–70.

23 Mary Kaldor, *Global Civil Society: An Answer to War* (Cambridge: Polity Press, 2003).

24 Jeffrey A. Winters, *Oligarchy* (Cambridge: Wiley Online Library, 2011).

extensions of national interest. Secondly, the state's role is constrained by virtue of the need to satisfy powerful state-producing interests (industries, investors, military, voters, media, etc.). The outcome of this power-brokering process creates winners and losers as the state "closes ranks" with these monied interests rather than producing policy geared toward common interests. This dynamic is especially acute today, where transnational capital dictates a large part of national policy, and where investors are far removed from those concretely affected by such policies.

The second half of this cycle thus points towards the re-invention of politics, governance, and democracy. The substance of this is a shift from the political infantilization of majority populations to a new politics of commons-based governance, where everyone can be a commoner, participating in creating, protecting, and maintaining commons that matter to them. Rather than mechanistically-defined lines of state power, we envision a network of diverse commons governance units, some at local, urban, and bioregional scales, and others at global scales, coordinated, and forming new structural synergies of power.[25]

Today, both capitalism and the state are intertwined in a structural synergy of power aimed at perpetuating the privilege of a "core" of wealthy and powerful people and groups at the expense of "peripheries." This dynamic is visible both within states and also transnationally through a complex system of harmonization between elites in core states and elites in peripheral states,[26] or — what Robinson refers to as a transnational capitalist class.[27] The harmonization of elites from core to periphery is a form of political enclosure whereby the futures most humans

25 Jose Ramos, "Liquid Democracy and the Futures of Governance," in *The Future Internet, Public Adminstration and The Futures of Governance,* eds. Jenifer Winter and Ryota Ono (Dordrecht: Springer, 2016), 173–91, at 173.

26 Johan Galtung, "A Structural Theory of Imperialism,'" *Journal of Peace Research* (1971): 81–117.

27 William I. Robinson, "What Is Critical Globalization Studies? Intellectual Labor and Global Society," in *Critical Globalisation Studies,* eds. Richard P. Applebaum and William I. Robinson (New York: Routledge, 2005), 11–18.

in the world and the ecosystems they depend on are thrown under the bus.[28]

2.3 Reimagining the Emergence of the Commons

These reorganizations help us to reimagine the re-emergence of the commons, and to posit a history and evolution of the commons, up to the current global challenge of reorganizing a planetary political economy. Here is the sequence that we propose:

1. The original format of the commons in both hunter-gathering and pre-capitalist class formations are the natural-resource commons, which connect the people to the land and its resources. Through conquest or enclosure, the commodification of land broke the relationship between traditional stewards and their commons.[29]

2. Under capitalism the dominant form of the commons is the social commons, as developed by the labor movement to ensure its survival in solidarity, i.e., the mutuals, cooperatives, and other forms that were eventually taken over by the welfare state and bureaucratized.

3. Under cognitive capitalism, with the invention of digital networks for the co-production of shared knowledge, it is the knowledge commons which comes to the fore. However, without capabilities for self-reproduction being vested in the commoners, most of these knowledge commons are subsumed under the new forms of netarchical capital — the new fraction of capital which directly exploits human cooperation (and relationality) and extracts value from it.[30]

---

28 Galtung, "Structural Theory of Imperialism." This is described more vividly towards the latter half of this chapter, in Scenario 3.

29 Many traditional societies have no ownership relationship with land, operating effective commons-type relations with their world, and are thus more "stewards" than "owners."

30 "Netarchical capitalism is a hypothesis about the emergence of a new segment of the capitalist class (the owners of financial or other capital), which

4. Under conditions of capitalist crisis and global urbanization, urban commons (and other territorial commons) become the locus where precarious workers merge physical infrastructures with knowledge commons, and urban culture merges with networked cooperation culture. Urban commons are a response to market and state failure in maintaining and constructing the infrastructures of social life.

5. Urban commons infrastructures, such as fablabs and coworking places, are not only places where the culture of the commons become embodied, tackling social-ecological transition concerns through experimentation with new provisioning systems. It is also where prototypal forms of production are invented, which prefigure the coming productive commons mode. This vision of the centrality of the urban should not mean a sole focus on the city however, but rather invite us to a bioregional and territorial vision, centered on organizing the provisioning systems for territories in ways that are compatible with the carrying capacity of the planet and the specific regions involved.

6. This model is called "cosmo-local production,"[31] or "Design Global, Manufacture Local."[32] This mode of production and exchange combines global cooperation in knowledge commons, for example, open design; and local fabrication in distributed local factories. These knowledge and production communities increasingly experiment with open and con-

---

is no longer dependent on the ownership of intellectual property rights (hypothesis of cognitive capitalism), nor on the control of the media vectors (hypothesis of MacKenzie Wark in his book *The Hacker's Manifesto*), but rather on the development and control of participatory platforms." *P2P Foundation Wiki*, s.v. "Netarchical Capitalism," http://wiki.p2pfoundation.net/Netarchical_Capitalism.

31 Jose Ramos, "Cosmo-localization and Leadership for the Future," *Journal of Futures Studies* 21, no. 4 (2017): 65–84.

32 Kostakis et al., "Design Global, Manufacture Local."

tributive accounting systems,[33] with open and participatory supply chains, etc. They show the potential future of a more fully organized commons-based society and economic system.

Recently, we asked a team of associates to study the Thermodynamics of Peer Production, to see how a systematic use of mutualization in physical production (open source), could actually diminish the human footprint on ecological systems. Their findings have confirmed the link between mutualization and radical lowering of the human footprint.[34]

So, to summarize our vision of the current conjuncture: we are now in a period of "phygital" convergence, i.e., the convergence of networked collective intelligence, which is expressed in global-local collaborations around all kinds of knowledge and their applications to local territorial contexts. However, we are at a point where citizen-commoners are starting to mutualize the use of resources,[35] but not yet the production of them. We are mutualizing the use of houses and cars, but not yet producing these physical resources in a commons-based fashion. This then seems to us the necessary focus of transition work, i.e., the strengthening of material-immaterial commons for provisioning, and the preparation of a better organized productive commons.

---

33 Michel Bauwens and Vasilis Niaros, *Value in the Commons Economy: Developments in Open and Contributory Value Accounting* (Berlin: Heinrich Böll Stiftung and P2P Foundation, 2017).

34 Celine Piques and Xavier Rizos, *Peer to Peer and the Commons: A Path Towards Transition: A Matter, Energy and Thermodynamic Perspective* (P2P Foundation Report, 2017), http://commonstransition.org/wp-content/uploads/2017/10/Report-P2P-Thermodynamics-VOL_1-web_2.0.pdf.

35 In a recent research project commissioned by the city of Ghent in northern Belgium, we found over 500 urban commons active in every area of human provisioning. The English executive summary of the report is available at Michel Bauwens and Jurek Onzia, "A Commons Transition Plan for the City of Ghent," *Commons Transition*, September 8, 2017, http://commonstransition.org/commons-transition-plan-city-ghent/.

3. The Commoner as Emergent Political Subject

The transition that we are experiencing works both across the dimensions of social learning/collective awakening and of personal learning/subjective awakening. The dimension of social learning takes place within historical and even macro-historical time frames of change. Through time, societies have experienced cultural and even civilizational transformations. Such transformations are recorded as collective memory, imbued in song, poetry, art, stories, and histories. For the individual, it is as difficult to get outside their own time frame and to experience historical social change as it is difficult for an ant foraging for food to realize that they are in someone's kitchen. Machiavelli discussed this as the "incredulity of mankind, who do not truly believe in anything new until they have actual experience of it."[36]

The individual, in dealing with the current planetary crisis, is likely to go through a number of phases.[37] First, utter confusion based on a litany of news and opinions. Second, powerful feelings of frustration, sadness, and even grief in the knowledge of the sheer magnitude of the crisis, the damage to ecosystems, the loss of species, de-humanization through inequality, and the threat of climate change. Thirdly, given this context, a person's sense of self — their identity — shifts. There are choices. A person may retreat to the old, strengthen the imperial self — the accumulator — in the face of existential threats. Or they may see how their fate and future is intertwined and interdependent with many others (indeed, that *they are* many others), and experiment with a new self and identity, as part of a commons. Fourthly, to be able to rise above fear and follow this higher self, individuals must be guided by empowering visions and pathways. There must be visible avenues based on grounded hope, reasonable analysis, and critical imagination. Finally, the indi-

---

36 Niccolo Machiavelli, *The Prince*, ed. M. Viroli (Oxford: Oxford University Press, 2008).

37 David Hicks, "Teaching about Global Issues, the Need for Holistic Learning," in *Lessons for the Future, the Missing Dimension in Education* (London: Routledge Falmer, 2002), 98–108.

vidual enters the realm of action, enmeshed in new communities and networks co-protecting and co-creating the planetary commons at various scales and dimensions.

The awakening we require at a personal level, which has the power to re-orient us as change agents, is contingent on making sense of historical and even macro-historical changes, grasping grand shifts and our role in the transformation of society through time. Therefore, one of the challenges in the transition towards a commons-based sociality is just this conceptualization of social change, which cannot be experienced directly by an individual through life experience, but is manifest through collective historical memory and a shared sociological understanding of change connected to images of the future.

In other terms, we are dealing with the de-colonization of the self. The shift needed is from "neo-liberal man," the rational, self-interested, economic accumulator, to "commoner," a community member whose actions reflect an embodied understanding of interdependence with others at various scales and in multiple dimensions. The specific shift in individual and collective group identity we are suggesting is one that is no longer centered on the dynamics of labor vs. capital, which is a category of socialism-capitalism, but rather centered on the dynamics of generative citizen-commoners, producers vs. extractors. We believe there is a sociological grounding to this. First of all, certainly in Western countries, after the de-industrialization *cum* globalization that started in the 1980s, the industrial working class is effectively in decline. Yet, even the global proletarization in the global South is not linked to a resurgence of socialism. On the contrary, different studies have shown an exponential growth of urban commons subsequent to the prior exponential growth of digital knowledge commons.[38] Contemporary

---

38 Tine de Moor, *Homo cooperans: Instituties voor collectieve actie en de solidaire samenleving* (Utrecht: Universiteit Utrecht, Faculteit Geesteswetenschappen, 2013), http://www.collective-action.info/sites/default/files/webmaster/_PUB_Homo-cooperans_EN.pdf; and see Fleur Noy and Dirk Holemans, "Burgercollectieven in kaart gebracht," *Oikos* 78, no. 3 (2016): 69–81, http://www.coopkracht.org/images/phocadownload/burgercollec-

precarious labor is very much linked to both an urban context and to a generalized connection with digital networks. In our view, it is this ongoing interconnection and the participation in the creation of urban commons infrastructures, linked to state and market failure, that creates the conditions for a new post-capitalist subjectivity, which can drives the ongoing growth in the creation of commons.

Personal awakening is contingent upon connecting personal experience with an understanding of broader social changes of which one is part. To know oneself and one's place in the world is to understand a bit about the past, the present, and the future, and about how one fits into the greater scheme of things. Yet, there is undoubtedly a materialist aspect to this, i.e., to the degree that exaggerated extraction of common wealth is enclosed by oligarchic elites, and to the degree that the capture of institutions paralyzes the state and the market's role in solving humanity's overshoot problems and the resulting social inequality, to that same degree, citizen-commoners are driven to common-ify vital infrastructures, create parallel solidarity mechanisms based on mutualization, and to undertake the organization of provisioning systems that more adequately deal with the necessity of socio-ecological transitions. All this feeds and strengthens post-capitalist commons-based transition activities.

3.1 Commoning as the Third Movement of the Anthropocene
By virtue of this second movement of the Anthropocene — our capacity to see ourselves as interdependent with other people and species for our wellbeing and common futures — the third movement of the Anthropocene is brought forth. This is a movement of "implication," whereby the person, through their emerging relational awareness, is "plied into" a shared concern. They become aware that they share with others a common interest. A commons has shifted from something implicit, real, but

tieven%20in%20okaart%20gebracht%20-%20fleur%20noy%20%20dirk%20holemans.pdf.

unidentified, to something explicit — its reality has been relationally formulated.

The explication of a commons, a domain of shared concern, is simultaneously the invocation of a community who must steward the good of that commons — commoning. A particular commons can only be as such because it is valued by a particular group of people. Because it is valued, that group tends to that commons — creating it, protecting it or extending it. In the case of a natural resource, it is the local inhabitants who want to protect such localized commons for their own use. These are the examples that Ostrom studied and gained fame for.[39]

In the case of public and social commons, these are created by political entities such as municipalities, states, and federal systems, which are meant to extend a common good to a whole political community. Universal healthcare is one example of such a public commons, where a public good that a political community cares for is created. Peer-produced commons are created by networks of participants, such as with open source software or sharing networks. These are not pre-existing commons, but rather, are created by that community from their own activity. Because a particular community, for example the Linux community, cares about this shared commons, they work to develop and protect it.

Finally, in the case of planetary life-support systems, the value of this as a commons is fundamentally implicit — that is, it does not appear valuable to a community until it is activated by virtue of a contextual shift. When the ozone layer became threatened due to certain industrial pollutants, which in turn fundamentally threatened human well being, the ozone layer became a commons for collective governance, an "object of commoning."[40] To enact ourselves as commoners is also to enact ourselves as protectors and governors of the commons in

---

39 Elinor Ostrom, *Governing the Commons* (Cambridge: Cambridge University Press, 1990).

40 Susan Buck, *The Global Commons: An Introduction* (Washington, DC: Island Press, 1998).

which we are implicated, and which we have explicated through language, speech, and practice.

For an issue as basic as climate change, the climate as commons represents the awakening of the individual to the fact that they/we share an atmosphere with seven billion others (and countless species) as a commons of concern. Through the accident of circumstance, such commoners have been "plied into" a shared concern. The planet's atmosphere has thus shifted from an implicit commons to an explicit commons. Commoning as an act of governance mirrors this movement of self awareness — those who share this commons for their mutual wellbeing and survival must make a shift toward becoming active protectors, shapers, and extenders of that commons. This is the movement from a *commons-in-itself* to a *commons-for-itself.* In practical terms, with respect to our atmosphere, everyone is a commoner, and this implies a radical democratization of planetary governance. This third movement of the Anthropocene thus depends on both an emerging awareness of our shared commons and an emergent subjectivity that responds to this awareness through commoning as a relationally charged form of action.

The transformation of subjectivity in the twenty-first century, of the experience and the definition of self, is the reawakening of our embodied relationality in respect to multiple categories of the commons, and its expression through our emergent practices of commoning. This can be from our connection to our local community or the resources that the local community manages for its wellbeing, but can also be in connection to what we experience in relation to the future of Earth's atmosphere and its suitability for human life — through which the community is a global one in which all of us, and our descendants, are all critical stakeholders.

4. Scenarios for a Commons Transition

We would like to offer three short scenarios that clarify the challenges we collectively face. For this, we employ a modified version of the integrated scenario methodology of Sohail Inayatul-lah[41] and scenario archetypes developed by Dator.[42]

The first scenario, "Catastrophe: Sleep Walking into Obliv-ion," is developed as a continuation of the dominant sys-tem — the structural synergy of power across capitalism, the state, and consumerism. The logic of capitalism and state power continues unimpeded by anti-systemic challenges. It is a future of extreme inequality amid ecological collapse, extreme privi-lege buttressed by innovations in social control, violence, and entertainment.

The second scenario, "The disciple of the 100 schools," ex-plores and develops what the first disowns — the transformative, idealistic, and ideological variants surrounding the commons. Post-capitalist variants can be over-ideologized and puritanical, and various "schools" compete, creating an incoherent societal transition that is not able to support livelihoods in a post-growth and ecologically constrained context.

The third scenario, "Ecologies of the Commons," develops an integration where the dominant system and the transformative/idealistic are interwoven, moving beyond the categorical purity and binary framing of the first two scenarios. It describes a pro-tocol commons that interconnects and creates synergies across a variety of forms, institutions, networks, businesses, academia, etc. These three high level scenarios are a segue toward discuss-ing more concrete strategies.

4.1 Scenario 1 — Catastrophe: Sleep-Walking into Oblivion

The extreme inequality of the twenty-first century between an emerging class of the super-rich, and the majority living in con-ditions of precarity, not only continues but accelerates into the middle of the century. Alongside this widening gap in prosper-ity, the wealthy become ever more policy-rich and the precariat

---

41 Sohail Inayatullah, "Six Pillars: Futures Thinking for Transforming," *Fore-sight* 10, no. 1 (2008): 4–21.

42 Jim Dator, "Alternative Futures at the Manoa School," *Journal of Futures Studies* 14, no. 2 (2009): 1–18.

have become even more policy-poor — state policy is determined by the interests of oligarchs, multinational corporations, and cashed up lobby groups.[43] Thus, while a combination of automation, robotics, and artificial intelligence (AI) increasingly eliminate jobs, the profits from this form of technological rationalization are offshored into tax havens. AI and automation create efficiencies and technical breakthroughs, but powerful companies continue to starve the state of revenue needed for a social transition. Despite warning signs, and many voices calling for change, the transnational capitalist class (a combination of the rich and the political classes that serve their interests) close ranks around the system that has guaranteed their success — they decide that the system must survive at all costs.

Yet, this hyper-inequality is also a powder keg. Dissidents multiply in the face of harsher economic conditions. The legitimacy of the capitalist-state formula must be maintained, and hence greater emphasis is put on green capitalism, the celebration of the billionaire businessman, and the celebration of the capitalist-innovator-disruptor. Alongside this, the big platform capitalists of the early twenty-first century begin to close ranks with the oligarchic elite.[44] Companies increasingly use their deep understanding of social interactions and predictive profiling to help the state neutralize and eliminate dissident threats. Increasingly, any outspoken voices against the system are considered to be sources of potential terrorism. Anti-systemic movements for equality, ecologically-minded change, and transformation are deemed to be terrorist insurgencies and lead

---

43 Martin Gilens and Benjamin I. Page, "Testing Theories of American Politics: Elites, Interest Groups, and Average Citizens," *Perspectives on Politics* 12 (2014): 564–81.

44 Frank Pasquale, "Two Narratives of Platform Capitalism," *Yale Law and Policy Review* 35 (2016): 309–19; Nick Srnicek, "The Challenges of Platform Capitalism: Understanding the Logic of a New Business Model," *Juncture* 23, no. 4 (2017): 254–57; Juliet B. Schor, "Does the Sharing Economy Increase Inequality within the Eighty Percent? Findings from a Qualitative Study of Platform Providers," *Cambridge Journal of Regions, Economy and Society* 10 (2017): 263–79.

to state repression. Individuals who "awaken" are neutralized early: with algorithms determining who is and is not a threat, surveillance becomes terror against any unlucky person.

There is an ontology in this scenario: surveillance by the state and the large netarchical firms that own and control the platform economy clearly have a vision of humans as subjects, which are "subjected" to the control of the state and corporate sovereigns. While neutralizing political activism internally, there must be the facade of democracy — hence the demonization of "non-democratic" states around the world. In order to maintain ideological and cultural control, cheap entertainment takes precedence, which keeps people from their higher purposes as commoners and global citizens, and leads to widespread nihilism.

Yet, green capitalism in this scenario cannot adequately deal with its own contradictions. The logic of economic growth continues unabated, carbon emissions continue to rise, impacts on oceans, forests, and other bioregions deepen, and corporate industrial externalities are not dealt with.[45] Because of this, in the mid-2040s, as predicted by the Club of Rome,[46] we experience genuine ecological collapse. Extreme weather severely disrupts food production, coastlines are inundated, the world is awash in hundreds of millions of climate and economic refugees, and broken financial systems do little to support any meaningful social transition.

The rich have retreated into pristine enclaves, serviced by middle-class attendants content to have livelihoods, while the majority poor are left with diminishing ecological and social futures and radical inequality amid ecological collapse. Because of the extreme inequality, it is a world of both high structural and real violence. For the poor there is the constant violence of competition for survival. For the middle class, there is a perpetual tightening and increasing struggle.

---

45 Piques and Rizos, *Peer to Peer and the Commons*.
46 Meadows, *The Limits to Growth*.

4.2 Scenario 2 — *The Disciple of the 100 Schools*

The legitimacy of capitalism and state power does not even survive the beginning of the twenty-first century. As wave after wave of financial crises hits, and an increasingly cash-starved state is unable to respond in any meaningful way, let alone to maintain its own coherence, the many social forces that had been waiting in the wings for decades come forth as contenders to guide social development.

Included in this are the many strands of thinking and practice disowned by capitalist industrial modernity: postcolonial, deep ecology, marxist, ecological economics, eco-feminism, anarchism, autonomism, socialism, etc. While each is an expression of a social ill and of social pain, the historical suffering that each represents does not become an opening and pathway to embracing a multiplicity of other types of suffering. Instead the pain closes out all other forms of suffering, magnifying its own.

Each of these social alternatives and social movements are thus marked by hard boundary-setting and a degree of ideological closure: each believes its anti- and counter-systemic solution is the true answer. Some completely disown any form of hierarchy or institutional power, others disavow any connection with markets and profit-making, others any male leadership, others any inclusion of "white people." There are many prophets preaching a disciplined adherence to a new way of life. Purity of body, mind, and relations is central. People don't want to appear "dirty" by being associated with various forms of "the enemy." These dynamics make internal conflict across the ideological divide commonplace and any kind of coherent social transition more difficult. For many, the historical legacy of capitalism and state power, and the many abuses in their names, are simply too great to forgive.

Instead of articulating the commons as a metalanguage, commons advocates attempt to create an ideologically consistent form of thinking and practice — a type of "commonism." This too makes the commons merely one of a number of other contenders in this new open space and contestation for change.

People have also retreated from commitments to nationhood and to a national community/identity. Rather than being stewards of the social commons, nations lose their status to other social groups that have formed new bases, trans-national affiliations and localized development. But this shift makes it impossible to campaign for the reintroduction of the state-based social commons of the mid-twentieth century (e.g. social democracies), for example: through new forms of Universal Basic Income or Assets. There are rich commons and poor commons — high social capital communities (in metro-cities) have the time and resources to create "their" commons, while poor communities are stuck in cycles of survival.

In this scenario, it can be seen that everything, taken to its absolute, runs the great danger of becoming oppressive. While this was true of the totalitarianism of the state form, historically represented by fascism and the Soviet system, we also must face the potential totalitarianism of the market, and yes — even of the commons.

One of the stronger movements of ideas, which is also well funded, is libertarianism — or more specifically, anarcho-capitalism — which finds many adherents amongst those that design, initiate, and use blockchain and cryptocurrencies such as Bitcoin, and which have conducted massively successful Initial Coin Offerings. This current of thought and practice designs technological systems to allow for "distributed markets" that allow any individuals, without centralized mediation, to exchange with each other directly and to make agreements based on smart contracts. It is a worldview that only sees individuals, atomized in their relations, but who are able to make agreements that are validated by blockchain technology. This political point of view is fundamentally technocratic, seeking solutions in technology because it lacks trust in human governance — hence the quest for, and support for, "trustless" systems.

We also know, as every child who has played *Monopoly* knows, that competition for scarce resources through market mechanisms leads to oligarchic results. Competition leads to winners and losers who, at each round, can accumulate more resources than their opponents and consequently have more chance of winning the longer the game goes on due to the reliance on greater and greater resources. Hence, an egalitarian-sounding idea: "let's all start as equal traders over blockchain systems," is a recipe for hyper-capitalism and for the near-total commodification of social life. Furthermore, this development is internally hostile to any measure that can rebalance the distribution of power and wealth, for example, through mechanisms arrived at by democratic governance and which would balance the natural outcomes of these exchange mechanisms.

In fact, the refusal to take into account any democratic governance mechanisms paradoxically leads to authoritarian outcomes once conflicts arise. Furthermore, these systems are also designed to be opaque to external controls and are used to massively evade taxation as a redistributive mechanism. For all these reasons, and despite the utopian charge of such movements, they work as a preparation for even more totalizing neoliberalism, i.e., the absolute domination of market forms, enhancing their control to ever more detailed and microscopic levels. Hence, the seemingly utopian efforts, based on the the anarcho-libertarian assumptions behind the blockchain, paradoxically lead to further enclosures as whole life worlds and the ecologies they are embedded in are ensnarled into "smart" contracts.

The commons too may have its own radical absolutization and generalizations. Common-ism becomes the tendency to want everything as a commons and to be radically opposed to any market or state form.[47] Moreover, these points of view come with a predilection for the assembly format of decision-making and full consensus, creating lowest-common-denominator effects, enforcing a radical collectivism that runs counter to individual preferences and freedoms, but also imposes very heavy processing costs. (This is one of the reasons that assemblies of-

---

47 The emerging literature on the urban commons supports the notion that commons are constructed across domains of state, markets, citizens, and other domains, see Christian Iaione, "The CO-City: Sharing, Collaborating, Cooperating, and Commoning in the City," *American Journal of Economics and Sociology* 75, no. 2 (2016): 415–55.

ten do not last very long, because participants get exhausted, or assemblies lead to the tyranny of structurelessness, i.e., to the domination by a minority of strong leaders who can sway the collective consensus.)[48]

Both the right-wing capitalistic form of anarchism, and the left-wing version, where collectives instead of individuals make agreements to constitute society, tend to ignore the societal field in which they operate, which limits the sphere of choices. There is no conception of a common good across a territory, which sets a framework on the coexistence of different value communities, and no conception of common good institutions, which may be necessary to guarantee common freedoms (and restraints). This results in the rejection of the democratic-state form and a refusal to think through its further democratization. Anarcho-capitalism and the value-sensitive design of the block-chain points to an ontological vision of humans as traders or as micro-capitalists, but otherwise, excludes a re-assembling of the social based on protocols of commoning.

Between the ideological purity of post-capitalist movements and the anarcho-capitalism of the blockchain, there is little co-herence across communities and sectors, and building collabo-rations and powerful synergies is too hard. There is not enough "gravity" or "glue" to bind or stop the powerful centrifugal forces from pulling apart. Because of this, in the context of degrowth economies and ecological constraints, standards of living drop significantly, and people live lives of frugality and discipline supported by the networks and groups to which they belong.

4.3 Scenario 3 — Ecologies of the Commons
In the mid-2030s, in the wake of major financial crises that crashed economies throughout the world, and which states could not find a way through, intensive cosmo-localization strategies are initiated ubiquitously. The first quarter of the century lays the groundwork for this through the creation of

---

48 Jo Freeman, "The Tyranny of Structurelessness," *Berkeley Journal of Sociology* 17 (1972–73): 151–64.

a "metalanguage" for the commons. Such metalanguage allows people to see how they are implicated in a number of commons, and helps to overcome the lack of political and cultural coherency experienced by twentieth-century movements. This is followed by the development of practical frameworks for generating synergies of the commons, a strategy that is early on termed "Ecologies of the Commons."[49]

The diversity of commoning activity is established early on.[50] Based on the experience of urban commoning from around the world,[51] which conceptualized a quintuple-helix strategy,[52] those behind building the framework and strategy for a commons transition abandon notions of "essential commoning" (that there is a "true" way for commoning), and instead focus on appreciating the broad variety of commoning strategies from around the world, and on creating practical mechanisms for exchange between ontologically distinct commoning entities, processes, and projects. This new approach expresses an understanding that synergies are possible between anchor institutions, universities, governments, businesses, and citizen-based groups and projects, even while each is quite different in form and purpose. Efforts are made to construct a language and body of concepts that can be understood by a variety of projects and organizations, which allow them to "talk to each other" in the language of commoning, and which enable processes of meta-systemic co-design — the development of new commons-based synergies.

Ecologies of the Commons dovetails with efforts to create an ecology of the left, where different social projects, movements,

49 Michel Bauwens and Jose Ramos, "Re-imagining the Left through an Ecology of the Commons: Towards a Post-capitalist Commons Transition," *Global Discourse* 8, no. 2 (2018): 325–42.

50 David Bollier and Silke Helfrich, eds., *The Wealth of the Commons: A World Beyond Market and State* (Amherst: Levellers Press, 2012); David Bollier and Silke Helfrich, *Patterns of Commoning* (Amherst: Off the Common Books, 2014).

51 Neal Gorenflo, ed., *Sharing Cities: Activating the Urban Commons* (San Francisco: Shareable, 2017).

52 Iaione, "The CO-City."

and ideologies can see how they are part of a broader process of social change.[53] Rather than a factionalism, people see themselves as part of an ecology of knowledges and of a "knowledge democracy,"[54] each knowledge forming an important aspect of how the new world needs to be constructed, but in relation to the variety of other knowledges and their contextual application.[55]

As these strategies mature and their positive effects are experienced, people begin to talk about the "protocol commons," the complex metalanguage and architecture required to form commons-based synergies — which in itself must be protected and extended. The protocol commons helps in the reinvention of the nation-state as a community — indeed it saves it.[56] State-created social commons are still seen as fundamentally critical in providing basic support across populations; however they are not seen as completely exclusionary, as nations have to see themselves as part of a community with other nations to support the development and protection of our global commons (for example, atmosphere and security). The role of the state transforms — now it is seen as the partner state or a partner city charged with supporting citizens as innovators, protectors, and

53 Boaventura de Sousa Santos, *The Rise of the Global Left: The World Social Forum and Beyond* (London and New York: Zed Books, 2006).

54 Boaventura de Sousa Santos, *Democratizing Democracy: Beyond the Liberal Democratic Canon* (London: Verso, 2007).

55 Lonnie L. Rowell and Eunsook Hong, "Knowledge Democracy and Action Research: Pathways for the Twenty-First Century," in *The Palgrave International Handbook of Action Research,* eds. Lonnie L. Rowell et al. (New York: Palgrave McMillan, 2017), 63–68. See also the "bricolage"-based approach in Per Olsson et al., "The Concept of the Anthropocene as a Game-Changer: A New Context for Social Innovation and Transformations to Sustainability," *Ecology & Society* 22, no. 2 (2017): art. 31.

56 Whereas scenario one sees a false construction of national community as a bulwark against anti-systemic movements, and in scenario two we see the weakening or abandonment of the idea of nationhood; in this scenario the state is seen as a critically important platform for commoning, but as relationally embedded.

maintainers of a variety of commons.[57] The protocol commons allows the state, and the various institutions embedded within the state, to understand the language that describes how the state sits within a broader ecology of societal transition, as well as the architecture that governs this system. This transformation is driven by new institutions that are in charge of public-commons cooperation at all scales, converging with the players responsible for regenerative market forms.

While it was just an experimental form in the early part of the twenty-first century, by mid-century, the partner state becomes a nuanced and powerful approach to creating synergies between a diversity of citizen-initiated projects and the enabling structures that allow this diversity to thrive and to create value. Institutions are reimagined as structures that exist to enhance the agency and creative potential of the variety of actors within civil society. This hyper-diverse and complex composition of structures, groups, individuals, and technology creates mutant synergies of the commons unimaginable years earlier. The ecologies of the commons are ever more diverse, complex, resilient, and generative — they cannot be pigeonholed into one category or another.

This vision stands for the human as citizen-commoners (or inhabitants-commoners, if we want to avoid the exclusionary character of national citizenship). Indeed, in this vision, citizens become productive commoners who contribute to the common good. We envisage a society where the core are productive civil societies, where citizens belong and co-produce all kinds of commons; where they are members of economic entities which create livelihoods in an ethical market; and where the infrastructural organizations that support digital and urban commons are reflected in a new vision of the state as enabling a "partner state."

---

57 Jose Ramos, Michel Bauwens, and Vasilis Kostakis, "P2P and Planetary Futures," in *Critical Posthumanism and Planetary Futures,* eds. Debashish Banerji and Makarand R. Paranjape (New Delhi: Springer India, 2016).

The protocol commons — the metalanguages for the commons, architecture and citizen-network-institutional synergies that generate value — begins by articlating a "cosmo-local production infrastructure" across four layers:

a) Layer 1 — Protocol Cooperativism Governance
The first layer is based on protocol cooperativism, which creates dynamic synergies between cities, networks, institutions, and civil society organizations. Protocol cooperativism generates the possibility of a cosmo-local institutional layer. We imagine global for-benefit associations which support the provisioning of infrastructures for urban and territorial commoning. These are structured as global public-commons partnerships, sustained by leagues of cities which are co-dependent and co-motivated to support these new infrastructures and to overcome the fragmentation of effort that benefits the most extractive and centralized "netarchical" firms. Instead, these infrastructural commons organizations co-support MuniRide, MuniBnB, and other applications necessary to commonify urban provisioning systems. These are global "protocol cooperative" governance organizations.

b) Layer 2 — Open Design Commons
The second layer consists of the actual global depositories of the commons applications themselves, a global technical infrastructure for open sourcing provisioning systems. They consist of what is globally common, but allow contextualized local adaptations, which in turn can serve as innovations and examples for other locales. These are the actual "protocol cooperatives," in their concrete manifestation as usable infrastructure.

c) Layer 3 — Localized Platform Cooperatives (and others commons-based platforms)
The third layer are the actual local (urban, territorial, bioregional) platform cooperatives, i.e., the local commons-based mechanisms that deliver access to services and exchange platforms, for the mutualized use of these provisioning systems. This is the

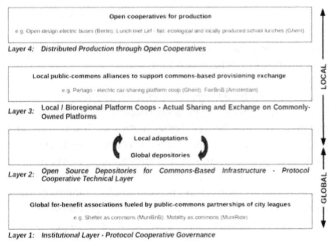

Figure 1. City-supported cosmo-local production infrastructure. (Source: P2P Foundation / Michel Bauwens http://wiki.p2pfoundation.net/Towards_a_Global_Infrastructure_for_Commons-Based_Provisioning)

layer where the Amsterdam FairBnb and the MuniRide applications of the city of Ghent, for example, organize the services for the local population and their visitors. It is where houses and cars are effectively shared.

d) Layer 4 — Open Cooperatives
The fourth layer is the actual production-based open cooperatives, where distributed manufacturing of goods and services produces the actual material services that are shared and mutualized on the platform cooperatives.

5. Institutional Design for a Commons-Centric Transformation

5.1 Towards a Public-Commons Framework for the Anthropocene
To close our heuristic loop for this chapter, we can consider a third movement of the Anthropocene — the planetary-coordinated response to an emerging awareness of ourselves as commoners, through some specific strategies for how we enact cosmo-local commoning. We see cities as a critical strategic locale of transformation to enact public-citizen commons synergies and transformation. While this does not exclude the multifaceted dimensions of commoning, the general logic of our proposals is to put forward realistic but important institutional innovations that can lead to successfully achieving basic ecological and social goals of general equity and wellbeing. For this, we conclude with specific strategies for the further progress and expansion of the urban commons, which can then be extended outward. We propose public-social or public-commons-based processes and protocols to streamline cooperation between the City and commoners in every field of human provisioning.

Figure 2 shows the basic collaboration process between commoners and the public-good institutions of the "partner city."

As we can see, commons initiatives can forward their proposals and need for support to a City Lab, which prepares a "Commons Accord" between the city and the commons initiative, modeled after the Bologna Regulation for the Care and Regeneration of the Urban Commons. Based on this contract, the city sets up specific support alliances which combine the commoners and civil society organizations, the city itself, and the generative private sector, in order to organize support flows.

This first institutional arrangement described here allows for permanent ad-hoc adaptations and the organization of frameworks to enable more support for the common-based initiatives. But just as importantly, this support needs to be strategized in the context of the necessary socio-ecological transitions, which is the purpose of the second set of proposals, as outlined in the following figure:

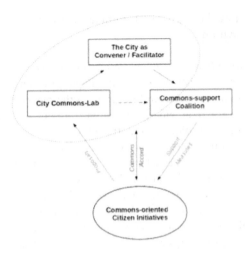

Figure 2: The basic processes for public-commons collaboration (Source: Commons Transition / Michel Bauwens, http://commonstransition.org/commons-transition-plan-city-ghent)

Figure 3 describes a cross-sector institutional infrastructure for commons policy-making and support, divided into "transitional platforms," or as we call them on the figure, "Sustainability Empowerment Platforms." The model comes from the existing practice in Ghent around food transition, which is far from perfect but nevertheless has the core institutional logic that can lead to more successful outcomes in the future.

The city of Ghent has created an initiative called *Gent en Garde,* which accepts the five aims of civil-society organizations active in food transition (local organic food, fairly produced) that works as follows: the city has initiated a Food Council, which meets regularly and contributes to food policy proposals. The Council is representative of the current forces at play and has both the strength and weaknesses of representative organizations, but it also counts in its membership the "urban food working group," which mobilizes those effectively work-

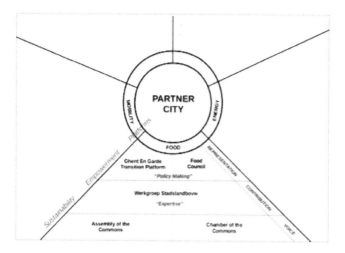

Figure 3: A public-commons institutional design for the social and ecological transition (Source: Commons Transition / Michel Bauwens, http://commonstransition.org/commons-transition-plan-city-ghent/)

ing at the grassroots level on that transition. The group follows a contributive logic, where every contributor has a voice. This combination of representative and contributive logic can create a super-competent Democracy+ institution that goes beyond the limitations of representation and integrates the contributive logic of the commoners. This model mixes representative logic and its legitimacy, and the expertise available in public institutions, but, crucially, augments them with the contextually-rich experience and expertise of the grassroots experts. The model is further augmented with the expertise of the generative businesses that are engaged in the necessary socio-ecological transitions.

But how can the commoners exert significant political weight so that political and representative institutions will actually "listen" to them? This requires "voice" and self-organization. We therefore propose the creation of an Assembly of the Commons for all citizens active in the co-construction of commons, and a

Chamber of the Commons for all those who are creating livelihoods around these commons, in order to create more social, economic — and ultimately political — power for the commons.

This essential process of participation that we have seen in food transition can be replicated across the transition domains, obtaining city and institutional support for a process leading to Energy as a Commons, Mobility as a Commons, Housing, Food, etc. These "transition arenas" or "sustainability empowerment platforms" integrate the goals and values necessary for a successful socio-ecological transition and allow for a permanent dialogue amongst all the stakeholders involved.

With this, we conclude, the model provides the minimal generic structures that we believe a partner city needs in order to support a transition towards commons-based civic and economic forms being integrated in democratic structures of representation, enriching the city and complementing its structures, while stimulating the individual and collective autonomy of its citizens organized as commoners.

5.2 A Three-Pronged Strategy Involving the Simultaneous Transformation of Civil Society, the Market and the State Forms

But how do we get from the current market-state and market-city configurations to commons-centric institutions? We believe that the model of the *Energiewende* in Germany shows a strategy for social, political, and institutional change that has been shown to work. We therefore propose a strategy in three phases:[58]

- The first phase is the emergence and formation of alternative commons-based seed forms that solve the systemic issues of the current dominant political economy. For example, the

---

58 This strategy is a simplified version of what is described in the "multi-level perspective" literature of social change, a heuristic model distinguishing and articulating the complex dynamics between the "niches," "regimes," and "landscape" levels of "socio-technical systems": Frank W. Geels, "Ontologies, Socio-technical Transitions (to Sustainability), and the Multi-level Perspective," *Research Policy* 39 (2010): 495–510.

carbon-producing activities of fossil fuel extraction need to be replaced by a strategy focusing on the development and expansion of renewable energy. We are seeing that successful transitions, such as those in Germany, depend on a large element of civic mobilization around commons-centric models of provisioning, such as the emergence of community-owned energy cooperatives. In this first phase, the focus is on promoting commons alternatives and their interconnection into integrated sub-systems, first of all within and then across provisioning systems. This emergence and expansion of commons-based alternatives is matched by the necessary growth of social, and eventually, political power. For example, in the case of *Energiewende,* the growth of energy co-ops was matched by the political power of the Greens, and Merkel's realization, after Fukushima, of the dead-end and dangers of nuclear power.[59]

- The second phase is a regulatory and institutional phase in which the right frameworks are put in place. Without proper frameworks and supportive regulations, the commons-centric model would have remained marginal and grown much more slowly. But once the feed-in tariff was in place, the new models could expand to the broader population, as they were "facilitated" by incentives that made the commons-based alternative economically interesting for non-idealistic citizens.

- The creation of the proper regulatory support and new institutional design creates the basis for the third phase, i.e., the normalization of the new practices from the margins to become the new normal. In this phase, generative market forms support the continuing expansion of commons-centric prac-

---

59 Tadzio Mueller, "Diversity Is Strength, the German *Energiewende* as a Resilient Alternative," *Source Network*, 2017, http://thesourcenetwork.eu/wp-content/themes/showcase-pro/images/Diversity%20is%20Strength%20-%20FINAL.pdf.

tices, with support from the institutional frameworks of the partner state or partner city.

6. Conclusion

Our era asks for no less than for us to collectively reimagine the way that we live our lives, our cities, polities, and our political economies. The hollow argument that "there is no alternative" is both callous in its disownment of future generations, and blind to the creative and generative power of citizens and communities forging new paths by walking them. Indeed, the seeds of change that demonstrate the powerful logics of commons and commoning are no longer confined to obscure pockets of "alternative" and "pre-industrial/pre-modern" forms. Actually, today they are globally distributed, networked, and highly visible. Our challenge is straightforward. At a cultural level, we need to "slip into" and to support communities and organizations that provide the emotive platforms for commoning, and to support others to make this emotional and cultural transition. Economically, we need to use and develop new mutualizing strategies that entwine relocalism with global knowledge commons and solidarity — cosmo-localization. And politically, we need to build a protocol commons that can allow the myriad movements, organizations, and communities to see how they/we are implicated into Ecologies of the Commons that provide both practical value and the basis for human flourishing. Our world has outworn the old clothes; but into the future, we will take our core — the human dignity that emerges when we see the truth of who we are, others in us and us in others — even as we sew our new garments by hand.

6

Beating the Bounds: Inside the Struggle to Make Open Source Seed

Maywa Montenegro de Wit

1. Introduction

C.R. Lawn knows what primitive accumulation feels like.[1] As founder of the Fedco Seeds cooperative, he saw fungicide treatments become ubiquitous in the 1980s, and decided to stop selling seeds laced with the hazardous chemicals. In the 1990s, as GMOs came online, he placed a moratorium on the technology out of concern for unknown risks. Nine years later, when Monsanto bought out Seminis — Fedco's largest supplier of vegetable seeds — Fedco began boycotting the company because, as Lawn explains, "we could not in good conscience sell their varieties." The chemicals, the GMOs, and the patents, Lawn says, are part of a broader phenomenon: "We have privatized our common wealth in the hands of the few at the expense of the common good."

---

1   An earlier version of this chapter appeared in Maywa Montenegro de Wit, "Beating the Bounds: How Does 'Open Source' Become a Commons for Seed?" *The Journal of Peasant Studies* 46, no. 1 (2019): 44–79.

C.R. Lawn and his Fedco growers and packers are not alone in these deliberate rejections of seed enclosures. They are part of a movement gaining traction in many parts of the world, Global North and South, that refuses to adopt the dominant wisdom: that agrobiodiversity is best managed as private property; that breeding innovation will not occur in the absence of patents, variety protections, and other intellectual property (IP) rights; and that "improved seeds" result from individual ingenuity, rather than from collective knowledge, gleaned in and through experience with the land. From India to Peru, France to the Philippines, social movements are now advancing a bold discourse of seed freedom, seeking to reclaim what has been appropriated, privatized, and separated from the everyday and practical experience of farmers and farmer-breeders.

This chapter traces a novel expression of seed freedom that emerges from something old: the concept of a "commons." Conventionally defined as social or natural resources not owned by anyone, but over which a community has shared and equal rights, the commons go back many centuries in agrarian history, their enclosures marking a crucial juncture in the transition from feudalism to capitalism.[2] I add to the burgeoning new commons literature by looking at commons as a biocultural form, specifically in relation to seeds. Scholarly emphasis to date has been primarily on rules and institutions of resource management, following the principles of a well-governed commons.[3] My argument is that seeds turn our attention to the politics and practices of access to means of reproduction. We consider how community rules, values, and practices of making new seed varieties — or plant breeding — are at once driven and shaped by a larger political economic order. We explore how seed diversity is gained and/or lost through histories of legal, scientific, and biological enclosure.

---

2   E.P. Thompson, *Whigs and Hunters: The Origin of the Black Act,* 1st edn. (Harmondsworth: Penguin, 1975).

3   Elinor Ostrom, *Governing the Commons: The Evolution of Institutions for Collective Action* (Cambridge: Cambridge University Press, 1990).

Following recent contributions to commons scholarship, I emphasize commons as a living, dynamic field of practice — not simply a resource divided amongst people, but a social transformation developed in and through the practices of *commoning*.[4] Moving from noun to verb, this formulation also puts greater emphasis on the people and communities intrinsic to the commons — not just on the seed, but on farmers, seed savers, and plant breeders.

This chapter traces the origins and early development of the Open Source Seed Initiative (OSSI), which seeks to "free the seed." Founded in 2012, OSSI disavows traditional intellectual property rights and proposes that plant genetic materials can be shared within a "protected commons," with access rights guaranteed by a simple moral pledge. In the US, OSSI now includes 38 breeders, 52 seed companies, and 407 varieties.[5] It is a project, I argue, that reflects the characteristics of a growing transnational commoning movement. Yet, challenges remain for OSSI to gain wider legitimacy for "free seed," to build trust in a moral pledge, and to establish fair and just guidelines for what kinds of seed — and thus, which communities — can participate in making the commons and reap its benefits.

In the story that follows, I briefly sketch my theoretical framework. I then relate OSSI's experiences in three cases, each framed as a question of repossession:

Un-Enclosing IP: How does OSSI create an alternative to patents and other forms of IP? What challenges has it faced in this journey so far?

---

4   Massimo De Angelis, "Separating the Doing and the Deed: Capital and the Continuous Character of Enclosures," *Historical Materialism* 12, no. 2 (2004): 57–87; Peter Linebaugh, *The Magna Carta Manifesto: Liberties and Commons for All* (Berkeley: University of California Press, 2008); Peter Linebaugh, *Stop, Thief! The Commons, Enclosures and Resistance* (Oakland: PM Press, 2014); Silvia Federici, *Caliban and the Witch*, 2nd rev. edn. (New York: Autonomedia, 2014); David Bollier, *Think Like a Commoner: A Short Introduction to the Life of the Commons* (Gabriola: New Society Publishers, 2014).
5   These figures are current as of April 2018.

Commoning Knowledge: In what ways do open source principles help repossess seed knowledge for common use? Whose expertise is central to commoning? Where does this knowledge exist?

Global Seed Systems: Do open source processes work in different geographical and cultural contexts, and if so, how? How does OSSI intersect and engage with other social movements, like seed sovereignty, for the repossession of common wealth?

2. Commons: From Tragic Herdsmen to Cooperating Commoners

For two generations, the very idea of the commons has been dismissed as a misguided way to manage resources: Hardin's so-called "tragedy of the commons."[6] It should come as no surprise, really. Affirming competition as the defining characteristic of human relations, Hardin's logic — spelled out in a 1968 essay — fitted perfectly into the then-congealing neoliberal designs. Yet, starting in the 1970s, Elinor Ostrom became interested in a heterodox question: what happens when communities cooperate to manage their resources? Gathering data on so-called "common pool resources" (CPR) — openly accessible resources over which no one has private property rights, Ostrom's team surveyed the institutions and strategies that peoples around the world were using to govern fisheries, forests, communal landholdings, and other CPRs vulnerable to over-exploitation and free-riding. The overwhelming evidence pointed to communities working together to manage their resources sustainably. The key, Ostrom wrote, was figuring out how to "organize and govern themselves to obtain continuing joint benefits when all face temptations to free-ride, shirk, or otherwise act opportunistically."[7]

---

6   Garrett Hardin, "The Tragedy of the Commons," *Science* 162, no. 3859 (December 13, 1968): 1243–48.

7   Ostrom, *Governing the Commons*, 29.

A new generation of scholarship has built upon Ostrom's work to apply her principles to many different forms of commons, including: knowledge commons,[8] digital commons,[9] cultural and civic commons,[10] and global commons.[11] Yet Ostrom still operated within the standard economic framework, which assumes some basic precepts about "rational actors" and functionalist decision-making in the design of a commons. She did not treat capitalist structures in depth, nor did she treat the micro-scale psychological dynamics or interpersonal relationships that might animate a commons. As Bollier puts it, Ostrom's scholarship laid the groundwork for a profound reconceptualization of economic analysis and the role of the commons in it — "without taking the next step: political engagement."[12]

I extend an emergent field of so-called "new commons" scholarship to study seeds within structural conditions of enclosure, reclamation, and expansion. Extending Ostrom's analysis and complementing neo-Marxian analysis over the past twenty years, this field connects working class struggles with social movements that are resisting new — and reversing old — separa-

8   Yochai Benkler, *The Wealth of Networks: How Social Production Transforms Markets and Freedom* (New Haven: Yale University Press, 2006); Michael J. Madison, Brett M. Frischmann, and Katherine J. Strandburg, "Constructing Commons in the Cultural Environment," *Cornell Law Review* 95 (2009): 657–710.

9   Lawrence Lessig, *Free Culture: How Big Media Uses Technology and the Law to Lock Down Culture and Control Creativity* (New York: Penguin Press, 2004); Benkler, *The Wealth of Networks*.

10 David Bollier, *Silent Theft: The Private Plunder of Our Common Wealth* (New York: Routledge, 2003); Yochai Benkler, *The Penguin and the Leviathan: The Triumph of Cooperation over Self-Interest* (New York: Crown Business, 2011).

11 Peter Barnes, *Who Owns the Sky? Our Common Assets and the Future of Capitalism* (Washington, DC: Island Press, 2001); John Vogler, "Global Commons Revisited: Global Commons Revisited," *Global Policy* 3, no. 1 (February 2012): 61–71.

12 David Bollier, "Commoning as a Transformative Social Paradigm," *The Next System Project*, April 28, 2016, http://thenextsystem.org/commoning-as-a-transformative-social-paradigm/.

tions from social wealth.[13] With the understanding that the neo-liberal state often colludes with capital to continuously privatize and enclose resources,[14] I join the new commoners in linking state to market to civil society processes — and in making a provocative claim: that rather than simply being a resource or place to share, commons represents a process — an active thing that people do. As historian Peter Linebaugh underlines: there is no commons without the commoners, no commons without commo*ning*.[15]

What this understanding further suggests is that the best place to study commoning — the place where its energy is most palpable — is often not within formal institutions. Instead, we should look to social movements — an eclectic cadre of Indigenous Water Protectors, European Transition Towns, and Venezuelan *comuneros* — that have embraced the commons as a paradigm for social change. Evident in these social movement articulations is that seeing the commons as the "resource" offers only a blinkered view. To make better sense of the dynamic whole, it helps to envision the commons as a triad:

resource + community + social protocols = commons

In my research on OSSI, I consider the resource as seeds, linking culture to biology in a "biocultural" resource. I consider the people as the plant breeders, scientists, and small seed-company owners who compose the OSSI community, and the social protocols as the rules, norms, and customs that they collectively negotiate to defend against enclosure of seed. To explore how

---

13 De Angelis, "Separating the Doing and the Deed"; Silvia Federici, *Caliban and the Witch*; Michael Perelman, *The Invention of Capitalism: Classical Political Economy and the Secret History of Primitive Accumulation* (Durham: Duke University Press, 2000); David Harvey, *The New Imperialism* (Oxford: Oxford University Press, 2003).

14 Amanda Huron, *Carving out the Commons: Tenant Organizing and Housing Cooperatives in Washington, D.C.* (Minneapolis: University of Minnesota Press, 2018).

15 Massimo De Angelis, Nate Holdren, and Stevphen Shukaitis, "The Commoner No. 11 — Reinfusing the Commons," *Mute,* June 20, 2006.

the social protocols of a commons are (re)negotiated, I anchor this analysis in political ecology — a field that begins with the assumption that politics are inevitably ecological, and that relations with the environment are intrinsically political.[16] Central to political ecology is, as Watts proposes, "a sensitivity to environmental politics as a process of cultural mobilization, and the ways in which such cultural practices — whether science, or traditional knowledge or discourses, or risk, or property rights — are contested, fought over and negotiated."[17]

3. Beating the Bounds

In medieval times, according to historian Linebaugh, the British monarchy and forest bureaucracy would regularly "beat the bounds" — perform "ceremonial walks about a territory for asserting and recoding its boundaries."[18] These walks were vital in mapping the complex and shifting geography of Crown holdings — and largely served to enlarge royal jurisdiction. But if the perambulation was a kind of mapping, it was also an act of contestation. Peasants would walk the perimeters of a forest or piece of open field — "If they came upon a private fence or hedge that had enclosed the commons, the commoners would knock it down, re-establishing the integrity of their land."[19] Before physical maps were ubiquitous, such boundary-beating served several purposes: marking territory, policing borders, and serving as a public delineation of place and community identity. The practice has survived for centuries in Welsh and English parishes, where on special days of the year, processional parties pass through the landscape, with men striking bounds with a stick — a willow branch known as a "wand" — and even

16 Paul Robbins, *Political Ecology: A Critical Introduction,* 2nd edn. (Malden: J. Wiley & Sons, 2012).
17 Michael Watts, "Political Ecology," in *A Companion to Economic Geography,* eds. Eric S. Sheppard and Trevor J. Barnes (Oxford: Blackwell, 2000), 257–74, at 259.
18 Linebaugh, *The Magna Carta Manifesto,* 74.
19 Bollier, *Think Like a Commoner,* 138.

bumping the heads of young boys against particular landmarks like gravestones and fences "so that they would remember."[20]

Commoners in medieval Europe variously employed boundary beating as physical mapping of space, territorial defense, and performative acts of community, collective memory, and shared responsibility. It is in this multifaceted spirit that I look to how boundary beating is occurring around seed in old and new manifestations. As corporations build unprecedented control over the formal seed supply, commoners are pulling up IP hedgerows and knocking down GMO fences; they are rewriting "feed the world" narratives; and bumping heads to reverse encroachments into farmers' seed. OSSI's approach, simply put, is one that beat boundaries for the commoners instead of the kings. This is their story.

4. Un-enclosing IP: From Open-Source Licenses to a Moral Economy Pledge

Pacing the stage energetically, rural sociologist Jack Kloppenburg laid out the seed crisis facing many a farmer today. Despite a wide variety of farming scales, customs, and practices, he told an audience at the University of California, Berkeley, most growers — from Guatemalan peasants to Iowa growers — are experiencing one thing in common: they confront their seeds as industrial commodities. Rather than enjoy the freedom to replant from a previous season, they are structurally shackled to Monsanto-Bayer or Dow-DuPont, with little choice but to purchase patented, highly priced, non-renewable seed.

Well known to this academic audience as the author of *First the Seed,* a landmark work on the history of biotechnology development, Kloppenburg has spent half a lifetime researching

---

20 Su-ming Khoo, Lisa K. Taylor, and Vanessa Andreotti, "Ethical Internationalization, Neo-Liberal Restructuring and 'Beating the Bounds' of Higher Education," in *Assembling and Governing the Higher Education Institution,* eds. Lynette Shultz and Melody Viczko (London: Palgrave Macmillan, 2016), 85–110.

such problems. But this was a different, solutions-focused provocation. Seed movements worldwide are roundly condemning monopoly gene giants, the injustice of patenting, and the rapid rollout of new GMOs. A more radical stance, he offered, might be to move from a defensive posture to an offensive one: not only to impede processes of dispossession, but to open up paths for repossession.

OSSI was conceived as a project of repossession — a move to steal back the proverbial goose. Founded in 2012, its organizational structure includes a board of directors and a wider network of OSSI-affiliated public plant breeders, freelance breeders, small seed companies, and nonprofits. Many of the freelance breeders are also farmers and company owners, blurring the conventional divisions of labor in US seed systems. In response to the past hundred years of seed enclosures, OSSI's self-stated commitment is to the "promoting and maintaining of open access to plant genetic resources worldwide." The Pledge promoted by OSSI is an agreement by users to "ensure that germplasm can be freely exchanged now and into the future."[21] But the Pledge at the heart of the OSSI commons — and more importantly, OSSI *commoning* — did not start out that way. It is the product of years of negotiations that illustrate the give-and-take of practical commoning, the disputes that shape a commons from inside and out, and how its boundaries can bend without breaking.

4.1 Enclosing Seed and Agri-Food Systems

The macroeconomic picture against which OSSI struggles has been detailed elsewhere and need not be rehearsed again here, except in broad strokes.[22] Since the 1930s, plant hybridization

---

21 Claire H. Luby et al., "Enhancing Freedom to Operate for Plant Breeders and Farmers through Open Source Plant Breeding," *Crop Science* 55, no. 6 (2015): 2481–88, at 2481.

22 Jack Kloppenburg, "Re-Purposing the Master's Tools: The Open Source Seed Initiative and the Struggle for Seed Sovereignty," *The Journal of Peasant Studies* 41, no. 6 (November 2, 2014): 1225–46, at 1225; Philip H. Howard, *Concentration and Power in the Food System: Who Controls What We Eat?* (New York: Bloomsbury, 2016); Maywa Montenegro de Wit, "Stealing

has affected biological enclosures of seed to finance the growth of a robust private seed industry. The growth and elaboration of intellectual property rights since the 1930s — through legislation, treaties and US Supreme Court rulings — has made law the handmaiden of biotechnology, creating a legal mechanism for enclosures of seed. The 1961 establishment of the Union for the Protection of New Varieties of Plants (UPOV) in Europe, followed by the 1970 Plant Variety Protection Act (PVPA) in the United States, instituted exclusive plant breeders' rights (PBR) but with important exemptions: breeders could still use protected varieties for further breeding and research, and farmers were free to save, exchange, and reproduce seed. Since 1985 (*Ex Parte Hibberd*),[23] utility patents have become especially prevalent in the US, enabling the private sector to expand ownership of genes, gene sequences, tissues, seeds, and whole plants. Unlike PVP rights, utility patents prohibit breeding, research, and seed saving on a patented cultivar, crippling both farmers' and plant breeders' freedom to operate. Today, as Luby et al. note:

> Commercial maize cultivars are generally protected by dozens of patents on specific traits, license agreements, contracts, and trade secrets, allowing developers to own and manage the intellectual property associated with their work. "Bag tag" licenses and associated "technology use/stewardship agreements" for modern maize cultivars specify that users cannot save, replant, use as a parent, or conduct research with the seed.[24]

---

into the Wild: Conservation Science, Plant Breeding and the Makings of New Seed Enclosures," *The Journal of Peasant Studies* 44, no. 1 (2017): 169–212.

23 *Ex parte Hibberd,* USPQ 443 Board of Patent Appeals and Interferences (1985): 443–48.

24 Luby et al., "Enhancing Freedom to Operate for Plant Breeders and Farmers through Open Source Plant Breeding." The authors focus on corn, an agro-industry favorite, alongside soybeans, canola, cotton, and wheat. But the IP regime that companies employ, says Goldman, is now trickling down to "specialty crops" — fruits, vegetables, nuts, and horticultural

Intellectual property incentives, in turn, have been a dominant factor in seed industry consolidation over the past 30 years, a trend documented in powerful synergies among stronger IP protections, anemic antitrust laws, and the dominance of top firms "at the expense of freely competitive industry."[25] As of 2015, just six seed and chemical corporations — BASF, Bayer, Dow, DuPont, Monsanto, Syngenta — were collecting more than USD 65 billion annually from selling their seed traits, chemicals, and bio-technologies.[26] Together they controlled 75% of the pesticide market, 63% of the seed market, and more than 75% of private-sector research in crops and pesticides. Mergers in 2015–2017 tightened that control yet further: Bayer acquired Monsanto, DuPont merged with Dow Chemical, and the Chinese state-owned chemical company ChemChina acquired Syngenta for a record $43 billion. DowDuPont subsequently spun off its agricultural businesses into a new company called Corteva Agriscience dedicated to seeds, agricultural chemicals, and traits – including those produced with CRISPR-Cas technology, for which Corteva is a global IP leader. ChemChina-Syngenta has now combined with the giant firm Sinochem, creating a patent powerhouse that analysts suggest will funnel substantial state-backed public research into proprietary holdings.,[27] extreme consolidation is well underway.

---

crops — through a complex of patents, licenses and bag tags (Goldman interview, June 17, 2017).

25 Philip H. Howard, "Visualizing Consolidation in the Global Seed Industry: 1996–2008," *Sustainability* 1, no. 4 (December 8, 2009): 1266; Philip H. Howard, "Intellectual Property and Consolidation in the Seed Industry," *Crop Science* 55, no. 6 (2015): 2489. See also Howard's revised seed industry visualization, updated to 2018, https://philhoward.net/2018/12/31/global-seed-industry-changes-since-2013/.

26 ETC, "Breaking Bad: Big Ag Mega-Mergers in Play," ETC Group Communiqué, December 2015, http://www.etcgroup.org/sites/www.etcgroup.org/files/files/etc_breakbad_23dec15.pdf.

27 Al Root, "DowDuPont Is Splitting Into 3 Companies. Here's Everything You Need to Know," *Barron's*, April 29, 2019, https://www.barrons.com/articles/dowdupont-spinoff-dow-dupont-corteva-51556552428; "ChemChina, Sinochem Merge Agricultural Assets: Syngenta," *Reuters*, January 5, 2020, https://www.reuters.com/article/us-chemchina-sinochem-syngenta/

While this concentrated structure is fully elaborated in most industrialized countries, seeds now offer the opportunity to transform agrarian economies globally. Markets for many patented, genetically engineered crops are now saturated in the US, Canada, the European Union, and Australia, pressing agrochemical firms to seek new frontiers of accumulation. Their target is tens of millions of peasant and small-scale farmers in the Global South who still save, replant, share, exchange, and sell their own seeds.[28] Toward enabling these enclosures, the UPOV framework has been a particularly effective instrument. Many developing country governments are being pressured to join UPOV through multilateral free trade agreements (such as the Trans-Pacific Partnership), bilateral treaties, and other foreign aid contracts. In doing so, they agree to implement strict IPR and marketing laws, effectively recognizing scientists as makers and rightful owners of seed, while ignoring the historical and ongoing contributions of farmer knowledge and farmer work.

4.2 The Digital Commons Inspiration

As suggested by its name, the Open Source Seed Initiative drew crucial inspiration from a field often considered remote from farmers' concerns: computer science. In the early 1980s, MIT professor Richard Stallman recognized that proprietary software could restrict people's ability to access and use software—and consequently, to innovate. Stallman's stroke of genius was to invert the copyright license, using intellectual property to make software contractually non-proprietary. This innovation, sometimes called "copyleft," is today celebrated as a landmark hack around copyright law. It ensures everyone the freedom to copy, modify, or distribute a program as they see fit,

---

chemchina-sinochem-merge-agricultural-assets-syngenta-idUSKBN-1Z40FZ; Jon Cohen, "Fields of Dreams," *Science* 365, no. 6452 (August 2, 2019): 422–25.

28 An estimated 90 percent of the seeds that peasant farmers plant every year come from their own bins or are bartered with neighbors in local markets: Shawn McGuire and Louise Sperling, "Seed Systems Smallholder Farmers Use. Food Security," *Food Security* 8, no. 1 (2016): 179.

as long as they apply the same copyleft license to their creation. In this way, the free license propagates, making more and more software shareable and legally protected. It achieves a so-called "viral" character.

The success of this digital commons was a key inspiration for OSSI's development. Frank Morton, a plant breeder and owner of Wild Garden Seed in Oregon explains it this way:

> I first heard of "open source" from my Linux-loving son, Taj, sometime before he created our website at age 13. That was 2003, so I guess this Open Source Seed notion has been rattling my cage for over a decade. But that is about all, because I have never been able to create the legal mechanism in my head that would allow me to share or market an original open-pollinated seed variety to others without the real possibility that some bad actor could patent it out from under me.[29]

Morton and other small-scale amateur breeders, I would later discover, have been releasing their seed into the public domain for decades, allowing others to freely use their seeds. Yet public domain operates more like an open access regime than a governed commons. The reality remains that if a breeder's original varieties are not protected by a utility patent or plant variety protection (PVP), they can be scooped up and protected as IP by someone else. Organic vegetable breeders like Morton have so far avoided such bioprospecting, "sailing by," as he puts it, with only a few varieties pirated from him. But he does not consider himself "out of the woods," since the imminent threat is not theft of whole varieties, but the patenting of individual traits. After the US Supreme Court declared in *JEM Ag Supply v. Pioneer Hi-Bred*[30] in 2001 that "novel traits" of plants could be subject to

---

29 Frank Morton, "Open Source Seed: A Farmer-Breeder's Perspective," in *Organic Seed Growers Conference Proceedings,* ed. Kristina Hubbard (Corvallis: Organic Seed Alliance, 2014), 147.

30 *J.E.M Ag Supply v. Pioneer Hi-Bred International, Inc.,* 122 S. Ct. 593 (2001), rehearing denied, 122 S. Ct. 1600 (2002).

utility patenting, the gates burst wide open for enclosures at the genetic level.

Despite this gene-grab occurring beneath their feet, Morton and several like-minded farmer-breeders have found the easy solution extremely unpalatable:

> So does that mean we should hoard our beans, lock 'em up with PVP and patents? Not allow others to see, breed, or make comparisons to our stuff? That's no fun, and you can't get started in plant breeding with an attitude like that.[31]

Facing this dilemma of wanting to share but risking free appropriation, in April 2010, Morton got together with Jack Kloppenburg and Irwin Goldman, a plant breeder at the University of Wisconsin-Madison, to explore prospects for developing an open-source seed. This meeting generated much enthusiasm, leading to a second meeting in Minneapolis in early 2011. By then, the commoners had expanded to include several more public university breeders, additional farmer-breeders, one organic seed company, representatives from Northern and Southern indigenous communities, and the institutional support of a few nonprofits, including the Organic Seed Alliance, a prominent US advocacy and education network. They called themselves the Open Source Seed Initiative, or OSSI, and began figuring out how to craft legally defensible, open source plant germplasm licenses. Just as in software, the idea was to create what they dubbed a "protected commons." It would allow for free sharing, saving, replanting, trading, and breeding of seeds. It would also allow selling of seeds, since copyleft means free from IP, not from price. But it would carry one pivotal restriction — the inability to restrict sharing.

For about 15 months, OSSI labored intensively to make the licenses work. By late 2013, however, it was evident that the licensing approach had reached an impasse. Their lawyers could — and indeed did — craft two forms of open-source seed

---

31 Morton, "Open Source Seed," 147.

licenses. But unlike software code, for which the code-writer automatically receives copyright protection, the creation of novel genetic sequences does not immediately grant the plant breeder an analogous right. This biological difference in seeds made it legally tricky to use copyright law to assure seed sharing. More importantly, OSSI's farmer affiliates were put off by tactics that, from their perspective, replicated those of "gene giants" such as Monsanto. The lawyers had solved the copylefting problem with dense and intricately worded licenses, but how were the farmers supposed to propagate eight-page contracts on 3x4-inch packets of seeds? And how were they supposed to understand the thick technical language that was required to make the licenses robust in court proceedings? OSSI's seed companies felt likewise: even if the lawyers could shorten the contracts, the whole approach would repel rather than attract their customers.

As they struggled with this tactical problem, OSSI encountered yet another dilemma, this one within its own plant breeding community. OSSI's breeders as a whole felt dedicated to a goal of maximally unencumbered flow of plant genetic resources. Yet within the group there was a rift: some breeders argued in favor of completely "free seed," while others felt that breeders need to be rewarded monetarily for their efforts.

On the free-seed side we had university breeders like Irwin Goldman and his protégé Claire Luby, for whom commoning via OSSI represented a chance to bring back the "freedom to operate" that he and his colleagues had traditionally enjoyed as land-grant breeders.[32] Goldman, Luby, and their colleagues hoped to rekindle the culture of sharing materials between labs — and even between campuses — without worrying about who owns what, who will get what, and whose innovation is proprietary. Other land-grant-breeders, however, were more skeptical of going all in with free seed licenses. Especially with declining levels of state support for agricultural research (and within that for conventional plant breeding), royalties are seen as a lifeline;

---

32 Luby et al., "Enhancing Freedom to Operate for Plant Breeders and Farmers through Open Source Plant Breeding."

many breeders rely directly on that revenue for maintenance of their breeding programs.

OSSI nearly collapsed under the weight of this early community dissension. The Organic Seed Alliance, which had been hoping to generate revenues from royalty-bearing licenses, decided to pull its support. Several breeders peeled off, leaving just five or six people. For several months, the remaining members struggled with the disappointment of likely defeat.

The holdouts, I came to realize, were doing their own form of "beating the bounds." Not, of course, in the literal sense of bushwhacking and head bumping, but in terms of defending the commons using a variety of social protocols. The original license was one such protocol, intended to defend the OSSI commons against the incursion of intellectual property. As they struggled to refine the social protocol (would it bear royalties? would it be free?), those protocols fed back to shape the composition of the community itself. OSSI went through a type of population bottleneck with this licensing experiment, as the crisis stoked by struggles over licenses dramatically reduced the size of its community. But those left standing were more united in their ethical commitments. They understood that gaining the trust of the small-scale farmers and seed companies — its future commons community — was more important than allaying the concerns of lawyers and royalty-seeking breeders. OSSI took a leap and decided to abandon the conventional path that licenses had come to represent.

4.3 From Open-Source Licenses to a Moral Economy Pledge

The pivotal moment, Morton said, was going back to first principles: "Our most central concern," he explained, "is that the users of seed must never restrict the use of seed by others to create new varieties and adapt seed for the benefit of future generations."[33] In place of a license, OSSI crafted a Pledge that reads:

---

33 Morton, "Open Source Seed," 148.

You have the freedom to use these OSSI seeds in any way you choose. In return, you pledge not to restrict others' use of these seeds or their derivatives by patents, licenses or other means, and to include this Pledge with any transfer of these seeds or their derivatives.

This Pledge is printed on every packet of OSSI seed today. It reflects, OSSI suggests, the underlying rationale of E. P. Thompson's "moral economy." Looking at eighteenth-century peasant uprisings over the price of bread, Thompson argued that the riots were less about bread per se than about emergent capitalism abridging customary social protocols. "The men and women in the crowd," he wrote, "were informed by the belief that they were defending traditional rights and customs; and, in general, that they were supported by the wider consensus in the community."[34]

Thinking about the Pledge in terms of a moral economic system, Kloppenburg told me, was also partly inspired by the radical invocations of black feminist author Audre Lorde. Instead of trying to use the "tools of the master" — that is, the legal contract — to dismantle the master's house, the Pledge means tossing out those tools and making your own. OSSI wanted to build a whole new house from the foundation up.

What the Pledge has *not* tossed out from the license phase is the central premise of functioning as a "protected commons" — that is, ensuring that materials are freely available and exchanged but are protected from appropriation by those who would monopolize them. Passed along with each seed packet, the Pledge commits all users to honor four basic freedoms:

1. The freedom to save or grow seed for replanting, or for any other purpose.
2. The freedom to share, trade, or sell seeds to others.

---

34 E.P. Thompson, "The Moral Economy of the English Crowd in the Eighteenth Century," *Past and Present* 50, no. 1 (1971): 76–136, at 78.

3. The freedom to trial and study seed, and to share, or publish information about it.
4. The freedom to select or adapt the seed, make crosses with it, or use it to breed new lines and varieties.

According to legal experts with whom I spoke, the moral Pledge represents interesting tradeoffs with state-backed judicial enforcement. Legally, holders of patents and copyrights are in a much stronger position to enforce control over seeds. In a moral pledge, enforcement usually cannot be backed by the courts through litigation or by prosecution; the enforcement would happen through the practices of the body issuing the Pledge, such as by excluding a violator from its community and resources. So, for example, if Monsanto-Bayer were to successfully patent an OSSI seed that the open source group was seeking to protect, what would happen? Very likely, the courts would uphold the patent to the exclusion of OSSI and its breeders, but the US Patent Office might not accept the patent application if OSSI showed evidence that the breeders had created and used a variety for some time. The new IPR claim would depend on the novelty of the invention, prior use, and practice history.

The courts might also treat the Pledge as defensible under contract law. After all, the Pledge is a contract, in the sense that everyone who takes OSSI seeds agrees to obey the conditions set in the Pledge. Every time a variety is passed on, a new contract is being made between OSSI and the chain of people using the seed. The question, then, is whether this "softer" contract would outweigh an attempt to patent the seed, which would violate the contract. This question arises regardless of the Pledge or the license approach, since the share-alike commitment in both cases only bind the two contracting parties and not third parties.[35]

When I put these queries to Kloppenburg — will the Pledge have any power? why abandon the surer route of the law? — he

---

35 Selim Louafi et al., "Open Source for Seeds and Genetic Sequence Data: Practical Experience and Future Strategies," CIRAD Policy Brief: Agricultural Research for Development, December 2018.

expressed a logic and strategy that I have come to recognize as emblematic of commoners' pragmatism. "I feel comfortable doing it and I'm glad we did it," he said. "The Pledge is much simpler and much more powerful as a discursive tool." By comparison, "the license approach is cumbersome [and] over-legalized in our view." And besides, he said, "the Pledge *may* well be legal. We say that it *could* be legal. Our current attorneys say, 'Treat it as legal until somebody tells you it isn't.'"[36]

5. Commoning Knowledge: Redefining Seed and Breeding Expertise

On April 17, 2014, in solidarity with International Peasant's Day, OSSI officially re-launched under this Pledge. OSSI's seven plant breeders at the time celebrated with release of 37 open-source varieties. Today, OSSI includes some 38 plant breeders, 52 small seed companies and more than 400 varieties. The *particular* way in which OSSI has expanded leads to the second part of our story — OSSI as a knowledge commons. What is it doing to re-possess knowledge? Who owns the expertise within OSSI?

When OSSI was first founded in 2012, the answer was clear: professional scientists. Its community was mostly comprised of public sector breeders affiliated with land grant schools such as Washington State University, Oregon State University, and the University of Wisconsin-Madison. Soon, however, it became apparent that the center of gravity of the OSSI community was shifting: away from the formal sector of universities, labs and extension, and toward the informal sector of independent farmer-breeders and gardener-breeders.

Carol Deppe (Fertile Valley Seeds), Frank Morton (Wild Garden Seed), Jonathan Spero (Lupine Knoll), Loretta Sandoval (Zulu's Petals), and Joseph Lofthouse (Lofthouse Farms) are just a few of the plant breeders who comprise a quietly expanding movement of "freelance" organic plant breeders in the US. In fact, they used to call themselves "amateur breeders" but have

---

36 Kloppenburg interview, December 7, 2016.

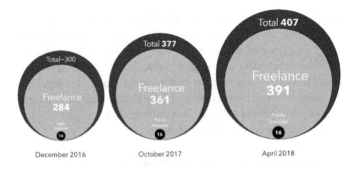

Figure 1. OSSI pledges over time. The number of crop varieties released into the OSSI commons by US public university breeders remained stable at 16 between December 2016 and April 2018, while the number from freelance breeders grew by 107 new seed varieties, or roughly 35 percent.

started to use the term "freelance" in recognition of their expertise. Self-taught and fiercely Do-It-Yourself, they are generally less driven by money than by curiosity, less driven by expanding patent portfolios than by self-renewal. To get along, many operate small direct-to-consumer companies, earning income from selling seed-breeding materials and finished varieties. They tend to specialize in open pollinated seed, or OPs, and in varieties specifically adapted to low external-input organic systems.

Geographically, the freelancers form a diffuse network, with a notable hotspot in Washington State and Oregon and single farm-company outposts in Virginia, North Carolina, Illinois, Maine, Michigan, New York, Utah, the UK, and Australia, among others. They are, of course, distinct from one another in important ways. Their entries into breeding range from subsistence farming to supplying niche vegetables to restaurants in the Bay Area. Some are lone seedsmen and seedswomen, while others participate collectively. Some are relative newcomers to breeding, whereas others have been at it for almost 50 years.

As a group, these informal breeders have contributed all but 16 of the total 407 OSSI-pledged varieties.[37] And as can be seen in Figure 1, over time, the number of seeds pledged by public sector players has remained stagnant at 16, while the number coming in from the informal sector continues to grow and grow. This raises the obvious question: why have these freelancers risen to prominence?

Part of the answer, I found, is that they represent an existing culture of commoning: freelance breeding networks were not born in 2014, after all. Many grassroots seed-saving, exchange, and breeding groups are thriving in spite of (and perhaps because of) the heavily corporatized seed sector. Organizations like the Seed Savers Exchange, now an OSSI partner, have survived for decades, even while fewer and fewer US growers today reuse seed let alone attempt to breed. For folks who are part of these networks, OSSI is not such a radical ideological shift; sharing is already the norm, rather than the exception.

Oregon breeder Carol Deppe told me that "[p]atents are often considered immoral" and inconsistent with an understanding of seed as the heritage of humankind. David Podoll of Prairie Road Organic Seed in North Dakota corroborates: "Seeds are a sacred thing. Everything we have now is built on farmers selecting seeds for millennia. All of that genetic diversity is a great gift. Seeds should not be owned, patented, or controlled."[38]

Hand-in-glove with this existing culture goes an existing *practice* of opposing intellectual property. As mentioned earlier, I discovered that freelancers have long been releasing their new varieties in the public domain. Yet, the problem with putting seeds into public domain is that others can scoop up your seeds; it is essentially an open access regime. What OSSI represents to freelancers, then, is the chance for more protection over their varieties than is currently offered by public domain, without having to adopt morally repugnant IPR solutions.

---

37 Luby interviews, between 2016 and 2018.
38 David Podoll, "Prairie Road Organic Seed," *Open Source Seed Initiative: Plant Breeders,* November 5, 2014; Deppe interview, August 2016.

The other reason that freelancers have risen into prominence within OSSI is the flipside of this coin: the constraints on participation faced by public-university breeders. Public-sector breeders today face an onerous IPR thicket: of patents, trade secrets, licensing arrangements, and material transfer agreements. In addition, they confront the structural backdrop of Bayh-Dole, a law passed in 1980 that granted universities the ability to claim ownership rights over taxpayer-funded innovations. Now that universities own this intellectual property, they can sell these rights to the private sector — and they have. Research published in 2012 indicates that private funding of land-grant schools has been outpacing federal funding for decades.[39] As you can imagine, Bayh-Dole put significant backwards pressure on the upstream breeding pipeline — what was valuable for corporations to commercialize began to discipline what public-university researchers would pursue.

Insofar as OSSI goes against this now-entrenched model, it represents not only a potential loss of capital for universities from any specific open-sourced variety, it challenges the whole setup: the propertizing of knowledge, the revenue stream from intellectual property, and the public-private partnerships that increasingly keep universities afloat.

The power of this structural lock-in has surprised even the breeders. In 2014, Goldman told NPR radio that he expected many public-sector scientists would join the open source effort.[40] But, as Goldman told NPR and later told me, the use of OSSI germplasm poses a huge pragmatic challenge for university breeders: because any *derivatives* of OSSI seeds are also open source, the university would not be able to claim IP rights over, say, the product of a cross between university-owned germplasm and OSSI-pledged germplasm. "This means that as a breeder," Goldman explained, "I would have to have two sepa-

---

39 FWW (Food and Water Watch), "Public Research, Private Gain: Corporate Influence Over University Agriculture," San Francisco, 2012.

40 Dan Charles, "Plant Breeders Release First 'Open Source Seeds,'" NPR: The Salt, April 17, 2014.

rate breeding programs: one for OSSI and a 'protected' program for the university."

This does not mean that university breeders cannot participate at all. In 2016, for example, Luby and Goldman released eight new carrot populations into OSSI. Carrying names that represent root color (Red, White, Purple, and Yellow) and market classes (Chantenay, Nantes, Danver, and Ball), these carrots represent a push against mainstream land-grant practices. Typically, breeders will develop cultivars or inbred lines that are genetically stable and homogeneous — types well-suited for monoculture systems. The goal here, Luby and Goldman explained, was the opposite: "to take commercially available cultivars that had the freedom to operate and create diverse carrot populations."[41] To do this, they identified 95 different carrot cultivars and, with the 87 not restricted by existing IPR, developed open source populations that can now be used by anyone breeding. The colorful carrots, they indicate, are "the first example of crop germplasm that has been collected, characterized, and bred specifically for entry into an open source commons."[42]

Still, Goldman told me, such work remains the exception rather than the norm. For these releases to happen, the University of Wisconsin-Madison had to forfeit institutional ownership of the germplasm, signifying that the breeders could dispose of the varieties in any way they chose. Yet this is not necessarily a likely outcome for most germplasm. Public breeders, he reckoned, may have some success in obtaining university permission to use germplasm in crosses that the university never intends to license, "but this is unlikely to occur when the cultivars are of high commercial value."[43]

41 Claire Luby and Irwin Goldman, "Release of Eight Open Source Carrot (*Daucus Carota* Var. *Sativa*) Composite Populations Developed under Organic Conditions," *Horticultural Science* 51, no. 4 (2016): 448–50, at 448.
42 Claire Luby and Irwin Goldman, "Improving Freedom to Operate in Carrot Breeding through the Development of Eight Open Source Composite Populations of Carrot (*Daucus Carota* L. Var. *sativus*)," *Sustainability* 8, no. 5 (May 14, 2016): 479.
43 Goldman interview, July 17, 2017.

In summary, while university breeders have been instrumental to OSSI's formation, they have been less vital to its ongoing growth. For all the reasons sketched above — scientific culture, structural lock-ins, the challenges of managing a separate breeding program, and the value of the germplasm in question — the university system has not been a particularly fertile space for the commons to grow. By contrast, the existing culture and non-proprietary practices of freelancers have made open source something of an intuitive step forward.

5.1 Promiscuous Pollination

Joseph Lofthouse, you might say, has been commoning all along, releasing seeds to his community with no claims to intellectual property and a fierce resistance to corporate control. Lofthouse and the other freelance breeders are also beating the bounds, I suggest. Insofar as they are moving plant breeding back into the informal sector, they are reclaiming farms and living landscapes as legitimate sites of seed production. Insofar as their seeds come to embody vernacular knowledge and on-farm expertise, they are fending off the enclosures of knowledge that ripple throughout the broader neoliberal project — where property is "normal" and sharing is not.

Lofthouse is a self-described subsistence farmer, specializing in landrace breeding. He grew up on a farm in Paradise, Utah, gardening and milking a cow on a farm first established by his grandfather's grandfather, more than 150 years ago. Before the Green Revolution, a variety of local wheat developed by Lofthouse senior was the most widely-planted wheat in northern Utah and Southern Idaho. Lofthouse Jr. still grows that wheat today, alongside other varieties he has coaxed back from ancient origins. Rather than "depend on faraway distant mega-companies for seeds," he told me, he has decided to restore the age-old practice of creating his own.

But "create" is an uncomfortable verb for Lofthouse, who prefers terms like "guarding" and "stewarding" when speaking of seeds. He also tends to defer to his ancestors — tipping his hat to their collective endeavors in contributing to the heritage of seed. This has created some tricky issues with the OSSI paperwork he must fill out in order to release his varieties. You are supposed to fill in the blank claiming that you are creator of a new variety, he explained. You must be the "breeder, agent, or coagent" with the express authority to release the seed. The variety must be biologically "novel." But Joseph doesn't really believe in individual creators of seed, nor does he consider his seeds to be novel. So, he told me, he compromises, sometimes signing 10K — by which he means "10,000 years' worth of illiterate plant breeders who created this variety."

For Lofthouse, who took a vow of poverty 17 years ago, there is simultaneous freedom and security in subsistence breeding. Freedom from the bland taste and nutritional vacuum of industrial food; security in the stability of harvests that may not yield maxima but are steadier over time; freedom, in turn, from food insecurity, which also fosters emancipation from the power that corporations and the state have over farmers. As Lofthouse told me: "I'm kind of an anarchist, and so what corporations do, or what governments do doesn't really matter to me, because I'm going to grow my seeds the same way I always grow my seeds."[44]

Traditional crops are the key to Lofthouse's breeding strategy. Much as peasant and indigenous farmers around the world still do, Lofthouse works with landrace varieties, crops with high genetic variability purposefully maintained as a diverse gene pool to enable their adaptation to territorially specific conditions. In Lofthouse's case, Paradise, Utah, demands that seeds can thrive in a cold arid climate. In his seed catalog, he explicitly tells his customers that these seeds are best for "irrigated desert, super-dry air, sunlight-drenched, cold radiant-cooled nights, short-season, and high-altitude clayish, limestone-based lake bottom soil."

If Lofthouse is specific about the ecological conditions he breeds for, he is even choosier about the social characteristics: "Home gardeners, plant breeders, and small-scale market growers who welcome diversity of shape, taste, texture, color, size,

---

44 Lofthouse interview, November 12, 2016.

and maturity dates may love my seeds," he prints clearly in his catalog. "My seeds are *unsuitable* for commercial farms or large operations that require uniformity, predictability, or stability."[45]

You may wonder how landraces of wheat and corn come to be grown in Utah, given that their origins are Mesopotamia and the Yucatán, respectively. This is where Lofthouse's method of "promiscuous pollination" comes in, a practice that reverses the stabilization of traits that have occurred with modern breeding: he allows plants to swap pollen freely rather than restrict who mates with whom.

Using this technique in 2009 to develop a new cantaloupe landrace, Lofthouse began by gathering 90 different varieties of cantaloupe over a three-year period.[46] The seeds came from his own farm, from surrounding farms, and from online mail orders. He then planted these together to make an original "mass cross" — without, he emphasizes, keeping track of which varieties went where. The seed produced by this mass cross were the beginnings of a new melon landrace. From there, it was a practice of observation and culling. Some varieties were entirely destroyed by soil microbes before they germinated. Some grew slowly and did not produce any fruit. Others grew passably and yielded a small bit of fruit before first frost, while still others grew vigorously, producing loads of melons that ripened on the vine well before the cold came in. Importantly, a collaborator in the valley did the same thing. They swapped seeds over the years and produced "Lofthouse-Oliverson Landrace Muskmelon."

This method of promiscuous pollination is remarkably similar to "evolutionary breeding" techniques now recognized as cutting-edge in the scientific community. Pioneering researchers, including Salvatore Ceccarelli and Kevin Murphy, approach such work as complexity science. Rather than refine varieties with stable traits, they allow nature to do the evolutionary work:

---

45 Joseph Lofthouse, "For Sale: Genetically-Diverse Promiscuously-Pollinated Landrace Seeds Grown by Joseph Lofthouse in Cache Valley in the Rocky Mountains," 2017, http://garden.lofthouse.com/seed-list.phtml.

46 Joseph Lofthouse, "Adaptivar Landraces," 2017, http://garden.lofthouse.com/seed-list.phtml.

by placing seeds in dynamic settings of shifting biotic and abiotic pressures, amidst complex trophic webs of predators and prey, they allow crops to adapt *to* diversity. Rather than create genetically simplified and stable seeds for monoculture systems, they allow complex ecosystems to breed complex seeds.

Lofthouse had never heard of evolutionary breeding when I asked him about it, but he understood. Moreover, he suggested, it is the *people* who benefit: "When I plant genetically diverse crops and allow them to promiscuously pollinate," he said, "they are creating lots of variation in taste, texture, color, and odor. When I save seeds from specific plants that taste best to me, I am moving the population in the direction of what tastes best to me and to my community."[47]

Of course, there are wrinkles in Lofthouse's open-source story that he is quick to point out. Unlike freelancer Deppe, for example, he is not particularly blown away by the "restriction to end all restrictions" of the OSSI Pledge. "It has no teeth," he suggested to me, implying that the Pledge will be ignored by large corporations who will do what they will. Nor is Lofthouse pleased that his great-great grandfather's heirloom wheat — not being "novel" — cannot be pledged. Yet he likes OSSI for other reasons. He values the relationships that come through the open-source network. Deppe corroborates this view, telling me that OSSI is helping bring dispersed freelance breeders into a more close-knit community, under the label, the logic, and the public recognition of a protected commons.

In this way, I suggest, the Pledge may well constitute a "legal hack." It is not quite legal — yet. But it has provided the impetus for OSSI to expand what De Angelis and colleagues call the "life flow," the "incessant activities of commoning, of (re)producing in common."[48] For OSSI, that means freeing the seed — making sure that genes in at least some seed can never be locked away by intellectual property rights. In Lofthouse's

---

47 Joseph Lofthouse, "Landrace Gardening: Do It for the Taste," *Mother Earth News,* April 27, 2016.

48 De Angelis et al., "The Commoner No. 11 — Reinfusing the Commons."

case, it means practicing promiscuous pollination to generate locally adapted, resilient varieties. For Deppe, it revolves around education — teaching gardeners and farmers how to breed their own seed varieties, reclaiming knowledge that US growers have nearly lost. For Luby, Goldman, and Kloppenburg, it means reviving norms around reciprocity and sharing within universities and between scientists and the public.

On this foundation, the legitimacy of commoning can expand — and a Pledge that is not yet legally enforceable can become so. Maybe it will become legal by widespread cultural assent — "common sense" — and eventually guide institutions of lawmaking. Maybe, as Illich reminds us, the requisites for formal legality become moot as commoning activities become rooted, richly recognized, and legitimated under vernacular law. The term "vernacular" comes from an Indo-Germanic root that implies "rootedness" and "abode," Illich muses in *Shadow Work*. But while Roman scholars attached the idea to vernacular language — a designation that stuck — for Illich it was about much more than local speech. The vernacular domain, as Illich calls it, is the realm of everyday life where people create and negotiate their own sense of things:

> We need a simple straightforward word to designate the activities of people when they are not motivated by thought of exchange, a word that denotes autonomous, non-market related actions that by their nature escape bureaucratic control, satisfying needs to which, in the very process, they give specific shape. [...] By speaking about vernacular language and the possibility of recuperation, I am trying to bring into awareness and discussion the existence of a vernacular mode of being, doing, and making in a future society [that] might again expand all aspects of life.[49]

---

49 Ivan Illich, *Shadow Work* (Boston and London: M. Boyars, 1981), 49–50.

For commoners like Lofthouse, there is freedom and power in the vernacular domain. Reproducing seeds, he says, has little to do with legal defensibility of the Pledge.

> If some corporation comes in and says that they own my seeds or whatever, I'll still just keep growing my seeds, because I've lived in poverty for decades and I have nothing they can take from me. So, I mean, they have no power.[50]

6. ossi and the Global Seed System

This brings us to the challenges of expanding open source to other countries, especially in the Global South. From the start, ossi has been interested in how open source will play out globally. To begin taking the pulse of global South civil society organizations, in 2011 Kloppenburg attended the fourth meeting of the International Plant Treaty in Bali, Indonesia, and met with several members of La Via Campesina (lvc). A few lvc members, Kloppenburg recalls, thought the idea of open source "was appalling" — though other members were more interested. Two years later, Kloppenburg flew to Mexico City to introduce ossi to potential allies. etc Group and grain representatives, he told me, expressed serious misgivings about the utility of an open source approach for indigenous and peasant communities.

Some of these concerns could be seen in a report by grain and lvc published in 2015 which critiqued open source licenses as "tools of intellectual property" and "not necessarily appropriate for seeds or for small farmers."[51] As Ramón Vera-Herrera of grain explained to me, the problem was not really about "the license or no license." The problem was the whole notion of reducing social and ecological relations to things. Especially in agriculture, he said, "what we call seeds, as you well know, is a

---

50 Lofthouse interview, November 12, 2016.
51 grain and La Vía Campesina, "Seed Laws That Criminalize Farmers: Resistance and Fight Back," March 2015, 43.

vast thread of social relations."[52] "How," he asked me, "can we get into a contract the vast complexity of life?"

Several related concerns, Vera-Herrera and other informants explained to me, grow from this basic disjuncture. First is that "open source" is strongly associated with computer technology, data, and information systems. This can pose particular challenges amongst peasant and indigenous communities skeptical of technological solutions. In contrast to the *territorial* concepts of sovereignty seen among many such communities — where seeds are rooted spatially, culturally, often spiritually — we often find in open source an *a-territorial* notion of resources. Unmoored from land or place, open source tends to be associated with radically unrestricted movement and fungibility. Indigenous peoples are seldom thrilled by the idea of unbounded freedoms for anyone to remix, reuse, and repurpose as they see fit.

Second is an issue of science and power. My interviewees indicated that much scientific manipulation is steeped in hubris — disrespectful (and indeed ignorant) of the scales and types of transformation it imposes. Especially when paired with the "viral" nature of open source sharing, genetically modified germplasm, synthetic biology products, and now CRISPR-edited organisms that could suffuse the seed and crop system, OSSI would then be displacing diverse seed and agroecological knowledge rather than sustaining them.

Third, there is the issue of law and governance. "Positive law" as developed by Western capitalist societies, informants told me, tends not to respect customary law, and efforts to translate customary arrangements into positive law often undermine them. Any attempt by OSSI, then, to build contractual licenses would therefore follow in this paradigm — likely displacing the very types of informal and "vernacular law" upon which commoning thrives.

---

52 Ramón Vera-Herrera, "Ejercer Nuestros Saberes Es Su Mejor Protección," *Biodiversidad,* August 2016, http://www.biodiversidadla.org/index.php/layout/set/print/layout/set/print/Principal/Secciones/Documentos/Ejercer_nuestros_saberes_es_su_mejor_proteccion; Vera-Herrera interview, January 2017.

For GRAIN and their allies, then, the point is that the attempt to codify seed reproduction is itself dangerously reductive. Yes, OSSI currently forbids GMOs from entering the commons. Yes, it has already abandoned the license in favor of the informal, vernacular Pledge. But my informants insisted I was overlooking a subtler form of codification inscribed in the OSSI protocols. In order to release a variety as open source, one must first affirm that the variety is "new." One must also claim authority over a variety in order to release it. All the freedoms of access and use that OSSI provides require first passing through an ontological keyhole tailor-made for Western scientific ideas about germplasm and property. One must first be an owner and creator in order to give seeds away.

6.1 From Commoning Seed to Seeding Many Commons

None of these concerns are unfamiliar — Kloppenburg recognizes the critiques. Unfortunately, the contradictions are not so easily fixed by relaxing the commons rules. If the Pledge guidelines are amended so as to include Native and heirloom seeds, for example, OSSI risks inadvertently becoming the bio-prospector. What gives OSSI the right to decide who among the countless cultivators of Brandywines or Cherokee Purple tomatoes should have the authority to pledge them? And why should OSSI allow one Navajo or Pueblo farmer to pledge a corn variety that belongs not to her individually (as she herself believes) but to her territory, community, and ancestry? To be seen as enabling biopiracy — which remains one of the most deeply resented expressions of colonial and imperialist "gene grabbing" — makes evident why OSSI would hesitate to relax guidelines on pledging heirloom and native varieties. "It has to be something novel," Kloppenburg told me. "Otherwise, we look like bad pirates too."[53]

---

53 Another reason OSSI requires that seeds be "new" is that it avoids the risk of IP infringement. As Kloppenburg describes, "Because we get novel material, the only way you can get it is through our channels, our chain of custody. It's one of our breeders who's pledged it." By the same rationale, the chain of custody protects OSSI seed from unauthorized use.

OSSI has, of course, investigated workarounds. In the case of heirlooms, they did so only to find that in addition to problems of uncertain origin, uncertain identities became an issue: heirloom varieties have many synonyms, opening up the chance for accidental duplication and inadvertent pledging of someone else's seed. With indigenous cultivars, the variables are even more complex, given communal, ancestral, and often sacred relations to seed. OSSI consulted with grassroots partners, including Seed Savers Exchange, who preferred that OSSI not include heirlooms, at least for the time being. Similarly, early consultations with indigenous communities in the US, Latin America, and Southeast Asia indicated these groups' preference for a "wait and see" approach. For many global South farmers, the concern is not only about unauthorized pledging of their varieties. It is also uncertainty over whether OSSI is vulnerable to being stolen *from*. Will the Pledge, as a moral economic construct, be respected by seed corporations and other proprietary interests? Will Lofthouse's concerns that the Pledge "has no teeth" sap the legitimacy through which a "protected" commons is protected?

OSSI's hope, for now, is that Monsanto-Bayer and other agrichemical companies will simply steer clear of the open source commons, because although corporations have access to OSSI materials, they cannot, under the Pledge, patent OSSI seed or any derivative product. Thus, breeding or engineering with OSSI germplasm is theoretically possible, but could potentially disrupt these companies' core business models, not to mention attract unpleasant publicity. In *Plant Breeding Reviews,* a team of Monsanto researchers hinted that they have little interest in tangling with open source seed, writing that if enforceable, OSSI

"If you've seen that variety out there and it doesn't have the OSSI logo on it, or it doesn't say OSSI pledge, then someone's taking it in a way that they shouldn't have taken it" (interview, December 7, 2016).

represents "one of the most restrictive forms of access" from their perspective.[54]

And yet, it remains the case that heirlooms, landraces, and indigenous people's seeds are particularly vulnerable to enclosure. They are especially in need of a protected commons — so what is there to do?

Rather than beat the US-specific OSSI Pledge into a pulp of contradictions, OSSI is now taking an alternate approach: seeding many commons. Open source is not a one-size-fits-all model. It is a set of principles that can be taken up, locally adapted, and made to work for and by communities globally. In this fashion, OSSI is moving towards what development scholar Arturo Escobar calls "commons in the pluriverse."[55] OSSI will share its experiences, struggles, and stories with other communities; it will offer inspiration over formulation, tested strategies, and solutions rather than a body of unified theory.

Some of this pluriverse action is already underway. In India, for example, the Centre for Sustainable Agriculture (CSA) has adapted the OSSI model to the conditions of Hyderabad and surrounding rural villages. An open source seed program helps farmers preserve seeds for traditional foods and supports participatory breeding projects to develop rice, eggplant, and millets that meet local needs.[56] Similarly, the German organization AGROECOL is launching an EU-appropriate open source system. In this case, the breeders and biodynamic farmers are designing formal licenses, not unlike those abandoned by OSSI. The Germans feel the licenses are feasible within their highly technocratic regulatory system — and may be more robust as an antidote to rigid UPOV rules. Meanwhile, partners in East Af-

---

54 David V. Butruille et al., "Maize Breeding in the United States: Views from Within Monsanto," in *Plant Breeding Reviews: Volume 39*, ed. Jules Janick (Hoboken: John Wiley & Sons, Inc., 2015), 199–282, at 223.

55 Arturo Escobar, "Commons in the Pluriverse," in *Patterns of Commoning*, eds. David Bollier and Silke Helfrich (Amityville: Common Strategies Group, 2015), 348–60.

56 CSA-India, "Open Source Seed Systems," *Centre for Sustainable Agriculture*, November 2014.

rica are beginning to pilot their own open source projects in Uganda, Tanzania, and Kenya, and plans are in the works for an ossi-indigenous platform specific to Native peoples.

7. Conclusion

In this chapter, I have traced the efforts of one new project to resist the long colonial and capitalist enclosures of seed. "Beating the bounds" is an active mode of resistance undertaken by members of the Open Source Seed Initiative in an attempt to repossess the commons. I have argued that such boundary beating moves us beyond a static "commons" and into the active form of commoning: the living practices of making rules, negotiating protocols, and re-evaluating the principles through which a commons adheres. By focusing on knowledge, I have followed these social practices through three related stories, from experimenting with legal structures to affirming plant breeding knowledge to articulating with the global seed system.

Beating the bounds also underlines that persistence is necessary — as enclosing is never a done deal. Indeed, since the time I conducted this research, new challenges have appeared on the horizon. The us Department of Justice in 2018 approved the buyout of the agrichemical giant Monsanto by the multinational life science company Bayer, cementing the third in a series of mergers that, according to Bayer, has created a "global leader in agriculture." At its launch, the new firm announced it would create a leading platform in "Digital Farming," provide an "integrated product portfolio across crops" with "a comprehensive offering of Seed and Crop Protection products," and have an annual innovation budget of 2.5 billion euros.[57] Meanwhile, at the university where I completed my PhD, gene editing is helping to propel the next generation of agricultural, pharmaceutical, and basic science research. The question "who owns CRISPR-Cas9?"

---

57 Bayer Corporation, "Bayer to Acquire Monsanto: Creating a Leader in Global Agriculture," 2016, https://www.advancingtogether.com/en/about-the-combination/compelling-strategic-rationale/.

is already a billion-dollar conundrum, pitting two universities into patent wars and sealing lucrative licensing deals for Du-Pont-Pioneer/Dow, Monsanto-Bayer, and Syngenta-ChemChina, among others.

However, there are many anti-enclosure developments too. In November 2019, the African Food Sovereignty Alliance gathered 44 women and men from 10 African countries (Zambia, Zimbabwe, Burundi, Malawi, Tanzania, Kenya, South Africa, Senegal, Eswatini, and Uganda) to develop "a common strategy for changing the prevailing narrative around seed in Africa, to one that recognizes smallholder farmers, their indigenous knowledge and their seed systems that are the fundamental basis of Africa's food system."[58] This meeting carried forward the decolonial and feminist ethic voiced by peasant agroecologists who convened in Rome the year prior: At FAO headquarters, they fought to assure that agroecology's core tenets — valuing indigenous wisdom, cultivating complex social-ecological systems, enabling women's full participation in the social and political life of their communities — are not instrumentalized by formal uptake in the international policy arena.[59] Commoning implicitly, if not explicitly, runs through each. I will therefore be watching — and participating — as OSSI seeks to promote a pluriverse of seed commons rather than establish or oversee a universal archetype, which would never succeed agroecologically or politically. These actually functioning commons are what Bollier suggests are the "staging areas" for post-capitalist systems and I agree. Like the OSSI commoners, I suggest that creating and protecting these staging areas will take much boundary-beating work. But in that activity, there are real possibilities of deconstructing dominant structures, there are real possibilities for commoned seed to grow.

---

58 AFSA (African Food Sovereignty in Africa), "Every Seed Has a Story – The Strategy," March 20, 2020, https://afsafrica.org/every-seed-has-a-story/.

59 La Vía Campesina, "Declaration at the II International Symposium on Agroecology, April, 2018 – Via Campesina English," April 8, 2018, https://viacampesina.org/en/declaration-at-the-ii-international-symposium-on-agroecology/.

7

Blockchain Technology: Toward a Decentralized Governance of Digital Platforms?

Primavera De Filippi and Xavier Lavayssière

1. Introduction

Over the past few decades, technological advances and, in particular, the development of modern information and communication technologies (ICT) have enhanced our capabilities to communicate and exchange information on a global scale. The advent of the Internet and digital technologies marked a shift from centralized communication systems (*one-to-many*) towards a more distributed and decentralized communication network (*many-to-many*), which has radically changed the way we work and organize ourselves. Originally designed as a re-silient telecommunication network that could resist a nuclear attack,[1] the decentralized structure of the Internet has also been found to be a key requisite to ensure the scalability and flexibility of the network.[2]

---

1 Paul Baran, *On Distributed Communications: I. Introduction to Distributed Communications Networks* (Santa Monica: Rand Corporation, 1964).
2 Manuel Castells, *The Internet Galaxy: Reflections on the Internet, Business, and Society* (Oxford: Oxford University Press, 2002).

As the Internet grew, it evolved into an open ecosystem for permissionless innovation, with a variety of new players deploying projects and initiatives that significantly disrupted the status quo.[3] On the one hand, the Internet provided new tools for companies and startups to experiment with innovative business models and economic practices that challenged the operations of established market players. On the other hand, it supported the emergence of commons-based communities relying on alternative legal regimes and new participatory models to promote openness and distributed collaboration.

Over time, as the Internet gained mainstream adoption, some companies and corporations established themselves as dominant players in this emergent ecosystem. While the building blocks of the Internet still consist, for the most part, of open and standardized protocols (e.g., TCP/IP, HTTP, SMTP) and open source software projects (e.g., Firefox, Linux, Apache, MySQL), services built on top of these protocols are mostly made up of centralized platforms and proprietary applications. Today, a few large online operators (e.g., Google, Facebook, Amazon) effectively dominate the Internet landscape by controlling the key online infrastructures through which users and companies interact with the network.

More recently, a new technology has emerged, together with a whole new set of promises for decentralization and disintermediation. By combining peer-to-peer technologies, game theory, and cryptographic primitives, blockchain technology[4]

---

3   Clark Gilbert, "The Disruption Opportunity," MIT *Sloan Management Review* 44, no. 4 (2003): 27–33.

4   Blockchain technology refers to a broader category of technologies (sometimes referred to as Distributed Ledger Technologies) that rely on a distributed ledger or database running on top of a peer-to-peer network. Following a particular protocol, nodes in the network can record transactions into a data structure (commonly, a series of data "blocks" which are linked to each other through cryptographic references forming a "chain"). The integrity of these transactional records is secured through cryptographic primitives and economic incentives designed to guarantee the tamper-resistance of the networked database. As a general rule, the technology can be used both for the deployment of public and open net-

makes it possible for people to experiment with new forms of peer-production and decentralized collaboration. Just as the Internet enabled users to communicate on a peer-to-peer basis, bypassing traditional intermediaries, Bitcoin and other block-chain-based applications enable users to exchange value directly with one another, relying on economic models and incentivization schemes that do not require the intervention of any trusted authority or intermediary middleman.

Yet, despite its promise to establish a more decentralized society with a novel economic order,[5] many of the blockchain-based networks or applications implemented thus far ultimately rely on market dynamics and economic incentives for distributed coordination. Indeed, consensus, in a large majority of existing blockchain-based networks, is established — at the protocol level — through a combination of code-based rules and game theoretical mechanisms that ultimately replicate the current economic order. This type of *governance by the infrastructure* has already shown its shortcomings, especially when it comes to promoting or preserving decentralization, mostly due to its inability to account for external political and economic forces that exist outside of a blockchain-based platform. We claim that, in order to ensure that these platforms cannot be co-opted by these external forces, a more comprehensive governance model must be elaborated — one that extends beyond the realm of pure algorithmically verifiable actions, and that supports or facilitates the *governance of the infrastructure.*

After providing a general overview of how the decentralized nature of the Internet enabled different models of innovation to emerge — in terms of both market-driven innovation (2.a) and distributed commons-based collaboration (2.b) — we will look

---

works (public blockchains) or for the creation of networks that are made available only to a restricted number of participants (permissioned blockchains). We will focus here on the former category of blockchains, insofar as they constitute a more relevant platform for permissionless innovation and peer-to-peer coordination.

5   Marcella Atzori, "Blockchain Technology and Decentralized Governance: Is the State Still Necessary?" *SSRN* (January 2, 2016).

at the potential for blockchain technology to incentivize new forms of decentralized collaboration (3.a) and to enable new distributed governance models (3.b). Finally, we will conclude by focusing on how the characteristics of blockchain-based platforms may benefit existing commons-based projects and initiatives, by providing new and more sustainable economic schemes (4.a) while ensuring a greater degree of control over shared digital platforms (4.b). Our thesis is that a carefully designed integration of blockchain technology with the operations of various commons-based initiatives — and in particular those related to the notions of the *sharing economy*[6] and *platform co-operativism*[7] — could significantly contribute to improving the governance and long-term sustainability of these projects. This could potentially lead to the establishment of a collaborative economy characterized by direct interactions among a disparate network of peers, without the need to rely on any trusted authority or intermediary middleman.

2. Internet and Permissionless Innovation

The advent of the Internet and digital technology marked the beginning of a digital revolution that led to significant social, economic, and cultural changes in modern societies. At the outset, the development of early Internet protocols was, for the most part, publicly funded through governmental initiatives, military projects and academic research.[8] Yet, the disruption brought about by the widespread deployment of the Internet network has been shaped by two different, yet interrelated, driving forces. On the one hand, a large variety of new companies and startups have been launched with a view to challenging the status quo, disrupting existing institutions and former incum-

---

6 Danielle Sacks, "The Sharing Economy," *Fast Company* 155 (May 2011): 88–93.

7 Trebor Scholz, *Platform Cooperativism: Challenging the Corporate Sharing Economy* (New York: Rosa Luxemburg Stiftung, 2016).

8 David D. Clark, "The Design Philosophy of the DARPA Internet Protocols," *ACM SIGCOMM Computer Communication Review* 18, no. 4 (1988): 106–14.

bents by using innovative services and novel business models. On the other hand, a series of commons-based initiatives has leveraged the power of this global communication network to build open ecosystems of distributed collaboration. Not only have some of these initiatives succeeded in challenging the status quo, they also inaugurated an entirely new paradigm of social organization based on peer-to-peer production and distributed collaboration.[9]

2.a Market-Driven Innovation
The Internet and modern information and telecommunication technologies have contributed to a significant shift in economic power from traditional "brick and mortar" to new companies that operate, almost exclusively, online. As a global infrastructure that comprises a series of open and standardized protocols, the Internet makes it possible for anyone to innovate on a worldwide digital platform without having to ask for permission from anyone.[10] New market players have been leveraging this new platform for "permissionless innovation,"[11] experimenting with new business models and managerial practices[12] that challenge the operations of traditional and more rigid incumbents.

Many Internet startups rely on specific business models designed to leverage network effects, gathering large user-bases by offering free, freemium, or low-cost services that often do not cover the costs of providing these services. In order to grow rapidly, these startups need to raise capital, often relying on competitive strategies and exclusionary practices in order to

9   Yochai Benkler, *The Wealth of Networks: How Social Production Transforms Markets and Freedom* (New Haven: Yale University Press, 2006).
10   Adam Thierer, *Permissionless Innovation: The Continuing Case for Comprehensive Technological Freedom* (Macon: Mercatus Center at George Mason University, 2016).
11   Vinton G. Cerf, "Dynamics of Disruptive Innovations," *Journal on Telecommunications and High Technology Law* 10 (2012): 21–31, at 21.
12   See, e.g., the "lean startup" methodology adopted by many early-stage Internet companies: Steve Blank, "Why the Lean Start-up Changes Everything," *Harvard Business Review* 91, no. 5 (2013): 63–72.

demonstrate their business model to investors. For instance, intellectual property (including patents and proprietary software) has often been weaponized to raise barriers to entry and undercut competition.[13] Moreover, because of the proprietary nature of these platforms — with limited interoperability and data portability — users find themselves locked into walled gardens, unable to shift from one platform to another without losing access their own data[14] or incurring other switching costs[15]. Finally, and perhaps most importantly, if many online platforms do not monetize their services directly by requiring users to pay a fee to access the platform, they do so indirectly, by monetizing their user-base through more personalized and targeted advertising campaigns.[16] With the emergence of increasingly large datasets, the development of new data-mining techniques, and the use of machine learning, the concentration of information into a few data centers controlled by a small number of large corporations has become a critical issue, jeopardizing privacy, individual autonomy, and, ultimately, competition.

Major players, such as Google and Twitter, are attempting to recreate an ecosystem for open innovation, by releasing open source libraries and APIs for third parties to build applications on top of their own platforms.[17] Yet, while this opens new pos-

---

13 Amar Bhidé, "The Venturesome Economy: How Innovation Sustains Prosperity in a More Connected World," *Journal of Applied Corporate Finance* 21, no. 1 (2009): 8–23.

14 Salil K. Mehra, "Paradise Is a Walled Garden? Trust, Antitrust and User Dynamism," *George Mason Law Review* 18 (2011): 889–952.

15 For instance, while some platforms might provide a mechanism for users to retrieve their data, data portability might nonetheless be limited because of a lack of standardization in data formats. See Janis Wong and Tristan Henderson, "The Right to Data Portability in Practice: Exploring the Implications of the Technologically Neutral GDPR," *International Data Privacy Law* 9, no. 3 (2019): 173–91.

16 As popularly put by Andrew Lewis, "if you are not paying for it, you are not the customer, you are the product being sold" (comment to "User-driven Discontent," *MetaFilter,* August 26, 2010, http://www.metafilter.com/95152/Userdriven-discontent#3256046).

17 Robert Bodle, "Regimes of Sharing: Open APIs, Interoperability, and Facebook," *Information, Communication and Society* 14, no. 3 (2011): 320–37.

sibilities for small players to enter into the market, these online operators ultimately seek to reinforce their dominant position by encouraging companies and developers to deploy new services or applications onto their platforms.

Similar issues lie at the core of the new "crowdsourcing" practices adopted by platforms such as Facebook, YouTube, Uber, and Airbnb. This new model of distributed production creates incentives for users to contribute value (e.g., by creating content or pooling their resources into a network) for the ultimate benefit of the platform operators. Under this model, users are not just passive consumers but rather become active contributors to a third-party platform. For instance, most of the content available on social networks such as Facebook or Twitter is not produced by platform operators but rather by companies and individuals interacting on top of these platforms. Operators rely on the production of their user base in order to offer a valuable service to the public at large. However, despite the significant value they provide to the platform, users are generally not remunerated for their contributions,[18] nor are they granted any kind of control or governance rights over the manner in which the platform will operate and evolve. On the contrary, because of the network effects inherent in these services, these platforms have grown increasingly centralized, with a few operators in charge of coordinating the contributions and activities of a large number of individual users. These operators are responsible for matching offer and demand (e.g., buyers and sellers, content producers and consumers), often collecting a rent — in the form of user data or a monetary fee — for every transaction

---

18 One notable exception is video sharing networks such as YouTube, where popular creators can gain revenues, which could be partially explained by the costs associated with video production. Still, the model nonetheless relies on an asymmetric relationship between content creators and platform operators. For more details, see Sonia Y. Song and Steven. S. Wildman, "Evolution of Strategy and Commercial Relationships for Social Media Platforms: The Case of YouTube," in *Handbook of Social Media Management,* eds. Mike Friedrichsen and Wolfgang Muhl-Benninghaus (Berlin and Heidelberg: Springer, 2013), 619–32.

they intermediate. Hence, this new model of production — often referred to via the misnomer of the *sharing* or *collaborative economy*[19] — has not significantly contributed to the establishment of a new economic order. Rather, it has turned out to be an even stronger instantiation of the capitalist mindset.[20]

2.b: Commons-Based Innovation

At the same time, a different kind of innovation has been taking place over the Internet, leveraging the new opportunities provided by this global communication network in order to create new platforms and applications, which are also meant to disrupt the status quo, albeit with a slightly different approach. Initiatives like GNU/Linux, the Apache HTTP server, and many other open source software projects were developed by a community of researchers and software engineers with the intention of creating a pool of shared resources that could complement or even replace some of the dominant proprietary platforms at the time. The same is true for large collaborative online projects, such as Wikipedia, OpenStreetMap, or other crowd-sourcing projects[21] designed to create a common and shared resource that remains available to all.

Commons-based innovation is concerned with maximizing the utility of software applications and online platforms built and operated by the community and for the community. Rather than trying to undercut the monopoly rents collected by dominant market players, these initiatives leverage the power of digital technologies to promote peer-to-peer collaboration through the creation of platforms and tools designed to further the needs

---

19 Sacks, "The Sharing Economy."
20 Chris J. Martin, "The Sharing Economy: A Pathway to Sustainability or a Nightmarish Form of Neoliberal Capitalism?" *Ecological Economics* 121 (2016): 149–59.
21 Planetary astronomy, for instance, increasingly relies on information provided by large number of amateurs cooperating online. See O. Mousis et al., "Instrumental Methods for Professional and Amateur Collaborations in Planetary Astronomy," *Experimental Astronomy* 38, nos. 1–2 (2014): 91–191.

of specific communities and the public at large. As opposed to most of the market-driven initiatives described above, this new form of innovation — sometimes described as *commons-based peer-production*[22] — operates according to a more open and co-operative approach, which is grounded on the principles of free and open source software.[23] In particular, in an endeavor to reduce the effects of monopoly rents on information established by intellectual property laws, and to ensure that information remains a common good accessible to all, early commons-based communities have elaborated new legal means of innovation, including free and open source licenses for software (see e.g., GNU General Public License, MIT License, BSD License, etc) and a suite of Creative Commons licenses[24] for creative works. The resources released under these licenses are not the exclusive property of one specific actor or intermediary operator. Rather, they are shared resources which are held in common by all community members and made available to the public at large.

While most commons-based initiatives are born out of grassroots community efforts,[25] some initiatives stem from the efforts of an industry's collective action[26] or of single privately-held

---

22 Benkler, *The Wealth of Networks*.

23 Eric S. Raymond, "The Cathedral and the Bazaar," *Philosophy & Technology* 12, no. 3 (1999): 23–32.

24 Creative Commons licenses are public copyright license, inspired from the Free and Open Source software licences, that enable the free distribution and reproduction of creative works, under specific conditions. They constitute a shift from the "all right reserved" default of copyright law, towards a more permissive regime of "certain rights reserved". For more details, see Lawrence Lessig, *Free Culture* (New York: Penguin Press, 2004).

25 See, e.g., the Apache HTTP server project, initiated by a collective of webmasters: Audris Mockus, Roy T. Fielding, and James D. Herbsleb, "Two Case Studies of Open Source Software Development: Apache and Mozilla," *ACM Transactions on Software Engineering and Methodology (TOSEM)* 11, no. 3 (2003): 309–46.

26 The Genivi Alliance, for instance, was founded in 2009 by BMW Group, Delphi, GM, Intel, Magneti-Marelli, PSA Peugeot Citroën, and Visteon in order to build open source infotainment software for vehicles.

companies.[27] Most community-driven initiatives are initially stewarded by one or more charismatic leaders[28] who establish the overall vision and modus operandi of the initiative, along with a small group of core contributors responsible for bootstrapping the project. It is only at a later stage of development — once a larger community has grown around the initiative — that the development and maintenance of these commons-based projects requires a more formalized and inclusive governance structure to manage the contributions of a large and distributed network of peers collaborating towards the production of a common resource. In the case of leading projects — such as GNU/Linux or the Apache HTTP server — which attract considerable interest from the industry, or in the case of projects initiated by private companies — such as ZEA partners or MySQL — a foundation is sometimes created around the project in order to receive and manage sponsorship or other forms of revenue with generally limited control over the development process.[29]

Indeed, as a general rule, the governance of commons-based communities is more open and participatory than that of many Internet startups, as the leaders or managers of commons-based initiatives only enjoy as much power as the community gives them. Specifically, the governance structure adopted by most of these initiatives has a strong meritocratic flavor, whereby those who contribute the most to the community are given the op-

27 For instance, MySQL was originated by the privately held MySQL AB Swedish company, whereas the Mozilla web browser emerged following the open source licensing of the Netscape browser's code. See Frank Hecker, "Setting Up Shop: The Business of Open-Source Software," *IEEE Software* (January–February 1998): 45–51; Eric von Hippel and Georg von Krogh, "Open Source Software and the 'Private-Collective' Innovation Model: Issues for Organization Science," *Organization Science* 14, no. 2 (2003): 209–23.

28 These charismatic leaders are sometimes described as "benevolent dictators": Jan Ljungberg, "Open Source Movements as a Model for Organising," *European Journal of Information Systems* 9, no. 4 (2000): 208–16 — such as Richard Stallman for the GNU project or Linus Torvald for the Linux kernel.

29 Paul B. De Laat, "Governance of Open Source Software: State of the Art," *Journal of Management & Governance* 11, no. 2 (2007): 165–77.

portunity to participate in the governance thereof. And if the managers were to abuse their powers or simply lead the project in a direction that is not in the best interests of the community, the community could simply "fork" the project into an alternative community operated according to different rules.[30]

Perhaps one of the biggest differences between market-driven and commons-based innovation lies in the economic models that underpin the two. While the former is mainly driven by the logic of profit maximization, the latter is driven by a combination of ideological values, a desire to maximize the utility of the products or services provided to the community and an expectation of individual returns or compensation (financial or otherwise). Nevertheless, although profits are not the main drivers for a large majority of commons-based initiatives, the ability to raise money and attract human resources remains an important precondition for their long-term sustainability. In that regard, many open source software projects secure funding through donations, and sometimes manage to earn a substantial amount of funds with related activities, such as product customization and support (e.g., RedHat), consulting (e.g., IBM), or connected cloud services (e.g., Wordpress). Software developers and engineers are also incentivized to contribute to these projects as a result of the informal benefits they might acquire through cooperation,[31] including new skills and visibility that may greatly enhance their position on the job market.

There are, however, many limitations to an open source approach. In particular, despite the relative success of the open source community and the predominance of open source software projects in the lower protocol layers of the Internet stack, commons-based peer-production suffers from a general lack of incentives and difficulty in coordination. First and

---

30 Such a fork, the reuse of code or content into a new project, is generally perceived as a healthy and intended process that enables people to build upon and adapt code to a different purpose, and has already happened in several open source communities and software projects; see, e.g., OpenOffice/LibreOffice, Debian/Ubuntu/Mint Linux, XFree86/XOrg.

31 Raymond, "The Cathedral and the Bazaar."

foremost, because of the open and non-proprietary character of these platforms, most of these initiatives are unable to raise funds from venture-capital firms and other sources. As a result, these projects are often under-funded, especially in their initial phases. Because of the lower economic incentives they provide, they sometimes do not manage to attract a sufficient number of contributors, in contrast to their more commercial and profit-driven counterparts. Secondly, even the most successful projects that have acquired mainstream adoption (e.g., GNU/Linux, Apache, Mozilla Firefox, etc.) suffer from the additional complexity of managing and coordinating a distributed network of contributors.

3. Blockchains and Distributed Coordination

Just as was the case with the Internet in the early 1990s, with the advent of Bitcoin in 2009, blockchain technologies have spurred a new wave of permissionless innovation and experimentation. The combination of existing technologies (including decentralized peer-to-peer networks and cryptographic primitives such as public-private key cryptography and cryptographic hash functions) has given rise to a new decentralized infrastructure for secure peer-to-peer transactions and distributed coordination.

As such, blockchain-based platforms are perceived by some to be a way to further the ideals of freedom and autonomy that the Internet ultimately failed to promote.[32] In light of the principles of decentralization and disintermediation that underpin the design of blockchain-based networks, a number of engineers, computer scientists, and entrepreneurs have begun to experiment with these new technologies, eager to implement decentralized applications that would operate, to a large extent, autonomously. Indeed, as opposed to traditional online platforms, administered by centralized operators or trusted authorities, Bitcoin and other blockchain-based applications operate in

---

32 Atzori, "Blockchain Technology and Decentralized Governance."

a more distributed manner, independently of any government or middlemen,[33] through a combination of novel incentivization schemes and distributed governance models. And because they are administered by a large number of peers located all over the globe, they are generally less affected by jurisdictional constraints than are their centralized counterparts.[34]

3.a Novel Incentivization Schemes

Born in the midst of the financial crisis of 2008, Bitcoin was the first decentralized payment system and virtual currency implemented on top of a blockchain-based network. The network was carefully designed to secure the scarcity of digital assets — the Bitcoin cryptocurrency — without relying on any trusted authority or centralized clearinghouse.[35]

Bitcoin was originally conceived by a pseudonymous entity, Satoshi Nakamoto, out of a desire to circumvent existing institutions — such as banks and other governmental institutions — which were seen as failing to protect the interests of regular citizens.[36] Most of the early Bitcoin adopters shared similar ideals, identifying themselves as "cypherpunks"[37] or as part of a specific breed of anarchism or libertarianism known as "crypto-anarchists" or "crypto-libertarians."[38]

---

33 Joseph Bonneau, Andrew Miller, Jeremy Clark, Arvind Narayanan, Joshua A. Kroll, and Edward W. Felten, "SoK: Research Perspectives and Challenges for Bitcoin and Cryptocurrencies," *2015 IEEE Symposium on Security and Privacy (SP)* (2015): 104.

34 Primavera De Filippi, "Bitcoin: A Regulatory Nightmare to a Libertarian Dream," *Internet Policy Review* 3, no. 2 (2014).

35 Satoshi Nakamoto, *Bitcoin: A Peer-to-Peer Electronic Cash System* (2008), http://www.bitcoin.org/bitcoin.pdf.

36 The first block of the Bitcoin blockchain contains the following quote: "The Times 03/Jan/2009 Chancellor on brink of second bailout for banks," possibly as an attempt to comment on the risks caused by fractional-reserve banking.

37 Jeremiah Bohr and Masooda M. Bashir, "Who Uses Bitcoin? An Exploration of the Bitcoin Community," *2014 IEEE Twelfth Annual International Conference on Privacy, Security and Trust (PST)* (2014): 94–101.

38 Henrik Karlstrøm, "Do Libertarians Dream of Electric Coins? The Material Embeddedness of Bitcoin," *Distinktion: Scandinavian Journal of Social*

Of course, despite the strong ideology surrounding the Bitcoin project, a significant number of people were motivated by more pragmatic reasons — trying to benefit from lower transactions costs for international transfers and reduced regulatory or corporate control over money transmission. But what really caused the system to take off and reach a much broader audience were the immediate gains provided by Bitcoin and other cryptocurrencies. The rapid increase in the value of these virtual currencies — whose price has increased, in the course of a few years, from a few dollar cents to hundreds or thousands of dollars[39] — has attracted new market players, including large corporations, startup entrepreneurs, speculators and "mining pools".[40] Mining operations, in particular, scaled from a hobby to large corporations investing in specialized equipment (e.g., ASIC computers[41]) and facilities to support the operations of

---

Theory 15, no. 1 (2014): 23–46.

39 In 2010, two pizzas were bought for 10,000 bitcoins, worth around than $40 at the time; whereas as of August 2017, one Bitcoin was valued above $4,000. Similarly, Ether, the native cryptocurrency on the Ethereum network was initially valued at $0.25 and was valued above $300 in August 2017.

40 A miner is a network node that not only verifies the validity of transactions executed on a blockchain-based network but also aggregates them into a "block" of transactions that will be append to the existing blockchain. On Proof-of-Work networks (such as Bitcoin and Ethereum), the mining process is used as a mechanism to ensure that no-one can coopt the network, unless they control more than 50% of the overall computational power of the network. Indeed, before publishing a block to the blockchain, miners need to find the solution to a cryptographic puzzle that requires a large amount of computational resources to solve, but that is relatively straightforward to verify, once found. Whenever a new block is published to the network, the miner of that block is rewarded with a fixed allotment of bitcoins, which halves every four years (today, the block reward amounts to 12.5 bitcoins per block). Miners are thus competing with each other, in order to be the first to find the solution to this cryptographic puzzle, and consequently to acquire the newly minted bitcoins associated with that block.

41 ASICS (Application-Specific Integrated Circuit Chip) are microchips specifically designed to perform a task, in this context, the hashing algorithm needed to successfully mine blocks on a Proof-of-Work blockchain.

these blockchain-based networks, receiving fixed allotments of virtual currency — the so-called *block reward* — in return.[42]

More recently, a few projects and initiatives have experimented with a new way of raising funds by selling blockchain-based tokens to the public at large. This practice — commonly referred to as a "token sale" or "Initial Coin Offering" (ICO) — has acquired considerable popularity in the last few years, reaching a cumulative investment of over 30 billion USD by the end of 2020.[43] The advantage of the ICO approach over the more traditional equity-based fundraising models is that it makes it possible for teams to raise funds without diluting control over a company or organization (as would normally happen through the sale of equity or shares). These new fundraising techniques make it possible to tap into a large pool of non-accredited investors who would not otherwise be able to invest in such early stage projects for both practical[44] and legal reasons.[45]

42 Whenever a block is published to the network, along with the solution to the cryptographic puzzle associated with that block, a fixed amount of cryptocurrency is created and attributed to the address of the miner of that block. Miners also collect the fees of each transaction included into the block.

43 Shadi Samieifar and Dirk G. Baur, "Read Me If You Can! An Analysis of ICO White Papers," *Finance Research Letters* (2020): 101427. N.B., this number might be difficult to evaluate as many ICOs management teams inflate their results for marketing purposes while other ICOs are not reported.

44 In addition to the obvious barriers to entry concerning the availability of funds, substantial complexity is involved in the process of deal-matching according to specific investment criteria, and the negotiation of acceptable investment terms. See Colin M. Mason and Richard T. Harrison, "Barriers to Investment in the Informal Venture Capital Sector," *Entrepreneurship & Regional Development* 14, no. 3 (2002): 271–87.

45 In the US for instance, under the Securities Act of 1933, a company that wants to issue securities to the public must register with the US Securities and Exchange Commission (SEC). An exception is introduced in Rule 501 of Regulation D, which allows for the sale of unregistered securities to accredited investors, who are considered able to bear the economic risk of investing in these securities.

The caveat is that the legal uncertainty surrounding these to-ken sales[46] created a high degree of legal uncertainty — both for token issuers, who might be found liable for the infringement of specific rules or regulations[47] — and for investors, who might fall into an unregulated ecosystem full of dubious projects and claims.[48] However, legal clarity has improved over time through law enforcement[49] and the enactment of new legal frameworks[50]. Besides, the volatility in the market price of these virtual curren-cies — some of which witnessed a value increase of over 10x in the period of just a the space of few months[51] — has attracted a

---

46 Token issuers might market these tokens in different ways, such as: "utility tokens," "asset-based tokens," "membership tokens," etc. Yet, regardless of the way they are defined by the token issuers, these tokens might be construed as different asset classes under different bodies of law. See, for the instance, the report of the SEC on the legal qualification of the DAO tokens as securities, available at https://www.sec.gov/litigation/investre-port/34-81207.pdf.

47 In China, for instance, following the ban on tokens sales by the People's Bank of China (see notice of April 9, 2017 available at http://www.pbc.gov. cn/goutongjiaoliu/113456/113469/3374222/index.html), several projects had to cancel or halt their operations. Similarly, following the issuance of the SEC report concerning the legal qualification of the DAO tokens (cf. *supra*), the Protostarr project was contacted by the SEC for an investigation of an alleged case of unregistered securities issuance. After consultation with multiple lawyers, the team decided to cease further operations and to refund all Ether collected to the original investors.

48 While these token sales represent a new opportunity for projects or initia-tives to raise the necessary capital to bootstrap themselves, they often operate in a regulatory gray area. While there are important benefits to the ability for non-accredited investors to participate in the economy of these projects, there are also significant concerns to the extent that unsophisti-cated retail investors run the risk of being defrauded or harmed by these highly risky and speculative instruments.

49 E.g., in the US, *Securities and Exchange Commission v. Telegram Group Inc. et al*, 19-cv-09439-PKC (S.D.N.Y. Oct 11, 2019).

50 E.g., in France, Loi n° 2019–486 du 22 mai 2019 relative à la croissance et la transformation des entreprises, available at https://www.legifrance.gouv.fr/eli/loi/2019/5/22/2019–486/jo/texte.

51 The value of cryptocurrencies has increased dramatically during the year of 2017. For instance, Bitcoin's value went from $1,200 in April 2017 to up to $4,800 in September 2017; Ethereum went from being worth less than $100 in May 2017 to being worth over $400 in June 2017; Ripple went from

large number of investors, traders, and speculators, who entered the game with an expectation of immediate returns, through a series of high-risk, high-profit investments. Most of these investors are not interested in the products or services associated with these tokens; they are merely speculating on the future value of the tokens, acquiring them for the sole purpose of subsequently reselling them on the market at a much higher price.

Blockchain technology thus provides new avenues for traditional market players, startups and commons-based initiatives to access new forms of capital and to engage in a variety of profit-making activities. Yet, in spite of the new opportunities it might provide to small players, a large part of the blockchain ecosystem — as it stands today — is an instantiation of a free-market economy built around game theoretical incentives and speculative dynamics, and devoid of any form of regulation or consumer protection. Besides, looking at how the blockchain ecosystem has evolved over the past few years, we witness an increasing number of financial institutions (including banks, investment firms, and insurance companies), a variety of large companies, firms, and corporations (such as Microsoft, IBM, and Samsung, amongst others) entering the space and leveraging the power of blockchain technology to further their own financial interests.

3.b Governance of Blockchain-Based Networks

The decentralization inherent in the design of most blockchain-based networks is a crucial element of disintermediation, which, however, also makes it more difficult to govern or regulate these platforms. By relying on the notion of "distributed consensus" as a new mechanism of distributed coordination, blockchain technology makes it possible to coordinate a large number of contributors without passing through a centralized intermediary or middleman. Yet, without any intermediary operator in charge of managing and administering the network, it becomes crucial to

---

$0.03 in April 2017 to $0.4 in May 2017; Litecoin went from $10 in April 2017 to over $80 in September 2017.

identify and analyze the different governance structures that can be (and have been) deployed on top of these distributed infrastructures and to examine how these can contribute to ensuring their resiliency and long-term sustainability.

The governance of blockchain-based networks can be distinguished into two different but interrelated categories: *on-chain* governance or *off-chain* governance. The former is done by encoding specific governance rules directly into the protocol that governs a particular blockchain-based network, so that these rules are automatically enforced by the technology itself (*governance by the infrastructure*). The latter is done by establishing a procedure for decision-making that operates outside of the network protocol (*governance of the infrastructure*).

At the protocol level, most blockchain-based networks have adopted a governance structure that relies on a combination of market-driven mechanisms and consensus protocols. In protocols that follow the Nakamoto consensus[52] the influence of each member of the network ultimately depends on their level of investment in a particular set of resources. This is the case, for instance, of the Proof-of-Work mechanism[53] adopted by Bitcoin and Ethereum, where decisions regarding the next block to be included into the chain are based on the quantity of computing power invested into the network, or the Proof-of-Stake mechanism adopted by other blockchain-based networks such as Peercoin or NXT, where voting power is based on the quantity of tokens held by a particular agent.[54] Network participants can

---

52 Chenxing Li, Peilun Li, Dong Zhou, Wei Xu, Fan Long, Andrew Yao, "Scaling Nakamoto Consensus to Thousands of Transactions per Second," *arXiv* preprint arXiv:1805.03870 (2018).

53 Nakamoto, *Bitcoin*.

54 In both types of blockchains, miners produce blocks and submit them to the network, which — after ensuring the validity of each block — will append them to the existing chain of blocks. Yet, not everyone is entitled to submit a new block to a blockchain-based network. The protocol is such that whoever is entitled to submit the next block will be determined according to either the amount of computing power they each have invested into the network (Proof-of-Work) or the number of tokens they hold (Proof-of-Stake).

also exercise a certain degree of decision-making power by accepting only (or rejecting) blocks that meet (or do not meet) certain criteria.[55]

A similar type of plutocratic governance can also be observed in the models adopted by a large number of blockchain-based applications — such as, most notably, the decentralized investment fund known as the DAO,[56] whose governance is structured around the number of tokens that each individual holds. Some blockchain-based networks — such as, for instance, Tezos[57] and Dfinity[58] — even went as far as implementing specific *on-chain* governance mechanisms allowing for token holders to vote for changes on the protocol of the blockchain itself.

Such a market-driven approach to governance makes sense — at least theoretically — because free market logics are, indeed, a powerful mechanism of indirect coordination that operate in accordance with the blockchain's logics of rough "distributed consensus." The game-theoretical models implemented

---

55 While only miners have the ability to forge and publish blocks to the network, full-node operators can also participate in specific on-chain voting mechanisms, e.g., by committing only to accept a specific type of blocks. Such a technique was used in 2017 to enable a user-activated Soft Fork of the Bitcoin blockchain, leading to the adoption of the SegWit improvement proposal.

56 Muhammad Mehar, Charlie Shier, Alana Giambattista, Elgar Gong, Gabrielle Fletcher, Ryan Sanayhie, Henry Kim, and Marek Laskowski, "Understanding a Revolutionary and Flawed Grand Experiment in Blockchain: The DAO Attack," *Journal of Cases on Information Technology* 21, no. 1 (2017): 19–32.

57 Tezos is a new decentralized blockchain that governs itself by establishing a true digital commonwealth — i.e., a group of people that chooses to be linked together because of their shared goals and interests. Tezos aims to have their token holders make decisions together to govern the platform and improve it over time. For more details, see http://www.tezos.com.

58 Dfinity is a blockchain protocol designed to enable decentralized networks to host high performance virtual computers of infinite capacity, with the aim of creating a "decentralized cloud" where smart contract software can be used to recreate a wide variety of systems. In contrast to other blockchain, Dfinity introduces the fundamental difference of governance by a novel decentralized decision-making system called the "Blockchain Nervous System" (or "BNS"). For more details, see http://dfinity.org.

into a blockchain protocol are of a strongly market-driven individualistic nature, as every individual is expected to behave in a rational manner in order to maximize individual utility and economic returns. Yet, these protocols rarely account for the fact that the ideal of a perfectly competitive market remains just an ideal; and that, in practice, markets can be easily manipulated by powerful actors, leading to collusion and market concentration.[59] Similarly, when left to the invisible hand of the market, blockchain-based applications are likely to evolve into increasingly centralized platforms, with the emergence of new intermediary operators and new potential incumbents.

Of course, not every rule and procedure can be transposed into a formal language and encoded into a set of protocol rules. Even where there is a formalized governance system implemented within the protocol of particular blockchain-based applications, there is always a point at which one needs to move away from the protocol in order to decide upon something that had not been accounted for within the protocol itself. For most blockchain-based networks, any decision regarding possible changes to the network's protocol has to be taken through an external decision-making process. Because most existing blockchain-based networks do not implement any formalized mechanism for *off-chain* governance, the process is generally done informally, in an ad-hoc manner. As a result, invisible powers emerge,[60] with decisions being made by a small handful of people with strong technical expertise, market power or charisma.[61]

In the case of Bitcoin, for instance, the long-standing scaling debate was dominated by a few software engineers and tech-

---

59 Georg J. Stigler, *The Organization of Industry* (Homewood: Irwin, 1968).

60 Primavera De Filippi and Benjamin Loveluck, "The Invisible Politics of Bitcoin: Governance Crisis of a Decentralized Infrastructure," *Internet Policy Review* 5, no. 3 (2016): 1–32.

61 Philipp Hacker, "Corporate Governance for Complex Cryptocurrencies? A Framework for Stability and Decision Making in Blockchain-Based Monetary Systems," in *Regulating Blockchain: Techno-Social and Legal Challenges*, eds. Philipp Hacker, Ioannis Lianos, Georgios Dimitropoulos, and Stefan Eich (Oxford: Oxford University Press, 2019), 140–66.

savvy individuals proposing alternative implementations and possible protocol changes to the underlying blockchain-based network.[62] Prominent figures in the debate also included a small number of highly influential individuals with strong visibility within the community, as well as several miners and mining-pools, which incurred substantial investments in specialized hardware devices for the mining of Bitcoin.[63]

Similarly, following the loss of over $50 million USD due to a vulnerability in the code of the DAO,[64] the Ethereum community had to take coordinated action to decide whether — and how — to fork the Ethereum network (i.e., whether or not to update its underlying protocol) in order to recover the funds. Yet, due to the lack of a formalized governance structure within the Ethereum community, it took several weeks for the community to agree on a coordinated course of action.[65] Ultimately, as it

---

62 Because the Bitcoin protocol only supports a limited number of transactions per block, increasing the scalability of the network ultimately requires a change in the protocol. The issue generated a long and heated debate (the so-called *scaling debate*), with different groups fighting over what would be the best way to allow for the Bitcoin network to process more transactions per second. Proposed solutions were to either increase the maximal size of a block or to provide news ways for a larger number of transactions to be settled into a block. In August 2017, inability to reach consensus as to the possible solutions to scalability resulted in a fork of the Bitcoin network into two separate networks: one increasing the block size limit from 1 to 8 MB (Bitcoin Cash) and the other implementing changes in the protocol to support scalability solutions such as the Lightning Network (through Segregated Witness modification). While the latter received vast support both before and after the fork, the Bitcoin scaling debate is, today, still an ongoing debate.

63 De Filippi and Loveluck, "The Invisible Politics of Bitcoin."

64 Shier et al., "Understanding a Revolutionary and Flawed Grand Experiment in Blockchain."

65 Quinn DuPont, "Experiments in Algorithmic Governance: A History and Ethnography of 'The DAO,' A Failed Decentralized Autonomous Organization," in *Bitcoin and Beyond (Open Access): Cryptocurrencies, Blockchains and Global Governance,* ed. Malcolm Campbell-Verduyn (London: Routledge, 2017), 157–77. Some actors from the Ethereum community attempted to gauge public opinion through a series of debates and discussions on online forums and social networks, largely led by the most prominent blockchain architects, software developers and early adopter in

became increasingly clear that the general consensus within the broader Ethereum community had converged towards the fork,[66] a new client was released with the relevant protocol changes and a specific activation schedule for the protocol change. While the fork was ultimately successful, the decision created significant controversy within the Ethereum community, which eventually led to the creation of an alternative version of the Ethereum network (*Ethereum Classic*) that still persists today.

These are just two examples of the difficulties encountered in the context of many blockchain-based networks when it comes to reaching consensus on issues related to changing the protocol or the infrastructure of these networks. Given the lack of a formalized governance structure, off-chain governance is generally much harder to achieve in a decentralized system than it is in the context of standard hierarchical systems. Moreover, because there are no formalized decision-making procedures in place, the system can easily be co-opted by established powers operating "behind the scenes."[67] As a result, there is often no transparency as to how decisions are made and little accountability as to who is responsible for their implementation.[68]

---

the Ethereum ecosystem. Others tried to refine their understanding about the degree of community support for the fork proposal via a more formal procedure mediated by an ad-hoc voting platform (CarbonVote) enabling Ethereum users to vote with their tokens.

66 Note that while the fork proposal was approved via CarbonVote by a significant majority (89% of the voters), this is not an accurate representation of the whole Ethereum community, because only a small percentage of Ether holders actually voted on the platform. Besides, even CarbonVote was only used as an informal signaling tool. Given the different stakeholders involved in the Ethereum community (each holding significantly different amounts of Ether), it is unclear whether the "one-Ether, one-vote" approach adopted in this case was the most appropriate tool to gauge public opinion.

67 De Filippi and Loveluck, "The Invisible Politics of Bitcoin."

68 Wessel Reijers, Iris Wuisman, Morshed Mannan, Primavera De Filippi, Christopher Wray, Vienna Rae-Looi, Angela Cubillos Vélez, and Liav Orgad, "Now the Code Runs Itself: On-Chain and Off-Chain Governance of Blockchain Technologies," *Topoi* (2018): 1–11.

Ultimately, these two models of governance — governance by the infrastructure through formalized market-based mechanisms, and *governance of the infrastructure* through a variety of ad-hoc decision-making mechanisms — significantly challenge the decentralized properties of existing blockchain-based networks. One the one hand, market-driven mechanisms are likely to lead to a centralization of power to those who engage in the accumulation of scarce resources. On the other hand, hidden power dynamics are likely to emerge from informal ad-hoc governance systems, characterized by a few (and sometimes concealed) "elite" members who can influence the system.[69] By removing the figure of the intermediary (e.g., the state or other centralized authority), these decentralized systems are providing new means for people to coordinate themselves in a distributed manner, but they are also foregoing the protective mechanisms that could ensure that these decentralized systems do not evolve, over time, into centralized or oligopolistic systems.

4. Blockchains for Digital Commons

Blockchain technologies were born and have grown at the confluence of various commons-based communities such as the frree and open source software movement and, more recently, the platform cooperativism movement.[70] The starting point, as noted above, was the public release of a white paper by the pseudonymous Satoshi Nakamoto presenting Bitcoin and its properties[71] — followed, a few months later, by the release of an open source implementation of the Bitcoin client[72]. Today, many

---

69 Jo Freeman, "The Tyranny of Structurelessness," *Berkeley Journal of Sociology* 17 (1972–73): 151–64.
70 Platform cooperativism is a movement tackling the limitation of the current sharing (i.e., micro-rental) economy by designing and offering alternative platforms owned and controlled by users. For more details, see Scholz, Platform Cooperativism.
71 Nakamoto, *Bitcoin*.
72 Bitcoin uses the MIT licence, available at https://github.com/bitcoin/bitcoin/blob/master/COPYING.

more blockchain-based projects have come into being, most of which are released under a free or an open source license. Yet, blockchain technology presents specific characteristics when compared to traditional open source projects. On the one hand, it offers a built-in incentivization system that rewards contributors for their participation in the network. One other hand, it provides the underlying infrastructure to incorporate specific governance rules into code, so as to manage community assets in a more automated and decentralized manner. This section will consider whether — and how — open source communities and other commons-based initiatives might benefit from these emergent technologies in order to support their operations and ensure their long-term sustainability.

4.a New Range of Economic Opportunities
The economic sustainability of common-based initiatives presents significant discrepancies, depending on their visibility, popularity and on the viability of their related business models.[73] While flagship projects — such as Linux and Mozilla Firefox[74] — receive reasonable amounts of funding, smaller projects or communities often lack mechanisms to compensate developers and contributors for their work. Because they are underfunded, these projects often fail to retain sufficient expertise to ensure the quality and maintenance of core Internet protocol

---

73 Brian Fitzgerald, "The Transformation of Open Source Software," *MIS Quarterly* 30, no. 3 (2006): 587–98.

74 The GNU/Linux project for instance is backed by a consortium of industry players (Linux Foundation 2015), while the Firefox browser received most of its funds from partnerships with search engines — mainly Google-then — which finance the development of the web browser in exchange for being listed as default choices for Internet search. Arrah-Marie Jo, "The Effect of Competition Intensity on Software Security: An Empirical Analysis of Security Patch Release on the Web Browser Market," *The Economics of Digitization: Proceedings of the 16th Annual Workshop on the Economics of Information Security*, 2017. This model is however precarious, as demonstrated by recent layoffs, see Mitchell Baker, "Readying for the Future at Mozilla," *The Mozilla Blog*, January 15, 2020, https://blog.mozilla.org/blog/2020/01/15/readying-for-the-future-at-mozilla/.

and related software.[75] In this section, we analyze how projects intend to leverage blockchain technology to offer new possibilities for funding and incentivizing users' contributions in commons-based projects.

As noted above, the Bitcoin network makes it possible for people to trade digital currency without passing through any intermediary operator. In order to ensure the long-term sustainability of the network, Bitcoin introduced the Proof-of-Work system that compensates users with digital currency proportionally to the utility they provide to the network. This inspired the design of many other blockchain-based networks, which all incorporate a similar incentivization scheme, using their own native digital currency to reward those who contribute resources to the network. As the value of these digital currencies is tied to the value of the services provided by the underlying blockchain-based platform, all network participants (including miners, developers, entrepreneurs, token holders, and speculators) have strong incentives to promote and enhance the utility of the platform.

Commons-based initiatives can leverage the characteristics of blockchain technology in order to sustain a growing community of contributors over time.[76] Indeed, by rewarding people with cryptocurrency and other blockchain-based tokens, commons-based initiatives have the opportunity to scale up and attract a larger pool of contributors — especially those who are not ideologically aligned with the underlying mission or objectives of the project, or who are not sufficiently satisfied with existing non-economic returns.

---

75 This is illustrated by the Heartbleed bug, a critical vulnerability found in 2014 in the Open SSL library which is at the core of securing most online communications.

76 Primavera De Filippi, "Translating Commons-Based Peer Production Values into Metrics: Toward Commons-Based Cryptocurrencies," in *Handbook of Digital Currency: Bitcoin, Innovation, Financial Instruments, and Big Data,* ed. David Lee Kuo Chuen (Amsterdam: Elsevier, 2015), 463–83.

For the sake of illustration, let us look at the various online platforms available for storing and sharing digital files. Up until now, users could either rely on centralized services provided by large cloud providers (like Dropbox or Google Drive) offering a basic service for free and requiring a premium for extra bandwidth or storage capacity; or they could participate in decentralized peer-to-peer networks (such as BitTorrent, for instance) without paying a fee[77] but without any guarantee as to the availability of their files. Projects such as the Inter-Planetary File System (IPFS)[78] offer an alternative solution for the storage and sharing of digital files in a secure and decentralized manner. IPFS is a peer-to-peer file system that comes with a specific incentivization system relying on a blockchain-based token (Filecoin) to reward network participants in proportion to the storage capacity they dedicate to the network. The system thus provides users with the possibility to pay extra in order to incentivize more network participants to host a specific file, thereby increasing the overall reliability of the system.

A similar model could be implemented, at a more generic level, to reward people who contribute value to a particular community, with specific digital currency or blockchain-based tokens that can be used to interact with that community.[79] While the value of these tokens might initially be very low, over time, as the community grows into a more structured project or initiative with an actual value proposition, early contributors can

---

77 Note that certain peer-to-peer applications actually require users to pay for the use of their software (e.g., Resilio).

78 IPFS is a decentralized file system whereby files are identified by their cryptographic hash and shared among participants in the network. Participants connected to the network can then retrieve files from any other participant using the hash as an address.

79 This is the case, for instance, with the Backfeed model, which relies on the notion of "Proof-of-Value" (as opposed to "Proof-of-Work") to reward people in proportion to the value they have brought to a particular community. For more details, see Alex Pazaitis, Primavera De Filippi, and Vasilis Kostakis, "Blockchain and Value Systems in the Sharing Economy: The Illustrative Case of Backfeed," *Technological Forecasting and Social Change* 125 (2017): 105–15.

spend these tokens in order to access the goods or services provided by the community, or — alternatively — they can sell these tokens on the secondary market, to whomever did not contribute to the community but would nonetheless like to access some of its goods and services. Such a model creates a positive incentive for people to contribute to a commons-based project on an ongoing basis because the more successful the project is, the greater utility (and value) these tokens will have.

However, despite the advantages that these models provide, one should be wary of the fact that, especially in the context of commons-based projects or initiatives, measuring and rewarding contributions can introduce biases in some of the participants' motivations. For instance, in most open source projects and peer-to-peer file-sharing networks, the motivations for users to contribute time and resources to these projects currently rely on non-monetary factors, mostly related to ideological values, social capital, or principles of reciprocity.[80] Indeed, for major commons-based initiatives like Wikipedia, Khan Academy, and Project Gutenberg, the lack of direct economic incentives does not actually hinder the success of the project. On the contrary, it could be argued that the introduction of market-driven mechanisms could actually jeopardize the established dynamics of peer-production, replacing them with an excessive degree of transactionality that might actually end up hindering, rather than supporting the long-term sustainability of the initiative.[81]

Even if one were to decide not to reward community members on a contribution basis, blockchain technologies can nonetheless be leveraged in order to raise the necessary funds to build and maintain a commons-based project or initiative. For instance, Bitcoin and its underlying blockchain protocol

---

80 Karim R. Lakhani and Robert G. Wolf, "Why Hackers Do What They Do: Understanding Motivation and Effort in Free/Open Source Software Projects," in *Perspectives on Free and Open Source Software,* eds. J. Feller, B. Fitzgerald, S. Hissam, and K.R. Lakhani (Cambridge: MIT Press, 2005).

81 Xiaoquan Zhang and Fen Zhu, "Intrinsic Motivation of Open Content Contributors: The Case of Wikipedia," *Workshop on Information Systems and Economics* 10 (January 2006): 4.

was originally developed and maintained by a small number of passionate developers, driven by an ideology — i.e., disrupting the current financial system — and by many of the same motivational drivers that characterize traditional open source software projects.[82] Over time, as the Bitcoin network has gained in popularity and adoption, the efforts of the initial contributors have been rewarded — albeit indirectly — through the appreciation in value of the Bitcoin digital currency. And because the value of Bitcoin is to a large extent correlated with the value of the Bitcoin network, token holders have an incentive to contribute to building or maintaining the network in order to increase its overall utility. [83]

The establishment of the token-sale model as a new funding mechanism emerged from the realization that, as a general rule, the digital tokens issued on a blockchain-based platform can be used as a means to fund the development and maintenance of that platform. Over the past years, a growing number of initiatives have been selling digital tokens or cryptocurrency to finance the development and growth of a particular blockchain-based platform or application. For instance, in July-August 2014, the Ethereum Foundation sold a large portion of the Ethereum native currency (Ether) in a public token sale, raising over USD 18 million worth of bitcoins at the time. The Foundation allocated the funds to a variety of people — including researchers, software developers, and marketers — in charge of ensuring the development, maintenance, and promotion of the Ethereum platform. Subsequently, the same model has been used by a large number of initiatives around the world, many of

---

82 Studies have identified various factors, but agree on the priority of non-monetary motivations such as a sense of creativity, intellectual stimulation, and learning. For more details, see: Lakhani and Wolf, "Why Hackers Do What They Do."

83 Recent projects have also adopted a similar soft launch such as Grin, an implementation of the Mimblewimble protocol, available at https://github.com/mimblewimble/grin/.

which have largely surpassed the amounts of traditional early-stage investment funding.[84]

The combination of token sales and internal incentivization systems offers interesting possibilities for bootstrapping, launching and sustaining the operations of certain commons-based platforms. While a token-based model is particularly suited to platforms managing scarce digital resources (such as digital currencies), it also applies in the context of collaborative platforms characterized by strong network effects, such as those coordinating individual workforce members, or managing the sharing of resources (such as flats, cars, or other personal items) amongst individual users. In these contexts, people can purchase digital tokens as a means to access specific resources, or they can share their resources within a community in order to earn tokens as a reward.

Nevertheless, despite these apparent benefits, financing a commons-based initiative through a token sale or by incentivizing contributors through the issuance of blockchain-based tokens presents several drawbacks in the long run. First — as opposed to the open source model adopted by many commons-based projects, which generally promote openness and inclusivity — *tokenization*[85] requires the adoption of an "exclusionary" model in order to assign an effective utility to the token. Second, many token sales rely on extensive marketing campaigns to increase the appeal of the project, creating strong expectations for the token holders with regard both to the future usability of the platform and to potential returns on investment — even if most of these projects are highly experimental, both technically

---

84 Perhaps the most notorious token sale sale was that of the DAO, launched in April 2016, which raised over USD 150 million's worth of ether in 28 days, making it the most successful crowdsale at the time. Among other examples, the Basic Attention Token (BAT) founded by Brendan Eich raised $35 million in a few seconds, Tezos raised $232 million, Bancor $153 million.

85 Tokenization refers to the process by which an ecosystem or a platform is organized to use a token, on a blockchain-based network, to exchange, measure, and store value.

and commercially.[86] Finally, the utility associated with these blockchain-based tokens might vary — ranging from profit or revenue sharing to specific governance or voting rights, in addition to the future ability to use these tokens to access a given product or service. Regardless of the economic model adopted, commons-based initiatives might thus be incentivized to promote market-driven dynamics, at the expense of their internal principles and ideological values.[87]

4.b New Tools for Commons-Based Governance

In order to succeed as a collaborative endeavor, commons-based platforms must come up with a specific governance model that accounts for the interests of all relevant stakeholders. Many commons-based projects and initiatives have established a set of social norms and community rules, mostly enforced as a result of individual stewardship, peer pressure, and other forms of social interaction. When the community grows beyond a certain point it becomes necessary to implement a more formalized governance structure, with a legal entity (e.g., a foundation) responsible for allocating resources and representing the community to the external world. While they are meant to serve the interests of all community members, such entities might end up prioritizing the interests of board members, eventually shifting the aims of the project and progressively losing community support.[88]

Moreover, centralized control over critical assets can impinge upon the values and long-term sustainability of many collaborative commons-based projects. Ownership of a particular website or domain name, access rights to a particular code repository in the case of open source software, or control over a publicly recognized brand or trademark, are all crucial to the proper operations of commons-based projects. Similarly, finan-

---

86 Indeed, a large majority of these projects are, at the time of the sale, more prototypes that serve an almost non-existent user base.

87 Arun Sundararajan, *The Sharing Economy: The End of Employment and the Rise of Crowd-based Capitalism* (Cambridge: MIT Press, 2016).

88 De Laat, "Governance of Open Source Software."

cial control over the way funds can be effectively disbursed plays a key role in the governance of these projects. Regardless of the governance structure adopted by each project, the party controlling these critical assets has the ability to leverage its position to increase its influence within the community.

One of the dangers associated with these elements of centralized governance is the risk of "corporate capture"[89] which might lead to a progressive "commodification" of the platforms[90] — as happened in the case of Couchsurfing after the non-profit organization was turned into a for-profit corporation.[91] A platform whose infrastructure relies on a decentralized blockchain-based network, with a clear on-chain and off-chain governance structure, could provide a solution to that problem, by ensuring that commons-based communities retain full control over the platforms they use. Indeed, because a blockchain-based platform is not owned or controlled by anyone, but is rather administered collectively by a distributed network of peers, the technology ensures that no one can take over control over these platforms after they have been deployed on a blockchain.

Another danger may stem from the inability to maintain a coherent and aligned vision within a community, leading to growing discontentment and potential opposition against the centralized authority managing a commons-based project. This could ultimately result in a "fork" — i.e., the community split-

---

89 Corporate capture generally refers to the means by which powerful economic actors exert undue influence over domestic and international decision-makers and public institutions. In this context, we refer to the situation in which market players might try to privatize a commons or influence the operations of existing commons-based initiatives, in order to bring them more in line with their commercial interests. For more details on the commodification of information commons, see Primavera De Filippi and Miguel S. Vieira, "The Commodification of Information Commons: The Case of Cloud Computing," *The Columbia Science and Technology Law Review* 16 (2014): 102–43.

90 Ibid.

91 Michel Bauwens, Nicolas Mendoza, and Franco Iacomella, *Synthetic Overview of the Collaborative Economy* (P2P Foundation, 2012), https://p2pfoundation.net/wp-content/uploads/2018/02/Synthetic-overview-of-the-collaborative-economy.pdf.

ting into two separate projects,[92] with a necessary reallocation of resources and assets between the two. Again, blockchain technologies could mitigate that risk by providing an open and shared infrastructure that anyone can use. As a result, even if the community were to disagree with a particular course of action, it could, for instance, trigger a vote or split into multiple communities operating according to their own value systems, but nonetheless interfacing with the same underlying technological platform.

As such, blockchain technologies create new opportunities for commons-based communities to experiment with new governance structures[93]. Indeed, although they require the contribution of multiple people to operate the network, blockchain-based platforms can be designed in a way that does not require an intermediary to manage the flow of contributions. By eliminating the need for any middleman, blockchain technology enables the creation of new community-driven blockchain-based organizations — commonly referred to as "decentralized collaborative organizations" — which are operated *by* the community and *for* the community and where every community member is simultaneously a contributor and an actual shareholder in the organization. While these organizations might be led by a charismatic leader in charge of stewardship of the organization, they are no longer subject to the whims of a benevolent dictator because they operate according to an infrastructure which is decentralized by design.[94]

---

92 While generally positive (*supra* note 29), forks are sometimes the result of a contentious issue or a simple failure in leadership. For instance, the OpenOffice project was forked — after having been neglected for a long time by Sun Microsystems and after having been repurchased by Oracle — to give birth to a new project (LibreOffice) built from the same code, and mostly with the same developers, but with an entirely different management structure.

93 Samer Hassan and Primavera De Filippi, "The Expansion of Algorithmic Governance: From Code Is Law to Law Is Code." *Field Actions Science Reports* 17 (2017): 88–90.

94 As opposed to traditional online platforms, which are managed and maintained by a centralized operator, decentralized blockchain-based

Yet, this is only a partial solution. While blockchain technology has strong potential, an important gap still needs to be filled to ensure the long-term sustainability of commons-based projects and initiatives. As described earlier, most of the decentralized blockchain-based applications deployed thus far ultimately rely on a series of distributed governance systems built around game-theoretical mechanisms and market-driven incentives. Due to the decentralization inherent in these systems — without an institution protecting them — they can be easily co-opted by established powers, accumulating the necessary resources (in terms of, for example, hashing power or tokens) to acquire more power and influence in the system. Major events and incidents such as the DAO's hack or the Bitcoin Cash fork also constitute an opportunity to reflect on the power mechanics resulting from the specific technical design of these decentralized infrastructures.

The blockchain ecosystem as a whole is currently exploring ways in which the governance of decentralized blockchain-based networks can be implemented in such a manner as to preclude the emergence of new intermediaries or centralized power dynamics. Yet, as the technology matures and spreads into the mainstream, the blockchain ecosystem is rapidly being occupied by small and large investors, speculators, and entrepreneurs — with very different interests and ideologies from the early adopters who belonged to the *cypherpunk* and *hacktivist* communities. In fact, rather than focusing on decentralization and disintermediation, these new players are mostly interested in capital accumulation and profit maximization. Hence, for

---

applications are both managed and maintained by a distributed network of peers, none of which has the ability to change or influence the operations of these blockchain-based systems, unless this is specifically provided for in the underlying protocol. Hence, by encoding a decentralized governance structure directly into the fabric of a blockchain-based system, it becomes difficult for any single party to unilaterally intervene in order to change the current and future operations thereof. See Sinclair Davidson, Primavera De Filippi, and Jason Potts, "Disrupting Governance: The New Institutional Economics of Distributed Ledger Technology," SSRN, July 22, 2016.

common-based projects or initiatives to thrive in this new environment, they need to experiment with alternative governance models that do not suffer from the same problems and drawbacks as many of the existing market-driven approaches.

We propose here a hybrid solution that might resolve some of the problems identified thus far. By combining a blockchain-based platform with existing instruments — such as institutional design, community-driven governance, and legal protections — common-based projects could leverage the power of blockchain technologies, while benefiting from the accumulated insights and experience of more traditional governance tools. Specifically, not only can blockchain-based networks support and facilitate the collective administration of any digital platform without a centralized point of control, they can also be used to create and manage a variety of activities or relationships that would otherwise require significant legal overhead. And because they already come with their own governance system, existing commons-based communities could transpose part of their current community rules and social norms into a set of code-based rules, incorporated directly into the underlying code of a blockchain-based applications. In doing so, they could shift some of their *off-chain* governance into a system of *on-chain* governance that is more transparent and no longer requires any third-party or centralized enforcement — because these rules are automatically enforced by the underlying technical infrastructure.[95]

Particularly relevant in this regard are the principles of *platform cooperativism*[96] for the establishment of collaborative plat-

---

95 On that point, it might be useful to distinguish between the governance of decentralized blockchain-based networks (usually governed through a Proof-of-Work or Proof-of-Stake protocol) and the governance of decentralized blockchain-based applications (or DApps) deployed on top of these platforms. Accordingly, while the underlying blockchain network might be governed through a series of market-driven mechanisms, the applications they run can feature their own governance models that operate according to completely different logics.

96 Those principle, as summarized by Scholz (in *Platform Cooperativism*), include participatory ownership, decent income and job security, transpar-

forms with more cooperative governance and more balanced revenue-sharing models than those currently adopted by many of the platforms of the "sharing economy." Shared ownership and democratic governance are, for instance, two key principles that are regarded as a prerequisite to ensure that everyone can reap the fruits of their own labor.[97] While their implementation might require extensive legal work and organizational overhead in a traditional context, both of these principles can be implemented through a blockchain-based platform that rewards contributors with tokens, decision-making power, and possibly even ownership rights in the platform.[98] Instead of relying on traditional legal means, and on the necessary processes that come along with them, the governance of these blockchain-based organizations could be done partially *on-chain,* through a transparent and self-executing system of rules. If properly designed, these systems could facilitate the move from the current crowdsourcing model, where large operators are in charge of a few centralized online platforms, towards a more cooperative model, where community members have a say in how these platforms should operate, and can benefit — in proportion to their individual contribution — from the economic returns generated by these platforms.

Yet, in order to operate properly, commons-based communities must retain the ability to rely on off-chain governance mechanisms for everything that cannot be properly transposed into code. First, organizations do not exist in a vacuum. While it might be possible to encode specific rules and regulations directly into a blockchain-based network, commons-based communities nonetheless need to interface with other organizations, market players and governmental institutions through off-chain interactions. Second, some norms require a particular degree of

---

ency and data portability, appreciation and acknowledgment of contributions, protective legal framework and worker protections against arbitrary behaviour, excessive workplace surveillance, and the right to log off.

97 Scholz, *Platform Cooperativism.*
98 Pazaitis, De Filippi, and Kostakis, "Blockchain and Value Systems in the Sharing Economy."

flexibility and ambiguity that cannot be provided by the formal language of code.[99] In particular, commons-based communities often need to account for a multiplicity of interests, promoting a particular vision of the general good while encouraging collaboration and trust among community members — none of which can be easily transposed into code. Lastly, as opposed to traditional blockchain-based networks, which are built around game-theoretical protocols and market-driven governance systems, commons-based communities also need to implement off-chain governance mechanisms necessary to preserve the coherence, values and long-term sustainability of the projects they support. Indeed, even if off-chain governance is, in many instances, much slower and more complicated to deal with than a system of automated on-chain code-based rules, it is almost always necessary to protect the system from external forces trying to use or bend the rules to their own advantage. In that regard, by delegating some of their off-chain governance to established institutions in the commons-based ecosystem (such as, for instance, the Free Software Foundation or the Mozilla Foundation), commons-based communities have been trying to ensure that no one can co-opt the system — whether from inside or outside the organization.

Hence, while blockchain technology provides the underlying architecture to decentralize the governance of many commons-based communities or platforms, the ultimate governance structure for these platforms should ideally include a mixture of on-chain governance rules (with regard to shared ownership and democratic governance) and off-chain protocols (with regard to institutional governance) to ensure the peaceful and orderly conduct of a large variety of commons-based projects or initiatives within the larger ecosystem.[100] Only then will it be

99 Primavera De Filippi and Samer Hassan, "Blockchain Technology as a Regulatory Technology: From Code Is Law to Law Is Code," *First Monday* 21, no. 12 (2016), https://firstmonday.org/article/view/7113/5657

100 Primavera De Filippi and Greg McMullen, "Governance of Blockchain Systems: Governance of and by the Infrastructure," HAL, February 22, 2019, https://hal.archives-ouvertes.fr/hal-02046787/document.

possible to build a more efficient, scalable, and resilient ecosystem that benefits from the best of both worlds: the transparency and accountability of decentralized blockchain-based systems on the one hand, and the flexibility, solidarity, and trust of social interactions and human collaboration on the other.

5. Conclusion

Over the years, the implementation of a global and decentralized telecommunication network has grown from a preliminary research project to become the main and most significant information system in the world. While the Internet, as a platform for permissionless innovation, has given rise to a great deal of innovation — in terms of information and communication technologies, novel economic models, and new mechanisms for social organization and coordination — the combination of market dynamics and network effects have led to a concentration of market power in the hands of a few operators, eventually turning the Internet into a network controlled and administered by a small number of incumbents.

Similarly, following the advent of Bitcoin in 2009, blockchain technology has enabled a new wave of innovation, empowering individuals and digital communities with an unprecedented tool for decentralized collaboration that comes along with built-in incentivization and reward mechanisms. While Bitcoin was created with the ambition of supplanting the current financial system, more generally, the decentralized nature of many blockchain-based applications has the potential to disrupt the business model of existing incumbents, both online and offline. Yet, most of the blockchain-based applications implemented thus far incorporate game theoretical protocols and market-driven incentives that actually exacerbate — rather than disrupt — existing dynamics of capital accumulation and speculation. The early, ideologically-driven individuals and communities that were originally responsible for building the blockchain ecosystem have thus progressively been supplanted by old and new market players, mostly driven by commercial gain and opportunistic motives.

Accordingly, it appears that, in the case of both the Internet and blockchain technology, recurring cycles of innovation have led to a temporary disruption in the status quo, only to replace it with a new set of incumbents that operate according to the same logics as before. Nevertheless, in addition to market-driven innovation, the Internet has also led to the emergence of radically new models of distributed production and collaboration — such as open source projects and other commons-based initiatives — operating according to a new set of principles and governance models, and which eventually succeeded in their desire to innovate beyond the current social and economic model.

In the same way, blockchain technology has enabled the emergence of new projects and initiatives designed around the principles of decentralization and disintermediation, providing a new platform for large-scale experimentation in the design of new economic and organizational structures. Yet, to be really transformative, these initiatives need to transcend the current models of protocol-based governance and game-theoretical incentives — which can easily be co-opted by powerful actors or lead to dissensus — and to come up with new governance models combining both *on-chain* and *off-chain* governance rules. The former can be used to support mechanisms of regulation by code, incentivization schemes and ownership over digital assets, whereas the latter are necessary to promote the vision, and facilitate the interaction of commons-based projects and initiatives with the existing legal and societal framework. Ultimately, whether or not blockchain technology will lead to the rise of a new economic order is not — solely — a technical matter; it is, first and foremost, a political question that requires an in-depth understanding of the social, economic, and political implications that different governance structures will bring to society.

8

Hacking the Law to Open Up Zones for Commoning

David Bollier

In recent years, the power and diversity of commoning in contemporary life has increased dramatically. Commoning is both an ancient and rediscovered social form that can be seen in the stewardship of forests, fisheries, and farmland, especially in subsistence and indigenous contexts. It lies at the heart of community land trusts, local currencies, mutual aid networks, and cohousing. It is embodied in community-supported agriculture, agroecology, and permaculture, and in digital spaces that produce open source software, hardware, and design. Commoning is at work in open access scholarly journals, crowdfunding tools, and platform cooperatives, and in academia, arts and culture, and many other realms.

Because commons are strongly inclined to respect ecological limits and devise fair-minded, flexible governance through inclusive participation, they hold great promise in dealing with many societal problems. However, commoning as a legal activity faces an uncertain future. Its practices and values are philosophically alien to many aspects of the liberal market and state and their mutual focus on individualism, calculative rationality, material gain, and market growth.[1] Commoning therefore has trouble gaining legal recognition and support. Indeed, the state is predisposed to ignore the commons, criminalize its activities, or exploit its resources in alliance with the business class.

The commons may be a pariah within the world of conventional politics because it challenges the foundational terms of ideological debate, which presumes that the market and state are ideological adversaries — the "private sector" battling the "public sector." This is a specious binary because market and state are in fact deeply interdependent and both subscribe to the grand narrative of "social progress through economic growth." The state looks to the market for economic growth, tax revenues, and social mobility for its citizens, while market players look to the state for a stable legal order, subsidies, state support and privileges, and the mitigation of market abuses (pollution, social disruption, inequality). State and market are so utterly symbiotic it is entirely warranted to speak about the *market/ state system*.[2]

From within this dominant worldview, it is almost a foregone conclusion that collective management of wealth would be seen as a "tragedy of the commons — " the over-exploitation and ruin of a resource.[3] To the guardians of the market/state, after all, individual agency and rights are supreme. Collective action is not perceived as feasible or attractive. By definition, human beings are defined as atomistic individuals, not as co-participants in

---

1   See, e.g., Patrick J. Deneen, *Why Liberalism Failed* (New Haven: Yale University Press, 2018).

2   For more on this theme, see, e.g., Neil Fligstein, *The Architecture of Markets: An Economic Sociology of Twenty-First-Century Capitalist Societies* (Princeton: Princeton University Press, 2001). See also David Bollier and Silke Helfrich, *Free, Fair and Alive: The Insurgent Power of the Commons* (Gabriola Island: New Society Publishers, 2019). I wish to thank my co-author Silke Helfrich for many of the ideas co-developed in this essay — and presented in our book *Free, Fair and Alive: The Insurgent Power of the Commons* — while stressing that I alone am responsible for the contents of this chapter.

3   Garrett Hardin, "The Tragedy of the Commons," *Science* 162, no. 13 (December 1968): 1243–45.

shared histories, cultures, interests, and values. When people are conceived of as "rational individuals" with boundless "incentives" to take as much as they can, it should not be surprising that heedless consumption and the reckless "externalization of costs" follows.[4]

Now, however, this convenient fiction is starting to fall apart. Critics are increasingly calling out the claim that a commons is simply a selfish free-for-all when, in fact, this scenario more accurately describes what we might call the *tragedy of the market*.[5] The commons is in fact a durable social form that orchestrates shared intentionality to steward wealth responsibly and inclusively over the long term. In a commons, people willingly negotiate rules of peer governance, resolve group conflicts, and enforce rules. They develop ways to pool and share (or divide up or mutualize) their collective wealth, without resort to a state Leviathan to maintain law, order, and personal safety.

Precisely because commoning is a stable, generative mode of governance and social organization, it represents a potentially disruptive alternative to the market/state system, whose dysfunctions are becoming more abundantly evident. As a social form, commoning does not have the same imperatives of market capitalism to maximize production, consumption, economic growth, and capital accumulation. Nor do commoners look primarily to liberal governance — centralized, hierarchical organizations, bureaucracies, amoral markets — to meet their needs. This is why they have been able to develop an astute perspective on the prevailing system. When they "withdraw" from market consumption — through, for example, their self-created software commons (Linux and scores of open source programs), healthier, more accountable local food markets (community

---

4   Margaret Stout, "Competing Ontologies: A Primer for Public Administration," *Public Administration Review* 72, no. 3 (May–June 2012): 388–98.

5   Among the critics of the "tragedy of the commons" fable are scholars associated with the International Association for the Study of Commons, members of the Degrowth movement, the Peer to Peer Foundation, and assorted activists and scholars working on commons-based projects for food, water, land, forests, fisheries, academia, and creative works.

supported agriculture, Slow Food, agroecology), and afford-able housing projects (community land trusts, co-housing, etc.) — they withdraw from the circuits of capitalism to create their own quasi-sovereign alternatives. Decommodifying access to essential resources and sharing the risks and benefits of self-provisioning are radical acts.

But as people attempt to grow the Commonsverse, a major challenge is imagining how law might affirmatively support commoning. Law in the modern liberal state is mostly geared to serve market priorities and norms through private property rights, legal privileges, state subsidies, and a prescriptive set of socio-legal identities such as "consumer," "producer," "business ex-ecutive," "investor." Given its deep institutional and legal com-mitments, we must ask whether modern states are truly capable of recognizing commoning in law, and in what forms.

In this essay, I wish to explore the tension between com-moning and modern state law, and suggest ways in which the two might become more functionally compatible. In the mid-term, the chief vehicle for reaching a *modus vivendi* will be crea-tive adaptations of existing law. I call these workarounds "legal hacks," a term that borrows from the world of software devel-opment, in which brilliant, eccentric programmers ("hackers") use whatever coding strategies are at hand to devise elegant so-lutions to difficult problems ("hacks").[6] Legal hacks have been proliferating in recent years as commoners discover that state legal institutions — legislatures, courts, regulatory bodies — are simply too closely aligned with corporate interests to offer genu-ine support to commons.[7] Hence the keen interest in some quar-ters in coming up with clever hacks of state law to protect the social practices of commoning.

---

6 Eric Raymond, *The New Hacker's Dictionary,* 3rd edn. (Cambridge: MIT Press, 1996).

7 See David Bollier's review of more than sixty legal hacks in "Reinventing Law for the Commons," *Heinrich Böll Stiftung,* September 4, 2015, https://www.boell.de/en/2015/09/04/reinventing-law-commons.

1. Commoning and the Problem with State Law

Let us start by unpacking the notion of *commoning*. Conventional economics and social sciences generally focus on *the commons,* the noun, not *commoning,* the verb. This reflects the prevailing epistemology of the standard economics and politics, which is focused on individual agents and the market exchange of goods and services. This worldview, obsessed as it is with market exchange, has only secondary concerns for human relationships, the inner wellbeing of people, care work, and the complex dynamics of ecosystems. The engine of market exchange, in short, is profoundly divorced from many realities of life itself. It is narrowly concerned with monetary transactions carried out via the price system, to which all else is considered peripheral.[8]

This helps explain why the commons has been mischaracterized for decades as an inventory of unowned resources. In a world of isolated, "utility-maximizing" individuals, *there is no social regime* for taking care of shared resources that we all depend upon. While the state throughout history has made game attempts to protect common wealth (as "public goods"),[9] the neoliberal economic regime has largely abandoned this commitment. "Private opulence and public squalor," in John Kenneth Galbraith's phrase, are the prevailing themes of policy and economics today. This is a natural outcome under free-market ideology, which usually regards public wealth as a free or under-leveraged resource whose value could be enhanced by converting it to market uses. The private appropriation and commodification of our shared wealth is seen as "progress" because value is purportedly maximized by expanding individual property rights and market activity. Given these premises, standard eco-

---

8   Karl Polanyi, *The Great Transformation* (Boston: Beacon Press, 1944).

9   Inge Kaul, Isabelle Grunberg, and Marc A. Stern, eds., *Global Public Goods: International Cooperation in the 21st Century* (Oxford: Oxford University Press, 1999); and Inge Kaul et al., eds., *Providing Global Public Goods: Managing Globalization* (Oxford: Oxford University Press, 2003).

nomics cannot help but conclude that commons (understood as unowned resources) are little more than "wastelands" awaiting the magic touch of the market.

Over the past ten to fifteen years, however, an emerging generation of activists and younger scholars has developed a very different narrative of the commons, with different ontological premises. They have rediscovered the commons as a *social system.* In open source software communities and community forests, for example, people realize that the heart of commoning consists of peer governance, provisioning, and social life.[10] Rather than assuming society is a libertarian free-for-all kept in check by a state Leviathan, commoners recognize the historical reality that self-organized institutions of cooperation can stymie free-riding and enclosure. This is the essential conclusion of Elinor Ostrom's landmark 1990 book, *Governing the Commons,* which painstakingly documents how human communities have created effective social institutions for the stewardship of shared wealth.[11] Ostrom won the Nobel Prize in Economic Sciences for this work in 2009.

Many scientists are increasingly concluding that the drama of making and maintaining commons has been a salient part of human evolution.[12] Even if the thought-categories and logic of modern economics cannot grasp this reality, history shows that commoning is something that human beings inevitably,

---

10 Bollier and Helfrich, *Free, Fair and Alive.*
11 Elinor Ostrom, *Governing the Commons: The Evolution of Institutions for Collective Action* (Cambridge: Cambridge University Press, 1990).
12 Samuel Bowles, *The Cooperative Species: Human Reciprocity and its Evolution* (Princeton: Princeton University Press, 2011); Martin A. Nowak, *Super Cooperators: Altruism, Evolution and Why We Need Each Other to Succeed* (New York: Free Press, 2011); David Sloan Wilson, *Does Altruism Exist? Culture, Genes and the Welfare of Others* (New Haven: Yale University Press, 2015); Yochai Benkler, *The Penguin and the Leviathan How Cooperation Triumphs over Self-Interest* (New York: Crown Business, 2011); Andreas Weber, *The Biology of Wonder: Aliveness, Feeling and the Metamorphosis of Science* (Gabriola Island: New Society Publishers, 2016).

irresistibly *do*.[13] While the culture of market industrialism and the modern state has eclipsed the very idea of the commons for nearly two centuries, the general social form remains remarkably persistent and alive. Its practices, ethical commitments, and traditions are still enacted by billions of people around the world, especially in subsistence and indigenous cultures. An estimated 2.5 billion people around the world manage about eight billion hectares of land through community-based ownership systems, according to the International Land Coalition,[14] and commons are pervasive in industrial countries of the North as well, even if they are not culturally visible.[15]

The ontological shift in understanding commons that is now underway — commons as social system, not as unowned resource — is significant because it helps reveal an important dimension of the commons that is widely overlooked. Commons are *alive* and *generative*. They are not an ideological abstraction. They are social vessels of lived experience that meet elemental human needs. Over generations, commoning manifests its own customary practices, social norms, and traditions. The ancient ways of indigenous peoples, the consensual agreements of wiki communities, the rules that people devise to manage a local currency — all are examples of socially grounded peer governance and provisioning. All are quasi-sovereign ways of meeting needs outside of the market and of state power. (There may be some

---

13 Thomas Widlok, *Anthropology and the Economy of Sharing* (New York: Routledge, 2017).

14 Fred Pearce, *Common Ground: Securing Land Rights and Safeguarding the Earth* (Land Rights Now, International Land Coalition, Oxfam, Rights + Resources, 2016). The report concludes: "Up to 2.5 billion people depend on indigenous and community lands, which make up over 50 percent of the land on the planet; they legally own just one-fifth. The remaining five billion hectares remain unprotected and vulnerable to land grabs from more powerful entities like governments and corporations."

15 See, e.g., David Bollier and Silke Helfrich, *Patterns of Commoning* (Amherst: Off the Common Books, 2014), http://www.patternsofcommoning. org and *The Wealth of the Commons* (Amherst: Levellers Press, 2012), http://www.wealthofthecommons.org

interaction with market and state, but mostly in minimal, transient ways.)

2. Commoning as Vernacular Law

In effect, commoning is itself a form of law because it serves to organize people into orderly wholes to achieve shared ends. People are able to generate consensual rules, practices, and ethical norms that preserve both shared wealth and the community. I call this form of law and governance *Vernacular Law,* taking a cue from social critic Ivan Illich who celebrated vernacular practice as a way to re-humanize people caught up in systems of institutional domination.[16]

Today, most forms of Vernacular Law have been eclipsed by positive law enacted by legislatures to serve the interests of capital and the market economy. Custom has little stature here. Intent on building globally integrated value-chains to enhance capital accumulation, the leaders of market capitalism regard Vernacular Law as a vestigial oddity, a bothersome "friction" impeding market efficiency and growth. Ecologically minded or locally committed behaviors are often seen as hostile to business interests, which is one reason why World Trade Organization treaties seek to supersede state, provincial, and local self-determination.[17] The mandarins of global trade regard the idea of subsidiarity — assigning authority at the lowest, most appropriate level in a system, or indeed, robust democratic sovereignty — as derailing the quest for a globally integrated system of commerce and law. (Not incidentally, it would also splinter and diminish corporate political influence over legislatures.)

---

16 See, e.g., Ivan Illich, *Medical Nemesis: The Expropriation of Health* (New York: Pantheon, 1976); *Deschooling Society* (1971; rpt. London: Marion Boyars Publishers, 2000); and *Tools for Conviviality* (1971; rpt. London: Marion Boyars Publishers, 2001). See also the chapter in this volume by Maywa Montenegro in which she mentions Illich.

17 Lori Wallach and Michelle Sforza, *Whose Trade Organization? Corporate Globalization and the Erosion of Democracy* (Washington: Public Citizen, 1999).

In the face of such realities, the idea that the commons can effect transformational change from within the market/state system may seem quixotic. After all, commoners are not a terribly well-organized or visible constituency, at least in the traditional political sense. Their influence in elections, political parties, policy, and law is barely discernible. However, the unappreciated power of commoning is its ability to incubate durable new forms of consciousness, culture, and (in time) political power.

In *The Human Condition,* Hannah Arendt wrote that power is something that "springs up between men when they act together and vanishes the moment they disperse."[18] By this reckoning, power arises whenever people come together and organize themselves, and so it is always capable of being "created" and expanded. In effect, that is what commoning does. It is a quasi-sovereign, living social organism that empowers people to know, act and be, in ways unknown to the market/state system. When a community builds and manages its own Wi-Fi system (Guifi.net in Barcelona), controls its coastal fishery through peer governance (Maine lobsterman), shares services with each other via a timebank (hundreds of places around the world), or uses a local currency to keep value within a community (scores of examples around the world), a meaningful shift in experience and consciousness occurs. People do not enact and reproduce their roles as consumers and producers, or even as state-focused citizens. They enter into commoning and its ethos, logic, and sense of inclusive fairness. Everyone who participates in commoning incrementally contributes to the growth of a different culture. A shared discourse makes shared intentionality more feasible.

This development has political implications over time because, in a world of commoning, people are quite emotionally attached to the "care-wealth" that they love and depend upon. They do not have relationships with commodities or resources, but with things that belong to them in a deeper sense: ancient

---

18   Hannah Arendt, *The Human Condition* (Chicago: University of Chicago Press, 1958), 200.

lands, beloved traditions, stable livelihoods, a sense of purpose and meaning. People's lives become somewhat more enmeshed with each other; new social circuits emerge and proliferate. The iron grip of capital recedes, if only a bit, as people recover a sense of the local, affective, and collective. Life becomes more relational, and not merely transactional. Commoning becomes an enactment of Thomas Berry's insight, "The universe is not a collection of objects, but a communion of subjects."[19] A sense of belonging and shared meaning emerges.

Commoners who manage their own fisheries, or contribute to open access scholarly journals, or steward scarce supplies of irrigation water, or participate in CSA farms, or contribute to mutual aid networks, tend to realize how their activities offer relief from the relentless demands of neoliberal capitalism. Many see the commons as counter-hegemonic, as McCarthy writes, because it asserts "collective ownership and rights against relentless privatization and commodification" and resists the "neoliberalization of nature."[20] Such ideas are not policy opinions; they are convictions based on personal experience.

Geographer Andreas J. Nightingale notes how Scottish fishermen who manage their fisheries have developed "nonrational subjectivities" that stand in stark contrast to the market-based "rationality" of state policymaking.[21] Working on small fishing vessels in the ocean is dangerous, difficult work, and so fishermen have learned the importance of cooperation and interdependence. Their lives are defined by "community obligations, the need to preserve kinship relationships [with fellow villagers], and an emotive attachment to the sea," writes Nightingale. Vernacular law is an attempt to validate and protect the "nonrational subjectivities" of local commoners. State law, by contrast,

---

19 Thomas Berry, *Evening Thoughts: Reflecting on Earth as a Sacred Community* (Berkeley: Counterpoint, 2015), 17.

20 James McCarthy, "Commons as Counterhegemonic Prospects," *Capitalism Nature Socialism* 16, no. 1 (2005): 9.

21 Andrea J. Nightingale, "Commons and Alternative Rationalities: Subjectivity, Emotion and the (Non)rational Commons," in Bollier and Helfrich, *Patterns of Commoning,* 297–308.

often attempts to use law to impose a very different worldview on people using rigid rules and coercion. The crude limitations of state law are especially evident in clashes with indigenous peoples. In her account of conflicts between Maori communities and the New Zealand state over how ocean fisheries shall be used, scholar Anne Salmond notes that disagreements are not really political, economic, or policy-based. They are ontological. She calls the decades of conflict over the proper uses of ocean spaces as "ontological collisions at sea."[22] Where the state sees extractive resources, the Maori see living systems and sacred beings.

One reason that Vernacular Law is so potentially powerful is because commoning reveals that power — which is presumed to inhere in state institutions and officials — really resides in all of us, if only we can organize the collective institutions, social practices, and shared language to sustain it. Power is revealed as more immanent than we may imagine it to be. As geographers J.K. Gibson-Graham memorably put it, "If to change ourselves is to change our worlds, and the relation is reciprocal, then the project of history making is never a distant one but always right here, on the borders of our sensing, thinking, feeling, moving bodies."[23] Commoning is significant in catalyzing and manifesting this inner awareness while building new archipelagos of proto-political power. One sees this in various transnational federations: diverse digital commoners that work loosely with each other (Creative Commons, free and open source software, open access scholarly publishing, open science, and more);[24] coordination among indigenous peoples worldwide (UN Working

---

22 Anne Salmond, "The Fountain of Fish: Ontological Collisions at Sea," in Bollier and Helfrich, *Patterrns of Commoning*, 309–29.

23 J.K. Gibson-Graham, *The End of Capitalism (As We Knew It): A Feminist Critique of Political Economy* (Minneapolis: University of Minnesota Press, 2006), xvi.

24 David Bollier, *Viral Spiral: How the Commoners Created a Digital Commons of Their Own* (New York: New Press, 2007).

Group on Indigenous Populations);[25] the global peasant-farmer network known as La Via Campesina; the Brazilian Landless Rural Worker Movement (known by its acronym MST);[26] the fledgling network of urban commoners, especially in European cities;[27] the Transition Town movement seeking to relocalize economies.[28]

While these movements often feel compelled to seek supportive, or at least non-threatening, policies from state power, their primary long-term goal is the exercise of Vernacular Law. This means having the capacity to function as living social organisms capable of addressing unique situational realities using flexible, self-determined practices. A vexing question arises for conventional law and commoners alike: Can law in its current forms can provide sufficient authority and "epistemological awareness" to help commoning flourish? Belgian scholar Serge Gutwirth explains the challenge:

> The commons demand a law that takes seriously the way they weave practices, sensibilities, modes of cooperation, vernacular habits, and interdependence into a local and self-sustainable, thus dynamic, whole… The commons demand an inductive topic and "becoming" law, rather than the one we know, which is abstract, axiomatic, deductive. The "law of the commons" would rather have case-law and customs, than legislation and "doctrine" as sources, since they [commons] generate their own law responding to the practical

---

25 Roxanne Dunbar-Ortiz, *An Indigenous Peoples' History of the United States* (Boston: Beacon Press, 2014).

26 Angus Lindsay Wright, *To Inherit the Earth: The Landless Movement and the Struggle for a New Brazil* (Oakland: Food First Books, 2003).

27 Shareable, *Sharing Cities: Activating Urban Commons* (San Francisco: Tides Center/Shareable, 2018).

28 Rob Hopkins, *The Transition Handbook: From Oil Dependency to Local Resilience* (Cambridge: UIT Cambridge Ltd., 2014). See also https://transitionnetwork.org.

constraints of the interdependence of those who are engaged in their becoming.[29]

Conventional law posits universal principles that are presumptively binding in all localities and circumstances. But Vernacular Law enacted by commons recognizes a great many behaviors and circumstances that are local, time-specific, and not capable of being generalized. It is precisely the imposition of a rough-hewn universal law designed to impose state priorities and power that commoners find objectionable.

3. Market/State Enclosures and the Necessity of Legal Hacks

As commoners chafe under the terms of the market/state order — and as the market/state itself aggressively expands its regime of individual property rights, market exchange, and the commodification of nature, social life, and beyond — state law is becoming an arena of intensified conflict. The trend is driven by global capitalism marching into the most remote corners of human and biophysical existence, often using new technologies. Nanomatter engineering, CRISPR genetic engineering of life, artificial intelligence, and data analytics that manipulate perception and behavior are among the tools being used to enlarge the imperium of the capitalist order, provoking social disruption and conflict in their wake. Enclosures are proceeding apace, too, through land grabbing, expansions of copyright and patent law, privatization of groundwater, plans to commercialize deep-sea minerals and the moon, and through corporate takeovers of the Internet infrastructure. Sometimes commoning is explicitly prohibited or criminalized, as we see with laws prohibiting seed sharing, information sharing, and music sampling. More typically, commoners find that their shared wealth — land, water,

---

29 Serge Gutwith and Isabelle Stengers, "The Law and the Commons," presentation at Third Global Thematic International Association for the Study of the Commons Conference on the Knowledge Commons, October 20–22, 2016.

forests, fisheries, genes, cultural heritage, and more — is simply seized by corporations, often with the full cooperation of the state.

An urgent practical question for commoners is how to stop enclosures and protect their commoning practices, if possible through law. *But can commoning be affirmatively protected via conventional state law while respecting the integrity of commoning as a post-capitalist social form?* Can Vernacular Law and modern law be artfully blended, if only as a makeshift venture?

The primary burden for imagining transformations along these lines will rest, as it always does, on the subaltern — in this case, on commoners. The guardians of the market/state order have little interest or expertise in exploring such change. Indeed, state power has a strong inclination to centralize and regularize control through bureaucratic systems and universal law, as political scientist James Scott has made clear:

> [T]he modern state, through its officials, attempts with varying success to create a terrain and a population with precisely those standardized characteristics that will be easiest to monitor, count, assess and manage. The utopian, immanent and continually frustrated goal of the modern state is to reduce the chaotic, disorderly, constantly changing social reality beneath it to something more closely resembling the administrative grid of its observation.[30]

While there is affirmative value in regularizing many aspects of a society, a state armed with digital surveillance technologies and bureaucratic systems can also assert far-reaching, authoritarian control over its population. Law is, of course, a vital instrument in this agenda.

But here we face a problem. Modern law is not equipped to recognize the role of customary practice or collective choices,

---

30 James C. Scott, *Seeing Like a State: How Certain Schemes to Improve the Human Condition Have Failed* (New Haven: Yale University Press, 1998), 81–82.

especially in the face of positive law. Nor are there any means for the state to "attribute rights to dynamic collectives without legal personalities," in Serge Gutwirth's words. Nor are there legal concepts or analytic traditions that can recognize commoning on its own terms.[31] As Gutwirth elaborates:

> Today there exists no right that can or could meet the needs of a collective that is characterized by "generative commoning," neither is it thinkable to consider the commoning practice as the source of the emergence and institutions of an entitlement that would protect the commoners as a collective against the claims of other rights holders (such as owners/proprietors), not even in terms of proportionality. So, what should be done in legal terms in order to protect and stimulate the culture of the collective intelligence that learns to detect and take into account, the consequences of one's activity for the others, for the commons?[32]

There is yet another issue, which has less to do with legal pragmatics than with state power itself. The state has a keen interest in asserting the supremacy of its terms of *legality* over and against the *legitimacy* of alternative orders claimed by commoners.[33] Political and corporate elites use state power — which includes formal law, bureaucratic rules, and jurisprudence — to fortify a market/state system around which their lives revolve. The guardians of state power, understandably, have a big stake in defending legality. They have far less interest in the vernacular norms, practices, and experiences of ordinary people that embody a different vision of "law." Commoners may not have legality on their side, but they often command a great deal of street cred.

---

31 Gutwith and Stengers, "The Law and the Commons."

32 Ibid.

33 This distinction was brought to my attention by Étienne Le Roy, who writes about it in "How I Have Been Conducting Research on the Commons for Thirty Years Without Knowing It," in Bollier and Helfrich, *Patterns of Commoning*, 277–96.

The discrepancy between legality and legitimacy is the space of vulnerability that holds opportunities for counter-hegemonic legal strategies, or legal hacks. Creative legal draftsmanship can often repurpose state law in ways not originally imagined or intended by lawmakers. The attempt to use law to serve different, unanticipated ends is not just a matter confined to the legal universe. The point is to hack out a new zone of legality from within existing law, and then to fill that zone with social and political action. This can leverage popular legitimacy and community practice to establish a "new legality." The remainder of this chapter will review several examples.

4. Creative Hacks on Copyright Law: Two Iconic Successes

Perhaps it is helpful to start with two of the most seminal and effective legal hacks in recent history — the General Public License (GPL) for software[34] and six Creative Commons (CC) licenses for digital and other content.[35] Copyright law is intended to privatize control over all creative works and information, based on the premise that would-be creators need the incentive of monopoly control over their work in order to produce in the first place and earn revenue. These two legal hacks, the GPL and CC licenses, dramatically reverse the intentions of copyright law by making works legally shareable in perpetuity, without any permission or payment required. The copyright holder merely affixes the license notice to his or her work (software code, music, text, etc.), which thereby grants formal legal permission to anyone to copy, re-use, modify, and share a work under the terms specified by the license.[36] Both of these hacks, instigated by Richard Stallman

---

34 GNU General Public License, https://www.gnu.org/licenses/gpl-3.0.en.html (GNU is the name of the project sponsored by the Free Software Foundation that issued the GPL). For a history of the GPL, see *Wikipedia*, s.v. "GNU General Public License," https://en.wikipedia.org/wiki/GNU_General_Public_License.

35 Creative Commons licenses, https://creativecommons.org/licenses.

36 For a history of the development of the Creative Commons licenses, see Bollier, *Viral Spiral.*

of the Free Software Foundation and Professor Lawrence Lessig and a merry band of legal scholars and activists, represent bold private hacks on a well-established legal form.

The introduction of the GPL in 1985 (and more significantly, its second iteration in 1991) and the CC licenses in 2004 has had an enormous impact in legalizing the sharing of works. Both have empowered people to share their works with the general public without having to pay the costs that cash-hungry market gatekeepers (such as publishers, broadcasters, or film studios) levy on creators. The licenses arrived just as network effects were becoming a significant marketplace and cultural phenomena. This is the idea, barely understood in the early 2000s, that making works freely available on open networks greatly *enhances* their value, rather than diminishing it. One wag, channeling Oscar Wilde, observed, "The only thing worse than being sampled on the Internet is not being sampled."[37]

The GPL gave rise to a burgeoning world of free software (meaning "freely available," not necessarily no-cost). In time, the GPL inspired the birth of a cousin, open source software, based on similar licenses that have revolutionized software development by decommodifying a central resource of the trade. The Linux computer operating system emerged out of nowhere to compete with proprietary systems like Windows, and countless open source programs have become the engines powering the Internet and digital marketplaces.

As for the CC licenses, they initially spurred a burgeoning video mashup and music remix scene, and went on to catalyze the rise of more than 12,000 open access scholarly journals,[38] the open educational resources (OER) movement,[39] open data

---

37 A classic text explaining the dynamics of network effects is Yochai Ben-kler's *The Wealth of Networks: How Social Production Transforms Markets and Freedom* (New Haven: Yale University Press, 2006).

38 The Directory of Open Access Journals listed 12,440 open access journals on January 9, 2019, containing more than 3.6 million articles, http://www.doaj.org.

39 See the OER Commons website, https://www.oercommons.org.

initiatives,[40] and open textbooks,[41] among many other projects to make knowledge more accessible. An estimated 1.4 billion works worldwide used the CC licenses in 2017, providing an enormous pool of legally shareable books, reports, Web content, photos, videos, music, and more.[42] Behind all this "open content," and not necessarily seen, are thousands of commoners engaging in a mode of provisioning known as "commons-based peer production."[43]

While the impact of the GPL and CC licenses has been enormous, the actual impact of legal hacks is variable and unpredictable. Some attempts fizzle, perhaps because they are not truly defensible in courts; others may have negligible impact because as a practical matter they may not attract people to participate in new zones of commoning. That said, many artfully designed and well-timed legal hacks do end up unleashing powerful social energies and even forge movements. One might say that the "master's tools" *can* be used to dismantle the master's house, at least in the sense that they may trigger a dynamic dialectic between law and social action. The jolts of new possibility caused by legal hacks may attract new players to a scene, induce creative experimentation, or in other ways open up new affordances for change. Consider how the fairly prosaic legal innovation of CC licenses have brought legal sharing to a variety of unexpected corners, including major websites such as Google Images, YouTube, Flickr, Wikimedia Commons, Jamendo, and Europeana.

The short history of the GPL and CC licenses is instructive in showing how, even though a legal hack may not effect a legal revolution or transform capitalism, it may nonetheless propel transformational behaviors. In the early 2000s, some left-

40 SPARC (Scholarly Publishing and Academic Resources Coalition), "Open Data," https://sparcopen.org/open-data/.

41 Open Textbook Network, https://research.cehd.umn.edu/otn.

42 Creative Commons, "State of the Commons 2017" report, https://stateof.creativecommons.org.

43 The term was coined by Yochai Benkler, author of *The Wealth of Networks*. See also *Wikipedia*, s.v. "Commons-based peer production," https://en.wikipedia.org/wiki/Commons-based_peer_production.

ists criticized the CC licenses as mere reformism because the licenses are based on capitalist property law (copyright). Yet the licenses' greatest impact may have been outside of the law, in building a diversified social, academic, and cultural movement based on everyday sharing practices. The true significance of legal hacks may lie in their capacity to facilitate social action and movements. That is no small thing when commoners, immured within a stifling market/state order, have few options but to play the cards they are dealt. Improvisation and opportunistic brilliance make the most of necessity. Progress does not proceed along straight lines, but from zigs and zags through an uncharted frontier. Sometimes the results are impressive.

5. Legal Hacks as a Strategy for Social Change

It may be premature to try to theorize about the dynamics of legal hacks or to develop a coherent typology of them. Part of the point is that unpredictable experience, not theory or other regularities, drives the process. It is not always clear when legal feasibility will intersect with social need and interest, nor how special circumstances and individual leadership may prove critical. Furthermore, the actual significance of a legal hack may not initially be known, and *post hoc* assessments may be skewed as well. The CC licenses are now so widely accepted and commonplace that an Internet user in 2019 might never realize that it took a heroic mobilization of law scholars and activists in the early 2000s to develop and popularize the then-daring idea.

With these caveats in mind, I wish to introduce other legal hacks to suggest the breadth of possibilities. I focus on three general areas — catalyzing new social norms, innovative organizational forms, and commons/public partnerships — which constitute a small subset of the areas for which legal hacks are being invented.[44]

---

44 Other areas include cooperative law, stakeholder trusts, urban commons, platform cooperatives, digital ledger technologies that enable "smart con-

5.1 Catalyzing New Social Norms

The GPL and CC licenses are clearly prime instances of using a legal hack to validate and popularize new social norms. There are others worth mentioning. The Open Source Seed Initiative (OSSI) — launched by a number of farmers, seed breeders, and others — clearly attempts to emulate the free licenses used by free and open source software. The OSSI license gives a user the right to share the seed and any future derivations so long as the user makes them available for public use. (A fuller description of the OSSI, by Maywa Montenegro, can be found in Chapter 7.) This license is a significant legal hack because it challenges the standard industry practice of locking up seeds through patents and subjecting their genetic information and use to restrictive proprietary licenses.

As Montenegro explains, a companion effort by like-minded farmers and seed breeders has chosen to eschew patent licensing and instead use a quasi-legal pledge to "ensure that germplasm can be freely exchanged now and into the future."[45] As Montenegro explains, the pledge abandons the putative power of formal law — legality — and boldly embraces moral suasion, normative practice, and public shaming as the best way to protect seeds from enclosure. In other words, commoning, not state law, is seen as the more practical, powerful tool. According to seed activist Jack Kloppenberg, "The Pledge is much simpler and much more powerful as a discursive tool [...]. The license approach is cumbersome [and] over-legalized in our view."[46]

The Community Environmental Legal Defense Fund (CELDF), based in Pennsylvania, has pioneered a fascinating strategy to use local ordinances to change social and political views.[47] Its general approach is to use municipal ordinances,

---

tracts," commons charters, and bold reinterpretations of the public-trust doctrine to force government action to combat climate change.

45 Claire H. Luby et al., "Enhancing Freedom to Operate for Plant Breeders and Farmers through Open Source Plant Breeding," *Crop Science* 55, no. 6 (2015): 2481.

46 Kloppenburg interview, December 7, 2016.

47 See Community Environmental Legal Defense Fund, https://celdf.org.

home-rule charters, and other legal strategies to preserve local governance over things that matter to the community. CELDF has, for example, helped communities enact local ordinances that recognize the "rights of nature," prohibit fracking, and ban big-box retailers Even though courts at the state and federal levels are unlikely to uphold many of these legal gambits, CELDF apparently sees them as a powerful way to provoke potential test cases and call into question the moral and political credibility of state law.

5.2 Organizational Forms

Within the framework of law that governs corporations, cooperatives, and nonprofits, for example, there is often sufficient leeway to develop legal regimes that are hospitable to commoning as a dynamic, evolving social form. One of the pioneering explorers of new possibilities is Janelle Orsi, founder of the Sustainable Economies Law Center, in Oakland, California. The SELC specializes in developing innovative governance regimes for cooperatives, digital communities, land trusts, shared housing, and other commons.[48] By changing the bylaws and financial structures governing cooperatives, for example, Orsi and her team attempts to build movement cooperatives, not just consumer cooperatives; decentralized organizations designed to grow from the grassroots; self-managed staff collectives; and permanent community ownership.[49] To enhance this process, SELC makes the boring, arcane aspects of organizational bylaws more accessible through plain English, cartoons, and diagrams. While such legal hacks may not sound dramatic, they are a frontier in rethinking organizational governance. They have also

---

48 Janelle Orsi, *Practicing Law in the Sharing Economy: Helping Build Cooperatives, Social Enterprise, and Local Sustainable Economies* (Chicago: ABA Publishing, 2012).

49 Janelle Orsi, "Legal Structures for Social Transformation," Sustainable Economies Law Center, January 18, 2019, https://www.theselc.org/transformativestructures. Among the organizations that have pioneered new bylaws are the East Bay Permanent Real Estate Collective, People Power Solar Cooperatives, and Loconomics.

started to raise ambitions for enlarging the scope of democratic peer governance.

One of the most creative uses of organizational forms to protect commoning may be the Indigenous Biocultural Heritage Area, or Potato Park, created by indigenous Quechua people of Peru. This is a *sui generis* legal regime that authorizes the Quechua to act as stewards of the unique biodiversity of the region, which features more than 900 different types of native potatoes.[50] By having a legal instrument that can be recognized by Peruvian courts to protect the agrobiodiversity of some 12,000 hectares, the Quechua have greater assurance that they can live in their ancient ways, in intimate reciprocal relationship with the land, each other, and the spirit world.[51] Equally important, the Quechua's legal protections help them protect their ancient commons against ag-biotech companies that wish to appropriate and patent the genetic information of rare varieties of potatoes.

5.3 Commons/public Partnerships

A favorite scheme for many neoliberal politicians is to create public/private partnerships, or PPPs, that attempt to address pressing social problems through businesses/government collaboration in building infrastructure, providing services and so forth. However, many PPPs amount to little more than disguised giveaways. The state showers generous sums on companies that take on traditional state functions such as running prisons, healthcare systems, and schools, or they buy the right to privatize revenues generated by public infrastructures such as tollroads, bridges, and parking garages.

---

50 David Bollier, "The Potato Park of Peru," in Bollier and Helfrich, *Patterns of Commoning*, 103–7.

51 The Potato Park does not have state recognition within either Peruvian national law or the International Union for the Conservation of Nature, but the IBCHA agreement is nonetheless legally compatible with existing systems of national and international law. In this respect, it provides some measure of legal protection bolstered by the moral claims of historical, traditional use rights. For more, see Bollier, "The Potato Park of Peru."

A clever twist on the public/private partnership is the *commons/public partnership* in which commoners act as working partners with municipal governments in tackling important needs. An early example of this is the Bologna Regulation for the Care and Regeneration of Urban Commons. This initiative of the municipal government of Bologna, Italy, established a system whereby the city bureaucracy provides legal, financial, and technical support to projects initiated by commoners. These projects have included the management of eldercare centers, kindergartens, and public spaces as well as rehabilitating abandoned buildings. The Bologna Regulation — developed by the Italian think tank LabGov — has evolved into the Co-City Protocols, a methodology for guiding co-governance initiatives.[52] The protocols are based on five design principles: "collective governance, enabling state, pooling economies, experimentalism, and technological justice."

The point of the Co-City Protocols as a legal innovation is to leap beyond the known limitations of bureaucratic administration and leverage the social and creative energies of commoning. Numerous cities in Italy have adopted the Protocols as a way to rethink and enlarge the relationship between city bureaucracies and residents. It is an insight that the City of Ghent, Belgium, has taken to heart as well. In 2017, it commissioned an intensive study of scores of commons-based projects within its borders. It wanted to learn how it might augment the work of a neighborhood-managed church building, a renewable energy coop, and a temporary urban commons lab that provides space to many community projects.[53] Any commons/public partner-

---

52 The protocols are based on "field-experiments designed, analyzed and interpreted by LabGov in several Italian cities, together with 200+ global case studies and indepth investigations run in more than 100 cities from different geopolitical contexts." See https://labgov.city/co-city-protocol.

53 Michel Bauwens, "A Commons Transition Plan for the City of Ghent," *P2P Foundation,* September 14, 2017, https://blog.p2pfoundation.net/a-commons-transition-plan-for-the-city-of-ghent/2017/09/14. Full report, in Dutch: Michel Bauwens and Yurek Onzia, "Commons Transitie Plan voor de stad Gent" (Commons Transition, June 2017), https://cdn8-blog.p2pfoundation.net/wp-content/uploads/Commons-transitieplan.pdf.

ships that result are likely to require legal hacks to define the shifting contours of state collaboration with commons.

6. Conclusion

The future impact of legal hacks in empowering commons and transforming state power remains an open question. Much will depend upon the beleaguered fortunes of the market/state system in the years ahead as well as on the tenacity of commoners in pressing for new modes of governance and provisioning. Still, as a mid-term strategy that seizes available opportunities to decriminalize commoning and create protected spaces for it, legal hacks are an important, promising tool. They can exploit state legality in unexpected ways to open new zones for commoning. And they can disrupt the inertia and staid thinking that so often afflicts mainstream political life, policymaking, and progressive activism.

Legal hacks stand as a way to revivify Vernacular Law, giving it standing and impact. This has great appeal in its own right. While legal hacks remain fairly rare and underdeveloped, they open up attractive ways for people to gain greater direct control over important aspects of their lives. They help people insulate themselves from the predatory forces of capital-driven markets. And hacks may also serve to weaken the influence of unaccountable state power, which indirectly helps strengthen democratic sovereignty.

Finally, legal hacks begin a process to bridge the chasm that separates state legality and vernacular legitimacy. At this point it is unclear where such a process might lead, and how rapidly. But legal hacks can be effective strategies for changing the exercise of state power, making it more supportive of commoning.

9

Thinking Law, Ecology, and the Commons

Vito De Lucia

1. Introduction

The commons have (re-)emerged in recent years as a rich and hopeful horizon of practices attempting to resist the increasing encroachment of capitalist modernity on natural ecosystems and communities. Recent literature identifies the commons as both a space of embodied political resistance against neoliberal (en)closures[1] and as a space of productive theoretical engagement for rethinking law with and through ecology.[2] Yet there are mul-

---

1   Ugo Mattei, *Beni Comuni. Un Manifesto* (Bari: Laterza, 2011); Maria Rosaria Marella, ed., *Oltre il Pubblico e il Privato. Per un Diritto dei Beni Comuni* (Bologna: Ombre Corte, 2012); Vito De Lucia, "Law as Insurgent Critique: The Perspective of the Commons in Italy," *Critical Legal Thinking*, August 5, 2013, http://criticallegalthinking.com/2013/08/05/law-as-insurgent-critique-the-perspective-of-the-commons-in-italy/.

2   Burns Weston and David Bollier, *Green Governance: Ecological Survival, Human Rights and the Law of the Commons* (Cambridge: Cambridge University Press, 2013); Fritjof Capra and Ugo Mattei, *The Ecology of Law. Toward a Legal System in Tune with Nature and Community* (Oakland: Berret-Koehler, 2015); Saki Bailey, Gilda Farrell, and Ugo Mattei, eds., *Protecting Future Generations through Commons,* Trends in Social Cohesion 26 (Council of Europe, 2014); Vito De Lucia, "Re-Embodying Law: Trans-

tiple epistemic and ontological ways to approach the commons, and it is not always entirely clear whether traditional commons[3] and new commons[4] occupy the same conceptual, epistemic, and legal horizon, and whether the commons have some innate ecological inclination or, like any other institutions, may align with a diverse array of political ecological projects. Additionally, it is equally unclear whether ecology is in fact capable of fueling a renovated engagement with law, given its "moral ambivalence,"[5] and the "alchemic"[6] as well as genealogical[7] complexities of its use towards different, and even conflicting ethical, political, and legal projects.

In this chapter, I engage precisely with the conceptual triangle formed by the commons, ecology, and law. The commons, as already tentatively outlined elsewhere,[8] are a suitable nexus for thinking law and ecology together in a manner that resists the prevailing narratives.[9] The commons, importantly for the purposes of this chapter, offers an institutional articulation of a responsive, and thus responsible, practice.[10] It acknowledges that technological progress — or the enticing promise it offers — cannot circumvent the reality that ecological catastrophe

versal Ecology and the Commons," in *Contributions to Law, Philosophy and Ecology: Exploring Re-Embodiments,* eds. Ruth Thomas-Pellicer, Vito De Lucia, and Sian Sullivan (Abingdon: Routledge, 2016), 161–91.

3   Peter Linebaugh, *The Magna Carta Manifesto. Liberties and Commons for All* (Berkeley: University of California Press, 2008).

4   Weston and Bollier, *Green Governance*; Marella, *Oltre il Pubblico e il Privato.*

5   Donald Worster, *Nature's Economy: The Roots of Ecology,* 2nd edn. (Cambridge: Cambridge University Press, 1994), 256.

6   Kevin deLaplante, "Environmental Alchemy: How to Turn Ecological Science into Ecological Philosophy," *Environmental Ethics* 26, no. 4 (2004): 361–80.

7   De Lucia, "Re-Embodying Law."

8   Ibid.

9   Such as that of sustainable development.

10 On responsive and responsible knowledge, see Lorraine Code, *Ecological Thinking: The Politics of Epistemic Location* (Oxford: Oxford University Press, 2006).

always remains a possibility,[11] if it is not already a reality.[12] In this respect, the practices of the commons, of necessity, remain on a tentative ontological terrain, embracing a relational and iterative methodology that responds to complexity, uncertainty, and the circumstances inherent in the realities and necessities of "epistemic location."[13] This dynamic relation forms the basis for understanding nature, both materially and legally, not as an object, thus rejecting the Cartesian view of nature as objectified *res extensa,* nor as a subject, thus rejecting (or at least problematizing) the transposition to nature of the logic of rights.[14] Nature, from the perspective of commoners, is not an inert biophysical object but a co-participant in a set of collaborative *relations.*[15] In these relations, humans have a crucial role. However, the prevailing ontology maintains a problematic division between what is natural and what is artificial. The perspective of the commons

---

11 This is a consideration that transposed onto the ecological plane Vico's general historical method of the "corsi e ricorsi," that is, of the circularity of history, on which, see, e.g., Roberto Esposito, *Living Thought: The Origins and Actuality of Italian Philosophy* (Stanford: Stanford University Press, 2012).

12 IPCC, *Special Report: Global Warming of 1.5 °C, Summary for Policymakers,* 2018, https://www.ipcc.ch/sr15/chapter/spm/; Francisco Sánchez-Bayoa and Kris Wyckhuys, "Worldwide Decline of the Entomofauna: A Review of Its Drivers," *Biological Conservation* 232 (2019): 8–27.

13 Code, *Ecological Thinking.*

14 In this respect see, e.g., Anne Louise Schillmoller and Alessandro Pelizzon, "Mapping the Terrain of Earth Jurisprudence: Landscape, Thresholds and Horizons," *Environmental and Earth Law Journal* 3, no. 1, (2013): 1–32, as well as De Lucia, "Law as Insurgent Critique" and Vito De Lucia, "Ocean Commons, Law of the Sea and Rights for the Sea," *Canadian Journal of Law and Jurisprudence* 32, no. 1 (2019): 45–57.

15 See, e.g., MariaChiara Tallacchini, *Diritto per la Natura. Ecologia e Filosofia del Diritto* (Turin: Giappichelli Editore, 1996) and François Ost, *La natura hors la loi. L'écologie à l'épreuve du droit* (Paris: La Découverte, 2003). They both speak of nature as an iterative project, and their ideas inspire my thinking. However, the terminology they use resonates too much with a master perspective where nature is directed, molded, and programmed, whereas I wish to emphasize the relational horizon that, while certainly asymmetrical, remains on a relational terrain that entails exchange, mutual shaping, etc., rather than the mobilization of resources towards a goal, as in a project.

offers, I argue, an alternative framing that integrates the two into an organic whole.

This chapter, it should be clear at the outset, is an exploration, and offers the reader no coherent framework, no complete theory, but only some reflections that reflect provisional, incomplete thinking.[16] The chapter will touch upon a number of arguably important aspects for thinking law beyond Law, where Law with a capital L is set to represent legal modernity, with its contingent (indeed genealogical) pedigree, yet universal aspirations.[17] In section 2, I will reflect on the notions of ecological thinking and epistemic location, two key insights drawn from the work of Lorraine Code, to which I add a transversal dimension, drawing out an intuition already present in Code's work, and more explicitly in Guattari's work on "three ecologies."

In section 3, I will try to locate the commons, which I will ultimately approach as a complex assemblage that exceeds, though without exhausting, any particular point of view. Thus, I will highlight key aspects that resonate with a transversal ecological mode of thinking, and arguably facilitate a way of thinking about law differently. In section 4, I further suggest that the commons do not operate according to a universal logic of ethics, but rather conform to *ethos* (a concept strongly linked to inhabiting a particular place) precisely because the commons *constitutively inhabit* a place, and their responsive and responsible normative texture — key elements of both transversal ecological thinking and of epistemic location — emerges from that very inhabiting. Subsequently, I briefly look at the ways in which the commons internalize the temporal dimension normatively, through the idea of plurigenerationality. In section 6, I try to bring together these ideas through some legal reflections that can accommodate the advantages of ecology as a mode of thinking — and of thinking law — through the lens of the commons,

---

16 See Esposito, *Living Thought.*

17 For an outline of the key features of legal modernity, of its thresholds and of its disembodied character, see, e.g., De Lucia, "Re-Embodying Law," and Vito De Lucia "Semantics of Chaos: Law, Modernity and the Commons," *Pólemos: Journal of Law, Literature and Culture* 12, no. 2 (2018): 393–414.

by way of further drawing out ideas already provisionally outlined elsewhere.[18] Finally, I present some final remarks, and raise some questions with respect to what limits the commons may have as a framework for thinking law and ecology together.

2. Transversal Ecological Thinking and Epistemic Location

We live in a time of ecological emergency. Unfolding ecological crises intersect and overlap at multiple scales and across multiple domains.[19] The devastating effects of human industrial presence on the planet are now painfully inscribed on the planetary body at the sedimentary and geological level.[20] Ecology, in this context, has acquired a central role. It is an important field of (scientific) knowledge, as it allows understanding of how ecosystems work, and allows and legitimates human interventions towards the conservation of nature.[21] Ecology, though, also represents an important philosophical horizon due to its capacity to fundamentally problematize the categories of (legal) moder-

---

18 De Lucia, "Re-Embodying Law."
19 See, e.g., Millennium Ecosystem Assessment, *Ecosystems and Human Well-being: Synthesis* (Washington, DC: Island Press, 2005); Stuart Butchart et al., "Global Biodiversity: Indicators of Recent Declines," *Science* 328, no. 5982 (2010): 1164–68; FAO, *State of the World's Forest,* 2011, http://www.fao.org/state-of-forests/en; UNEP, *The Fifth Global Environment Outlook, GEO-5: Environment for the Future We Want* (DEW/1417/NA, 2012); World Ocean Review, *The Future of Fish: The Fisheries of the Future* (Maribus, 2013); David Azoulay et al., "Plastic and Health: The Hidden Costs of a Plastic Planet," *Center for International Environmental Law,* 2019, https://www.ciel.org/plasticandhealth/.
20 A proposal to formalize the Anthropocene as a new geological unit within the Geological Time Scale is under development by the "Anthropocene" working group of the Subcommission on Quaternary Stratigraphy, with a view to presenting it for consideration to the International Commission on Stratigraphy (the largest scientific organization within the International Union of Geological Sciences), available at http://quaternary.stratigraphy.org/workinggroups/anthropocene/.
21 See on this Vito De Lucia, "Critical Environmental Law and the Double Register of the Anthropocene: A Biopolitical Reading," in *Environmental Law and Governance for the Anthropocene,* ed. Louis Kotzé (Oxford: Hart Publishing, 2017), 97–116.

nity.[22] Ecology raises complex questions because of its double epistemic role — as a science and as a normative framework that both represents (epistemologically) and demands (culturally and, crucially, legally) a paradigm shift. It is also an "alchemic" source of a variety of ethical orientations,[23] and is fundamentally affected by a "moral ambivalence."[24] Ecology, moreover, is also affected by an irreducible complexity.[25] Thus, ecology is the object of discursive contestations, and is claimed as a source of legitimacy by a variety of political projects, each aimed at imposing their hegemonic dominance.[26] Indeed ecology, through alchemic operations,[27] is able to underpin philosophical positions aimed at challenging the modern construction of nature; yet is also mobilized as a legitimating framework for the continued enforcement of nature as a modern category, and for its exploitation.[28]

---

22 In at least some of its forms, see, e.g., Tallacchini, *Diritto per la Natura*; deLaplante, "Environmental Alchemy."

23 Indeed, ecology is able to underpin both anthropocentric and ecocentric ethics, see, e.g., deLaplante, "Environmental Alchemy" for a general illustration of these alchemic possibilities. See also Tallacchini, *Diritto per la Natura,* which illustrates how ecology supports all hues of environmentalism.

24 Worster, *Nature's Economy,* 256.

25 Frank Golley, *A History of the Ecosystem Concept in Ecology: More Than the Sum of Its Parts* (New Haven: Yale University Press, 1993); Greg Mitman, *The State of Nature: Ecology, Community, and American Social Thought, 1900–1950* (Chicago: University of Chicago Press, 1992); Vito De Lucia, "Competing Narratives and Complex Genealogies: The Ecosystem Approach in International Environmental Law," *Journal of Environmental Law* 27, no. 2 (2015): 91–117, specifically in relation to how this complex genealogy manifests in international environmental law.

26 Anne Bell, "Non Human Nature and the Ecosystem Approach: The Limits of Anthropocentrism in Great Lakes Management," *Alternatives Journal* 20, no. 3 (2004): 20–25; De Lucia, "Competing Narratives and Complex Genealogies."

27 deLaplante, "Environmental Alchemy."

28 Eric Darier, ed., *Discourses of the Environment* (Oxford: Blackwell, 1999); Bell, "Non Human Nature."

If the discourse of ecology inspires an apparent radicaliza-
tion of legal theory,[29] it also enables new biopolitical regimes
that, aimed at the regularization of the provisions of ecosystems,
goods, and services, ultimately subjugate nature.[30] What is ecology then? Ecology, I suggest, is best and most usefully understood as a mode of thinking. Additionally, ecology is a *transversal* mode of thinking that crosses many disciplinary boundaries.
Understood in this manner, ecology becomes a critical political and legal methodology that irritates and disarticulates the
fragmented epistemic and legal ideology of modernity. I suggest, drawing on Felix Guattari and Lorraine Code, that ecology requires us to think "transversally,"[31] that is, thinking must
simultaneously embrace the natural, technical, social, and psychological planes. Ecological thinking, in its transversal mode,
helps subvert the neat separation of the personal, the social, and
the natural, and thus allows the formation of transversal links
between the material world, social practices, legal rules, ecosystems, and international capitalism.[32]

A central insight that ecology has made evident (despite all
its ambiguities and contestations) is the instability of knowledge. Ignorance and uncertainty are no longer simply a lack to
be filled, but acquire a specific epistemic and normative role,[33]

---

29 For a comparative discussion of two such legal philosophical approaches,
see Vito De Lucia, "Towards an Ecological Philosophy of Law: A Comparative Discussion," *Journal of Human Rights and the Environment* 4, no.
2 (2013): 167–90.

30 Vito De Lucia, "Beyond Anthropocentrism and Ecocentrism: A Biopolitical Reading of Environmental Law," *Journal of Human Rights and Environment* 8, no. 2, (2017): 181–202; Vito De Lucia, "A Critical Interrogation of
the Relation between the Ecosystem Approach and Ecosystem Services,"
RECIEL 27, no. 2 (2018): 104–14; Vito De Lucia, "Bare Nature: The Biopolitical Logic of the International Regulation of Invasive Alien Species," *Journal
of Environmental Law* 31, no. 1 (2018): 109–34; See also, more generally,
Darier, *Discourses of the Environment.*

31 Felix Guattari, *The Three Ecologies* (London: Continuum, 2008), 29.

32 Code, *Ecological Thinking,* 19.

33 Kristen Shrader-Frechette, "Methodological Rules for Four Classes of Scientific Uncertainty," in *Scientific Uncertainty and Environmental Problem
Solving,* ed. John Lemons (Oxford: Blackwell, 1996), 12–39; Code, *Ecologi-*

which derives from an endemic (and perhaps insuperable) uncertainty that arises from the complexity of non-linear and cross-scalar ecological processes.[34] Every decision, then, carries with/in it specific normative, ethical and political commitments arising from both scientific and legal processes;[35] and knowledge and values reflect both objective and subjective perspectives.[36] This situation has prompted scholars to describe law, and environmental law more specifically, as postmodern,[37] hot,[38] irreducibly mired in genealogical tensions, and situated between competing narratives.[39]

If knowledge is uncertain, unstable and negotiated, it then becomes important, as Latour suggests, to focus on matters of

cal Thinking; Kevin deLaplante, "Is Ecosystem Management a Postmodern Science?" in Ecological Paradigms Lost: Routes of Theory Change, eds. Beatrix Beisner and Kim Cuddington (Burlington: Elsevier Academic Press, 2005), 397–414.

34 See, e.g., Serge Gutwirth and Eric Naim-Gesbert, "Science et droit de l'environnement: Réflexions pour le cadre conceptual du pluralisme de vérités," Revue interdisciplinaire d'études juridiques 34 (1995): 33–98. See also Nicolas De Sadeleer, Environmental Principles: From Political Slogans to Legal Rules (Oxford: Oxford University Press, 2008).

35 MariaChiara Tallacchini, "A Legal Framework from Ecology," Biodiversity and Conservation 9, no. 8 (2000): 1085–98, at 1095.

36 Subjective biases may arise from personal biases; from social or cultural preferences; and/or from methodological choices that themselves carry an axiological dimension. Methodological operations such as extrapolation from one context to another "are never neutral and univocal, but are always influenced by values and goals": ibid., 1096. See also Kristen Shrader-Frechette, Risk and Rationality. Philosophical Foundations for Populist Reforms (Berkeley: University of California Press, 1991), and Shrader-Frechette, "Methodological Rules," 12–39.

37 De Sadeleer, Environmental Principles, esp. 251.

38 Elizabeth Fisher, "Environmental Law as 'Hot' Law," Journal of Environmental Law 25, no. 3 (2013): 347–58, at 347–48.

39 De Lucia, "Competing Narratives and Complex Genealogies." Some, however, still maintain that "science has the answers," placing a different kind of responsibility on law: that of implementing those answers: Christina Voigt, "The Principle of Sustainable Development. Integration and Ecological Integrity," in Rule of Law for Nature: New Dimensions and Ideas in Environmental Law, ed. Christina Voigt (Cambridge: Cambridge University Press, 2013), 146–57, at 153.

concern and not on matters of fact.[40] Law, no longer defensible as a *technical* domain, must exploit the productive potential of epistemic instability and accept, as Tallacchini suggests, "the responsibility to solve problems which science cannot decide and that are linked to uncertain outcomes."[41] It will be important, then, to emphasize the central role of what Lorraine Code calls "epistemic location" for the creation, negotiation, and circulation of ecological knowledge — "down on the ground," as Code aptly puts it.[42] Epistemic location links knowledge with the physical, social, and political location of the knower, as well as with her values and background, and with the specificities of the situation and place where knowledge is produced.[43] In this sense "the nature and conditions of the particular 'ground', the situations and circumstances of specific knowers, their interdependence and their negotiations," all become relevant and even crucial factors.[44] Code further suggests that truth is no longer a regime, but a "truth to,"[45] a form of interpretation (rather than of verification) that is "textured and responsive,"[46] as well as "responsible [to] local sensitivity."[47] Indeed, ultimately truth is a form of life responsive to the embodied world and a form of responsible knowledge, meaning a form of knowledge cognizant of the "multiply contestable" nature of categories and taxonomies that impose permanent closures on the living world.[48]

Another important effect of the epistemic location of ecological thinking is that formal science, for all its recognized "force,"[49] needs to be situated in the particular place where its

40 Bruno Latour, "An Attempt at a 'Compositionist Manifesto'," *New Literary History* 41 (2010): 471–90, at 478.
41 Tallacchini, "A Legal Framework from Ecology," 1095.
42 Code, *Ecological Thinking*, 5.
43 Ibid., esp. 177.
44 Ibid., 5–6.
45 Ibid., 7.
46 Ibid.
47 Ibid., 8.
48 Ibid., 50.
49 I use "force" here rather than "truth" deliberately, having in mind Hornborg's work (Alf Hornborg, *The Power of the Machine: Global Inequalities*

regime of truth is to leave traces and marks. Only in this manner can scientific knowledge be responsive and responsible.
Epistemic location recognizes precisely science's character of
"determined abstraction," to use a Marxian concept.[50] If abstraction is a necessary operation of thought, its effects are always
produced within a particular social and ecological fabric and in
a particular historical place and time. Knowledge thus must be
situated (or perhaps re-situated, following the Marxian method
of the concrete-abstract-concrete circle); it must be embedded
and integrated in the richness of life's problematics. Only then
will it be able to be responsible and respond to life's demands.[51]

3. Locating the Commons

The commons, I suggest, is precisely an example of practices
that are located on particular grounds. However, what are the
commons? This may seem to be an unnecessary question at

---

of Economy, Technology, and Environment (Walnut Creek: Altamira Press,
2001)) on the relation between the truth of techno-science and the global
capitalist system. Hornborg identifies an intimate, inevitable link between
industrial technology and the unequal exchange relations that facilitate
the extraction, appropriation, and accumulation of ecological and social
resources in a world system aligned along a core-periphery continuum.
It is capitalist accumulation "*which made industrial technology possible
to begin with,*" 46 (emphasis in the original). "If specific technologies
require and reproduce specific forms of social organization," continues
Hornborg — and it is well worth quoting at length — "it is no less true that
industrial technology as a general phenomenon requires and reproduces
a specific world order [...] technological knowledge is 'true' (i.e., 'works')
only within a restricted social space. The social definition of what is technologically feasible is not external to technology but [...] intrinsic to it,"
107. In other words, machine productivity in itself, disjointed from global
accumulation practices, cannot exist.

50 See, e.g., Karl Marx, "Introduction (1857)," in *A Contribution to the Critique of Political Economy,* trans. N.I. Stone (Chicago: Charles Kerr, 1904),
264–313.

51 On this see, e.g., Giorgio Borrelli, "Semiosis and Discursivity of the Commodity Form," in *Material Discourse: Materialist Analysis: Approaches in
Discourse Studies,* eds. Johannes Beetz and Veit Schwab (Lanham: Lexington Books, 2018), 129–44, at 132.

best, and frivolous at worst. Of course, we generally know what the commons are.[52] In the standard analysis pioneered by Elinor Ostrom and her colleagues, the commons are resources or resource domains managed by a community of users over which it has a series of use rights.[53] The rights may be local (a field or a parking lot), international (a regional sea), or global (the Earth's atmosphere or the high seas),[54] and they may entail use rights over resource domains held in common, held privately, publicly, or to which no one has title (the so-called *res communes omnium*).

Yet this sort of description, which effectively conflates a diverse array of legal regimes under the same narrative of the commons,[55] remains in many ways silent about key elements that I wish to emphasize in this chapter. These elements may help facilitate a certain shift in perspective that will in turn allow for re-assessing, from a critical legal theoretical perspective, how the commons offers a rich repository of ideas for thinking law beyond Law. However — and this is something we will return to in the conclusions by way of a word of caution — it is important to keep in mind that commons *per se* do not offer any guarantee. They do not represent ideal forms or models of collective arrangements that will successfully ferry us out of the unfolding ecological crises. They rather, and more modestly, of-

---

52 Yet there are many voices discussing the commons, and there seems to be as much overlap as difference in perspective, political point of view, and legal theorizing. See, e.g., Weston and Bollier, *Green Governance;* Mattei, *Beni Comuni;* Marella, *Oltre il Pubblico e il Privato;* Michael Hardt and Antonio Negri, *Commonwealth* (Cambridge: Belknap Press of Harvard University Press, 2009); De Lucia, "Re-Embodying Law."

53 See, e.g., Susan Buck, *The Global Commons: An Introduction* (Washington, DC: Island Press, 1998).

54 Ibid., 5–6.

55 A conflation, and a confusion, which I discuss in some more detail, with respect to the international and global level, in Vito De Lucia, "The Concept of Commons and Marine Genetic Resources in Areas beyond National Jurisdiction," *Marine Safety and Security Law Journal* 5 (2018): 1–21, at 11.

fer hope of a re-emerging sensibility for (legal) pluralism, multiplicity, complexity, and difference.

A commons, I suggest then, is not (only) a resource. Common goods, or resources, are obviously an important element of the commons, and indeed central in conventional academic perspectives.[56] Yet to establish an equivalence between commons and resource means, arguably, delimiting the scope and complexity of a commons to an economic dimension. While this maneuver may be analytically useful in some circumstances, it denies much of the richness of the idea of commons. It precludes a novel reading of law that may respond to a series of slippery questions raised by our current ecological juncture. In this sense, the term "resource" or "goods" denotes a particular orientation that circumscribes the "vulnerable living world"[57] and makes it ready for a utilitarian deployment. That such resources are held, or used, in common may or may not change anything in and of itself. We have seen, for example, that the legal regime of the Common Heritage of Mankind as applied to deep seabed mineral resources[58] and marine genetic resources has not significantly impeded their exploitation by capital.[59]

A commons is not (only) a resource domain either. Places and spaces are important elements for most (though not all) commons.[60] Yet neither places nor spaces alone are sufficient for

---

56 Indeed, the Italian movement of the commons starts from the idea of common goods ("beni comuni"). See, e.g., Mattei, *Beni Comuni* and Marella, *Oltre il Pubblico e il Privato*.

57 Anna Grear, "The Vulnerable Living Order: Human Rights and the Environment in a Critical and Philosophical Perspective," *Journal of Human Rights and the Environment* 2, no. 1 (2011): 23–44.

58 UNCLOS, Part XI. However, some commentators consider that the environmental dimension is an important element of the common heritage principle, see, e.g., Kemal Baslar, *The Concept of the Common Heritage of Mankind in International Law* (The Hague: Nijhoff, 1998).

59 De Lucia, "The Concept of Commons and Marine Genetic Resources."

60 It is sufficient to think of knowledge, software, other digital commons, or even law, to understand the place-less-ness of certain commons, see, e.g., Weston and Bollier, *Green Governance* or Marella, *Oltre il Pubblico e il Privato*.

describing a commons. They constitute only one element among the many that may characterize or constitute a commons.

A commons is not (only) a mode of production either. As Hardt and Negri emphasize, production is certainly an important dimension, as it focuses on the dynamic aspect of the social practices of the commons on the one hand, and on the other hand, on the exploitation by capital of cooperative forms of production.[61] Capital operates here in its predatory inflection, bent on extracting rent (rather than profit), as it "seeks to capture and expropriate autonomously produced common wealth" that is external to the capitalist production form.[62] Yet this dimension for seeing the commons, while valuable, focuses primarily on the social practice of labor, and is thus also limited in its scope.

What are commons then? And what is the role of each of these perspectives in finding some sort of frame that can capture the complexities of the commons? I have argued elsewhere that a defining characteristic of the commons is that they resist taxonomic closure.[63] Commons cannot be subsumed under a "universal template" since each particular commons "is grounded in particular, historically rooted, local circumstances."[64] Yet it is possible to capture the complexity, multiplicity, and "slipperiness" of commons. Commons produce knowledge and law "down on the ground,"[65] and that, accordingly, is where the commons must be met. This means that while abstract taxonomies may offer some guidance, they remain unable to capture, restrain, contain, and ultimately represent the commons as resisting practices or "insurgent critiques."[66] Down on the ground, then, commons are a complex, variable, shifting assemblage of peoples, things, places, beliefs, norms, and practices. In other

---

61 Hardt and Negri, *Commonwealth*. See also Antonio Negri, "Il Comune come Modo di Produzione," *EuroNomade,* June 10, 2016, http://www. euronomade.info/?p=7331.
62 Hardt and Negri, *Commonwealth,* 141.
63 De Lucia, "Re-Embodying Law," 169.
64 Weston and Bollier, *Green Governance,* 126.
65 Code, *Ecological Thinking,* 5.
66 De Lucia, "Law as Insurgent Critique"; De Lucia, "Re-Embodying Law."

words, any commons is variously comprised of a particular ground (a geophysical dimension); common goods (a material, which may not always have an immediately economic dimension); practices of commoning (e.g., labor); a community of commoners carrying out these practices (what Negri would call a "multitude;"[67] yet, importantly, the community of commoners may also include nonhuman living entities);[68] the natural (in the sense of the "vulnerable living world"[69]) aspects of which a place and/or the resource base is comprised; and the rules and relations regulating and linking in multiple ways the interactions between each of these elements, and between the commons and its external world (be that other commons, other institutions such as the State etc.). These rules and relations comprise the normative and regulative element — that is, law. In this respect, as an instantiation of a situated practice, it is precisely in a particular grounded reality that the commons know and produce law. The commons, thus, are epistemically located, and produce knowledge as well as law. Knower and known are organically connected in a constant, dynamic, and iterative relation with one another. Law becomes thus both responsive and responsible.

4. From Ethics to Ethos

The commons, we have seen, can be — indeed should be — understood as a complex assemblage that reflects transversal ecological thinking through epistemic location. The commons, however, also has an ethical dimension — often a crucial underpinning for environmental legal arguments. Regardless of whether the current debates between anthropocentrism and

---

67 Hardt and Negri, *Commonwealth*.
68 See in this respect Margherita Pieraccini, "Beyond Legal Facts and Discourses: Towards a Social-ecological Production of the Legal," in *Contributions to Law, Philosophy, Ecology*, eds. Thomas-Pellicer, De Lucia, and Sullivan, 227–43.
69 Grear, "The Vulnerable Living Order."

ecocentrism can or should be displaced,[70] ethics remains a key parameter because it informs and guides law and legal discourse. It is also entangled in multiple and "alchemic" ways, as we have seen, with ecology. Yet what the idea of epistemic location tells us is that ethics, when posited in universal forms, cannot become grounded, which is to say, *embodied* in a particular ground. Indeed, as Zygmunt Bauman has observed, modern ethics is entirely focused on articulating a universal code.[71] Thus, modern ethics (and especially its applied versions) is not sufficiently able to accommodate difference, diversity, ambiguity, and contingency, or indeed any tentative, iterative mode of situated, responsive, and responsible action.

What I propose, then, is to shift from ethics to ethos, and see how that may offer a different, located, underpinning for conceptualizing and enacting law.

In its original meaning, ethos arises out of dwelling, and it is firstly captured through the "loud" particularity of mythos.[72] Ethos is deeply connected to a place: ἤθεα ἵππων, suggested Homer, the dwelling place or the habitat of horses.[73] The use of the word *ēthos* in the famous fragment 119 of Heraclitus of Ephesus, "*ēthos anthrōpōi daimōn*" indicates precisely the dwelling place, the abode, said Heidegger.[74] Further, ethos indicates the specific dwelling of man in the nearness of his *daimōn,* which can be translated as god, power, or spirit. Interpreted historically — thinking in a Greek way, not in a modern one — Heidegger explicitly observes — man's abode, the "open region in which the human being dwells,"[75] his local world, is animated by

---

70 See, e.g., De Lucia, "Critical Environmental Law."
71 Zygmunt Bauman, *Postmodern Ethics* (London: Wiley-Blackwell, 1993).
72 In its original etymological meaning of utterance, hence the reference to sounds ("loud").
73 James Baumlin and Craig Meyer, "Positioning Ethos in/for the Twenty-First Century: An Introduction to Histories of Ethos," *Humanities* 7, no. 3, (2018): 1–26, at 12.
74 Martin Heidegger, "Letter on Humanism," in *Pathmarks*, ed. W. McNeill (Cambridge: Cambridge University Press, 1998), 239–76, at 269.
75 Ibid.

enchanted lives.[76] What Heidegger does here is to emphasize an historical understanding of a word, rather than the modern one, which helps us to understand the Greek fragment as reflecting Heraclitus' sense that the good fortune of a man is related to his character ("character" being a common modern translation of "ethos").[77] However, the character of any human being is linked to the world in which he or she is born and raised, with all its particular climatic, geophysical, and ecological conditions. One's abode, family, and community have a significant influence on one's character.[78]

Nomos — a term more directly associated with law[79] — implicates the material constitution of a community in its orientation on a territory, but most significantly in its structured order.[80] *Ethos* by contrast emphasizes more specifically a dialectical orientation, a relation with the territory — with the terrain, with the *terroir,* to use an enological term — and with the natural world, a relation that is mutually constitutive. The relationship with the territory entailed by *nomos,* linked to the pasture and to the spatial configuration and delimitation of a community *inter se,* takes with *ethos* the character of an emergent self-image of the community, shaping its identity and values, as well as its very character. But this self-image is a reflection: the community sees itself in its surrounding habitat. The relation with the territory captured by *ethos* reflects the "nearness with god,"[81] with the enchanted lives animating the dwelling place of humans. In turn, the *nomos* reflects the materiality of the relationship, which crystallizes in regularities, ritual normativities, territorial demarcations, and the sacralization of spaces and places. Both

---

76 Ibid.

77 See, e.g., Daniel Graham, "Heraclitus," *The Stanford Encyclopedia of Philosophy* (Fall 2015 edition), https://plato.stanford.edu/archives/fall2015/entries/heraclitus/.

78 This linkage is, for example, crucially analyzed by Cuomo in his reflections: Esposito, *Living Thought.*

79 See, e.g., Carl Schmitt, *The Nomos of the Earth in the International Law of the* Jus Publicum Europaeum (New York: Telos Press, 2006).

80 Through an "original, constitutive act of spatial ordering," ibid., 78.

81 Heidegger, "Letter on Humanism."

terms however, express a fundamental relation between habit and place, implying the localization of human activities.

Refined over time and through practice, *nomos* has come to mean custom, convention, or (positive) law, while *ethos* has come to mean "disposition, character, or fundamental values peculiar to a specific person, people, culture, or movement."[82] These conventions articulate and manifest possibilities and proprieties of socio-technical configurations, and thus mold both natures and cultures in particular ways. Different *ethē* (and here we can use the plural to indicate a plurality of localized abodes, a plurality of commons) map to different sets of dispositions and values. Furthermore, through their epistemic location, they also significantly express different relational engagements with particular natures. They are the different symbolic, cultural images of the constitutive diversity of a multiplicity of natures.

This is not to say that these *ethē* engage with unadulterated, pure forms of nature (which do not exist), nor that they are not afflicted by conflict. Not at all. Rather, the complex assemblage of the commons is always the material and symbolic/interpretive result of ongoing dialectical relations among its constitutive elements, as mentioned above. *Ethos* in this respect reflects the idea of ecology as a mode of thinking, and epistemic location reflects the appropriate modality for producing a responsive and responsible knowledge (and law).

The idea of *ethos* indeed reflects a localized, "on the ground" appreciation of the difference of circumstances. It acknowledges the fact that, contrary to the binary logic of western modernity, there is never a right/wrong answer, but rather an ensemble of possibilities, each with its own set of tonalities and shadows. Law recapitulates itself as an exercise in finding the good and equitable principle and outcome (*jus est ars boni et aequi*)[83]

---

82 *The American Heritage Dictionary of the English Language,* s.v. "ethos," http://dictionary.reference.com/browse/ethos.

83 Ulpianus D. 1.1.1, *Corpus Iuris Civilis, Vol. I, Iustiniani Digesta,* Mommsen Edition, https://droitromain.univ-grenoble-alpes.fr/Corpus/digest.htm.

in particular circumstances[84] rather than a fixed set of binary choices such as legal/illegal, true/false, and good/bad, which subsumes the world into a universal matrix of control, as per legal modernity's ideo-ontological template.[85]

In this respect, a related notation is perhaps in order. What shall we make of the distinction between justice as an ethical concept and justice as a legal concept (or indeed as a concept resting on the notion of *ethos*)? The tensions between the two — and the inevitable relation that somehow binds them — have always permeated thinking about law. Aristotle first articulated the distinction in detail.[86] But there is no reason (nor space) to discuss that framework in the context of this chapter. What I rather want to emphasize briefly here is a key juncture in the genealogical history of justice that, parallel to the momentous transition from orality to literacy,[87] pre-dates Aristotle's *Ethics*, and the delineation between the ethical and juridical justice that he adopts therein.

In this respect, Erik Havelock[88] provides us with an excellent account of the transition from a Homeric, "orally" embedded conception of *justices* (in the plural) to a Platonic "literate," and abstracting[89] conception of *Justice* (in the singular). In the fluid (Homeric) oral world, what one must relate to is not Justice, but rather *justices,* in the plural. "These plural justices" according to Havelock, "have no connection with an a priori set of principles, but rather are processes aiming at the conservation of existing mores or at the restoration of the propriety of human relationships."[90] However, there is no prescription as to

---

84 Or what used to be called "the nature of things." See Michel Villey, *La formation de la pensée juridique moderne* (Paris: PUF, 2003).

85 On the idea of ideo-ontology, see De Lucia, "Re-Embodying Law."

86 Aristotle, *Nicomachean Ethics* (Kitchener: Batoche Books, 1999).

87 For details I can only point the reader to, e.g., Walter Ong, *Orality and Literacy,* 2nd edn. (London: Routledge, 2002).

88 Erik Havelock, *The Greek Concept of Justice: From Its Shadow in Homer to Its Substance in Plato* (Harvard: Harvard University Press, 1978).

89 I use the present participle to emphasize the dynamic beginning of a process of disembedding, rather than its static completion.

90 Havelock, *The Greek Concept of Justice,* 181.

what, generally speaking, the mores and customs ought to be: that is rather a task left to the community. In Homer, "Justice, as the name of a social principle of universal dimension, or of a moral sense fundamental to our human nature, may be wholly absent."[91] And in fact the root of the adjectival derivation of *dikē, dikaios* (the just person) represents "a man who does the appropriate thing," in the sense of following the proper customs and processes, hence fulfilling the expectations of the community.

This is closely linked to the concept of *aretē* (excellence, quality, virtue) as that set of qualities necessary to function well in one's social role. Justice, then, maps onto "what one has a right to expect of human behavior, in given cases from given types of people:"[92] a fully localized, embodied, and situated notion. Havelock continues by highlighting how "in oral thought [justice] remains a method, not a principle."[93] It is pragmatic and consists of a process of readjustment, a restoration of disrupted values and customs, so as to re-establish a fair pattern of relationships.[94] There is, moreover, no separation between justice as an idea and the activities that achieve it.

A justice so extremely embedded in its social and relational context is still familiar to Plato. Yet Plato's idea of justice becomes a singular, universal entity, and can be identified by "properties or attributes, categories or relationships, which are seen as permanent and not really subject to conditional changes, as justice itself."[95] Hesiod had already achieved an earlier key in-

---

91 Ibid., 191.

92 Ibid.

93 Ibid., 230.

94 And in fact in the Aristotelian view, the whole of Law is contained in the goal of (re-)establishing a fair pattern of relationships, an idea captured by the word *dikaion. Jus,* in the Roman legal world, had the same function, that is, it referred to an objective thing, to a fair distribution of benefits and burdens between concrete, particular human beings — rather than "equal legal subjects." See on this, at length, Villey, *La formation de la pensée juridique moderne,* and for a brief overview, Costas Douzinas and Adam Geary, *Critical Jurisprudence: The Political Philosophy of Justice* (Oxford and Portland: Hart Publishing, 2005), especially chapter 3.

95 Havelock, *The Greek Concept of Justice,* 313.

tellectual shift. In his *Works and Days*,[96] he managed to isolate justice as independent from an agent. Plato would later complete this analytical shift more fully by turning justice into an entity, into a "thing which is,"[97] while at the same time firmly making it singular: Justice. By intellectually providing justice with an essential character, by applying the verb "to be" to it, justice is made independent of human agency. The effect of this analytical shift was effectively to detach justice from the realm of particular experiences, and transform it into a general, abstract, and universal (or universalizable) ideal.[98]

In this respect, justice in its juridical, plural, processual mode is clearly aligned with the idea of commons outlined here. It emerges from an epistemic location, and is aligned with the framework of *ethos* where norms do not respond to a binary logic, but possess the soft flexibility that characterizes an immanent mode of law that *happens* in the world. Unlike Law, law doesn't attempt to order the world, but rather to respond to it in a careful ("full of care") and responsible manner.

5. Plurigenerationality

Having discussed the spatial dimension at some length, this section offers reflections on the manner in which the commons normatively internalize the temporal dimension. The commons is, I suggest, *plurigenerational,* which is to say, links generations

---

96 Hesiod, *Works and Days* (London: Penguin Classics, 2018).

97 Havelock, *The Greek Concept of Justice,* underlines how the key step was that of using the verb "to be," assigning to Justice the dimension and properties of an entity, a being, a thing with independent agency.

98 The realm of particulars remains the domain of equity, or *epieikeia.* Aristotle would call it particular justice. It must be noted that some argue for the Platonic idealization of Justice, its derivation from absolute, transhistorical natural norms as the first critical theory of Justice, targeted at disentangling the individual from the asphyxiating hold of the community. Again, there are no right/wrong answers, only process and tentative attempts, see Villey, *La formation de la pensée juridique moderne.*

together in a plural, collective dimension.[99] In this sense, this term deliberately marks its incommensurability with the increasingly popular concept of an *intergenerational* space, and of an intergenerational justice.[100] The idea of plurigenerationality implies an inclusive orientation, drawing on plurality as the key semantic and conceptual indicator. Intergenerationality, by contrast, has a more exclusionary orientation insofar as it implies that different subjects may have competing rights-claims over the same object (the natural resources of the Earth, the climate etc.).[101] The intergenerational relation is articulated in terms of individual rights-holders, and its legal operationalization usually hinges on the idea of guardianship to protect the interests of future generations as against current generations. Intergenerationality presupposes in this respect two separate subjects of rights — the present generation and future generations — each collective and also individualized.[102]

A plurigenerational perspective is quite different because it maintains both currently living generations (elderly, adults, youngsters, children) and future generations within the same horizon of commoning. Commoning always already includes

---

99 This is a felicitous expression found in Paolo Grossi, "La Proprietà e le Proprietà nell'Officina dello Storico," *Quaderni Fiorentini per la Storia del Pensiero Giuridico Moderno* 17 (1988): 359–422, 365.

100 See for example the seminal work of Edith Brown-Weiss, *In Fairness to Future Generations: International Law, Common Patrimony, and Intergenerational Equity* (New York: Transnational Publishers, 1989), or more recently in Joeng Tremmel, ed., *Handbook of Intergenerational Justice* (Cheltenham: Edward Elgar, 2006).

101 The question always hinges on "rights," even when the conclusion is that "future generations cannot be said to have any rights,'" thus, e.g., Wilfred Beckerman, "The Impossibility of a theory of Intergenerational Justice," in Tremmel, *Handbook of Intergenerational Justice*, 53–71.

102 This is indeed the usual framework within which lawsuits that have sought to protect the interests of future generations — youth and generations unborn — have been articulated; see, e.g., "The Philippines: Supreme Court Decision in *Minors Oposa V. Secretary of the Department of Environment and Natural Resources (DENR)* (Deforestation; Environmental Damage; Intergenerational Equity)," *International Legal Materials* 33, no. 1 (1994): 173–206.

the future in its present practices in the same way that the past — as manifested through practices, knowledge-sharing, memories, histories, and affects — is also always included in its present. It is in this sense, for example, that some forms of traditional commons are vested not in the individual, nor in a separate corporate entity (town, municipality, etc.), but rather in the "incessant concatenation of generations" of commoners.[103] Furthermore, commoners do not "discount" the past, as modern capitalist discourse does. They rather make it present in everyday life and culture through their practices. Presence, as Patrick Glenn emphasizes with respect to the notion of tradition, is crucial in establishing continuity and in inclusively framing ways of doing things as meaningfully traditional, rather than as merely habitual.[104] Contrary to modern perceptions, traditions are operational mechanisms that mobilize "the past in order to invent a future,"[105] never losing sight of their participation in a whole that is contingently concretized in the present, while exceeding it.

This inclusive plurigeneretional perspective is in many ways inherently part of the practices of commoning, and it is one of the constitutive elements of the commons. When Ugo Mattei observes how, in Alpine villages, one generation would cut trees for seasoning so that their grandchildren would be able to use them as construction material, it becomes evident how the commons links generations across time (rather than juxtaposing them in an adversarial relation). Practices such as "intergenerational seasoning"[106] help constitute commons and

---

103 Grossi, "La Proprietà e le Proprietà nell'Officina dello Storico," 364, my translation. The original reads "incessante concatenazione delle generazioni di consorti."

104 Patrick Glenn, *Legal Traditions of the World: Sustainable Diversity in Law,* 2nd edn. (Oxford: Oxford University Press, 2004), esp. 1–29.

105 Ibid., esp. 23, and related footnote 57.

106 Ugo Mattei, "Future Generations Now! A Commons-based Analysis," in Bailey, Farrell, and Mattei, *Protecting Future Generations through Commons,* 9–26, at 11.

continuously reproduce them.[107] Mattei describes these practices in terms of "intergenerational duties,"[108] though I would
rather call them plurigenerational, in the sense outlined above.
This plurigenerational perspective is not only relevant in small,
temporal and spatial circumstances, as Mattei also observes;[109]
such plurigenerational perspective is arguably crucial as well for
global challenges such as addressing climate change, though this
aspect cannot be further explored here.

6. Plural Institutionalism

Inhabiting a place (be it a place on a mountain, in a forest, a city,
or a particular occupied and reclaimed building), a commons
generates a form of "responsible knowledge,"[110] a social practice and a juridical institution. The legal-modern form of law,
constructed as an autonomous field of knowledge and practice,
is disarticulated. The complex assemblages that constitute the
commons resonate then, as already outlined elsewhere,[111] with
a theory of law known as institutionalism.[112] Law is (re-)located,
animated by organized social practices, and inhabits a location

---

107 Ibid.
108 Ibid.
109 Ibid.
110 Ibid., 50.
111 De Lucia, "Re-Embodying Law."
112 A theory elaborated by Italian legal theorist Santi Romano. Romano
   considers institutions to be the springboard of any juridical phenomenon,
   Santi Romano, L'Ordinamento Giuridico, 2nd edn. (Florence: Sansoni,
   1946). Romano thus radically identifies the social and the legal (so that
   neither has causal, logical or temporal priority). A legal order ("ordinamento giuridico"), from this perspective, "is the concretisation of a social
   fact [...] the effectiveness of its structure:" Filippo Fontanelli, "Santi
   Romano and L'ordinamento giuridico: The Relevance of a Forgotten Masterpiece for Contemporary International, Transnational and Global Legal
   Relations," Transnational Legal Theory 2, no. 1 (2001): 67–177, at 79. This is
   not the place for elaborating on Romano's theory. For an English account
   of his theory see ibid., and Massimo La Torre, Law as Institution (London
   and New York: Springer, 2010), esp. 98–115, where La Torre discusses Romano's theory and then compares it with MacCormick and Weinberger's
   (new) institutionalism.

which situates the point of view — with all its advantages and limitations. The commons, from this perspective, are *institutions*. The term "institution" here refers to the specific notion of institution elaborated by Italian legal philosopher Santi Romano. Romano describes an institution very broadly as "every social entity or body" that has a significant enough measure of stable pattern, form and/or organization.[113] Romano theorizes the social and the legal as coterminous: neither has causal, logical, or temporal priority. A legal order,[114] from this perspective, "is the concretisation of a social fact [...] the effectiveness of its structure."[115] This emphasis on social fact and on effectiveness, it is useful to note, well captures a dimension that, especially in relation to the new commons, has been singled out as crucial: the dimension of conflict. Mattei in particular has emphasized the element of conflict, partly due to the Italian experience where indeed conflict, struggle, and resistance were salient, operative dimensions.[116]

Romano, however, tended to close his institutional theory around the all-encompassing institution of the State, integrating all other institutions within a hierarchical structure.[117] The commons on the other hand point to a much more radical orientation:[118] social practices are always already legal practices,[119] and law is therefore a form of *living* law. Any order including competing social forces and legal claims, from this perspective,

---

113 Romano, *L'Ordinamento Giuridico,* my translation.

114 This translates Romano's "*ordinamento giuridico.*" For problems relating to this translation, see Fontanelli, "Santi Romano and L'ordinamento giuridico."

115 Ibid., 79.

116 Mattei, *Beni Comuni.*

117 Thomas Schultz, *Transnational Legality: Stateless Law and International Arbitration* (Oxford: Oxford University Press, 2014), 61, citing Italian legal scholar Tarello. This position seems close to that taken by Weston and Bollier, to the extent that, while they recognize the normative capacity of the commons, they imagine it couched within and enabled by the structures of formal State law: Weston and Bollier, *Green Governance.*

118 Weston and Bollier, however, do not necessarily see antagonism between the commons and the State: Weston and Bollier, *Green Governance.*

119 Thus Romano, *L'Ordinamento Giuridico,* 8; Mattei, *Beni Comuni.*

is not subsumed within a higher structure (such as the State). It takes rather the form of a complex and complementary assemblage constituted through this conflict, always ambiguously balancing and re-balancing.

The legal architectural model for this radical institutionalism is not the Constitutional State, but a bottom-up federalism, without a center and without a top.[120] And while the role of the State can be, as some suggest, re-aligned with vernacular[121] or post-sovereign[122] modes of governance, it is suggested here that it is not the State that remains crucial, but multiplicity and plurality, including plurality of governance scales and arrangements. In that respect, this institutional perspective further points in the direction of a radical legal pluralism.[123] If the social is always already juridical, and each social institution carries and re-produces its particular legality, the world is traversed by overlapping juridical institutions carving their own constituent space through the production of a plurality of ecologically situated legal habits, a multiplicity of legalities co-extensive with the socio-ecological institutions which form, self-recognize and act in the world. In this respect, the commons are practices and institutions grounded on particular habitats and features of the world, and are constituted by and through them as both complex assemblages and legal institutions. As such, commons produce knowledge and law "down on the ground."[124] Importantly,

---

120 There is a clear genealogical referent for this model, namely the Roman municipal republican model. There is no space to delve into this here, and I can only point to some key literature, such as, e.g., Pierangelo Catalano, *Populus Romanus Quirites* (Turin: Giappichelli, 1975), and Giovanni Lobrano, *Res Publica Res Populi. La Legge e la Limitazione del Potere* (Turin: Giappichelli, 1997).

121 Weston and Bollier, *Green Governance*.

122 Bradley Karkkainen, "Post-Sovereign Environmental Governance," *Global Environmental Politics* 4, no. 1 (2004): 72–96.

123 This is, in many ways, an inevitable consequence. Romano in fact derived legal pluralism from his institutional account of law.

124 Code, *Ecological Thinking*, 5.

this idea of legal pluralism includes also non-human legalities and normativities.[125]

The commons are, importantly, a provisional and functional category: the emphasis and the relevant subjectivities shift according to the needs for achieving particular goals. In this sense, commons as a form of law offer a way to take account of the problem of ecological shiftiness,[126] disarticulating the nature/cultural divide that entrenches the particular political epistemology of modernity and that fixes living and non-living entities as either subjects or objects. The commons thus also "allows," conceptually as well as legally, multispecies and multi-being assemblages.[127] They sanction a transversal composition of law, a composition that may include under the operative framework of the legal person — perhaps in terms that approximate the Roman legal category of *universitas* — humans, multiple species of non-human beings, rivers, rocks, mountains, etc.[128]

Yet, we may be compelled to ask, how can a rock participate? Isn't a rock's position always mediated by a human representative? Inevitably, the human perspective mediates and speaks for others. That is certainly an insuperable limitation of the human perspective. That will also lead to contestations. Epistemic location, however, in facilitating responsive and responsible knowledge and law, may facilitate responsive and responsible representation.

Another important notation: whether the legalities the commons as institutions produce are capable of being legally effective, under which conditions, and to what degree, remains a

---

125 For an outline of the argument for an inclusive legal pluralism that is able to accommodate the normativity produced by non-human actors, see, e.g., Pieraccini, "Beyond Legal Facts and Discourses."

126 De Lucia, "Re-Embodying Law." See also Tallacchini, *Diritto per la Natura.*

127 Rafi Youatt, "Anthropocentrism and the Politics of the Living," in *Reflections on the Posthuman in International Relations: The Anthropocene, Security and Ecology,* eds. Clara Eroukhmanoff and Matt Harker (Bristol: E-International Relations, 2017), 39–49, at 44.

128 And here we must bear in mind the distinction — but also the similarities — between biological life and animacy. See Alfred Gell, *Art and Agency: An Anthropological Theory* (Oxford: Clarendon Press, 1998), 122.

question that does not detract from their character as legal institutions. It is, however, a different law, a law inside Law, against Law, beyond Law — where the second term Law, capitalized, represents legal modernity, the hegemonic yet narrow mode of legality that dominates conceptually, philosophically, as well as materially, our current juncture. As Paolo Grossi suggests however, there is no Law, but only a series of juridical experiences that supersede one another.[129] What is coming is impossible to predict. What is being resisted, however, is evident before our eyes: Law in its current hegemonic form. The commons offers a counterpoint because it operates on a multiplicity of levels. In and of themselves, commons operate as a constituent force — a dynamic that never succumbs to — yet never exceeds — its own closure. This reflects the fact that the process of the production of law is not removed from the iterative, transversal, living practices that both constitute and respond to law simultaneously. The way in which this constituent force, this dynamic legal productivity, is articulated and managed will often determine the resilience of a commons, as Ostrom has shown in her research.[130]

The ways in which the commons operates against law is perhaps best described as an irritant force, a *pouvoir irritant*.[131] The notion of *pouvoir irritant* perhaps better fits in a global scenario where the classic concept of constituent power, which typically aims at enacting the revolutionary reset of a constituted State, of its institutions and of its Law,[132] is historically (rather than perhaps politically) out of reach. As Kirsch suggests, "[f]rom the perspective of the international legal order, invocations of

129 Paolo Grossi, "Storia di Esperienze Giuridiche e Tradizione Romanistica," *Quaderni Fiorentini per la Storia del Pensiero Giuridico Moderno* 17 (1988): 533–50.
130 Elinor Ostrom, *Governing the Commons: The Evolution of Institutions for Collective Action* (Cambridge: Cambridge University Press, 1990).
131 Nico Krisch, "*Pouvoir Constituant* and *Pouvoir Irritant* in the Postnational Order," *International Journal of Constitutional Law* 14, no. 3 (2016): 657.
132 A legacy that arguably remains present also in Teubner's "distributed" re-articulation of constituent power in terms of societal constitutionalism: Gunther Teubner, *Constitutional Fragments: Societal Constitutionalism and Globalization* (Oxford: Oxford University Press, 2012).

constituent power [...] [appear] mostly as an unexceptional, political irritant."[133] Here, however, the logic of a transversal legal pluralism — that is, a pluralism that is articulated in a variety of interactional directions — may offer useful ideas; however these ideas cannot be explored further here for reasons of space, and will need to form the basis of a future research agenda. The question that remains, however, is: what can the commons offer for thinking law *beyond* Law?

7. Conclusions

What to make of these tentative, exploratory reflections on the commons? Can the commons simply, and perhaps naively, be thought of in terms of an exclusively positive contribution to the task of thinking law ecologically, and of thinking law beyond and against Law today? Certainly not. This chapter is a contribution to thinking, speaking, and imagining differently. And it is a contribution to retrieving ideas that may populate a new imaginary for law. As Pieraccini has suggested, today "[t]he task for legal scholars is [to] produce a new language" so as to disentangle law and legal strategies "from the constraints imposed by the tradition of [modernity]."[134] Yet the commons, both historically and normatively, remain fully capable of failure and open to conflict. If modernity, however, constructs thresholds separating conflict and order, war and peace, reason and passion,[135] a new vision of law must embrace the ambiguities that traverse life. The commons must acknowledge that conflict, and the way it is approached, is the basis of an always-provisional order that, itself, must be carefully maintained in a responsive and responsible manner.[136] This is, perhaps, the key strength of a perspective of the commons. But what can we bring forward from the reflections offered in this chapter?

---

133 Krisch, "*Pouvoir Constituant* and *Pouvoir Irritant*," 674.
134 Pieraccini, "Beyond Legal Facts and Discourses," 17.
135 See De Lucia, "Re-Embodying Law" and De Lucia, "Semantics of Chaos."
136 See on this, Esposito, *Living Thought*.

In a commons understood as a socio-ecological institution, law emerges not from the will of a subject, nor is it entirely independent of human agency; law emerges through a relation between the various elements constituting each commons. Law, moreover, is not found, arguably, by measuring it against a binary law/non-law, but rather through a qualitative assessment. We return to the idea that law is the art of discovering what is good and equitable, or, to use the language of ecological thinking, law is measured against whether it is responsive and responsible.

The plurigenerational dimension of the commons outlined above is also inserted into this re-framing of law. The commons function as transtemporal relational hubs. Additionally, through their complexity, commons function as the connective legal tissue that joins together not only the traditional planes of the political, the social, and the legal, but also the ecological. What results is a transversal institutional model that hinges on the key aspects of both epistemic location and of ethos. A law attuned to an inhabited place, that emerges as responsive and responsible through epistemic location, resonates in multiple ways with natural law. However, natural law in this context has none of the characteristics typical of modern rationalist natural law, based on universal, immutable principles. And it is certainly not an ethical framework. A natural law as it may emerge from these reflections, is attuned to *ethos* and emerges from the observation of the regularities of nature, culture, and their interactions. It embodies their responses and affectivity, and animates the relations that constitute and are constituted through the commons as complex assemblages. Law thus acquires an "ethological" meaning. Not a universal natural law, but a situated one, in both time and space. The commons, as socio-ecological institutions, integrate a multiplicity of perspectives, not only those of the participating humans. Indeed, the legal pluralism that underpins the commons is significant because it also incorporates non-human legalities and normativities. The commons, further, can be thought of as a functional legal category that allows us to move from rights to duties and from duties to rights, where the allocation of legal personhood is not fixed, and is based on necessity and usefulness, rather than on the fixed, objective criteria of modernity that delineate subjects and objects absolutely. The commons, ultimately, articulates a mode of legality that is incommensurable with hegemonic forms of Law. Commons perform and produce law through their practices, and their "legal productivity" draws upon all elements of each commons assemblage.

However, the commons offer no guarantees, and may only offer what they are: a set of plural practices of resistance and recalcitrance. What then if the best the commons can offer is to *infect* or *irritate*[137] modern law? Can they offer a global template for thinking law beyond Law? Or can they "merely" offer localized instances of their strength of inhabiting particular grounds — a strength that is also a key limitation in terms of theorizing? Do we need theorizing?

---

137 Krisch, "*Pouvoir Constituant* and *Pouvoir Irritant*."

10

CommonsWealth: The Difference Engine: Complexity and Generativity — New Ontological Foundations

Paul B. Hartzog

Being in Relation

Complexity is a condition, a structure, a dynamical system, in which it is not merely the elements of the system that are relevant, but, sometimes more importantly, their arrangement, their relations to each other; here complementary, there juxtaposed. The study of complex systems seeks to find deep structural insights in the universe, order out of chaos, and a hidden meaning in the assemblages of things. For this chapter, a Table of Contents is offered as a crucial lens on the relations between elements, just as the embryo allows us to see in its entirety the structure of the future organism: although the details have not yet emerged, the distilled structure reveals understandings about what is yet to be explored.

1. Introduction

1.1 The Difference Engine
In 1822 Charles Babbage designed his Difference Engine, a machine for making calculations.[1] Shortly thereafter, the communication revolution began with the first electric telegraph. The resulting era of mechanization, and eventually computerization, along with instantaneous communication, ushered in a new era with new ways of thinking and organizing, ultimately resulting in the emergence of the Internet, a global network for sharing and connecting everything from information to people. Interactions once spread across space and time now produce aggregate effects that take place on timescales that are perceptible to human beings. Like a flock, or swarm, the parts act not in unison, but complementarily, not like a machine, but like a living organism.

Commons, cooperation, and complex systems synergize in a way that leverages diversity and difference into an effect that I call "The Difference Engine." At the intersection of social and technological change there is a nexus of activity that embraces a radical new politics, not as an engagement with a beleaguered anarchy of nation-states, but rather through new modes of social, political, and economic production. Confronted by the radical reality of a world of inequality, climate change, and economic collapse perpetuated by legacy modes of being, technologically mobilized individuals have crafted an equally radical response: new modes of being that are diverse and evolving, fluid and anarchical. Because its own internal organization is complex and adaptive, the difference engine calls into being an equally complex and adaptive new form of social, political, and economic space. This new space is ontologically generative in the sense that it continually creates and activates new forms of difference, resulting in a "perpetual revolution." It is crucial that we learn to understand this new politics as a space where we empower,

---

1   *Wikipedia,* s.v. "Difference engine," https://en.wikipedia.org/wiki/Difference_engine.

recognize, and celebrate horizontality and diversity, rather than seek to impose a conformance to hierarchy and similarity.

This constellation of recently-emerged factors provides us with a set of lenses onto an evolving new reality. This new reality is dynamic and non-linear, and like the new reality itself, the means to understanding it is also non-linear. Understanding must happen as a gestalt, where seemingly separate elements, when brought into proximity with each other, suddenly make possible a new experience formed by the relationships that the parts have with each other. Because a simple linear argument cannot convey such a gestalt, this writing presents the parts in no particular order, to be thought of more as a constellation. In auto-catalytic reactions, for example, it is only when all of the necessary chemicals are present that the reaction begins spontaneously. Likewise, in this chapter, only when all of the pieces are apparent, can their previously hidden relations be brought to light to reveal the emergent gestalt that is the dynamic evolving whole.

The goal of this revelation is both descriptive and normative. Descriptively, it offers understanding. The world seems increasingly chaotic, with global collapse looming ever closer on the horizon. Despair is not far behind. However, by revealing that though we are now living in closer engagement with constant change, these changes are not chaotic, but are instead a scientific discipline called "complexity," we also discover hope. Complex adaptive systems are understandable, and though we may not be able to control them, we can utilize a deeper understanding of their dynamics and principles in order to harness their energy and direct it towards our goals, as long as those goals do not conflict with the dynamics and principles of the system. In a nutshell, a kayaker does not seek to control the river, but simply moves with its flows and currents, avoiding obstacles, and drawing energy from it on her journey. In politics, economics, and society, we, too, can harness complexity to create a more harmonious, mindful, and just civilization.[2]

Epistemologically, there is ample room to debate why and how we can and should attempt to justify faith in unpredictable but understandable complex adaptive systems. Fortunately, Umberto Eco has provided some comfort for those who seek to cultivate new conversations and directions:

> There is only the risk of contradiction. But sometimes you have to speak because you feel the moral obligation to say something, not because you have the "scientific" certainty that you are saying it in an unassailable way.[3]

2. Commons and Commoning

2.1 *The Centrality of Ontology: Tragedy and Perception*

Commons come in a wide variety of kinds, but they are typically defined as shared resources of some kind. Some commons are naturally occurring physical resources such as forests or fish populations. Other commons are conceptual, such as information. Others are rhetorical tools: "Internet technology is a part of the global commons," claims the Tokyo Declaration on Global Commons.[4]

Historically, there have been many attempts to clarify the ontology of commons. Roman Law recognized the following four categories of property:

- *res nullius*
- *res communes*
- *res privatae*
- *res publica*

---

2   Robert Axelrod and Michael D. Cohen, *Harnessing Complexity: Organizational Implications of a Scientific Frontier* (New York: Basic Books 2001).

3   Umberto Eco, *Travels in Hyper Reality: Essays* (San Diego: Harcourt Brace Jovanovich, 1986), xii.

4   "Tokyo Declaration on Global Commons," *Environmental Policy and Law* 29, no. 5 (1999): 249–50.

While "res privatae" and "res publica" are easily recognized as referring to privately and publicly owned and managed resources, the other two are less obvious. "Res nullius" refers to things that are not owned or managed by anyone, and are, as a result, "open access." At that time in history, one might consider the fish in the sea to be a "res nullius" resource. "Res communes," however, refers to resources which *were* collectively managed, not through a public or private proxy, but through the actions of the group itself.

In 1968, Garrett Hardin wrote "The Tragedy of the Commons."[5] One of the most frequently cited articles ever written, it set the stage for decades of misunderstandings. Ontologically, it uses the term "tragedy" in the original Greek sense of a situation which, because of its own internal trajectory, cannot be avoided or overcome. A tragedy, for the Greeks, is not a tragedy because no one took action, but, rather, is the following-to-conclusion of an inexorable set of affairs *for which no diverting action exists.* The tragedy is inevitable. Oedipus is fated to kill his father and to marry his mother, and even actions taken to prevent the tragedy only serve to seal his fate. Although Hardin's article itself simply attempts to show the cause leading to overgrazing livestock on a commons, the framing of this as a tragedy has led to decades of pessimistic misunderstandings and irresponsible avoidance. Notably, the article incorrectly conflates "commons" with "open access" resources rather with than "collectively managed" resources, mistaking "res communes" for "res nullius."

Later, scholar Elinor Ostrom, eventually a recipient of the Nobel Prize in Economics for her work on commons, wrote *Governing the Commons.*[6] In *Governing the Commons,* and her subsequent decades of work, Ostrom shows how groups have cooperated to collectively manage resources across cultures worldwide throughout time. Her body of work, along with the

---

5   Garrett Hardin, "The Tragedy of the Commons," *Science* 162, no. 3859 (1968): 1243–48.
6   Elinor Ostrom, *Governing the Commons: The Evolution of Institutions for Collective Action* (Cambridge: Cambridge University Press, 1990).

generations of scholars she inspired, is a catalog of findings in case studies of commons solutions, as well as the ongoing analysis necessary to identify patterns, both successful and unsuccessful, that can be generalized into effective strategies. Moreover, Ostrom specifically points out the harm brought about by representing commons dilemmas as a "tragedy" because of the role of human perception in achieving cooperation. The perceived cost of solving a collective-action dilemma can prevent those trapped in it from making a move to escape.

So, the task ever since has been to change the ontology of commons from one that offers only a single tragic narrative, to one that recognizes and celebrates a diversity of framings and solutions. Instead of merely accepting the dominant narrative, i.e., that "private" (market) and "public" (state) solutions are the only routes at our disposal, by embracing commons-thinking we can design a wide variety of solutions, tailor-made to the situation at hand, and thereby also having a higher likelihood of success. Ostrom's repeated finding was that "communities of individuals have relied on institutions resembling neither the state nor the market to govern some resource systems with reasonable degrees of success over long periods of time."[7]

2.2 Rivalrousness and Excludability

Resources are typically analyzed in relation to two key properties: rivalrousness and excludability. Rivalrousness is the degree to which one person's uses diminishes others' use. In other words, when the consumption of a good results in less of that good remaining for others, via depletion, then the good is said to be rivalrous, or subtractable. A clear example would be any natural resource like trees or oil. Alternatively, knowledge goods are non-rivalrous: the knowledge you learn does not reduce the amount of knowledge remaining for others to learn.

The principle of excludability refers to the ease with which the beneficiaries, i.e., users, of a good can be prevented from accessing the resource in question. We tend to mobilize exclud-

---

7   Ibid., 1.

able resources as either private or toll goods and charge money for access. For non-excludable goods, however, we tend to manage them as "common pool" resources or public goods, both of which will be considered to be types of commons for the purposes of this discussion.

The crucial thing about these categories is that they, like commons themselves, are fluid. Their attributes are not given, but are a byproduct of how they are conceptualized and in what contexts they are framed. It is worth looking at this in more detail.

> In most situations, *excludability is a human artifact* rather than an unalterable natural condition.[8]

To illustrate the importance of ontology, we need to look at how technology allows us to move resources into and out of commons status. For a first example, we can look at the use of frequency spectrum in the United States. The number of radio frequencies available for broadcasting is essentially unlimited, but by creating a licensing regime and providing enforceable proprietary allocation of certain frequencies, a governmental and business strategy was able to turn a non-rivalrous resource into a rivalrous one. More recently, technology has emerged that allows devices to inspect the locally available frequency spectrum for unused bandwidths and then broadcast in those regions at short range for medical devices and other tools. There are also ways to turn otherwise non-rivalrous resources into rivalrous ones. When knowledge is limited to a particular book, then when someone has that book, there is literally less knowledge available for others. Atoms are rivalrous, but bits are not, unless they are forced to be. Furthermore, excludability is also affected. When knowledge is packaged into scientific journals that are only available at cost, then potential beneficiaries are excluded. Just as fences partitioned the once-open prairie, so, too, can

---

8   Oran Young, *The Institutional Dimensions of Environmental Change* (Cambridge: MIT Press, 2002), 142.

Digital Rights Management partition the knowledge commons. Fortunately, we can also use technology to go the other way. We might choose to take excludable resources such as books, and choose to make them non-excludable using the realities of digital technology and the Internet. Specifically, when a user downloads a file from the Internet or from another digital source, that file is *copied* to the destination, leaving the original file for others to access.

Furthermore, in a merely anthropocentric analysis of commons, the user pool is assumed to be humans. However, whale populations are important and valid user pools of the krill shrimp fields in the southern oceans, which they consume. While human user pools may be excluded from these resources by using laws, fishing licenses, and such, there is no applicable analogy for animal populations. Moreover, efficient excludability on land is treated as if it were fundamentally different than oceanic or atmospheric excludability. Unfortunately, however effective a fence may be in excluding the human user pool from a parcel of a land, this fragmentation approach fails to take into account migratory birds, transboundary pollution, water table contamination, as well as a whole host of other factors.

In addition, the "efficiency" of excludability is never defined. Efficient in what regard? A *reductio ad absurdum* makes the point best: one can imagine a world where all humans wear masks that allow the wearer to breathe, perhaps based on their credit rating, thus efficiently excluding the anthropocentric user pool from the common pool resource. There is nothing technologically unsound about this option, nor is it economically outrageous. Its real-world feasibility, however, is somewhat lacking. So again, is efficient excludability an issue of technology, cost-effectiveness, political willpower, or some other hazy notion that perhaps enables the discussion to advance some concepts at the expense of others?

The crucial reality here is that there is no one singular reality. The properties of commons are not some extrinsic "given" but, rather, are as variable as the concepts we deploy to operationalize them. In some situations, commons management runs afoul of "collective action" problems, namely that collective management will not occur when decision-making, management, and monitoring are costly.[9] In recent years, however, technology has greatly reduced the costs of collective organizing, and has thereby yielded new forms of commons and "commoning" practices.

2.3 Technologies of Cooperation and the Emergence of Commons-Based Peer Production

A crucial global economic phenomenon is the rise of commons-based peer production. "Technologies of cooperation" enable people to self-organize more easily.[10] Volunteer work such as Wikipedia and open-source software were early indicators of powerful new ways of organizing labor and capital. Later, analyses of "commons-based peer-production" showed the logic and forces behind its successes — for example, how sharing commons to support work is radically cost-effective.[11] Some commons in which peer production is gaining a foothold are food, energy, "maker culture," health, education, news, culture, housing, transportation, and even currency. Clearly, our thinking about production, property, and even politics must evolve to reflect the growing participatory economy of global stewardship and collectively-driven "platform cooperatives."[12]

The rise of 3D printing and the Internet of Things combined with participatory practices yields new forms of value production, paralleling new forms of value accounting and exchange. We witness a "Cambrian explosion" of new currency species, like Bitcoin, and innovative trust technologies to support them: blockchain, holochain, and other distributed ledgers. Just as

---

9   Mancur Olson, *The Logic of Collective Action, Public Goods, and the Theory of Groups* (Cambridge: Harvard University Press, 1971).

10 Howard Rheingold, *Smart Mobs: The Next Social Revolution* (Cambridge: Perseus Publishing, 2002).

11 Yochai Benkler, "Coase's Penguin, or, Linux and the Nature of the Firm," *The Yale Law Journal* 112, no. 3 (2002): 369–446.

12 Trebor Scholz and Nathan Schneider, *Ours to Hack and to Own: The Rise of Platform Cooperativism, A New Vision for the Future of Work and a Fairer Internet* (New York: OR Books, 2017). Also, Michel Bauwens, *P2P Foundation,* https://p2pfoundation.net

twentieth-century electrical infrastructure remained fragmented until standards enabled a connected network, new infrastructure matures when separate solutions merge and the parts of the emergent system reinforce the stability of the whole.

Moreover, commons-based peer production is organized into networks that practice "agile" modes of production. These new forms of social organization show two key characteristics:

1. They operate intelligently by means of "information commons," i.e., information about the system that is available to the members, and
2. They operate in a fluid, dynamic way.

Whether we look at the "smart mobs" of crowds protesting the WTO in Seattle, or the "pop-up" infrastructures of food, shelter, and medical care during the Occupy Movement, we see similar processes. Open-source production of software and hardware employs a process called "agile development," which has spilled over into education in the form of "agile learning" practices. That smart mobs and agile networks behave so much like flocks and swarms is no accident. In fact, there is a field of research that studies the presence of these patterns across many disciplines, and it is to that study of "complex adaptive systems" that we must now turn.

3. Complex Adaptive Systems

3.1 The Edge of Chaos
Complex adaptive systems have been called "small pieces loosely joined."[13] They are a network of creative parts that function as a whole. By being neither overly rigid nor overly flexible, they are able to perpetuate themselves in sometimes highly volatile environments. Complex systems are composed of a diversity of interdependent pieces, that adjust to each other on a landscape.

---

13 David Weinberger, *Small Pieces Loosely Joined: A Unified Theory of The Web* (Cambridge: Perseus Publishing, 2002).

What parts exist, how they can adapt, and how they are connected all factor into a complex system's properties.

The study of complex adaptive systems has enjoyed considerable attention in recent decades. Chaos theory reveals that out of turbulence and nonlinear dynamics, complex systems emerge: order from chaos. We learned that complex systems are poised on the "edge of chaos" and generate "order for free".[14] They are composed of many parts connected into a flexible network. As matter and energy flow through, the systems spontaneously self-organize into increasingly complex structures. These systems, continuously in flux, operate "far from equilibrium".[15] Beyond critical thresholds, differences in degree become differences in kind: "More is different."[16]

Complexity science reveals the difference between prediction and attraction. We can know that a marble in a bowl will reach the bottom of the bowl even though we cannot predict its exact path because of sensitivity to initial conditions. Deterministic chaos means path dependence, where future states are highly influenced by small changes in previous states. A typical example is the lock-in of the now-standard "QWERTY" keyboard.

Complex adaptive systems, then, are a specific kind of system, found across many disciplines: economics, biology, ecology, genetics, politics, sociology, epidemiology, physics. The findings of complex adaptive systems reveal the hidden order behind everything from traffic jams to economic crashes, from synchronized fireflies to internet networks.[17]

---

14 Stuart A. Kauffman, *At Home in the Universe: The Search for Laws of Self-Organization and Complexity* (New York: Oxford University Press, 1995) and Stuart A. Kauffman, *The Origins of Order: Self Organization and Selection in Evolution* (New York: Oxford University Press, 1993).

15 Ilya Prigogine and Isabelle Stengers, *Order Out of Chaos: Man's New Dialogue with Nature* (Toronto: Bantam Books, 1984).

16 Philip W. Anderson, "More Is Different: Broken Symmetry and the Nature of the Hierarchical Structure of Science," *Science* 177, no. 4047 (1972): 393–96.

17 John H. Holland, *Hidden Order: How Adaptation Builds Complexity* (Reading: Addison-Wesley, 1995) and Steven H. Strogatz, *Sync: The Emerg-*

3.2 Networks

Because complex systems are networks, we can see "network effects."

- Metcalfe's Law describes how adding another node to a network increases the value of all other nodes exponentially, because many new pairs of connections are possible.[18] In economics in particular, this is called "increasing returns to scale."[19]
- Reed's Law goes even farther, because new groups can be formed — not merely new pairwise linkages — and exhibits a much greater geometric growth.[20]

In addition to network effects, network topology also plays a key role. Some kinds of network are robust to random failures but are vulnerable to selective damage, i.e., network failures that harm or remove nodes possessing a higher centrality. Furthermore, "centrality" means different things inside different network topologies and depending on how it is defined and measured. Network structure also affects the frequency and magnitude of cascades across the network. Like avalanches in sand piles, power laws create "self-organized criticality" wherein systems minimize the frequency of large changes by allowing a higher frequency of small changes.[21]

3.3 Information Landscapes

Complex systems constitute and also occupy "fitness landscapes," exhibit cycles of growth and decline, are punctuated by explosions of diversity and periods of stasis, and show waves

_____
ing Science of Spontaneous Order_ (New York: Theia, 2003).
18 *Wikipedia,* s.v. "Metcalfe's Law," https://en.wikipedia.org/wiki/Metcalfe%27s_law.
19 W. Brian Arthur et al., *The Economy as an Evolving Complex System II* (Reading: Addison-Wesley, 1997).
20 *Wikipedia,* s.v. "Reed's Law," https://en.wikipedia.org/wiki/Reed%27s_law.
21 Per Bak, *How Nature Works: The Science of Self-Organized Criticality* (New York: Copernicus, 1996), 33–48.

of ebb and flow, seen, for example, in traffic patterns. On fitness landscapes, algorithms that pursue merely maximization, without the capacity to learn from remote information on the landscape, get stuck in local optima. Without diversity and sharing, there is no possibility for improvement. Swarms can escape fitness traps when they not only read information from the landscape but also write to it, creating shared information environments, such as when ants lay down chemical trails for other ants to follow.[22]

Landscapes and occupants impart selection pressures on each other. Good employees and good jobs both outperform bad ones. Agents and strategies evolve. Because landscapes are constantly shifting, adaptation can become maladaptation when selection pressures change. The buffalo's strategy to frighten off wolves was to turn broadside and make itself appear as large as possible, a strategy that proved all too fatal when confronted by rifle-wielding pioneers.

3.4 Dynamics and Time

Complex systems operate across a variety of timescales. When we study the spread of disease through a forest, we see a slow progression of infected trees. However, when we study the spread of fire, we see the same pattern enacted much faster.

Thus, complex systems and their dynamics are not new. What is new is that human systems have accelerated to the point where political, economic, and social changes now occur rapidly enough to appear within the threshold of human perception. We change from slow social movement to an era of "smart mobs."[23] Consequently, while it may be true that we did not need the tools of complex systems in the past because change was slow or infrequent and did not require a dynamical viewpoint, the current speed of change demands a new lens.

---

22 Deborah Gordon, *Ants at Work: How An Insect Society Is Organized* (New York: Free Press 2011).

23 Rheingold, *Smart Mobs.*

3.5 Difference and Diversity

Complex systems generate diversity through cycles of adaptation. The diversity of the parts leverages simultaneous exploration of new avenues of evolution. As discoveries emerge, the benefits of these advantageous adaptations provide pathways for the beneficial evolution of the whole.

Scott Page's work has shown that for complex problems, having a diverse set of resources is more effective. Having a few experts can result in "groupthink," when what is needed is for a variety of creative and different approaches to thinking outside the box.[24] You can do a lot with a hammer, but a toolbox full of hammers is only useful if all you ever confront are nails. More importantly, as an ontology, a toolbox full of hammers is likely to become a lens that causes you to see all problems as nails, rather than in some other way, just as public/private and commons narratives shape our approaches to resource management.

4. Negotiating Difference: Normality vs. Power

4.1 Normality: The Bell Curve

Figure 1 shows the bell curve, also called a "normal distribution." It contains a central peak, an average. Moreover, that center average is meaningful, since it is representative of the rest of the curve. The average is the highest point on the curve; i.e., it has the most points directly underneath it, and most of the other points under the curve lie near the average as well. That's what a normal distribution means.

More interestingly, we can describe two axes of marginalization and oppression. First, the horizontal axis demonstrates *marginalization*. As populations move away from the center average, they are increasingly marginalized. Second, the vertical

---

24 Scott Page, *The Difference: How the Power of Diversity Creates Better Groups, Firms, Schools, and Societies* (Princeton: Princeton University Press, 2008); Scott Page, *Diversity and Complexity* (Princeton: Princeton University Press, 2010); Scott Page, *The Diversity Bonus: How Great Teams Pay Off in the Knowledge Economy* (Princeton: Princeton University Press, 2017).

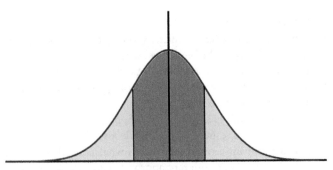

Figure 1. Bell Curve / Normal Distribution

axis demonstrates *oppression*. As populations move away from the center average, they are increasingly oppressed. Minority realities do not get addressed because the system caters to the center average.

The bell curve represents a system which includes:

- mass politics,
- mass culture,
- mass society,
- mass production,
- mass marketing.

In a bell-curve civilization, everything is produced using 1) large amounts of 2) similar elements. The reign of "one size fits all" — in everything from culture and media to physical objects — leaves little room for customization in accordance with difference, diversity, or individual expression.

4.2 Power: The Long Tail

Figure 2 shows a "power law" distribution, or "long tail." Complex systems, such as the one we are now experiencing globally, are organized according to power laws, not normal distributions. There are a few high points at the top, but most of the activity (the area under the curve) is in the long tail. The long

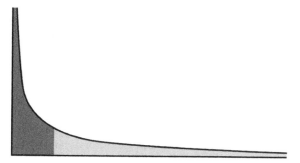

Figure 2. Power Law / Long Tail Distribution.

tail constitutes such a huge proportion of the whole because it is populated with such a large array of diverse elements.

Under the long tail, we can also describe an average, but in this graph, that average is meaningless. The average is not the highest point on the curve. It is not even an important point. In addition, the rest of the points under the curve do not lie near the average. In fact, the average is not representative of the system as a whole in any meaningful way.

The long tail represents a system which includes:

- politics of difference,
- global subcultures,
- overlapping societies,
- customized production,
- niche marketing.

In a long-tail civilization, everything is produced using 1) small amounts of 2) different elements. Creation is bespoke(n). Everything — from culture and media to physical objects — can be customized in accord with difference, diversity, or individual expression.

4.3 The Difference
The key distinction between these two systems lies in how they deal with difference. Under a bell-curve society, if you select any

two people or groups at random, they are *more likely to be similar than different*. Under the long tail, however, if you select any two people or groups at random, they are *more likely to be different than similar*. This has profound consequences for everything from production to politics.

To reiterate, under a mass-oriented society, mass culture produces mass media for mass consumption, and mass production produces large quantities of identical units. "Normal" is a meaningful distinction. Diversity is eschewed in favor of homogeneity. We do not have to be concerned with our ethics in the presence of the Other when we create a society in which that Other is marginalized and oppressed.

However, under the long tail, the *norm* is to be *different*. Under the long tail, to conform is to be non-conforming. "Normal" is no longer a meaningful expression. When encounters with difference become commonplace, then we are confronted, both individually and collectively, with a civilizational crisis. Consequently, living together and crafting a healthy civilization becomes a choice and a commitment, not something that we do by default simply because we are similar. This is sometimes neither comfortable nor easy, but it is mindful of the Other.

5. Politics: The Postmodern Failure of Imagination

5.1 *Towards the Many*

> [What postmodernists] cannot imagine is a nontotalizing system or structure that nonetheless acts as a whole.[25]

The key questions, then, asked by many social and political thinkers in the 20th century, concern the alternatives to mass society, with its mass production and mass culture and mass politics. Many of these initial forays brought to light important factors that set the stage by cultivating a heightened sense of

---

25 Mark C. Taylor, *The Moment of Complexity: Emerging Network Culture* (Chicago: University of Chicago Press, 2001), 65.

awareness. Although these thinkers could not offer new positive or meaningful alternatives, they did begin to articulate that something that needed solving was on the horizon of our perception. With the arrival of the Internet, global complexity skyrocketed, along with cultural interpenetration. Suddenly, complex systems and commons-thinking emerged as fields of study with direct relevance to new conditions.

5.1.1 Despair: From One to None

After World War II and the revelation of the Holocaust, philosophers struggled to come to grips with how the principles of the Enlightenment could have led to such a mind-bogglingly epic human disaster. The answer came in the recognition that monolithic totalizing ontologies could, and did, lead to immense tragedy. In fact, given that singular ontologies have no systemic mechanisms to balance or act as a "check" on their central dogmas, one might even assert that, given time, it is inevitable that they would encounter circumstances to which they could no longer adapt. Like the cave cricket, their very excellence at being themselves makes them severely fragile to changes in their environment.

If, according to Adorno and Horkheimer, the Enlightenment, as a programme, results in the "disenchantment of the world,"[26] and is therefore totalitarian at its core, then what is necessary to restore balance and freedom is nothing less than what Morris Berman calls "the reenchantment of the world."[27] Unfortunately, the answer to the inexorable tragedy of monolithic meta-narratives was, for the post-modernists, an invitation to an even deeper tragedy.

The necessary first step, which the post-modernists wholeheartedly embraced, was the utter rejection of monolithic meta-narratives and totalizing systems. It is no accident that

---

26 Max Horkheimer and Theodor W. Adorno, *Dialectic of Enlightenment* (Stanford: Stanford University Press, 2007), 1–4.

27 Morris Berman, *The Reenchantment of the World* (New York: Cornell University Press, 1981).

these rejections occurred not merely in social theory but also in mathematics, physics, and computing as well. The zeitgeist had arrived, and the naive faith in Science's capacity to offer clear and final answers was its sacrificial lamb on the altar. Three examples demonstrate the shift:

- First, where Russell and Whitehead had claimed that mathematics would soon be complete, Kurt Gödel's subsequent "Incompleteness Theorem" showed that mathematical systems can never be both coherent and complete. When complete, they must contain self-contradiction, and when coherent, they remain incomplete.
- Second, Heisenberg, Bell, and other physicists revealed the inadequacy of classical mechanics in favor of a new "quantum" mechanics, which relied *at its foundation* on indeterminacy and uncertainty, not merely as inaccuracies that might be resolved by future developments, but rather as fundamental properties of reality. Even Einstein was shocked by this turn of events, although his own discoveries had destroyed the firm foundations of classical Newtonian physics in light of his new physics of relativity.
- And third, Alan Turing demonstrated in computing that "the halting problem" had no solution. In a nutshell, he showed that recursive statements in computing produced the same kinds of intractability as Godel's Incompleteness.

All of these examples are, in essence, variations on the statement "This sentence is false," which, by virtue of its self-reference, results in a kind of quasi-real condition. The truth or falsehood of the statement remains in a kind of perpetual metastasis, like quantum physicist Erwin Schrödinger's oft-discussed cat, frozen between being and non-being, not neither but both, just as light is both a wave and a particle depending on the consciousness of the observer. What all of these revelations initiated was deep thinking about the role that the observer's ideas, definitions, lenses, and preconceptions play in perception. The previously-held belief that the world was both objective and external was thrown into a cosmic disarray against the revelation of subjectivity and interiority.

Unfortunately for the philosophers, this revelation could only result in wholesale rejection of the One. What is clear, in hindsight, is that in the postmodern zeal to do away with the tyranny of the One, the only alternative provided is a vacuous and nihilist Zero. The Zero, however, offers us nothing. While it was true that everything was now uncertain, the discussions at the time could offer nothing new, no real alternative, now that rejection was required.

There are deep ramifications to insisting on rejection without offering alternatives, i.e., a negative assertion without a balancing positive assertion — deconstruction without construction. Both are what William Connolly defines as "ontopolitical interpretation:" Connolly clarifies that "to say that either something is fundamental or that nothing is fundamental, then, is to engage in ontopolitical interpretation."[28] More important, however, is understanding the consequences:

> Fundamental [political] presumptions fix possibilities, distribute explanatory elements, generate parameters within which an ethic is elaborated, and center (or decenter) assessments of identity, legitimacy, and responsibility.[29]

While it has been claimed that an honest despair is better than a false hope, in this case such a claim rests on a mistaken ontology, namely, that there is no non-nihilist alternative to totalizing systems. It is this claim that we must transcend.

5.1.2. Hope: From One to Many

There is an opposing alternative to The One, however, that is not The Zero. It is, rather, The Many. Moreover, the reason the post-

---

28 William Connolly, *Ethos of Pluralization* (Minneapolis: University of Minnesota Press, 1995), 1.
29 Ibid., 2.

modernists missed it is all too clearly articulated by the Mark Taylor quote that began this section, worth repeating here:

> [What postmodernists] cannot imagine is a nontotalizing system or structure that nonetheless acts as a whole.[30]

The crucial failure, then, is one of imagination. Construction, design, vision: these all rest on imagination. We have already seen that complex systems cannot be understood by taking them apart. A dynamic system, like an organism, deconstructed, cannot simply be re-constructed. What is necessary is to imagine new assemblages and new dynamics. Continuing, Bruno Latour has noted (citing Callon):

> The universalists defined a single hierarchy. The absolute relativists [postmodernists] made all hierarchies equal. The relative relativists, more modest but more empirical, point out what instruments and what chains serve to create asymmetries and equalities, hierarchies and differences.[31]

Latour likewise suggests that modernity is a One, against which is arrayed post-modernity's Zero. Modernity provides a singular meta-, which postmodernism resists not merely in substance but in definition, i.e., it does not resist that particular meta- but all "metas" on principle. When we accept that the opposition between One and Zero is not adequate, and that a second opposition between One and Many is available, then we have suddenly at our disposal, a "third estate," an alternative site for construction, a vast field of potentiality that we can investigate further. The logic is as follows:

---

30 Taylor, *The Moment of Complexity*, 65.

31 Michel Callon, "Techno-economic Networks and Irreversibility," in *A Sociology of Monsters: Essays on Power, Technology and Domination,* ed. John Law (London: Routledge, 1991), 132–64, 138, cited in Bruno Latour, *We Have Never Been Modern,* trans. Catherine Porter (Cambridge: Harvard University Press, 1993), 113.

- if what we may call the "Ontology of the One" rejects what is not itself— *by positing a radical commensurability by which only that which is its Self is valued, and all that is Other is devalued,*
- and what we may call the "Ontology of the Zero" rejects everything— *by positing a radical incommensurability by which nothing can be valued at all,*
- then the alternative "Ontology of the Many" succeeds because it rejects nothing (out of hand) — *by positing a perpetual flux of commensurables and incommensurables by which subjects/objects, Nature/Society, humans/nonhumans, are continually constructed, deconstructed, and reconstructed, in other words, e-value-ated.*

To be fair, systems-thinking was not terribly well known at the time, being relatively new, and is even now still not well-used among philosophers and social theorists. Fortunately, great strides have been made in understanding genetic networks, computer networks, ecological networks, and complex systems in general. The time has come to move theory-construction beyond a "post-" anything into a description of an emerging polity that can describe "a nontotalizing system or structure that nonetheless acts as a whole." In so doing, we can subsequently realize our current condition as a "pre-"condition, and thereby gather energy and focus on understanding precisely what it is *toward which we are moving,* and into we which we are evolving. We are certainly in a time of transition, where the old has not yet given way, but neither has the new coalesced. After transition comes transformation, where the system as a whole crosses a requisite threshold, and the phase change exhibited by complex systems (discussed earlier) occurs with great rapidity.

Our primary difficulty as a disenchanted world now rests in our struggle with the narratives we have been given — narratives that tell us what options exist, what pathways are sensible, and what is "real" in the sense that it is possible or achievable within something called "reality." The narrative formerly required by the rejection of The One was The Zero. With a new understanding comes the possibility of a new narrative, but we have been conditioned against that narrative in many ways. We have been told at least since Machiavelli that "a multitude without a head is useless."[32] Even Aristotle suggests that the ideal polis must not be so large that the citizens cannot hear its herald's voice, thus firmly anchoring the governable to the idea of communications, but also to the idea of a monolithic collective "voice" embodied in a singular herald.[33] To craft a new narrative, the lenses of commons-thinking and complex systems are crucial, but we need one more piece, namely, that of understanding how diverse multitudes could possibly function as a viable polity.

5.2. The Agony of the Multitude

5.2.1 Complex Multitudes

Hardt and Negri gave us a first attempt at describing this new "multitude."

> The people has traditionally been a unitary conception. The population, of course, is characterized by all kinds of differences, but the people reduces that diversity to a unity and makes of the population a single identity: "the people" is one. The multitude, in contrast, is many. The multitude is composed of innumerable internal differences that can never be reduced to a unity or a single identity — different cultures, races, ethnicities, genders, and sexual orientations; different forms of labor; different ways of living; different views of the world; and different desires. The multitude is a multiplicity of all these singular differences.[34]

> Network organization [...] is based on the continuing plurality of its elements and its networks of communication in such

---

32 Niccolò Machiavelli, *Discourses on Livy* (Chicago: University of Chicago Press, 1998), XLIV.

33 Aristotle, *Politics* (Mineola: Dover Publications, 2000), 1326b.

34 Michael Hardt and Antonio Negri, *Multitude: War and Democracy in the Age of Empire* (Penguin Books 2005), xiv.

a way that reduction to a centralized and unified command structure is impossible. The polycentric form of the guerrilla model thus evolves into a network form in which there is no center, only an irreducible plurality of nodes in communication with each other.[35]

The multitude [...] is composed of innumerable elements that remain different, one from the other, and yet communicate, collaborate, and act in common.[36]

In parallel with their recognition of network forms of sociality and vast arrays of difference, Hardt and Negri also note the absence of commons-thinking in contemporary politics, which is wholly apparent through the relentless focus on merely two historical choices. They urge us to move "beyond private and public":[37]

In the social, in other words, the tendency is to make everything public and thus open to government surveillance and control; and in the economic, to make everything private and subject to property rights.[38]

Thus is raised a seeming paradox, namely, how a system can function that exhibits both commonality and difference at the same time:

The challenge posed by the concept of multitude is for a social multiplicity to manage to communicate and act in common while remaining internally different.[39]

The multitude, by contrast, is not unified but remains plural and multiple. This is why, according to the dominant tradi-

---

35 Ibid., 82.
36 Ibid., 140.
37 Ibid., 202.
38 Ibid., 203.
39 Ibid., xiv.

tion of political philosophy, the people can rule as a sovereign power and the multitude cannot. The multitude is composed of a set of singularities — and by singularity here we mean a social subject whose difference cannot be reduced to sameness, a difference that remains different.[40]

The concept of multitude, then, is meant in one respect to demonstrate that a theory of the economic class need not choose between unity and plurality. A multitude is an irreducible multiplicity; the singular social differences that constitute the multitude must always be expressed and can never be flattened into sameness, unity, identity, or indifference.[41]

Perhaps inadvertently, Hardt and Negri's work cries out for an engagement with commons and complex systems, pieces of the puzzle that are relevant throughout. For example:

The common does not refer to traditional notions of either the community or the public; it is based on the communication among singularities and emerges through the collaborative social processes of production.[42]

[T]his production of the common is neither directed by some central point of command and intelligence [...] but rather it emerges [...] in the social space of communication. The multitude is created in collaborative social interactions.[43]

In fact, the entirety of their thesis reverberates with the importance of complex systems and peer-to-peer relations in relation to commons-thinking. This is particularly notable in their understanding of the role of technology, as well as in their use of specific words like "self-organization."

---

40 Ibid., 99.
41 Ibid., 105.
42 Ibid., 204.
43 Ibid., 222.

In this new world of networks, the "commons-based" social production [...] is politics, insofar as it generates the raw material of political action and propels the self-organization and decision-making that creates wealth and social equity.[44]

Again, it is worth underscoring that the wants and needs of the diverse multitude, both physical ones as well as expressions of selves calling for recognition, cannot be served by any overarching singular entity, such as the traditional nation-state. In sharp contrast to Hardt and Negri's description of the multitude, the origin of the state is a construction stemming from the idea of a unifying identity of a "people." In this origin, one particular axis of difference assumes the representation of the totality, and all other forms of difference remain outside the system. This totalizing distinction, à la Schmitt, is the "us/them" or "friend/enemy" distinction, which is totalizing precisely because it exists without regard to or in relation to the particular properties that characterize any given "us" or "them."[45] Even the presence of national borders is not sufficient to exhaustively articulate the properties that constitute what makes something part of an "us" or part of a "them." This essential ambiguity is of primary importance to sustaining the distinction.

In *Parchment, Printing, and Hypermedia,* Ron Deibert notes that:

The heterogeneous nature of postmodern social epistemology, and the overlapping layers of political authority... would all act as strong constraints against the emergence of a single mass identity. It is more likely that this sense of a global imagined community would coexist in a complex montage of overlapping and fluid multiple identities.[46]

---

44 Ibid., 350.
45 Carl Schmitt, *The Concept of the Political* (Chicago: University of Chicago Press, 2007).
46 Ron Deibert, *Parchment, Printing, and Hypermedia* (New York: Columbia University Press, 1997), 16.

So, Ernesto Laclau posits, given the complex heterogeneity of global society, as the state system declines there is no possibility of the emergence of a new state-like entity because the diverse multitudes possess no overarching singular criterion of difference around which a new state could crystallize.[47] There is no possibility of a monolithic "us" to juxtapose with an equally monolithic "them" contained within the diversity of a long-tail society. Rather, there are, recursively and self-referentially, only multitudes of "us"s and "them"s, interpenetrated and overlapping. There is not only the Multitude, but multitudes of Multitudes. Thus, there is no possibility for the emergence of a state that could inculcate in a singular fashion the heterogeneous values of the diverse multitude.

Moreover, there are two additional ramifications to this level of complexity.

- First, Alexander Wendt claimed that a world-state was "inevitable" because of the need for a singular authoritative entity that could provide social and political recognition.[48] The very definition of "authority" is at play, insofar as the act of recognition "authors" who we are. With a little imagination though, we can easily see that a peer-to-peer form of recognition satisfies the demand but is in keeping with what we know from complex systems. The multitudes can recognize *each other* through horizontal networks rather than relying on a vertical hierarchy. Authority is distributed throughout the network.[49] Interestingly, new forms of distributed authority have also emerged in technological networks using systems such as "blockchain" and "holochain" innovations.

47 Ernesto Laclau and Chantal Mouffe, *Hegemony and Socialist Strategy: Towards a Radical Democratic Politics* (London and New York: Verso, 1985) and personal conversation with Ernesto Laclau.

48 Alexander Wendt, "Why a World State Is Inevitable," *European Journal of International Relations* 9, no. 4 (2003): 491–542.

49 Paul B. Hartzog, "Panarchy Is What We Make of It: Why a World State Is Not Inevitable," 2004, https://www.academia.edu/2409728/Panarchy_Is_What_We_Make_of_It_Why_a_World_State_Is_Not_Inevitable.

- Second, networks of multitudes that are interpenetrated and overlapping significantly decrease the likelihood of war. Since no particular axis of difference can acquire the necessary salience of an us/them distinction, there is no enemy. A multitude of differences reduces all differences to merely one among many. Distinctions remain, but the heart cannot hate the liver, nor kill it — at least not without killing the whole.

What is significant here is that according to this logic, once the Multitude arrives, because of the sheer diversity under its long tail, it can never coalesce into some new stable unified state-like entity. In other words, the system is autopoietic *as is*. As new criteria of difference emerge and vanish, the complex un-whole that exists will never rigidify into something that can be opposed, i.e., it cannot become a new hegemony — not a discursive hegemony, nor a cultural one, nor a statist one. All that remains is an endless play of difference.

For political theorists for whom community is equated with identity and similitude, this is a death knell for civilization. We should be thankful, then, that *we no longer have to envision nor construct a polity on those terms.* Instead, we must look to other more radical forms of social and political theory for clues as to what lies ahead. By what means can a multitude of differences persist as a functional whole? Mark Taylor may be correct that the post-modernists could not imagine it, but *we must.*

5.2.2 Beyond Agonism

We realize at this stage that the structural reality of a "long tail" civilization, when juxtaposed with the political reality of the emergent multitude, reveals a synergy, a synchronicity. This synchronicity manifests in both modes as a continuous flux of diversity in which we are constantly confronted by the omnipresence of the Other, by differences that cannot be subsumed into a singular identity.

Such a realization is fundamentally agonistic, which is to say it shares much in common with the political theory of "agonism" or "agonistic pluralism," but the concept also goes beyond these.

Agonism emphasizes the importance of critical debate within a democracy, noting that the "polis" is not necessarily a place where we come to agree, but rather to disagree: "Consensus is indeed necessary but it must be accompanied by dissent [...] [D]isagreement should be considered as legitimate and indeed welcome."[50]

The agon itself, however, is a celebration of the struggle for ideas against each other, and in that context, we need to be wary that evolutionary adaptation is not a contest with winners and losers. Rather, as we have seen, "winning" only occurs within particular contexts, and carries evolutionary costs. To be a winner in one context is to be a loser in another. Adaptations can, and do, become maladaptive when the environment changes. For this reason, "survival of the fittest" is more accurately dubbed "survival of the fitters,"[51] and "winning" is often "winning by playing."[52]

Consequently, a new politics of the kind needed here must not only empower the continued emergence of new forms of difference, but much more importantly, must not subsume those differences into a totalizing condition via a monolithic centralized authoritative eidolon[53] that recognizes differences only when they are in accord with already-recognized differences (i.e., only when they are immediately beneficial to it). For example, the recognition of the particular social, political, and economic conditions of "women of color" must not be accepted

---

50 Chantal Mouffe, *The Democratic Paradox* (London and New York: Verso, 2000), 113.

51 Tom Malloy, "Curtain of Dawn," 1987, unpublished, cited in Alfred Seegert, *Ontology Recapitulates Ecology: The Relational Real in Evolution and Ecophilosophy,* Master's Thesis, University of Utah, 1998.

52 Paul B. Hartzog, "Winning by Playing: A Political Economy of Networks," 2004, https://www.academia.edu/2409729/Winning_By_Playing_A_Political_Economy_of_Networks.

53 From the Greek *eidolon*. An *eidolon* is both an idealized form of a person or thing as well as being a phantom, illusion, or specter. In this context, the point made is simply that the Enlightenment dream of perfect governance via a "monolithic centralized authority" was always not only a mere fantasy but also one without actual substance.

simply because "women" and "people of color" are already-recognized political conditions. In this example, "women of color," like all new forms of difference, exist *in and of themselves* and not merely as derivatives of existing conditions. Donna Haraway warns us of "seductions to organic wholeness through a final appropriation of all the powers of the parts into a higher unity."[54]

William Connolly, too, points out that it is not enough simply to define a set of pluralistic categories and then declare the "end of history," thinking that we have settled on a final ontology that is all-inclusive of diversity.

> The conventional understanding [of pluralism] first misrecognizes the paradoxical relation between a dominant constellation of identities and the very differences through which the constellation is consolidated and, second, misrecognizes new possibilities of diversification by freezing moral standards of judgment condensed from past political struggles.[55]

Rather, we must first realize that the dynamics of the new system spontaneously generate new and novel forms of diversity as a part of its functional maintenance, via autopoiesis. Second, we must then proceed to articulate a politics that is not only sustainably open to the emergence of those new forms and categories, but moreover, is capable of perpetually seeking out and recognizing new persons and groups, and is able to incorporate the new elements, not by subsuming them into existing categories, or by repressing them in favor of entrenched mechanisms, but by adjusting the system's characteristics to in order to evolve even more new modes of being and expression.

In addition, in contrast to Schmitt, Connolly claims that

---

54 Donna Haraway, "A Cyborg Manifesto: Science, Technology, and Socialist-Feminism in the Late Twentieth Century," in *Simians, Cyborgs and Women: The Reinvention of Nature* (New York: Routledge, 1991), 149–81, at 150.

55 Connolly, *Ethos of Pluralization*, xiv.

> You do not need a wide universal "we" (a nation, a community, a singular practice of rationality, a particular monotheism) to foster [...] governance of a population. Numerous possibilities of intersection and collaboration between multiple, interdependent constituencies infused by a general ethos of critical responsiveness drawn from several sources suffice very nicely.[56]

That the system is ontologically generative of new axes of differentiation may not come as a surprise, but it is even more crucial to see how that generativity is recursive, resulting in ever-increasing possibilities. Recalling the properties of networks mentioned above, new entities create *by their very existence* the possibility of new interactions and new associations: "When the cultural conditions of pluralization are reasonably intact, differentiation along some lines opens up multiple possibilities of selective collaboration along others."[57]

Such a multitude, then, is the precise opposite of the totalitarianism of which Giorgio Agamben warns us:

> Modern totalitarianism can be defined as the establishment [...] of a legal civil war that allows for the physical elimination not only of political adversaries but of entire categories of citizens who for some reason cannot be integrated into the political system.[58]

Fortunately, such a new civilization is made possible by The Difference Engine. The keystone of such a system lies in the realization and joyful enactment of the paradox of cultivating difference while at the same time producing the common. Just as for every instance of competition a form of cooperation is occurring at a higher level, for every form of difference there are

---

56 Ibid., xx.

57 Ibid., 197.

58 Giorgio Agamben, *State of Exception*, trans. Kevin Attell (Chicago: University of Chicago Press, 2008), 2.

higher forms of commonality — but to discover and recognize these forms requires challenging and reflective work.

Finally, the difference engine upon which future society relies, demands of us a complementary ethic of the Other. This new ethic cannot rely on axes of similarity or identity upon which to ground moral considerability, but rather, must engage with the omnipresent proximity of the radical Other in a field of constantly emerging difference. In embracing such an ethic, Umberto Eco encourages us to remember that we are capable of "finding in the multiplicity […] no longer a wound that must, at whatever cost, be healed, but rather the key to the possibility of a new alliance and of a new concord."[59]

However, by also embracing a more-than-agonistic worldview, multiplicity is not merely something to create alliances and concordance, but is also a thing to be celebrated as the artistic expression of the diversity of being in the world. Difference becomes not a thing to resolve in the sense of coming to a conclusion, but a thing to resolve (in the word's other sense), which is to disunify a whole into a diversity of parts in precisely the way light passing through a prism *resolves* into a spectrum of colors. With this kind of resolution one can see more, not less, and the previously perceived reality is revealed as a partial condition that, if not illusory or fraudulent, is at the very least reduced to only one of many ways of perceiving a complex reality.

Donna Haraway, too, celebrates the irony of this paradox of the irresolution of non-totalizing parts and wholes:

> Irony is about contradictions that do not resolve into larger wholes, even dialectically, about the tension of holding incompatible things together because both or all are necessary and true. Irony is about humour and serious play. It is also a rhetorical strategy and a political method.[60]

---

59 Umberto Eco, *The Search for the Perfect Language,* trans. James Fentress (Malden: Wiley-Blackwell, 1995), 351.
60 Haraway, "A Cyborg Manifesto," 149.

So what is ultimately at stake here is nothing less than a new vision of politics, a new definition of political life, or more accurately, a new definition of life qua politics. Certainly, the idea that living is itself political stretches back to the early political philosophers (Aristotle, Plato, etc.). Interestingly, it is Arlene Saxonhouse's insights in *Fear of Diversity* about Aristotle and ancient Greek life and politics that provides us with illumination:

> Diversity previously had meant the need for suppression or destruction, epistemological and political. For Aristotle it means life, epistemologically and politically.[61]

> The political art is to understand the need for diversity within the city and not to fear it, to acknowledge that it is the diversity that, while building the city, can never bring about a city that has escaped the conflicts of political claims.[62]

This political art is nothing less than the means to forge a new political association, complex and diverse, free and just.

5.3. *The Difference Engine and CommonsWealth*
5.3.1 Manifesto for a New Civilization

> We have never had to deal with problems of the scale facing today's globally interconnected society. No one knows for sure what will work, so it is important to build a system that can evolve and adapt rapidly.[63]

In conclusion, we find ourselves again at the beginning. Elinor Ostrom wrote the quote above on the last day of her life. It is

---

61 Arlene Saxonhouse, *Fear of Diversity: The Birth of Political Science in Ancient Greek Thought* (Chicago: University of Chicago Press, 1992), 232.

62 Ibid.

63 Elinor Ostrom, "Green from The Grassroots," *Project Syndicate,* June 12, 2012, https://www.project-syndicate.org/commentary/green-from-the-grassroots.

no accident that Elinor Ostrom, whose life's work is most responsible for giving us a half-century's worth of insights into the commons, was also responsible for deep thinking about the appropriate social structures to create a thriving commons-based civilization. For decades, she, along with her husband Vincent, crafted and articulated a political theory of "polyarchy." Polyarchy is many-centered, diverse, and most-importantly, not ruled by elites, i.e., a "-cracy." The themes of polyarchy are deeply in accord with complex adaptive systems. Ostrom's work on polyarchy challenges and encourages us to move "beyond panaceas," and to focus on broadening participatory culture, as well as promoting diversity and cooperation.[64]

The task of cultivating an entirely new civilization might at first seem daunting, but Umberto Eco shines a light forward, in a way that is conspicuously reminiscent of much of our earlier discussion:

A member of an archaic culture who acknowledges the limits of his own model and compares it to the one that is being formed as an alternative, from inside or outside his model, is creating […] in a positive sense, "counter-culture." Counter-culture is thus the active critique or transformation of the existing social, scientific or aesthetic paradigm […]. It is the only cultural manifestation that a dominant culture is unable to acknowledge and accept. The dominant culture tolerates parasitic counter-cultures as more or less innocuous deviations, but it cannot accept critical manifestations which call it [the dominant culture] into question. Counter-culture comes about when those who transform the culture in which they live become critically conscious of what they are doing and elaborate a theory of their deviation from the dominant model, offering a model that is capable of sustaining itself.[65]

---

64 Derek Wall, *Elinor Ostrom's Rules for Radicals: Cooperative Alternatives beyond Markets and States* (London: Pluto Press, 2017).
65 Umberto Eco, "Does Counter-culture Exist?" trans. Jenny Condie, in *Apocalypse Postponed: Essays by Umberto Eco* (Bloomington: Indiana University Press 2000), 115–28, at 124.

Insofar as both "culture" and "counter-culture" are defined by the currently prevailing system, so, too, are the possibilities for future civilization defined and constrained by the "hegemonic discourse."[66] Whereas a rebellion is defined by what it resists, a productive, generative, and positive way forward requires a more creative approach than mere opposition.

Here, then, is where we find clues and possibilities in Hannah Arendt's work. Hannah Arendt's definition of power is something that exists whenever individuals come together for a common activity: power, she says, is not simply possessed by groups (in the sense that they could be divested from it) but is rather "inherent in the very existence of political communities."[67] Power is constituted by the very fact of a group's existence. In other words: "[P]ower springs up between men when they act together and vanishes the moment they disperse."[68]

The mobilization of that collective power takes one of three forms:

- First, power can operate *on behalf of* current systems.
- Second, power can operate *in opposition to* current systems.
- But most importantly, power can exist as "third way" alternatives that reject both the dominant and oppositional structures, and instead operate *in parallel to* current structures.

Most contemporary analysis maintains that *only the first two constitute political activity.* But it is this very blind spot that offers hope for the emergence of truly revolutionary commons-building and human cooperation. New cooperating collectives are not of interest *only* when they intersect with traditional nation-states or economic structures. Whether we call it "pan-archy," or "polyarchy," or "heterarchy," or "plurilateralism," or

---

66 Antonio Gramsci, *Selections from the Prison Notebooks* (London: Lawrence & Wishart, 1971).

67 Hannah Arendt, "On Violence," in *Crises of the Republic* (New York: Houghton Mifflin, 1972), 103–84, at 151.

68 Hannah Arendt, *The Human Condition* (Chicago: University of Chicago Press, 1958), 200.

"cosmopolitanism," or "polycontexturality," or "neo-medieval-ism," or "mobius web governance," or "p2p [peer- to-peer] so-ciety," or "global civil society," the Multitude manifests through mechanisms of social governance that function independently of and in parallel to state governing.[69]

> What is absolutely essential to recognize, however, is that it is not the entanglements and overlaps with states and the state system that make efforts in global civil society "political" [...] [A]ctivism does not simply become politically relevant when it intersects with state behavior [...]. At stake in this analysis, then, is the concept of [...] politics.[70]

So, although many writers about citizen networks note their an-ti-systemic roots, it is also true that commoning activities such as open-source and Wikipedia are not primarily anti-systemic in their formation or motivations, despite the obviously system-transforming capacity of their innovative modes of production. When faced with the constraints of existing structures, it is of-ten the case that people will choose to, or be compelled to, turn aside and create something new on their own. So, from Hannah

---

69 Paul B. Hartzog, "Panarchy: Governance in the Network Age," 2005, https://www.academia.edu/210378/Panarchy_Governance_in_the_Net-work_Age; Kyriakos M. Kontopoulos, *The Logics of Social Structure* (Cambridge: Cambridge University Press, 1992); Niklas Luhmann, *Social Systems, Writing Science* (Stanford: Stanford University Press, 1995); Raimo Vayrynen, "Reforming the World Order: Multi- and Plurilat-eral Approaches," in *Global Governance in the 21st Century: Alternative Perspectives on World Order,* eds. Bjorn Hettne and Bertil Oden (Goth-enburg: Almqvist and Wiksell International, 2002), 110–11; David Held, "Cosmopolitanism," in *Governing Globalization: Power, Authority, and Global Governance,* eds. David Held and Anthony G. McGrew (Cam-bridge: Polity, 2002), 305–24, at 305; Hedley Bull, *The Anarchical Society: A Study of Order in World Politics* (New York: Columbia University Press, 1977); James N. Rosenau, *Distant Proximities: Dynamics Beyond Globaliza-tion* (Princeton: Princeton University Press, 2003); Michel Bauwens, *P2P Foundation,* http://www.p2pfoundation.net.

70 Paul Wapner, "Politics Beyond the State: Environmental Activism and World Civic Politics," *World Politics* 47, no .3 (1995): 311–40.

Arendt we gain insight into the ability of groups to undermine undesirable political and social practices, *not by attacking them, but by simply engaging in some other practice that, by its very nature, calls the existing practices into question and, eventually, to account.*

Our capacity to recognize and understand those new practices is informed by our knowledge of commons and complex systems. From that knowledge, we can begin to formulate a set of agile commoning principles that foster adaptability.[71]

- Build shared commons infrastructure.
- Improve information flow.
- Enable rapid innovation.
- Encourage participation.
- Support diversity and citizen empowerment.

By now it should be clear that agile practices also imply that we do not need to know the way in advance. The entire point of a complex adaptive system is that by optimizing its flexibility it maintains the best chance of continued existence. Creating the wealth of the commons, and studying how to go about it, can also be fluid. More hearts and minds are called for:

> A person who creates a new discipline does not have the task of enumerating all the problems connected with it. His task is to specify the subject of the discipline and its various branches and the discussions connected with it. His successors, then, may gradually add more problems, until the discipline is completely (presented).[72]

---

71 Paul B. Hartzog, "The Future of Economics: From Complexity to Commons," *OECD Insights*, January 9, 2017, http://oecdinsights.org/2017/01/09/the-future-of-economics-from-complexity-to-commons/.

72 Ibn Khaldun, *The Muqaddimah: An Introduction to History*, trans. Franz Rosenthal and N.J. Dawood (Princeton: Princeton University Press, 1967), 459.

The task before us is this: to co-create a system that is in perpetual flux — agile, dynamic, adaptive, evolving. The discipline is to explore cooperation, commons, and complexity with compassionate hearts and minds. The goal is to use what we learn in order to cultivate a society of "commoners" for whom the continued harmonious sustainability of a regenerative and thriving civilization is our collective endeavor. Only endless creativity in both arts and sciences will help us. Only a civilization that generates and celebrates difference will survive.

To re-emphasize, The Difference Engine produces benefits on two levels:

1. First, *diversity improves functionality.* A diverse system is more able to successfully respond to disruptions and to discover new pathways forward.
2. Second, *diversity is more just.* A compassionate civilization does not merely tolerate difference for its utility, but, rather, actively *encourages* it, *empowers* it, and *celebrates* it. Differences exist for their own sakes. Perpetual wonder needs no other justification.

For those who need a reason, the first should suffice, and for those who do not, the second is obvious.

Infinite Diversity in Infinite Combinations […] the elements that create truth and beauty.[73]

This, then, is the Great Work, to which we must dedicate ourselves.

This is the civilization that we must work towards.

This is the Difference Engine.

This is CommonsWealth.

---

73 *Memory Alpha*, s.v. "IDIC," http://memory-alpha.wikia.com/wiki/IDIC.

11

Resisting Anthropocene Neoliberalism: Towards New Materialist Commoning?

Anna Grear

1. Introduction

Materiality lies inescapably at the heart of the commons, and this chapter explores the idea that a New Materialist onto-epistemology might offer an important contribution to the power of commoning as ontological politics.[1] In particular, the chapter explores what it might mean to think of non-human actants as commoners — that is to say, to think of non-human actants (both organic and inorganic) as lively partners in commons entanglements. What might that mean for the ongoing challenge of living together, as commoners, in a world facing multiple crises?

Bollier and Helfrich suggest that commons, which are found all over the world, express a deep and irrepressible human longing and that "the process of *commoning* — of joint action, of cre-

---

1   Escobar insists that the commons should be understood as just such a politics: Arturo Escobar, "Commons in the Pluriverse," in *Patterns of Commoning,* eds. David Bollier and Silke Helfrich (Amherst: Off the Common Books, 2014), 348–60.

ating things together, of cooperating to meet shared goals — is ubiquitous."[2] What happens, then, when we imagine commons to be ubiquitous because they are first and foremost a living mesh of processes of living-together reflecting the nature of lively materiality itself? What happens when we take that as far as embracing the "agency" of inorganic matter, not stopping at the boundaries of "life?" What insights, ontological, epistemological, and ethical, emerge? What gains might there be for a political ecology of the commons?

The discussion in this chapter has the following structure: First, I briefly introduce commons, commoning, and the idea of "nature" as a fractious frontline between opposing forms of ontological politics. Next, I position the urgency of ontological politics in relation to the Anthropocene-Capitalocene. Finally, I bring the commons into conversation with New Materialism in order to think about the potential implications of embracing non-human actants as commoners. Might the kind of ethical and epistemological attentiveness introduced by New Materialist ontology produce ways of living *against* the deadening objectifications performed by neoliberalism, and further underline the potency of the commons as a better way of living together in the present planetary situation?

2. Commons, Commoning and the Fractious Space of "Nature"

It is clear that for many commons scholars, commons structures express normative principles governing cooperatively designed human social relationships and are firmly located in human communities. Helfrich and Haas, for example, offering an authoritative account of commons relationalities in 2008, identified four central normative principles governing the social relationships at the heart of the commons, all of which are, in context, envisaged as governing the relations between human

---

2 David Bollier and Silke Helfrich, "Overture," in *Patterns of Commoning*, eds. Bollier and Helfrich, 1–12, at 1.

commoners: "fair access," "equitably shared benefit," "responsibility for preserving the resource," and "democratic and transparent decision-making."[3] Helfrich and Haas define commons as

> a shared ownership relationship, which, at the same time, entails a shared responsibility and shared beneficiary relationship. This relationship does not exist "in and of itself," that is, it is not inherent in the resource or the good. It is a social convention; it is law and norm, whether formal or informal. Or it is a behavioural pattern. In other words, the commons is fundamentally about social relationships. Commons are not the resources themselves but among individuals and a resource and individuals and each other.[4]

The definition offered by Helfrich and Haas, no matter that it accurately reflects core features of many commons, would be unlikely to go uncontested. Commons scholarship is, indeed, an increasingly lively arena. Commons certainly embrace archaic forms, but there is also an explosive multiplicity of newer commons and modes of commoning.

New forms of commoning are now so diverse that McCarthy, reviewing the field, claims that he is uncertain "how much these many new 'commons' might have in common."[5] McCarthy's central focus is on the way in which new commons forms and movements depart from earlier forms of commons understood, in the relevant scholarship, as common pool resources

---

3   Silke Helfrich and Jorg Haas, *The Commons: A New Narrative for our Times* (Heinrich Boll Stiftung, 2008), 7–8, http://commonstrust.global-negotiations.org/resources/Helfrich%20and%20Haas%20The_Commons_A_New_Narrative_for_Our_Times.pdf.

4   Ibid., 5. It is important to note that Helfrich has since developed a broader conception of the ontology of the commons as "differentiated relational ontology:" See David Bollier and Silke Helfrich, *Free, Fair and Alive: The Insurgent Power of the Commons* (Gabriola Island: New Society Publishers, 2019), ch. 2, "The Onto-Shift Towards the Commons".

5   James McCarthy, "Commons as Counterhegemonic Projects," *Capitalism Nature Socialism* 16, no. 1 (2005): 9–24, at 10.

and common property regimes.[6] These forms of commons, first canvassed in academic scholarship in response to Hardin's famous 1968 article, "The Tragedy of the Commons,"[7] reflect early theoretical models of the commons offered by scholars such as Ostrom.[8]

According to McCarthy, the new commons movements depart from the understandings "refined and advocated in a large and robust line of research over the past few decades"[9] in three main respects: first, they move beyond the older scholarly understandings; secondly, the kinds of commons being generated in the new commons movements are more eclectic than the "fisheries, forests and agrarian landscapes"[10] characterizing the typical subjects of the earlier research; and thirdly, new commons dynamics emerge from a far wider array of actors. McCarthy's analysis leads him to conclude that what the new commons movements *do* share — notwithstanding their myriad forms, foci and modes of expression — is "their assertion of collective ownership and rights against relentless privatization and commodification" and their movement away from traditional commons concerns with common property regimes in a heterogeneous tide of resistance against the "neoliberalization of nature."[11]

If the youthful, insurgent energies of the newer commons movements are best to be understood as a wave of resistance to neoliberalism's reduction of "nature" to a privatized, finan-

---

6   See, for an account of this scholarship, Elinor Ostrom, Joanna Burger, Christopher B. Field, Richard B. Norgaard, and David Policansky, "Revisiting the Commons: Local Lessons, Global Challenges," *Science* 283, no. 5412 (1999): 278–82.

7   Garrett Hardin, "The Tragedy of the Commons," *Science* 162 (1968): 1243–48.

8   See, for example, Elinor Ostrom, *Governing the Commons: The Evolution of Institutions for Collective Action* (Cambridge: Cambridge University Press, 1990).

9   McCarthy, "Commons as Counterhegemonic Projects," 10.

10   Ibid.

11   Ibid., 11.

cialized resource,[12] then much turns on the ability of commons formations to resist neoliberal capture.

It seems that it is difficult for anything at all to resist neoliberal capture. Indeed, the commons, despite the fact that commons are sometimes assumed to be inherently anti-neoliberal, already shows signs of partial capture. Caffentzis, for example, demonstrates how the notion of the "commons" is deployed to "describe very different, indeed conflicting, purposes and realities" by those invoking it,[13] actively canvassing the possibility that the commons is deployed, indeed, as "Neoliberalism's Plan B."[14]

Caffentzis reads the resurgence in commons thinking and action as the being result of a convergence between reactions to challenges facing capitalism and socialism respectively. He argues that the imperative for capitalist deployment of the commons (reflected in various contemporary vocabularies and initiatives related to "social capital," the "business community," etc.) reflects the need for capitalism itself to mediate the more self-destructive logics of neoliberalism and to "propose other models for participating in the market, besides individualism or corporatism."[15] This, then, is commons deployed as capitalist rehabilitation. Meanwhile, the anti-capitalist commons impulse pushes back against the failures of socialism and communism to offer genuinely collective modes of social organization. Anti-capitalist invocations of the commons, argues Caffentzis, draw upon the inspiration of older, archaic and pre-capitalist commons while simultaneously embracing the rise of the new com-

---

12 Catherine Corson and Kenneth I. Mcdonald, "Enclosing the Global Commons: The Convention on Biological Diversity and Green Grabbing," *The Journal of Peasant Studies* 39, no. 2 (2012): 263–83.

13 George Caffentzis, "The Future of 'The Commons': Neoliberalism's Plan B, or the Original Disaccumulation of Capital?" *New Formations* 69 (2010): 23–41, at 23.

14 Ibid. This is the title of the article and the central concern of Caffentzis's analysis.

15 Ibid., 23.

mons, "especially in ecological-energy spaces and in computa-tional-informational manifolds."[16]

Caffentzis argues that the fact that the mantle of the com-mons is so easily applied or extended to so many variant situ-ations, and the fact that commons projects are so ubiquitous, generates a certain level of ambiguity, and that the simultaneous deployment of the commons to "deal with the crisis and limits of both neoliberalism and socialism/communism/nationalism" explains "both the surprising popularity of the term and the confusion it induces."[17]

For Caffentzis, this confusion hinges, in part, upon a criti-cal failure in commons discourse: the assumption made among anti-capitalists that commons thought and praxis is "inevitably anticapitalist — " a failure — in short — to recognize the co-ex-istence of two kinds of commons: "(1) pro-capitalist commons that are compatible with and potentiate capitalist accumulation and (2) anti-capitalist commons that are antagonistic to and subversive of capitalist accumulation."[18]

In order to illustrate his claim about pro-capitalist commons, Caffentzis delineates the strategy of the World Bank and other institutions of global neoliberal capitalism to subvert anti-capi-talist agendas. He suggests that there was a capitalist need to ad-dress popular resistance to the privatization of common prop-erty, a need that led to a neoliberal acceptance of commons (for example, of agrarian and forest commons) as being "at least as a stop-gap, transitional institution when revolts of the landless or the devastation of forests become destabilizing to the general exploitation of a territory or population."[19] In certain discursive and regulatory formations, therefore, commons can become tools of capitalist accumulation — or minimally, can be de-ployed to legitimize/facilitate an agenda of neoliberal capitalist predation. Caffentzis's argument on this point has considerable

16 Ibid., 24.
17 Ibid., 25.
18 Ibid.
19 Ibid., 29.

resonance with other critiques of neoliberal agendas, including those addressing neoliberal strategies in the face of climate and environmental crises and a range of related issues. Dehm, for example, convincingly argues that the features of the carbon offset scheme REDD+ (Reducing Emission from Deforestation and Forest Degradation) — which relies upon the communal efforts of indigenous peoples living in and around forests, as well as upon rights-based interventions such as tenure reform and free, prior, and informed consent — tend to operationalize the capture of indigenous forest communities within the neoliberal Green Economy.[20]

The subversion of resistance and critique, and the capture by neoliberal agendas of collective initiatives and alternative ways of being, living and thinking, is a strategy exposed time and again by critiques of neoliberal governance interventions.[21] Neoliberalism's highly interventionist construction of the preconditions for its market system, its extensive construction of capital and finance-friendly environments,[22] and its production of neoliberal subjects in the service of its imperatives, form the logic driving the application of adaptive strategies to the subversion of commons, and this logic is evident in the World Bank's eager recruitment of "'common property management groups among the 'civil society' institutions."[23] Neoliberal exploitation of the productivity of the commons is transparent in such initiatives and developments, and Caffentzis points out that the

20 Julia Dehm, "Indigenous Peoples and REDD+ Safeguards: Rights as Resistance or as Disciplinary Inclusion in the Green Economy?" *Journal of Human Rights and the Environment* 7, no. 2 (2016): 170–217.

21 For example, that provided by Timothy W. Luke, "On Environmentality: Geo-Power and Eco-Knowledge in the Discourses of Contemporary Environmentalism", *Cultural Critique (The Politics of Systems and Environments, Part II)* 31 (1995): 57–81. See also, for an extensive and celebrated Marxist deconstruction of neoliberalism, David Harvey, *A Short History of Neoliberalism* (Oxford: Oxford University Press, 2005).

22 Robert Fletcher, "Neoliberal Environmentality: Towards a Post-Structuralist Political Ecology of the Conservation Debate," *Conservation and Society* 8, no. 3 (2010): 171–81.

23 Caffentzis, "The Future of 'The Commons'," 32.

Common Property Resource Management Group (CPRNet) was founded by the World Bank as early as 1995 precisely for the purpose of integrating commons organizations "into the larger project of making the world safe for neoliberalism."[24]

Making the world safe for neoliberalism involves, among other things, the extensive governance, regulation, technification, and financialization of "nature" as "natural resources."[25] Meanwhile, constructions of "nature" are also pivotal to the commons. "Nature" is at the heart of the older, archetypal commons taking the form of "fisheries, forests and agrarian landscapes;"[26] central to "nature"-centered practices of traditional indigenous commoners; and pivotal to multiple new commons the world over.[27] Indeed, as noted above, anti-capitalist "new commons," for all their dynamic heterogeneity, converge in resistance to the "neoliberalization of nature."[28] "Nature" thus forms a materio-semiotic frontline, not only between the two competing versions of the commons identified by Caffentzis but of a global ontological struggle between anti-capitalist commons and neoliberalism's biopolitical/necropolitical agenda. Accordingly, "Nature," increasingly forced to "speak" as "environment,"[29] forms a decisive zone of contestation across which a life and death struggle over the meanings and forms of co-living and the status of life itself now takes place. (It is also, as will be noted later in this chapter, a construct widely deployed for the oppression and marginalization of humans (and non-humans) constructed as being non-rational by Eurocentric ontology and epistemology.)

---

24 Ibid.
25 Sian Sullivan, "Green Capitalism, and the Cultural Poverty of Constructing Nature as Service-provider," *Radical Anthropology* 3 (2009): 18–27; Rupert Read and Molly Scott-Cato, "A Price for Everything? The Natural Capital Controversy," *Journal of Human Rights and the Environment* 5, no. 2 (2014): 153–67.
26 McCarthy, "Commons as Counterhegemonic Projects," 10.
27 Even a brief survey of the multitudinous forms of commoning discussed in Bollier and Helfrich, *Patterns of Commoning,* reveal the radical intimacy between the living order and commons communities.
28 McCarthy, "Commons as Counterhegemonic Projects," 11.
29 Luke, "On Environmentality," 59–63.

The totalizing ambition of neoliberalism's agenda is well captured by Luke's Foucauldian analysis of the Worldwatch Institute,[30] which emerges as a particularly salient example of the ambivalence of "progressive" narratives such as (in Luke's case) environmentalism and (in the World Bank example above) the commons.

Luke records that in a Worldwatch Institute publication, Brown, Flavin, and Postel reject "a narrow economic view of the world"[31] and argue that "growth is confined by the parameters of the biosphere."[32] The Institute's aim, reflected in its publication, Luke writes, is to "meld ecology with economics to infuse environmental studies with economic instrumental rationality and defuse economics with ecological systems reasoning."[33] While the ostensible aim of this double-headed strategy is apparently to ensure that economic growth cannot be decoupled from its substrate in natural systems and resources, it ultimately articulates a strategy expressing the WorldWatch Institute's "vision of geo-power and eco-knowledge as the instrumental rationality of resource managerialism working on a global scale."[34] In this process, "Nature" is reduced to a cybernetic system of four planetary biophysical systems supplying the global resources for the human population and translated into technical data for the management and capture of life itself as an object of ecological hyper-control.

The ambivalence of this strategy is both striking and familiar. As De Lucia has pointed out, when environmental interventions are read through the lens of Foucauldian biopolitics, even ecologically-driven critiques become legible as "a new set of normalizing strategies extending the scope of biopolitical technologies of power from human populations to the entire natural

---

30 Ibid., 71–80.
31 Ibid., 71.
32 Ibid.
33 Ibid., 72–73.
34 Ibid., 73.

world."[35] Of course, control of population and environment has long been interlinked. As Rutherford puts it, "the definition and administration of populations simultaneously requires the constitution and management of the environment in which those populations exist and upon which they depend."[36] It is this bottom line that explains the central focus of both pro- and anti-capitalist commons on "nature," and why "the environment" has become the core fulcrum point of ontological — and ontic — struggles.

Luke suggests that the Worldwatch writers are engaged in nothing less than a struggle to shift "the authorizing legitimacy of truth claims used in policy analysis away from economic terms to ecological terms [...] [thereby] working to reframe the power/knowledge systems of advanced capitalist societies."[37] In this light, the neoliberal deployment of the commons, and its related recruitment and regulatory disciplining of communities and indigenous practices as modes of neoliberal governance, are entirely predictable.

The struggle between neoliberalism (with its deployment of pro-capitalist commons) and the anti-capitalist commons movement centers — in the final analysis — on the present and future of life on the planet. On the one hand, a global control system made up of a complex assemblage of actors, regulatory mechanisms and calculative market structures marshals and reduces life to informatics — to privatized, propertized, financialized, market-friendly processes and products — deploying ecological mechanisms of managerialism. On the other hand, all over the planet, human commoners of multiple kinds explicitly resist such logics, urgently seeking to express a radically

35 Vito De Lucia, "Beyond Anthropocentrism and Ecocentrism: A Biopolitical Reading of Environmental Law," *Journal of Human Rights and the Environment* 8, no. 2 (2017): 181–202, at 194.

36 Paul Rutherford, "The Entry of Life into History," in *Discourses of the Environment*, ed. Eric Darier (London: Blackwell Publishers, 1999) 37–62, at 45, cited in De Lucia, "Beyond Anthropocentrism and Ecocentrism," 194.

37 Luke, "On Environmentality," 74.

different kind of ontology and to reject the neoliberalization of nature.[38]

Emphasizing the "intrinsic value" of "nature" is thus a familiar theme in commons scholarship, though it is unclear how many commons scholars pay attention to the instability of nature as a referent[39] — or to its historical, oppressive deployments as a system of marginalization. Notwithstanding the instability of "nature" as a referent, one thing seems clear: the reduction of "nature" to spaces of acquisition, capitalist accumulation, and aggressive eco-managerialism as "environment" fully reflects the "environing" (encircling and controlling)[40] governance strategies identified by Luke as central expressions of eco-knowledge and geo-power.[41] Neoliberal eco-governmentality expresses

> the continuous attempt to reinvent the forces of Nature in the economic exploitation of advanced technologies linking structures in Nature to the rational management of its energies as geo-power, [which] is an ongoing supplement to the disciplinary construction of various modes of bio-power in promoting the growth [and control] of human populations.[42]

Such critiques resonate well with Caffentzis's analysis of the subversion of commons in the service of making the world secure for the neoliberal order. The sheer scale of ambition intrinsic to neoliberal eco-governmentality, and the totality of what is put at stake for lively systems and for human populations means

---

38 McCarthy, "Commons as Counterhegemonic Projects," 11.
39 "Nature" has an inherent semiotic instability for human beings. As Luke puts it, "different human beings will observe [Nature's] patterns, choosing to accentuate some while deciding at the same time to ignore others:" because of this, "Nature's meanings will always be multiple and unfixed:' Luke, "On Environmentality," 58.
40 Ibid., 63–65.
41 Ibid., 57.
42 Ibid., 58.

that it is now urgently necessary, with Escobar, to position anti-capitalist commons as sites and formations of a vibrant onto-logical politics[43] lined up against the ontological imperialism of an equally political neoliberalism.

3. Commons and Commoning as Ontological Politics

Escobar, primarily an anti-globalization social-movements scholar, argues that for commoners "the defense of territory, life and the commons are one and the same."[44] He addresses the "ontological dimension of commoning," arguing that "whereas the occupation of territories implies economic, technological, cultural, ecological and often armed aspects, its most funda-mental dimension is ontological:"[45] ontological occupation spawns "*ontological struggles.*"[46] These are struggles, as Escobar frames them, to maintain "multiple worlds" against the "One World World" imposed by the neoliberal market order.[47] Esco-bar imagines the commons in their anti-capitalist forms pitted against the neoliberal colonization of life-worlds. This is the commons and commoning as ontological struggle against "the merciless world of the global 10 percent, foisted upon the 90 percent and the natural world with a seemingly ever-increasing degree of virulence and cynicism."[48]

Weber, like Escobar, turns towards the question of commons ontology. Weber argues that the structure of reality itself — even the perception that yields it to the human being's gaze — is a commons[49] — and that the crisis signalled by the Anthropocene provides an opportunity to re-conceive of the "relationship be-

---

43 Escobar, "Commons in the Pluriverse."

44 Ibid., 352.

45 Ibid.

46 Ibid., 353. Emphasis original.

47 Ibid., 348.

48 Ibid., at 355–56.

49 Andreas Weber, "Reality as Commons: A Poetics of Participation for the Anthropocene," in *Patterns of Commoning,* eds. Bollier and Helfrich, 369–91.

tween humanity and nature" and to "reimagine our ontological condition."[50] Weber's response to this opportunity is to evoke what he calls "*Enlivenment*" as a post-Enlightenment (or "Enlightenment II") "ontology of aliveness, of coming to life, that is at once physical and intangible, and scientific and spiritual."[51] Weber argues, indeed, that the perspective of the commons is now indispensable to understanding "the relationship of humans to reality."[52] Weber, like Escobar, also assumes the anti-capitalist strain of commons theory, praxis, and activism. He also embraces non-dualistic indigenous cosmovisions and the need to reject the ontological colonization enacted by Enlightenment reductionism.

Taken together, the commons ontological framework offered by Weber and Escobar offers a corrective to the instrumentalist paradigm of "nature." The complexity-sensitive and pluriversal energies at the heart of the ontology intimated by Escobar and Weber, when read together, open a seam for depth-exploration of epistemic and ontological resistance to hegemonic neoliberal coloniality and the tyranny of the knowing "centre."[53]

While the instability of "nature" as a referent persists, it is clear that neither of these writers make the assumption that "nature" is intrinsically benign. The commons of "nature" remains full of tensions — with implications for the practice of ontological politics as process: Weber, for example, in his long essay *Enlivenment,* makes the point that his ontological proposal means that "[t]o be really alive means to be embedded in a mess that must constantly be negotiated."[54] Weber argues that binaries are

---

50 Ibid., 370.
51 Ibid., 372. See also Andreas Weber, *Enlivenment: Towards a Fundamental Shift in the Concepts of Nature, Culture and Politics* (Berlin: Heinrich Boll Stiftung, 2013).
52 Weber, "Reality as Commons," 371.
53 For particularly rich exploration of a distinctly post-Kantian de-centering of epistemology, see Lorraine Code, *Ecological Thinking: The Politics of Epistemic Location* (Oxford: Oxford University Press, 2006).
54 Weber, *Enlivenment,* 62.

to be replaced by an epistemic practice of embracing paradox and living with oppositionalities in a constant, flexible negotiation — an embrace of paradox central and necessary to the "poetic materialism" he proposes.[55]

Weber's account points the way towards an ontological politics unafraid of internal tension, complexity, paradox, and ambiguity. Does poetic materialism, however, go far enough? Might New Materialist onto-epistemology add something valuable the mix?

4. Encountering "Poetic Materialism" — An Existential Ecological Ontology

It seems important to address Weber's work because it offers a materialist ontology for the commons, and, at points, explicitly addresses the commons as praxis. His work invites engagement, therefore, in a chapter offering New Materialist insights that might contribute distinctive threads to the development of a more radical commons ontology.

In reading Weber — and the New Materialist authors I later discuss — I have chosen to keep in mind Bennett's argument that vocabulary is a precursor to, and pivotal for, the level of "discernment" intrinsic to appreciating the "active powers" of the more-than-human.[56] How, then, does Weber's vocabulary position the more-than-human for the commons? And what does his choice of language imply concerning the ontology of poetic materialism?

Weber argues, in *Enlivenment,* that at the heart of the commons are "diverse interests negotiating mutually acceptable outcomes, and individual actors coming to respectful terms with their habitat. This concept transcends the idea of a mere exchange of resources and covers many areas of human–human

---

55 Weber, *Enlivenment,* ch. 7, "Basic Principles of Enlivenment: Working with Paradoxes."

56 Jane Bennett, *Vibrant Matter: A Political Ecology of Things* (Durham: Duke University Press, 2010), ix. Emphasis added.

and human–nature interactions."[57] Weber's language here explicitly foregrounds "human-human" and "human-nature" interactions. It is immediately noticeable — and interesting — that there is no explicit equivalence given here to "nature-human" and "nature-nature" interactions. The linguistic formulation here seems potentially to foreground the human in a way that sits at nuanced variance with Weber's broader ontological framework, which openly embraces the meaningful and meaning-generative capacities of "other animate beings, which, after all share the same capacities [as humans] for embodied experiences and 'worldmaking.'"[58] Indeed, Weber's book *Enlivenment* explicitly places "other animate beings" alongside the human and explicitly centers his ontology on *life/zoē* — even proposing a new designation of the Anthropocene as the "*Zoocene.*"[59]

Weber offers what he calls a "wild naturalism" based on

> the idea of nature as an unfolding process of ever-growing freedom and creativity paradoxically linked to material and embodied processes. The biosphere is alive in the sense that it does not only obey the rules of deterministic or stochastic interactions of particles, molecules, atoms, fields and waves. The biosphere is also very much about producing agency, expression, and meaning.[60]

Weber's later works further develop this wild naturalism. Weber proposes a "poetic materialism," or "erotic ecology," primarily establishing his ontology by foregrounding embodied affective relationality, and by highlighting the interiority and "desire" of material entities for each other in terms reminiscent of panpsychism. In fact, Weber's panpsychic resonance seems close — in some respects — to the panpsychism presented by

---

57 Weber, *Enlivenment,* 67.
58 Ibid., 22.
59 Ibid., 67. The zoocene emphasises "life in its felt sense" and includes "the whole animate earth" (ibid).
60 Ibid.

Mathews in *For Love of Matter* — as "a subjectival dimension, to materiality."[61]

This subjectival dimension to materiality, in Weber's philosophy, is activated as an ethical and creative force through the phenomenon of "feeling":

> Emotional experience is not alien to the conception of an ecological commons but central to it. In an ethics of mutual ecological transformation, feeling is a central part. As inwardness is the necessary way bodies experience themselves, feeling is also a crucial component of an ecological ethics.[62]

Weber sees ecological commons as complex, rhizomatic, situated, sites of interactivity. These are characterized — as is his conception of "nature" more generally — by the "mutual transformation" of embodied agents. Weber argues that "Agency is always inscribed within a living system of other animate forces, each of which is both sovereign and interdependent at the same time"[63] — and that in a commons, humans are not "ruler[s]" but "attentive subject[s] in a network of relationships."[64] Every commons is, therefore, "a material and informal network of living, incarnate and meaningful connections, which constantly changes as it mutates and evolves —"[65] "a community (between humans and/or nonhuman agents)."[66]

Weber argues that the commons, because it does not conceptually detach commoners from the space of commoning, dissolves the nature/culture divide because it cancels the divide between the social and the ecological.[67] While it might be ob-

---

61 Freya Mathews, *For Love of Matter: A Contemporary Panpsychism* (Albany: State University of New York, 2003), 8.

62 Andreas Weber, *The Biology of Wonder: Aliveness, Feeling and the Metamorphosis of Science* (Gabriola Island: New Society Publishers, 2016), 802.

63 Ibid., 800.

64 Ibid.

65 Ibid.

66 Ibid., 795.

67 Ibid., 798–99.

jected that it would take more argument than this satisfactorily to establish that seeing the commons in this way dissolves the socio-ecological divide, it is clear that, in an important and central sense, Weber imagines commoning to be an active, affective community between humans and/or non-human agents.

This is all very promising.

However, at the same time, there is an elusive tenor of lingering human centrality in Weber's writing. Reading him more closely, this tenor seems to emerge from the "poetic" expression of his erotic ecological materialism — a communicative choice producing a subtle linguistic traction towards the centrality of human experience. Access to the "innermost core of aliveness" of matter, Weber argues, is "only possible through being involved in experiences and creative expression," and commoning is thus described as an eco-ethical set of practices, a "culture" facilitating the "self-realization of Homo sapiens [...] [as] the species-specific realization of our own particular embodiment of being alive within a common system of other living subjects."[68] It is important, here, to bear in mind that a central component of Weber's passionate eco-philosophical project is precisely to provoke an awakening to the "aliveness" revealed by "new biology" — and that his choice of poetic communication is key to that. It is also important to acknowledge that there is indeed a potent onto-political role for poetic communication and consciousness-raising. Nevertheless, it seems to me that there is a distinction that can and should be drawn between offering (an inescapably human) existential perspective on the lively inter-species entanglement of a commons, and positioning the commons as a vehicle for the "self-realization of Homo sapiens." The poetic formulations that Weber uses, moreover, seem to convey a subtle, lingering primacy of the human at odds with elements of his ontology. It seems that the "we" of the subtly central humanity is the almost inevitable offspring of the "I"-centered phenomenological poetics of Weber's communicative methodology.

---

68 Ibid., 799.

The flickeringly foregrounded human, to me at least, signals a subtle tension between the poetic and the analytical in Weber's writing. He is deliberately intimately present to the reader in his texts as a first person, emotional narrator. His poetic, experientially "felt" ontology is both discovered and shared with his readers through Whiteheadean shifts of perception — existential moments of personal transformative awareness: Weber's writing foregrounds the centrality of his own subjective human account of how he "feels" the relational and "inner" aliveness of his ontological poem-scape.

Clearly, such first-person intimacy is a powerful rhetorical strategy for awakening the sensibility of the reader to the biopoetic materialist ontology that Weber seeks to establish as the ground of his "erotic" ecological ethics. Nonetheless, this first-person "I" — and its apparent drift into a second-person collective human "we" — has the effect, linguistically, of rendering the (agentic) non-human the "other" in an "I-Thou" relation for which the human "I" retains a subtle priority at inconsistent and muted odds with Weber's broader ontological intuitions.

Such priority is also implicated in some of Weber's more general exhortations to transformative thinking. For example, his statement in *The Biology of Wonder* that "We must preserve living beings for life's sake, in order for life to be able to self-organize, to unfold, to experience itself,"[69] is a statement whose vocabulary and formulation makes materiality's self-organizing capacities and "self"-"experience" dependent on a prior exercise of agency by an apparently human "we." The language installs this "we" as a human collective whose agency must act to preserve living beings in order for life to be able to self-organize, to unfold, to experience itself. In context, Weber is addressing the environmental destruction wrought by the deadening objectification of traditional Western thought and science — but even so — this formulation of his point elevates human agency, almost rendering it a material precondition for "nature's" self-organizational capacities to function. This formulation hints

---

69 Ibid., 58–59.

at a kind of agentic overreach that ironically, echoes (without sharing other suppositions of) the agentic assumptions driving climate change and environmental destructiveness.

If, in the final analysis, Weber's commons is a form of situated, embodied relationality establishing an eco-ethical set of practices serving the "self-realization of Homo sapiens,"[70] it is little wonder that he defines a commons in terms of "human-human and human-nature interactions." Nevertheless, Weber's poetic existentialism breathes into being an ontology that, in most respects embraces an entangled meshwork of lively, agentic, human–non-human relations. He thus reaches (albeit inconsistently perhaps) beyond traditional conceptions of the commons in a welcome departure from the kinds of complexly constituted anthropocentrism haunting much of commons scholarship.

If we return to the definition offered by Helfrich and Haas,[71] we can clearly see the centrality of the social to the commons. Helfrich and Haas, recall, emphasize that "Commons are not the resources themselves but the set of relationships that are forged among individuals and a resource and individuals and each other."[72] There are two things of note here: first, the "social" at the heart of the commons is clearly a human "social." Secondly, the relationships at the heart of the commons, as formulated here, map onto Weber's "human-human and human-nature interactions." Unlike Weber's conception, however, these relationships are more reductively imagined, and closer to the subject-object assumptions of Cartesianism. The "individual" maps onto the "human," while "resource" maps onto "'nature'/non-human source of value, etc." — but the ontology implied by the language is the precisely the ontology that Weber seeks to replace with his poetic materialism.

The definition offered by Helfrich and Haas exposes the predominant operative conception of the commons for which commoners are human beings and for which human social relation-

---

70 Ibid., 799.
71 See n.4 above and related text.
72 Helfrich and Haas, "The Commons," 5.

ships lie at the center. Indeed, overall, it is difficult to read much commons scholarship without gaining the impression that there is in it a tension reflecting the possibility that anthropocentrism is simultaneously both rejected and re-installed: rejected at the overt surface, re-installed by the undertow of ontological assumptions — assumptions revealed by vocabulary.

This tension suggests the possibility that commons thinking — as yet — evinces a certain lack of theoretical settlement. Lack of settlement — in and of itself — is not a negative state of affairs, of course. It can be a sign of evolution and energy and can signal potential for future development. Commons and commoning are capacious enough to embrace a multitude of ontological visions. Escobar, for example, imagines "the pluriverse" — an excitingly rich figuration embracing numerous ways of living and seeing, numerous worlds that co-exist,[73] cross-fertilize, interweave, and co-negotiate. Moreover, the centrality of "relationality" to the commons — emphasized by so much commons scholarship — and so poetically by Weber — readily implies the importance of providing epistemic space for the ontological commitments of literally thousands of communities the world over, many of which already embrace consciously intimate engagements with lively "nature." Such epistemic space offers, in addition, a direct and important contrast with the systemic epistemic closure enacted by the neoliberal eco-governance order or — to borrow Escobar's language — by the "One world world."[74]

All that said, it seems productive to use the tensions and opportunities emerging from the possibility of subtle, internal contradictions in commons thinking as a space of indeterminacy, into which to offer some brief reflections concerning more-than-human commoners and the distinctive contribution of a "New Materialist" approach.

First, however, I want to position that reflection — briefly — in relation to what it is that the commons as ontological

---

73 Indeed, this is the title of Escobar's chapter: "Commons in the Pluriverse."
74 Ibid., 348.

politics is up against: is there a possibility that the situation in which onto-struggles now take place strengthens the appeal of a New Materialist theorization of more-than-human commons, commoning, and commoners?

5. The Urgency of Ontological Politics

To appreciate fully the decisive importance of commons as ontological politics, it seems important to locate reflection in the contemporary situation. This is, after all, the situation in which anti-capitalist commoning seeks to resist capitalist enclosures, appropriations and captures.

The contemporary era is often referred to as "Anthropocene," which is a widely deployed term for a "new age of man" in which the human species has become a geological, rather than just a biological, force.[75] The terminology is etymologically drawn from *anthrōpos* (man) and *kainos* (new) and was first popularized in 2002.[76] It is important to remember, however, that despite the notion that the "anthropos" of the Anthropocene is a species figuration, in reality, it is not.[77] Moreover, as Haraway has pointed out, the Anthropocene is intrinsically coupled with the scale of the "global," and the "global" is highly specific in its origins and development.[78] In reality, the Anthropocene reflects highly uneven historical processes of colonization[79] and ram-

---

75 Dipesh Chakrabarty, "The Climate of History: Four Theses," *Critical Inquiry* 35 (2009): 197–222.

76 It was first popularized by Crutzen: Paul J. Crutzen, "Geology of Mankind," *Nature* 415, no. 6867 (2002): 23.

77 Anna Grear, "Deconstructing Anthropos: A Critical Legal Reflection on 'Anthropocentric' Law and Anthropocene 'Humanity,'" *Law and Critique* 26, no. 3 (2015): 225–49.

78 AURA, "Donna Haraway, 'Anthropocene, Capitalocene, Chthulucene: Staying with the Trouble,' 5/9/14," *Vimeo*, June 8, 2014, https://vimeo.com/97663518, at 14.02. See Antony Anghie, *Imperialism, Sovereignty and the Making of International Law* (Cambridge: Cambridge University Press, 2005).

79 Andreas Malm and Alf Hornborg, "The Geology of Mankind? A Critique of the Anthropocene Narrative," *The Anthropocene Review* 1, no. 1 (2014): 62–69.

pant capitalist neo-coloniality.[80] So specific is the "global" folded into the Anthropocene that the "Anthropocene" is also identified by some as the "Capitalocene."[81]

I will use the term "Anthropocene-Capitalocene" to foreground the uneven origins and contemporary mal-distribution of Anthropocene climate and environmental fallouts; the fundamentally colonial capitalist imperatives driving the continuing structural dominance of the fossil-fuel economy;[82] extensive, and continuing, corporate enclosures in the Global South;[83] and the pervasive and expanding commodification and technification of "nature."[84]

So much is at stake. Neoliberalism is now the dominant engine of the Anthropocene-Capitalocene: it enacts violence extensively visited upon communities, individuals, places, animals, ecosystems, and other lively materialities either in the way of or (alternatively) in the sights of, neoliberal agendas. The colonizing of multiple life-worlds at stake in neoliberal accumulation reiterates, and builds on, earlier patterns of ontological (and epistemological) violence[85] underlying Eurocentric power

---

80 Max Koch, *Capitalism and Climate Change: Theoretical Discussion, Historical Development and Policy Responses* (Basingstoke: Palgrave Macmillan, 2012).

81 This proposal is offered, among others, by Haraway, in AURA, "Donna Haraway, 'Anthropocene, Capitalocene, Chthulucene: Staying with the Trouble,' 5/9/14"; Andreas Malm, *Fossil Capital: The Rise of Steam Power and the Roots of Global Warming* (London: Verso, 2016); Jason W. Moore, ed., *Anthropocene or Capitalocene? Nature, History, and the Crisis of Capitalism and the Crisis of Capitalism* (Oakland: PM Press, 2016).

82 Koch, *Capitalism and Climate Change*; Jerome Dangerman and Hans J. Schellnhuber, "Energy Systems Transformation," *PNAS* 110, no.7 (2013): E549–E558.

83 Corson and McDonald, "Enclosing the Global Commons."

84 Gernot Bohme, *Invasive Technification: Critical Essays in the Philosophy of Technology*, trans. Cameron Shingleton (London and New York: Bloomsbury, 2012).

85 Graham Huggan and Helen Tiffin, "Green Postcolonialism," *Interventions: International Journal of Postcolonial Studies* 9, no. 1 (2007): 1–11.

distributions of the international legal order.[86] More fundamentally, neoliberal accumulative rationalism ultimately relies — as Weber and Escobar both either state or imply — upon a central, binary set of severed ontological relations between "humans" and "nature," between "subject" and "object". Ontology is at the heart of the current sets of crises. The well-rehearsed, uneven, and entirely predictable mal-distributions of life and death characterizing the Anthropocene-Capitalocene thus draw upon the same fundamental ontological splits as have long operated in the service of Eurocentric, masculinist, colonizing power.[87] In the Anthropocene-Capitalocene, neoliberalism's biopolitical/ necropolitical logics are driving a potential terminus — including for human beings. As Stengers puts it in *In Catastrophic Times*,[88] human beings face, potentially "the death of what we have called a civilization [— and, she reminds us —] there are many manners of dying, some being more ugly than others."[89] Even death itself — the great leveler — is unevenly distributed, whether as terminus or process.

Neoliberalism actively exploits the notion that there is no other solution to the enormity of the problems confronting humanity — and, accordingly, constructs the illusion that there is no alternative to neoliberal managerial eco-governance on a planetary scale. Indeed, Stengers argues that even "radical uncertainty with regard to the catastrophes that [the current crisis] is likely to produce […] won't make the capitalist machine hesitate, because it is incapable of hesitating: it can't do anything other than define every situation as a source of profit."[90] The logics of consumptive capitalism will continue to insist — in

---

86 Dipesh Chakrabarty, *Provincialising Europe* (Princeton: Princeton University Press, 2007); Anghie, *Imperialism, Sovereignty and the Making of International Law,* 67.
87 Sam Adelman, "Epistemologies of Mastery," in *Research Handbook on Human Rights and the Environment,* eds. Anna Grear and Louise Kotzé (Cheltenham: Edward Elgar Publishing, 2015), 9–27.
88 Isabelle Stengers, *Catastrophic Times: Resisting the Coming Barbarism* (Luneburg: Open Humanities Press/meson press, 2015).
89 Ibid., 10.
90 Ibid., 9.

short — that "the techno-industrial capitalist path is the only one that is viable"[91] in the face of the Anthropocene-Capitalocene planetary crisis.

The ascendancy of such logic is already evident in the growing popularity of ethically dubious[92] commitments to geo-engineering as a way of techno-fixing the climate, irrespective of the risks involved.[93] Such hubristic strategies amount to a form of risky gambling with the futures of millions,[94] and reveal the vulnerability of "humanity in its entirety [to being] taken hostage" by capitalist profit making "solutions" for the otherwise (supposedly) insoluble: "In this way, an 'infernal alternative' [is] fabricated at the planetary scale: either it's us, your saviours, or it's the end of the world."[95]

Against such horizons, it is all the more urgent for commoning to offer multiple forms of resistance. The dangers for the commons, however, are pervasive: panoptic governance and neoliberal eco-managerialism already subvert, as we have seen, some commons for pro-capitalist ends, and in the final analysis, there is absolutely nothing to guarantee that any commons will be, or remain, immune from capture. Moreover,

[t]here isn't the slightest guarantee that we will be able to overcome the hold that capitalism has over us (and in this instance, what some have proposed calling "capitalocene," and not anthropocene, will be a geological epoch that is extremely short). Nor do we know how, in the best of cases, we might live in the ruins that it will leave us: the window of

---

91 Ibid.

92 Henry Shue, "Climate Dreaming: Negative Emissions, Risk Transfer, and Irreversibility," *Journal of Human Rights and the Environment* 8, no. 2 (2017): 203–26.

93 Sam Adelman, "Geoengineering: Rights, Risks and Ethics," *Journal of Human Rights and the Environment* 8, no. 1 (2017): 119–38.

94 Ibid.; Shue, "Climate Dreaming."

95 Stengers, *Catastrophic Times,* 9.

opportunity in which, on paper, the measures to take were reasonably clear, is in the process of closing.[96]

If the Anthropocene-Capitalocene leaves a window of opportunity in the process of closing, ontology as politics could not be more decisively important or timely — and commoning has never been more urgent as a dynamic of ontological resistance. What, then, might New Materialism offer to commons thought in the face of such struggles? And how does New Materialism offer agentic significance to the more-than-human? And why might that matter in the calculus of resistance to neoliberalism's voracious colonization of lifeworlds?

6. New Materialist Commoning

For New Materialist thinkers, all matter — including inorganic matter — and the artefactual — is agentic in the broad sense that there is, as Bennett puts it, a "capacity of things — edibles, commodities, storms, metals — not only to impede or block the will and designs of humans but also to act as quasi agents or forces with trajectories, propensities or tendencies of their own."[97] Bennett is explicit, moreover, about dissipating the organic/inorganic binary.[98] Her ontological proposal aims to challenge the "received concepts of agency, action, and freedom sometimes to the breaking point" and to "sketch a style of political analysis that can better account for the contributions of nonhuman actants."[99] Language is central to this task, and Bennett's work can, in part, be characterized as an exercise in strategic epistemic politics: She argues that her focus is on "the task of developing a vocabulary and a syntax for, and *thus a better discernment of,* the active powers issuing from non-subjects."[100]

---

96 Ibid.
97 Bennett, *Vibrant Matter,* ix.
98 Ibid., x; xviii.
99 Ibid., x.
100 Ibid., ix (emphasis added).

We have seen how challenging it is to find this vocabulary and syntax — and I have suggested that Weber's communicative methodology presents challenges to the ontological consistency of poetic materialism. Bennett's search for vocabulary, I suggest, does not present the same challenges for her — and her onto-epistemology does not adopt, or express itself through, an existentialist frame.

The ethical task at the heart of Bennett's proposal is "to cultivate the ability to discern nonhuman vitality, to become perceptually open to it"[101] — which on the face of it, chimes closely with Weber's ambition. For Bennett, the active powers issuing from non-subjects express the liveliness intrinsic to materiality that Bennett calls "thing-power," which is "an alternative to the object as a way of encountering the nonhuman world."[102] Matter is *materialization* and "things" have a productivity of their own. Being animate is, on this view, a matter of degree, and inorganic matter displays powers of self-organization and is "much more variable and creative than we ever imagined."[103]

For Bennett, however, matter's powers of self-organization do not rely on humans preserving "nature" or playing any other facilitative role. She uses the example of metal to communicate the liveliness of the inorganic,[104] drawing, in part, on Deleuze

---

101 Ibid., 14.

102 Ibid., xvii.

103 Ibid., 7.

104 Ibid., ch. 4 "A Life of Metal." Metal has its own "protean activeness" (59). "The crystal grains of, say, iron come in a large variety of sizes and shapes, depending on 'the space-filling pressures of their neighbours.' Though the atoms within each individual grain are 'arranged with regular array on a space lattice,' there are also 'imperfections in the array,' most notably the presence of loose atoms at the 'interfaces' of grains. These atoms 'belong' to none of the grains, and they render the boundaries of each grain porous and quivering: a grain of iron is not 'some kind of an enveloped entity,' as is 'a grain of wheat.' This means that the crystalline structure of metal is full of holes or 'intercrystalline spaces.' These 'vacancies' can be 'as important as the atom' in determining properties of a particular metal" (58–59), citing Cyril S. Smith, *A History of Metallography* (Chicago: University of Chicago Press, 1960) (original citations omitted). "Manuel De Landa points to another instance of a life of metal in the 'complex dynamics of

and Guattari who refer to "metal as the exemplar of vital materiality," a material exhibiting "the prodigious idea of Nonorganic Life."[105] Bennett suggests that metallurgists, artisans, mechanics, woodworkers, builders, cooks, cleaners, "(and anyone else intimate with things) *encounter* a creative materiality with incipient tendencies and propensities, which are variably enacted depending on the other forces, affects, or bodies with which they come into close contact."[106] Matter, as she puts it, drawing on a quotation from Massumi, is a "pressing crowd of incipiencies and tendencies."[107]

It is not necessarily easy for humans in the everydayness of ordinary embodied life to see these forms of liveliness, but Bennett argues that what we humans take to be objects only seem to be static because their "becoming proceeds at a speed or a level below the threshold of human discernment."[108] Bennett accepts that humans tend to distinguish things from persons, but points

---

spreading cracks' [...] the travel of which is "not deterministic but expressive of an emergent causality, whereby grains respond on the spot and in real time to the idiosyncratic movements of their neighbors, and then to their neighbors' response to their response, and so on, in feedback spirals" (59), citing Manuel De Landa, "Uniformity and Variability: An Essay in the Philosophy of Matter," paper presented at the "Doors of Perception 3" Conference, Netherlands Design Institute, Amsterdam, November 7–11, 1995.

105 Ibid., 55, citing Gilles Deleuze and Felix Guattari, *A Thousand Plateaus: Capitalism and Schizophrenia,* trans. Brian Massumi (Minneapolis: University of Minnesota Press, 1987), 411. Bennett argues that *A Thousand Plateaus* "is full of quickening, effervescent proto- and no-bodies [...] which are best described, in Spinozist terms as 'a set of speeds and slownesses between unformed particles [with] [...] the individuality of a day, a season, a year, a life'" (55), citing Deleuze and Guattari, *A Thousand Plateaus,* 262.

106 Ibid., 56, emphasis added.

107 Ibid., 57, citing Alan Latham and Derek P. McCormick, "Moving Cities: Rethinking the Materialities of Urban Geographies," *Progress in Human Geography* 28, no. 6 (2004): 701–24, at 701, where the authors, at 705, cite Massumi. (In original context, Massumi is speaking of the body's combination of actual and virtual: Brian Massumi, *Parables for the Virtual: Movement, Affect, Sensation* [London and Durham: Duke University Press, 2002], 30).

108 Bennett, *Vibrant Matter,* 58.

out that "the sort of world we live in makes it constantly possible for these two sets of kinds to exchange properties."[109] The liveliness here, however, is neither "transpersonal or intersubjective but impersonal, an affect intrinsic to forms that cannot be imagined (even ideally) as persons."[110] This embrace of the impersonal nature of material liveliness seems to be an important potential distinction between Bennett's ontology and that of Weber. Bennett's account of lively matter is also not strictly speaking *zoocentric* — even in an expanded sense that moves beyond a focus on the animal to something approaching a life force. Nor does Bennett posit an eco-romantic "I-Thou" relation with "nature" or with "natural forces." Her thought arguably takes materialism into register that eschews biocentrism as well as anthropocentrism.[111] Thus, while Bennett shares Weber's passion for awakening a perceptual responsiveness to non-human material agency, her mode of communication and her ontological framing seem more insistently to emphasize the agentic liveliness of non-human matter in a way that foregrounds the idea that "[t]he locus of agency" is "*always* a human-nonhuman working group"[112] — and this would be the case, presumably, even when the frame of attention is placed on human beings operating a "human-human" or a "human-nature" relationship. Inorganic and artefactual material actants are thus necessarily fully significant for "why collectives involving humans take the form they do."[113]

The kind of "distributed agency" that Bennett traces reflects the capacity to affect or to be affected that is typical of all matter. And this affect forms a central focus of New Materialist analyses,

---

109 Ibid., 10.

110 Ibid., 61.

111 Andreas Philippopoulos-Mihalopoulos, "Actors or Spectators? Vulnerability and Critical Environmental Law," in *Thought, Law, Rights and Action in the Age of Environmental Crisis*, eds. Anna Grear and Evadne Grant (Cheltenham: Edward Elgar, 2015) 46–75; De Lucia, "Beyond Anthropocentrism and Ecocentrism."

112 Ibid., xvii, emphasis added.

113 Levi R. Bryant, *The Democracy of Objects* (Ann Arbor: New Humanities Press, 2011), 23.

more broadly.[114] New Materialism foregrounds impersonal material processes of production that emerge as "assemblages" "in a kind of chaotic network of habitual and non-habitual connections, always in flux, always reassembling in different ways."[115] The centrality of the assemblage to New Materialist analysis links ontology to politics in a way that is particularly salient for the complexities of Anthropocene-Capitalocene planetary predicament. Since "there is nothing to prevent a relation conventionally thought of as 'micro' (e.g., a local transaction) and a 'macro' relation (e.g., a nation-state or a climate pattern) [being] drawn into an assemblage by an affective flow," New Materialist analysis is wide-ranging in focus. The affects of macro-structural projects (such as the international economy) can be drawn together with critical attention to "micro-powers of governmentality," and with a whole constellation of actants; biological urges; movements of herds or flocks; transits of toxins, viruses, nutrients, water, air; the physical infrastructure of a power supply, the movement of electrons, patterns of discourse, and so much more besides.

One particularly useful contribution to New Materialist thought for the Anthropocene-Capitalocene is offered by Alaimo in *Bodily Natures: Science, Environment and the Material Self*.[116] Alaimo's work foregrounds embodiment, materiality and interconnection (as Weber's does), but takes corporeal entanglements into an urgent political encounter with toxicity. Alaimo does not offer an eco-romantic theorization, though she does invoke the convergence of "concern and wonder" (terms Weber would embrace) that emerges when "the context for ethics becomes not merely social but material — the emergent,

---

114 Nick J. Fox and Pam Alldred, "New Materialist Social Inquiry: Designs, Methods and the Research-assemblage," *International Journal of Social Research Methodology* 18, no. 4 (2015): 399–414, at 401, citing Gilles Deleuze, *Spinoza: Practical Philosophy* (San Francisco: City Lights, 1988), 101.

115 Ibid., citing Annie Potts, "Deleuze on Viagra (or, What Can a Viagra-body Do?)," *Body and Society* 10 (2004): 17–36, at 19.

116 Stacy Alaimo, *Bodily Natures: Science, Environment and the Material Self* (Bloomington and Indianapolis: Indiana University Press, 2010).

ultimately unmappable landscapes of interacting biological, climatic, economic and political forces."[117] These unmappable landscapes are encountered in Alaimo's work through "trans-corporeality", a mode of encounter and analysis which, she argues, enables a "thinking across bodies" and a "movement across bodies" that "opens up a mobile space that acknowledges the often unpredictable and unwanted actions of human bodies, nonhuman creatures, ecological systems, chemical agents, and other actors".[118] Alaimo's emphasis on the "trans-" also demands "more capacious epistemologies" and, she suggests, "allows us to forge ethical and political positions that can contend with [...] late twentieth- and early twenty-first-century realities."[119]

Importantly, trans-corporeality brings corporeal theories, science studies and environmental theories into a complexly productive engagement, responding to the need for "modes of analysis that travel through the entangled territories of material and discursive, natural and cultural, biological and textual."[120] Analysis itself, in other words, is a trans-corporeal assemblage — and Alaimo is careful to acknowledge that the deep realities of trans-corporeality are already being registered in a wide range of intellectual, cultural, material spaces, in scholarship, activisms, art practices, and broader socio-cultural practices.

Alaimo rightly foregrounds the well-founded feminist suspicion of biology and of "nature" as constructs that have long been used to privilege Eurocentric, masculinist rationalism and concomitantly to denigrate women, indigenous peoples and all other humans (and non-humans) constructed as being less than fully rational. This critique of biology and "nature" is critical, I suggest, for thinking about onto-political alternatives — not least because the distributions of privilege and marginalization marking them are fundamental to the Anthropocene-Capitalo-

---

117 Ibid., 2.
118 Ibid.
119 Ibid.
120 Ibid., 3.

cene. There is, in short, a significant continuity between science, biology, "nature," and a highly unjust, gendered, raced, politics of juridical "neutrality" that needs overtly calling out. Alaimo signals an acutely injustice-sensitive aspect of feminist New Materialist work when she argues that "Perhaps the only way to truly oust the twin ghosts of biology and nature is, paradoxically, to endow them with flesh, to allow them to materialize more fully, and to attend to their precise materializations."[121]

Many of these materializations in the Anthropocene-Capitalocene necessitate an explicit focus on risk and toxicity. Alaimo places a strong epistemological and political emphasis on the trans-corporeal transit of toxins, a transit that is intimately local and simultaneously entangled with regulatory negligence, environmental degradation, and global patterns of social injustice.[122] Such trans-corporeal vectors necessitate an epistemological expansion, not just for tracing the ways in which "trans-corporeality often ruptures ordinary knowledge practices," but also for embracing "particular moments of confusion and contestation that occur when individuals and collectives must contend not only with the materiality of their very selves but with the often invisibly hazardous landscapes of risk society." [123]

This necessity for an epistemological shift reflects an immersive entanglement within "incalculable, interconnected material agencies that erode even our most sophisticated modes of understanding."[124] Citing Beck, Alaimo argues that, "Understanding the risks requires the 'sensory organs' of science — theories, experiments, measuring instruments — in order to become visible or interpretable as hazards at all."[125] Given that, as members of the risk society, we cannot "know" without such sensory organs, scientific knowledge becomes a pre-requisite for "survey[ing] the landscape of the self."[126] One implication,

---

121 Ibid., 6.
122 Ibid., 15.
123 Ibid., 17.
124 Ibid.
125 Ibid., 19.
126 Ibid.

therefore, of Alaimo's work is that an account of the self for the Anthropocene-Capitalocene must go beyond an existential account of human ontological entanglement with "nature," and must explicitly highlight the entanglements of the self in the structural assemblages of a trans-corporeal materiality that is emphatically marked by toxic risk. The risks at stake here also require understanding materiality itself as agential within a frame that brings into view the immense complexity of flows and forces at work: economic, political, juridical, cultural, climatic, spatial, chemical, viral, molecular, racial, sexual, extractive, appropriative, emissive, calculative, regulatory, and so on. And, as result, as Alaimo rightly points out, trans-corporeality "demands more responsible, less confident epistemologies."[127] It also means that "The self becomes unrecognizable in the material memoir [...] because self-knowledge in risk society demands 'scientific' understandings of a vast, coextensive materiality."[128]

Alaimo's account positions a powerful, critically-informed onto-politics firmly within the complex materialities of the Anthropocene-Capitalocene, in a feminist New Materialist reflection richly fed by strands of critical theory, literatures, themes, and activisms that are not foregrounded by Weber's poetic materialism. Alaimo's important argument concerning the extension of science as a necessary sensory organ for the trans-corporeal risk society contextualizes, by implication, existential poetics, with a critical injustice-sensitive framing. Such a framing, I suggest, is a non-negotiable component of living against the global networks of historical and contemporary injustice typifying neoliberalism's appropriative colonization of lifeworlds.

It is clear that New Materialism radically de-centers the human. It focuses, in De Landa's words, on the "idea that matter has morphogenetic capacities of its own and does not need to be commanded into a generating form."[129] How then, might we

---

127 Ibid., 22.

128 Ibid., 24.

129 Rick Dolphijn and Iris van der Tuin, *New Materialism: Interviews & Cartographies* (Ann Arbor: Open Humanities Press, 2012), 43.

construct New Materialist entanglements and "relationalities" for the Anthropocene-Capitalocene with commoning in mind?

One insight that we might follow, one Weber would undoubtedly share and endorse, is the idea that "all bodies are kin in the sense of inextricably enmeshed in a dense network of relations."[130] Haraway, arguably, has offered most to this particular thread, both in her alternative figuration for the Anthropocene-Capitalocene — the "Chthulucene" — and, in her emphasis on "staying with the trouble" and her call to active "kin-making."[131] Several commons-sustaining insights emerge, in particular, from Haraway's chapter on "Tentacular Thinking" in *Staying with the Trouble*.[132]

Haraway is deeply attentive to the multiplicity of connections at stake in contemporary planetary dilemmas. Without denying the ultimate sense in which everything is ultimately entangled, she insists that "nothing is connected to everything; everything is connected to something," meaning that while everything may ultimately be connected to everything else, the "specificity and proximity of connections matters — *who we are bound up with and in what ways.*"[133] This question of who we are bound up with in what ways, it seems to me, lies at the heart of commoning, and is rich with implication for the kind of embodied, situated awareness at the heart of Weber's commons ontology. In a commons, we could say, it matters how humans and other lively non-human commoners of all kinds — organic and inorganic — are understood to be bound up with each other, and in what ways. It matters whether human-non-human distributed agency/affect is made visible or invisible by the onto-epistemic framing in play. It matters how the incipiencies and propensities

---

130 Bennett, *Vibrant Matter,* 13.
131 Donna J. Haraway, "Tentacular Thinking: Anthropocene, Capitalocene, Chthulucene," in *Staying with the Trouble: Making Kin in the Chthulucene* (Durham: Duke University Press, 2016) 30–57.
132 Ibid.
133 Ibid., 31, n.2. Emphasis original. Here, Haraway is citing Thom van Dooren, *Flight Ways: Life at the Edge of Extinction* (New York: Columbia University Press, 2014), 60.

of the organic and inorganic actants meshed in a commons as-semblage might co-generate or co-shape normative relations in that particular assemblage.[134]

In the light of New Materialist onto-epistemology, human commoners are best seen as members of a "specifically endowed (but not special) environment-making species"[135] entangled with other specifically endowed, but not necessarily special, non-hu-man kinds of commoners. In this connection, it is useful to em-brace "sympoiesis" rather than "autopoiesis." Weber — writing in his analytical, biological, scientist mode rather than in his po-etic, existentialist mode — embraces autopoiesis for its emphasis on the capacity of organisms to self-produce: "organisms," while "no longer viewed as genetic machines, [are] basically [...] materially embodied processes that *bring forth themselves.*"[136] Haraway, however, in line with the assemblage thinking of New Materialism, prefers sympoiesis, precisely because rather than emphasizing the "self-producing," it emphasizes the "collective-ly producing." Haraway observes, moreover, that

> many systems are mistaken for autopoietic when they are really sympoietic. I think this point is important for think-ing about rehabilitation (making liveable again) and sustain-ability amid the porous tissues and open edges of damaged but still ongoing living worlds, like the planet earth and its denizens in current times being called the Anthropocene.[137]

134 Margherita Pieraccini, "Property Pluralism and the Partial Reflexivity of Conservation Law: The Case of Upland Commons in England and Wales," *Journal of Human Rights and the Environment* 3, no. 2 (2012): 273–87; An-dreas Philippoulous-Mihalopoulos, "The Triveneto Transhumance: Law, Land, Movement," *Politica and Societa* 3 (2012): 447–68.

135 Haraway, "Tentacular Thinking," 185, n.52.

136 Weber, *Enlivement,* 30, emphasis added. Haraway argues that "[autopoi-etic systems are hugely interesting — witness the history of cybernetics and information sciences; but they are not good models for living and dying worlds and their critters [...]. Poiesis is symchthonic, sympoietic, always partnered all the way down, with no starting and subsequently interacting 'units'" ("Tentacular Thinking," 33).

137 Haraway, "Tentacular Thinking," 33.

Sympoiesis also complicates the boundaries of assemblages and commons by emphasizing trans-corporeal flows of information, affect, and distributed agency: Sympoiesis refers to

> collectively-producing systems that do not have self-defined spatial or temporal boundaries. Information and control are distributed among components. The systems are evolution-ary and have the potential for surprising change.[138]

As Haraway argues, "[i]f it is true that neither biology nor phi-losophy supports the notion of independent organisms in en-vironments, that is, interacting units plus contexts/rules, then sympoiesis is the name of the game in spades."[139] Sympoiesis, in rejecting interacting units plus contexts and rules, and in em-phasizing the membranous, porous nature of system-entangle-ments, offers rich insights and questions for commons imagi-naries. Are commons sympoietic? Should they be understood as such? What is gained and lost in such an understanding? What about seeing them as "multipoietic?" Would the removal of the "sym-" open up a different space for critical reflection on power relations and struggles "internal" to commons in a way respon-sive to critical histories of exclusion? Do commons have self-defined boundaries, or are they more accurately to be conceived of as contingently identified assemblages with frayed and po-rous membranes, which underline the need for sustained atten-tion to questions of extension, membership, and power? How is the "skin" of any particular commons to be identified — and for which purposes? Who are the potential (human and non-human) commoners at stake in any given commons assem-blage — and in relation to what? If thinking of interacting units plus contexts and rules is out, how are commons normativities to be co-woven? What might such questions mean for digital commons? To what extent can who "we" are bound up with and

---

138 Ibid., citing M. Beth L. Dempster, "A Self-Organizing Systems Perspective on Planning for Sustainability," MA Thesis, University of Waterloo, 1998.
139 Haraway, "Tentacular Thinking," 33.

in what ways be de-localized in physical terms, but re-localized in material intimacies forged by trans-corporeal relationalities that overspill particular ground-based commons boundaries — such as is the case with cyber-commons? We could go on.

I think one important gain from framing a commons as an assemblage and/or as a site of sympoetic/multipoetic commoning is its focus on co-negotiation, contingency, and the need to analyse critically what counts and for whom and why in a messy play of world-making. It also means admitting, and tracing the full ethical implications of the fact that, in Bryant's words, the

> nonhuman [...] in the form of technologies, weather patterns, resources, diseases, animals, natural disasters, the presence or absence of roads, the availability of water, animals, microbes, the presence or absence of electricity and high speed internet connections, modes of transportation, and so on [...] and many more besides play a crucial role in bringing humans together in particular ways.[140]

Thinking of this kind is significant for a political ecology of the commons. It calls for fresh attention to the "graspings, frayings, and weavings, passing relays again and again, in the generative recursions that make up living and dying."[141] It invites an accounting for the "shifting states and capacities, which in turn produce further shifting states and capacities in a non-linear, rhizomatic way that spreads out in all directions sometimes in patterned ways, sometimes unpredictably."[142] It invites "tentacular thinking," which is the kind of thinking that moves along with spider-like feelers, rather than buying into outdated and

---

140 Bryant, *The Democracy of Objects*, 23–24.

141 Ibid., 33.

142 Anna Grear, "Foregrounding Vulnerability: Materiality's Porous Affectability as a Methodological Platform," in *Research Methods in Environmental Law*, eds. Andreas Philippoulos-Mihalopoulos and Valerie Brooks (Cheltenham: Edward Elgar, 2017) 3–28, at 23.

destructive illusions of ocularcentric human mastery (such as those driving neoliberal environmental governmentality).

As Haraway insists, it matters "what ideas we use to think other ideas."[143] Tentacular thinking inspires,

> ecology of practices, [a commitment] to the mundane articulating of assemblages through situated work and play in the muddle of messy living and dying. Actual players, articulating with varied allies of all ontological sorts (molecules, colleagues and much more) must compose and sustain what is and will be. Alignment in tentacular worlding must be a seriously tangled affair![144]

Commons are ideally placed to function as "on-the-ground collectives capable of inventing new practices of imagination, resistance, revolt, repair and mourning, and of living and dying well."[145] Commons are assemblages richly gifted with intimate possibilities for "staying with the trouble," staying willingly immersed in the messy incompletion of resistive, trans-corporeally aware, scientifically-sensing, living against the managerial coloniality of the Anthropocene-Capitalocene. Haraway's important invitation to "stay with the trouble" in this way is precisely what necessitates "making kin" of all kinds. There is an urgent need to learn "practices of becoming with" more-than-human collaborators. As Haraway puts it,

> We are at stake to each other. Unlike the dominant dramas of Anthropocene and Capitalocene discourse, human beings are not the only important actors in the Chthulucene, with all other beings able simply to react. The order is reknitted:

---

143 Haraway, "Tentacular Thinking," 34.

144 Ibid., 42.

145 Ibid., referring to the work of Philippe Pignarre and Isabelle Stengers, *La sorcellerie capitaliste: Pratiques de désenvoûtement* (Paris: La Découverte, 2005).

human beings are with and of the earth, and the biotic and abiotic powers of this earth are the main story.[146]

Haraway is right to argue that "diverse human and nonhuman players are necessary in every fiber of the tissues of the urgently needed Chthulucene story."[147] There are no guarantees of immunity from neoliberal subversion of commons, but actively turning towards more-than-human commoners — allowing them actively to co-shape the normative praxis of a commons — holds out a space, at least, where a resistive, alert, subversive onto-politics of radical inclusion and care might work against neoliberal reductionisms and objectifications. Certainly, "in an age where we are faced with the looming threat of monumental climate change, it is [now] irresponsible to draw our distinctions in such a way as to exclude nonhuman actors."[148] It seems vital to move beyond thinking and speaking of commons as "human-human" and "human-nature" relations and explicitly to embrace commoning as a "human-non-human" co-practice for which non-human commoners are active, generative contributors.

While eco-romanticism presents a powerful emotional appeal to the reader's sense of embodied entanglement, in the final analysis (and despite its potential to reach some who might not be moved by alternative vocabularies), it provides an incomplete answer to the global scale and complexity of the problems and dilemmas to which new commons movements are an insurgent response. And, as powerful and valuable as poetics is as a tool of existential awakening, it is not poetic materialism that ultimately offers the most critically informed, injustice-sensitive grounding for commons ontology in an age of systematic oppression. The trans-corporeal nature of climate risk and the toxic flows marking all planetary existence suggests the vital importance of a highly politicized and critical commons onto-epistemology, one alive to the potentially oppressive implica-

---

146 Haraway, "Tentacular Thinking," 55.
147 Ibid.
148 Bryant, *The Democracy of Objects,* 24.

tions of "nature" as a construct, alert to its pattern of historical injustices and their links with contemporary mal-distributions of risk, hazard, life, and death. New Materialism, perhaps especially as deployed by feminist New Materialist thinkers, arguably offers vocabulary, wide-ranging critical literacy, and accounts of an emergent onto-epistemology especially suited to re-grounding commoning as a form of human–non-human onto-insurgency against the multiple, pathological closures of the Anthropocene-Capitalocene.

Reference Bibliography

Adelman, Sam. "Epistemologies of Mastery." In *Research Handbook on Human Rights and the Environment,* edited by Anna Grear and Louis J. Kotzé, 9–27. Cheltenham: Edward Elgar Publishing, 2015.

———. "Geoengineering: Rights, Risks and Ethics." *Journal of Human Rights and the Environment* 8 (2017): 119–38. DOI: 10.4337/jhre.2017.01.06.

———. "The Sustainable Development Goals, Anthropocentrism and Neoliberalism." In *Global Goals: Law, Theory & Implementation,* edited by Duncan French and Louis J. Kotzé, 15–40. Cheltenham: Edward Elgar, 2018.

AFSA (African Food Sovereignty in Africa). "Every Seed Has a Story – The Strategy," March 20, 2020. https://afsafrica.org/every-seed-has-a-story/.

Agamben, Giorgio. *State of Exception.* Translated by Kevin Attell. Chicago: University of Chicago Press, 2008.

Alaimo, Stacy. *Bodily Natures: Science, Environment and the Material Self.* Bloomington and Indianapolis: Indiana University Press, 2010.

Anderson, Philip W. "More Is Different: Broken Symmetry and the Nature of the Hierarchical Structure of Science." *Science* 177, no. 4047 (1972): 393–96. DOI: 10.1126/science.177.4047.393.

Anghie, Antony. *Imperialism, Sovereignty and the Making of International Law.* Cambridge: Cambridge University Press, 2005.

Angus, Ian. *Facing the Anthropocene: Fossil Capitalism and Crisis of the Earth System.* New York: Monthly Review Press, 2016.

Arendt, Hannah. "On Violence." In *Crises of the Republic,* 103–84. New York: Houghton Mifflin, 1972.

———. *The Human Condition.* Chicago: University of Chicago Press, 1958.

Aristotle. *Nicomachean Ethics.* Kitchener: Batoche Books, 1999.

———. *Politics.* Mineola: Dover Publications, 2000.

Arrighi, Giovanni. *The Long Twentieth Century.* London and New York: Verso, 2010.

Arthur, W. Brian, et al. *The Economy as an Evolving Complex System II.* Reading: Addison-Wesley, 1997.

Atzori, Marcella. "Blockchain Technology and Decentralized Governance: Is the State Still Necessary?" *SSRN,* January 2, 2016. DOI: 10.2139/ssrn.2709713.

AURA. "Donna Haraway, 'Anthropocene, Capitalocene, Chthulucene: Staying with the Trouble,' 5/9/14." *Vimeo,* June 8, 2014. https://vimeo.com/97663518.

Axelrod, Robert, and Michael D. Cohen. *Harnessing Complexity: Organizational Implications of a Scientific Frontier.* New York: Basic Books, 2001.

Azoulay, David, et al. "Plastic and Health: The Hidden Costs of a Plastic Planet." *Center for International Environmental Law,* 2019. https://www.ciel.org/plasticandhealth/.

Bailey, Saki, Gilda Farrell, and Ugo Mattei, eds. *Protecting Future Generations through Commons.* Trends in Social Cohesion 26. Council of Europe, 2014.

Bak, Per. *How Nature Works: The Science of Self-Organized Criticality.* New York: Copernicus, 1996.

Baker, Mitchell. "Readying for the Future at Mozilla." *The Mozilla Blog,* January 15, 2020. https://blog.mozilla.org/blog/2020/01/15/readying-for-the-future-at-mozilla/.

Baran, Paul. *On Distributed Communications: I. Introduction to Distributed Communications Networks.* Santa Monica: Rand Corporation, 1964.

Barnes, Peter. *Who Owns the Sky? Our Common Assets and the Future of Capitalism.* Washington, DC: Island Press, 2001.

Barnet, Richard J. *Who Wants Disarmament?* Boston: Beacon Press, 1960.

Baskin, Jeremy. "Paradigm Dressed as Epoch: The Ideology of the Anthropocene." *Environmental Values* 24, no. 1 (2015): 9–29. DOI: 10.319/096327115X14183182353746.

Baslar, Kemal. *The Concept of the Common Heritage of Mankind in International Law.* The Hague: Nijhoff, 1998.

Bauman, Zygmunt. *Postmodern Ethics.* London: Wiley-Blackwell, 1993.

Baumlin, James, and Craig Meyer. "Positioning Ethos in/for the Twenty-First Century: An Introduction to Histories of Ethos." *Humanities* 7, no. 3 (2018): 1–26. DOI: 10.3390/h7030078.

Bauwens, Michel, "A Commons Transition Plan for the City of Ghent." *P2P Foundation,* September 14, 2017. https://blog.p2pfoundation.net/a-commons-transition-plan-for-the-city-of-ghent/2017/09/14.

———. *P2P Foundation.* http://www.p2pfoundation.net.

Bauwens, Michel, Nicolas Mendoza, and Franco Iacomella. *Synthetic Overview of the Collaborative Economy.* P2P Foundation, 2012. https://p2pfoundation.net/wp-content/uploads/2018/02/Synthetic-overview-of-the-collaborative-economy.pdf.

Bauwens, Michel, and Vasilis Niaros. *Value in the Commons Economy: Developments in Open and Contributory Value Accounting.* Berlin: Heinrich Böll Stiftung and P2P Foundation, 2017.

Bauwens, Michel, and Jurek Onzia, "A Commons Transition Plan for the City of Ghent." *Commons Transition,* September 8, 2017. http://commonstransition.org/commons-transition-plan-city-ghent/.

Bauwens, Michel, and Jose Ramos. "Re-imagining the Left through an Ecology of the Commons: Towards a Post-capitalist Commons Transition." *Global Discourse* 8, no. 2 (2018): 325–42. DOI: 10.1080/23269995.2018.1461442.

Bayer Corporation. "Bayer to Acquire Monsanto: Creating a Leader in Global Agriculture," 2016. https://www.advancingtogether.com/en/about-the-combination/compelling-strategic-rationale/.

Beck, Ulrich. "Climate for Change, or How to Create a Green Modernity?" *Theory, Culture & Society* 27, nos. 2–3 (2010): 254–66. DOI: 10.1177/0263276409358729.

———. "Emancipatory Catastrophism: What Does It Mean to Climate Change and Risk Society?" *Current Sociology* 63, no. 1 (2015): 75–88. DOI: 10.1177/0011392114559951.

———. *World Risk Society.* Cambridge: Polity Press, 1999.

Beck, Ulrich, Anthony Giddens, and Scott Lash. *Reflexive Modernization: Politics, Tradition and Aesthetics in the Modern Social Order.* Cambridge: Polity Press, 1994.

Beckerman, Wilfred. "The Impossibility of a Theory of Intergenerational Justice." In *Handbook Of Intergenerational Justice,* edited by Joeng Tremmel, 53–71. Cheltenham: Edward Elgar, 2006.

Bell, Anne. "Non Human Nature and the Ecosystem Approach. The Limits of Anthropocentrism in Great Lakes Management." *Alternatives Journal* 20, no. 3 (2004): 20–25.

Bellamy Foster, John, Brett Clark and Richard York. *The Ecological Rift: Capitalism's War on the Earth.* New York: Monthly Review Press, 2011.

Benjamin, Walter. "On the Concept of History." In *Selected Writings, Volume 4, 1938–1940,* edited by Howard Eiland and Michael W. Jennings, 389–400. Cambridge: Belknap Press of Harvard University Press, 2006.

Benkler, Yochai. "Coase's Penguin, or, Linux and the Nature of the Firm." *The Yale Law Journal* 112, no. 3 (2002): 369–446.

———. *The Penguin and the Leviathan How Cooperation Triumphs over Self-Interest.* New York: Crown Business, 2011.

————. *The Wealth of Networks: How Social Production Transforms Markets and Freedom.* New Haven: Yale University Press, 2006.

Bennett, Elena M., et al. "Bright Spots: Seeds of a Good Anthropocene." *Frontiers in Ecology and the Environment* 14, no. 8 (2016): 441–48. DOI: 10/1002/fee.1309.

Bennett, Jane. *Vibrant Matter: A Political Ecology of Things.* Durham: Duke University Press, 2010.

Berman, Morris. *The Reenchantment of the World.* New York: Cornell University Press, 1981.

Berry, Thomas. *Evening Thoughts: Reflecting on Earth as a Sacred Community.* Berkeley: Counterpoint, 2015.

Bhidé, Amar. "The Venturesome Economy: How Innovation Sustains Prosperity in a More Connected World." *Journal of Applied Corporate Finance* 21, no. 1 (2009): 8–23. DOI: 10.1111/j.1745–6622.2009.00211.x.

Blank, Steve. "Why the Lean Start-up Changes Everything." *Harvard Business Review* 91, no. 5 (2013): 63–72.

Bodle, Robert. "Regimes of Sharing: Open APIs, Interoperability, and Facebook." *Information, Communication & Society* 14, no. 3 (2011): 320–37. DOI: 10.1080/1369118X.2010.542825.

Bohme, Gernot. *Cameron Shingleton, trans. Invasive Technification: Critical Essays in the Philosophy of Technology.* London and New York: Bloomsbury, 2012.

Bohr, Jeremiah, and Masooda M. Bashir. "Who Uses Bitcoin? An Exploration of the Bitcoin Community." *2014 IEEE Twelfth Annual International Conference on Privacy, Security and Trust (PST)* (2014): 94–101.

Bollier, David. "Commoning as a Transformative Social Paradigm." *The Next System Project,* April 28, 2016. http://thenextsystem.org/commoning-as-a-transformative-social-paradigm/.

————. "Reinventing Law for the Commons." *Heinrich Böll Stiftung,* September 4, 2015. https://www.boell.de/en/2015/09/04/reinventing-law-commons.

———. *Silent Theft: The Private Plunder of Our Common Wealth*. New York: Routledge, 2003.

———. "The Potato Park of Peru." In *Patterns of Commoning*, edited by David Bollier and Silke Helfrich, 103–7. Amherst: Off the Common Books, 2014. http://patternsofcommoning. org/the-potato-park-of-peru.

———. *Think Like a Commoner: A Short Introduction to the Life of the Commons*. Gabriola: New Society Publishers, 2014.

———. *Viral Spiral: How the Commoners Created a Digital Commons of Their Own*. New York: New Press, 2007.

Bollier, David, and Silke Helfrich. *Free, Fair and Alive: The Insurgent Power of the Commons*. Gabriola Island: New Society Publishers, 2019.

———. "Overture." In *Patterns of Commoning*, edited by David Bollier and Silke Helfrich, 1–12. Amherst: Off the Common Books, 2014.

———. *Patterns of Commoning*. Amherst: Off the Common Books, 2014. http://www.patternsofcommoning.org.

———. *The Wealth of the Commons*. Amherst: Levellers Press, 2012. http://www.wealthofthecommons.org.

Bonneau, Joseph, Andrew Miller, Jeremy Clark, Arvind Narayanan, Joshua A. Kroll, and Edward W. Felten, "SoK: Research Perspectives and Challenges for Bitcoin and Cryptocurrencies." *2015 IEEE Symposium on Security and Privacy (SP)* (2015): 104–21.

Bonneuil, Christophe. "The Geological Turn: Narratives of the Anthropocene." In *The Anthropocene and the Global Environmental Crisis: Rethinking Modernity in a New Epoch*, edited by Clive Hamilton, Christophe Bonneuil, and François Gemenne, 17–31. Abingdon: Routledge, 2015.

Bonneuil, Christophe, and Jean-Baptiste Fressoz. *The Shock of the Anthropocene: The Earth, History and Us*. London: Verso, 2016.

Borrelli, Giorgio. "Semiosis and Discursivity of the Commodity Form." In *Material Discourse—Materialist Analysis:*

Approaches in Discourse Studies, edited by Johannes Beetz and Veit Schwab, 129–44. Lexington Books, 2018.

Boulding, Elise. "Futuristics and the Imaging Capacity of the West." In *Cultures of the Future,* edited by Magoroh Maruyama and Arthur M. Harkins, 146–57. The Hague: Mouton, 1978.

Bowles, Samuel. *The Cooperative Species: Human Reciprocity and its Evolution.* Princeton: Princeton University Press, 2011.

Brown, Wendy. *Undoing the Demos.* New York: Zone Books, 2015.

Brown-Weiss, Edith. *In Fairness to Future Generations: International Law, Common Patrimony, and Intergenerational Equity.* New York: Transnational Publishers, 1989.

Bryant, Levi R. *The Democracy of Objects.* Ann Arbor: New Humanities Press, 2011.

Buck, Susan. *The Global Commons: An Introduction.* Washington, DC: Island Press, 1998.

Bull, Hedley. *The Anarchical Society: A Study of Order in World Politics.* New York: Columbia University Press, 1977.

Burckhardt, Jacob. *Reflections on History.* 1868; rpt. Indianapolis: Liberty Classics, 1979.

Butchart, Stuart, et al. "Global Biodiversity: Indicators of Recent Declines." *Science* 328, no. 5982 (2010): 1164–68. DOI: 10.1126/science.1187512.

Butruille, David V., Fufa H. Birru, Marv L. Boerboom, Edward J. Cargill, Duane A. Davis, Prabhakar Dhungana, Gerald M. Dill, et al. "Maize Breeding in the United States: Views from Within Monsanto." In *Plant Breeding Reviews: Volume 39,* edited by Jules Janick, 199–282. Hoboken: John Wiley & Sons, Inc., 2015.

Butt, Ronald. "Mrs Thatcher: The First Two Years." *Sunday Times,* May 3, 1981. http://www.margaretthatcher.org/document/104475.

Caffentzis, George. "The Future of 'The Commons': Neoliberalism's Plan B, or the Original Disaccumulation of

Capital?" *New Formations* 69 (2010): 23–41. DOI: 10.3898/NEWF.69.01.2010.

Callon, Michel. "Techno-economic Networks and Irreversibility." In *A Sociology of Monsters: Essays on Power, Technology and Domination,* edited by John Law, 132–64. London: Routledge, 1991.

Camilleri, Joseph A., and Jim Falk. *The End of Sovereignty: The Politics of a Shrinking and Fragmenting World.* Hants: Edward Elgar, 1992.

Capra, Fritjof, and Ugo Mattei. *The Ecology of Law: Toward a Legal System in Tune with Nature and Community.* Oakland: Berrett-Koehler, 2015.

Castells, Manuel. *The Internet Galaxy: Reflections on the Internet, Business, and Society.* Oxford: Oxford University Press, 2002.

Castree, Noel. "The Anthropocene: A Primer for Geographers." *Geography* 100, no. 2 (2015): 66–75.

Catalano, Pierangelo. *Populus Romanus Quirites.* Turin: Giappichelli, 1975.

Cerf, Vinton G. "Dynamics of Disruptive Innovations." *Journal on Telecommunications and High Technology Law* 10 (2012): 21–31. https://dblp.org/rec/journals/jthtl/Cerf12.

Chakrabarty, Dipesh. *Provincialising Europe.* Princeton: Princeton University Press, 2007.

———. "The Climate of History: Four Theses." *Critical Inquiry* 35, no. 2 (2009): 197–222. DOI: 10.1086/596640.

Charles, Dan. "Plant Breeders Release First 'Open Source Seeds.'" NPR: *The Salt,* April 17, 2014.

"ChemChina, Sinochem Merge Agricultural Assets: Syngenta." *Reuters,* January 5, 2020. https://www.reuters.com/article/us-chemchina-sinochem-syngenta/chemchina-sinochem-merge-agricultural-assets-syngenta-idUSKBN1Z40FZ.

Clark, David D. "The Design Philosophy of the DARPA Internet Protocols." *ACM SIGCOMM Computer Communication Review* 18, no. 4 (1988): 106–14. DOI: 10.1145/52324.52336.

Code, Lorraine. *Ecological Thinking: The Politics of Epistemic Location.* Oxford: Oxford University Press, 2006.

Cohen, Jon. "Fields of Dreams." *Science* 365, no. 6452 (August 2, 2019): 422–25. DOI: 10.1126/science.365.6452.422.

Connolly, William. *Ethos of Pluralization*. Minneapolis: University of Minnesota Press, 1995.

Corson, Catherine, and Kenneth I. McDonald. "Enclosing the Global Commons: The Convention on Biological Diversity and Green Grabbing." *The Journal of Peasant Studies* 39, no. 2 (2012): 263–83. DOI: 10.1080/03066150.2012.664138.

Cox, Robert W., and Timothy J. Sinclair. *Approaches to World Order*. Cambridge: Cambridge University Press, 1996.

Crutzen, Paul J. "Geology of Mankind." *Nature* 415, no. 6867 (2002): 23. DOI: 10.1038/415023a.

Crutzen, Paul J., and Eugene F. Stoermer. "The 'Anthropocene.'" *Global Change Newsletter* 41 (2000): 17–18.

CSA-India. "Open Source Seed Systems." *Centre for Sustainable Agriculture,* November 2014. http://csa-india.org/wp-content/uploads/2014/11/Open_Source_Seed_Systems_1.0.pdf.

Dangerman, Jerome, and Hans J. Schellnhuber. "Energy Systems Transformation." *PNAS* 110, no. 7 (2013): E549–E558. DOI: 10.1073/pnas.1219791110.

Dardot, Pierre, and Christian Laval. *The New Way of the World: On Neoliberal Society*. London and New York: Verso, 2013.

Darier, Eric, ed. *Discourses of the Environment*. Oxford: Blackwell, 1999.

Dator, Jim. "Alternative Futures at the Manoa School." *Journal of Futures Studies* 14, no. 2 (2009): 1–18.

Davidson, Sinclair, Primavera De Filippi, and Jason Potts. "Disrupting Governance: The New Institutional Economics of Distributed Ledger Technology." *SSRN,* July 22, 2016. DOI: 10.2139/ssrn.2811995.

De Angelis, Massimo. "Separating the Doing and the Deed: Capital and the Continuous Character of Enclosures." *Historical Materialism* 12, no. 2 (2004): 57–87. DOI: 10.1163/1569206041551609.

De Angelis, Massimo, Nate Holdren, and Stevphen Shukaitis. "The Commoner No. 1—Reinfusing the Commons." *Mute*, June 20, 2006.

De Filippi, Primavera. "Bitcoin: A Regulatory Nightmare to a Libertarian Dream." *Internet Policy Review* 3, no. 2 (2014). DOI: 10.14763/2014.2.286.

———. "Translating Commons-Based Peer Production Values into Metrics: Toward Commons-Based Cryptocurrencies." In *Handbook of Digital Currency: Bitcoin, Innovation, Financial Instruments, and Big Data*, ed. David Lee Kuo Chuen, 463–83. Amsterdam: Elsevier, 2015.

De Filippi, Primavera, and Samer Hassan. "Blockchain Technology as a Regulatory Technology: From Code Is Law to Law Is Code." *First Monday* 21, no. 12 (2016). https://firstmonday.org/article/view/7113/5657.

De Filippi, Primavera, and Benjamin Loveluck. "The Invisible Politics of Bitcoin: Governance Crisis of a Decentralized Infrastructure." *Internet Policy Review* 5, no. 3 (2016): 1–32. DOI: 10.14763/2016.3.427.

De Filippi, Primavera, and Greg McMullen. "Governance of Blockchain Systems: Governance of and by the Infrastructure." *HAL*, February 22, 2019. https://hal.archives-ouvertes.fr/hal-02046787/document.

De Filippi, Primavera, and Miguel S. Vieira. "The Commodification of Information Commons: The Case of Cloud Computing." *The Columbia Science and Technology Law Review* 16 (2014): 102–43. https://hal.archives-ouvertes.fr/hal-01265175.

Dehm, Julia. "Indigenous Peoples and REDD+ Safeguards: Rights as Resistance or as Disciplinary Inclusion in the Green Economy?" *Journal of Human Rights and the Environment* 7, no. 2 (2016): 170–217. DOI: 10.4337/jhre/2016.02.01.

Deibert, Ron. *Parchment, Printing, and Hypermedia*. New York: Columbia University Press, 1997.

De Landa, Manuel. "Uniformity and Variability: An Essay in the Philosophy of Matter." Paper presented at the "Doors of Perception 3" Conference, Netherlands Design Institute, Amsterdam, November 7–11, 1995.

deLaplante, Kevin. "Environmental Alchemy: How to Turn Ecological Science into Ecological Philosophy." *Environmental Ethics* 26, no. 4 (2004): 361–80. DOI: 10.5840/enviroethics20042643.

———. "Is Ecosystem Management a Postmodern Science?" In *Ecological Paradigms Lost: Routes of Theory Change,* edited by Beatrix Beisner and Kim Cuddington, 397–414. Burlington: Elsevier Academic Press, 2005.

Deleuze, Gilles. *Spinoza: Practical Philosophy*. San Francisco: City Lights, 1988.

Deleuze, Gilles, and Felix Guattari, *Thousand Plateaus: Capitalism and Schizophrenia.* Translated by Brian Massumi. Minneapolis: University of Minnesota Press, 1987.

De Lucia, Vito. "A Critical Interrogation of the Relation between the Ecosystem Approach and Ecosystem Services." *RECIEL* 27, no. 2 (2018): 104–14. DOI: 10.1111/reel-12227.

———. "Bare Nature. The Biopolitical Logic of the International Regulation of Invasive Alien Species." *Journal of Environmental Law* 31, no. 1 (2018): 109–34. DOI: 10.1093/jel/eqy016.

———. "Beyond Anthropocentrism and Ecocentrism: A Biopolitical Reading of Environmental Law." *Journal of Human Rights and the Environment* 8, no. 2 (2017): 181–202. DOI: 10.4337/jhre.2017.02.01.

———. "Competing Narratives and Complex Genealogies. The Ecosystem Approach in International Environmental Law." *Journal of Environmental Law* 27, no. 2 (2015): 91–117. DOI: 10.1093/jel/equ031.

———. "Critical Environmental Law and the Double Register of the Anthropocene: A Biopolitical Reading." In *Environmental Law and Governance for the Anthropocene,* edited by Louis Kotzé, 97–116. Oxford: Hart Publishing, 2017.

———. "Law as Insurgent Critique: The Perspective of the Commons in Italy." *Critical Legal Thinking,* August 5, 2013. http://criticallegalthinking.com/2013/08/05/law-as-insurgent-critique-the-perspective-of-the-commons-in-italy/.

———. "Ocean Commons, Law of the Sea and Rights for the Sea." *Canadian Journal of Law and Jurisprudence* 32, no. 1 (2019): 45–57. DOI: 10.1017/cjlj.2019.2.

———. "Re-Embodying Law: Transversal Ecology and the Commons." In *Contributions to Law, Philosophy and Ecology: Exploring Re-Embodiments,* edited by Ruth Thomas-Pellicer, Vito De Lucia, and Sian Sullivan, 161–91. Abingdon: Routledge, 2016.

———. "Semantics of Chaos. Law, Modernity and the Commons." *Pólemos Journal of Law, Literature and Culture* 12, no. 2 (2018): 393–414. DOI: 10.1515/pol-2018–0022.

———. "The Concept of Commons and Marine Genetic Resources in Areas beyond National Jurisdiction." *Marine Safety and Security Law Journal* 5 (2018): 1–21.

———. "Towards an Ecological Philosophy of Law. A Comparative Discussion." *Journal of Human Rights and the Environment* 4, no. 2 (2013): 167–90. DOI: 10.4337/jhre/2013.02.03.

Dempster, M. Beth L. "A Self-Organizing Systems Perspective on Planning for Sustainability." MA Thesis, University of Waterloo, 1998. http://citeseerx.ist.psu.edu/viewdoc/download?doi=10.1.1.180.6090&rep=rep1&type=pdf.

Deneen, Patrick J. *Why Liberalism Failed.* New Haven: Yale University Press, 2018.

De Sadeleer, Nicolas. *Environmental Principles: From Political Slogans to Legal Rules.* Oxford: Oxford University Press, 2008.

Descartes, René. *Discourse on Method and the Meditations.* London: Penguin, 1968.

Descola, Philippe. *The Ecology of Others.* Chicago: Prickly Paradigm Press, 2013.

de Sousa Santos, Boaventura. *Democratizing Democracy: Beyond the Liberal Democratic Canon.* London: Verso, 2007.

———. *The Rise of the Global Left: The World Social Forum and Beyond.* London and New York: Zed Books, 2006.

———. *Toward a New Legal Common Sense: Law, Globalization and Emancipation.* Cambridge: Cambridge University Press, 2002.

de Sousa Santos, Boaventura, João Arriscado Nunes, and Maria Paula Meneses. "Opening Up the Canon of Knowledge and Recognition of Difference." In *Another Knowledge is Possible,* edited by Boaventura de Sousa Santos, xx–lxii. London: Verso, 2007.

Deudney, Daniel. *Bounding Power: Republican Theory from the Polis to the Global Village.* Princeton: Princeton University Press, 2004.

Diamond, Jared. *Collapse: How Societies Choose to Fail or Succeed.* New York: Viking, 2005.

Dolphijn, Rick, and Iris van der Tuin. *New Materialism: Interviews & Cartographies.* Ann Arbor: Open Humanities Press, 2012.

Dooren, Thom van. *Flight Ways: Life at the Edge of Extinction.* New York: Columbia University Press, 2014.

Douzinas, Costas, and Adam Geary. *Critical Jurisprudence: The Political Philosophy of Justice.* Oxford and Portland: Hart Publishing, 2005.

Dugard, John, Richard Falk, Ana Stanic, and Marc Weller. *The Will of the People and Statehood.* Report at the request of Esquerra Republicana de Catalunya, October 30, 2017.

Dunbar-Ortiz, Roxanne. *An Indigenous Peoples' History of the United States.* Boston: Beacon Press, 2014.

DuPont, Quinn. "Experiments in Algorithmic Governance: A History and Ethnography of 'The DAO,' a Failed Decentralized Autonomous Organization." In *Bitcoin and Beyond (Open Access): Cryptocurrencies, Blockchains and Global Governance,* edited by Malcolm Campbell-Verduyn, 157–77. London: Routledge, 2017.

Eco, Umberto. "Does Counter-culture Exist?" Translated by
     Jenny Condie. In *Apocalypse Postponed: Essays by Umberto
     Eco*, 115–28. Bloomington, Indiana: Indiana University Press,
     2000.

———. *The Search for the Perfect Language*. Translated by
     James Fentress. Malden: Wiley-Blackwell, 1995.

———. *Travels in Hyper Reality: Essays*. San Diego: Harcourt
     Brace Jovanovich, 1986.

Escobar, Arturo. "Commons in the Pluriverse." In *Patterns of
     Commoning*, edited by David Bollier and Silke Helfrich,
     348–60. Amherst: Off the Common Books, 2014.

Esposito, Roberto. *Living Thought: The Origins and Actuality of
     Italian Philosophy*. Stanford: Stanford University Press, 2012.

ETC. "Breaking Bad: Big Ag Mega-Mergers in Play." ETC Group
     Communiqué, December 2015. http://www.etcgroup.org/
     sites/www.etcgroup.org/files/files/etc_breakbad_23dec15.
     pdf.

Ex parte Hibberd. "227 USPQ 433." Board of Patent Appeals and
     Interferences, 1985.

Falk, Richard. "After 9/11: The Toxic Interplay of
     Counterterrorism, Geopolitics, and World Order."
     Presented at Workshop on "Is there an After After 9/11?"
     Orfalea Center on Global and International Studies,
     University of California Santa Barbara, January 20–21, 2018.

———. "Challenging Nuclearism: The Nuclear Ban Treaty
     Assessed." July 14, 2017. https://richardfalk.wordpress.
     com/2017/07/14/challenging-nuclearism-the-nuclear-ban-
     treaty-assessed/.

———. "Nobel Peace Prize 2017: International Campaign to
     Abolish Nuclear Weapons (ICAN)." October 8, 2017. https://
     richardfalk.wordpress.com/2017/10/08/nobel-peace-prize-
     2017-international-campaign-to-abolish-nuclear-weapons-
     ican/.

———. "Ordering the World: Hedley Bull after 40 Years." In
     *The Anarchical Society at 40: Contemporary Challenges and
     Prospects*, edited by Hidemi Suganami, Madeline Carr, and

Adam Humphreys, 41–55. Oxford: Oxford University Press, 2017.

———. *Predatory Globalization: A Critique.* Cambridge: Polity Press, 2000.

———. *Power Shift: On the New Global Order.* London: Zed Books, 2016.

———. *The Declining World Order: America's Imperial Geopolitics.* New York and London: Routledge, 2004.

———. *The Great Terror War.* Northampton: Olive Branch Press, 2003.

———. "The World Ahead: Entering the Anthropocene?" In *Exploring Emergent Thresholds: Toward 2030,* edited by Richard Falk, Manoranjan Mohanty, and Victor Faessel, 19–47. Delhi: Orient Black Swan, 2017.

Falk, Richard, and David Krieger. *The Path to Nuclear Zero: Dialogues on Nuclear Danger.* Boulder: Paradigm, 2012.

FAO. *State of the World's Forests.* 2011. http://www.fao.org/state-of-forests/en.

Federici, Silvia. *Caliban and the Witch: Women, the Body and Primitive Accumulation.* 2nd revised edition. New York: Autonomedia, 2014.

Fisher, Elizabeth. "Environmental Law as 'Hot' Law.'" *Journal of Environmental Law* 25, no. 3 (2013): 347–58. DOI: 10.1093/jel/eqt025.

Fiske, Alan P. *Structures of Social Life: The Four Elementary Forms of Human Relations: Communal Sharing, Authority Ranking, Equality Matching, Market Pricing.* New York: Free Press, 1991.

Fitzgerald, Brian. "The Transformation of Open Source Software." *MIS Quarterly* 30, no. 3 (2006): 587–98.

Fitzpatrick, Peter. *The Mythology of Modern Law.* Abingdon: Routledge, 1992.

Fletcher, Robert. "Neoliberal Environmentality: Towards a Post-Structuralist Political Ecology of the Conservation Debate." *Conservation and Society* 8, no. 3 (2010): 171–81. DOI: 10.4103/0972–4923.73806.

Fligstein, Neil. *The Architecture of Markets: An Economic Sociology of Twenty-First-Century Capitalist Societies.* Princeton: Princeton University Press, 2001.

Fontanelli, Filippo. "Santi Romano and L'ordinamento giuridico: The Relevance of a Forgotten Masterpiece for Contemporary International, Transnational and Global Legal Relations." *Transnational Legal Theory* 2, no. 1 (2001): 67–117.

Fox, Nick J., and Pam Alldred. "New Materialist Social Inquiry: Designs, Methods and the Research-assemblage." *International Journal of Social Research Methodology* 18, no. 4 (2015): 399–414. DOI: 10.1080/13645579.2014.921458.

Freeman, Jo. "The Tyranny of Structurelessness." *Berkeley Journal of Sociology* 17 (1972–73): 151–64.

Fukuyama, Francis. *The End of History and the Last Man.* New York: The Free Press, 1992.

FWW (Food and Water Watch). "Public Research, Private Gain: Corporate Influence Over University Agriculture." San Francisco, 2012.

Galtung, Johan. "A Structural Theory of Imperialism." *Journal of Peace Research* (1971): 81–117. DOI: 10.1177/002234337100800201.

———. "Arnold Toynbee: Challenge and Response." In *Macrohistory and Macrohistorians,* edited by Johan Galtung and Sohail Inayatullah, 120–27. New York: Praeger, 1997.

Geels, Frank W. "Ontologies, Socio-technical Transitions (to Sustainability), and the Multi-level Perspective." *Research Policy* 39 (2010): 495–510. DOI: 10.1016/j.respol.2010.01.022.

Gell, Alfred. *Art and Agency: An Anthropological Theory.* Oxford: Clarendon Press, 1998.

Ghosh, Amitav. *The Great Derangement: Climate Change and the Unthinkable.* London: Penguin 2016.

Gibson-Graham, J.K. *The End of Capitalism (As We Knew It): A Feminist Critique of Political Economy.* Minneapolis: University of Minnesota Press, 2006.

Gilbert, Clark. "The Disruption Opportunity." *MIT Sloan Management Review* 44, no. 4 (2003): 27–33.

Gilens, Martin, and Benjamin I. Page. "Testing Theories of American Politics: Elites, Interest Groups, and Average Citizens." *Perspectives on Politics* 12 (2014): 564–81. DOI: 10.1017/S1537592714001595.

Gill, Stephen, ed. *Global Crises and the Crisis of Global Leadership.* Cambridge: Cambridge University Press, 2012.

Gimpel, Jean. *The Medieval Machine: The Industrial Revolution of the Middle Ages.* New York: Penguin Books, 1977.

Glenn, Patrick. *Legal Traditions of the World: Sustainable Diversity in Law.* 2nd edition. Oxford: Oxford University Press, 2004.

Golley, Frank. *A History of the Ecosystem Concept in Ecology: More than the Sum of Its Parts.* New Haven: Yale University Press, 1993.

Gordon, Deborah. *Ants at Work: How an Insect Society Is Organized.* New York: Free Press, 2011.

Gorenflo, Neal, ed. *Sharing Cities: Activating the Urban Commons.* San Francisco: Shareable, 2017.

Graeber, David. *Debt: The First 5000 Years.* New York: Melville House Publishing, 2012.

Graeber, David, and David Wengrow. "How to Change the Course of Human History (At Least, the Part That's Already Happened)." *Eurozine,* March 2, 2018. https://www.eurozine.com/change-course-human-history/.

Graham, Daniel. "Heraclitus." In *The Stanford Encyclopedia of Philosophy* (Fall 2015 edition), edited by Edward Zalta. https://plato.stanford.edu/archives/fall2015/entries/heraclitus/.

GRAIN and La Vía Campesina. "Seed Laws That Criminalize Farmers: Resistance and Fight Back," March 2015. http://viacampesina.org/en/images/stories/pdf/2015-Seed%20laws%20booklet%20EN.pdf.

Gramsci, Antonio. *Selections from the Prison Notebooks.* London: Lawrence & Wishart, 1971.

Grear, Anna. "The Vulnerable Living Order: Human Rights and the Environment in a Critical and Philosophical

Perspective." *Journal of Human Rights and the Environment* 2, no. 1 (2011): 23–44. DOI: 10.4337/jhre.2011.01.02.

———. "Deconstructing Anthropos: A Critical Legal Reflection on 'Anthropocentric' Law and Anthropocene 'Humanity'." *Law and Critique* 26, no. 3 (2015): 225–49. DOI: 10.1007/s10978-015-9161-0.

———. "Foregrounding Vulnerability: Materiality's Porous Affectability as a Methodological Platform." In *Research Methods in Environmental Law,* edited by Andreas Philippopoulos-Mihalopoulos and Valerie Brooks, 3–28. Cheltenham: Edward Elgar, 2017.

Greenfield, Adam. *Radical Technologies.* London and New York: Verso, 2017.

Grossi, Paolo. "Storia di Esperienze Giuridiche e Tradizione Romanistica." *Quaderni Fiorentini per la Storia del Pensiero Giuridico Moderno* 17 (1988): 533–50.

———. "La Proprietà e le Proprietà nell'Officina dello Storico." *Quaderni Fiorentini per la Storia del Pensiero Giuridico Moderno* 17 (1988): 359–422.

Guattari, Felix. *The Three Ecologies.* London: Continuum, 2008.

Gunderson, Ryan. "Commodification of Nature." In *The International Encyclopedia of Geography: People, the Earth, Environment and Technology,* edited by Douglas Richardson, 1–20. Chichester: John Wiley & Sons, 2016.

Gutwirth, Serge, and Eric Naim-Gesbert. "Science et droit de l'environnement: Réflexions pour le cadre conceptual du pluralisme de vérités." *Revue interdisciplinaire d'études juridiques* 34 (1995): 33–98.

Gutwirth, Serge, and Isabelle Stengers. "The Law and the Commons." Presentation at Third Global Thematic International Association for the Study of the Commons Conference on the Knowledge Commons, October 20–22, 2016.

Hacker, Phillip. "Corporate Governance for Complex Cryptocurrencies? A Framework for Stability and Decision Making in Blockchain-Based Monetary Systems." In *Regulating Blockchain: Techno-Social and Legal Challenges,* edited by Philipp Hacker, Ioannis Lianos, Georgios Dimitropoulos, and Stefan Eich, 140–66. Oxford: Oxford University Press, 2019.

Hamilton, Clive. *Defiant Earth: The Fate of Humans in the Anthropocene.* Cambridge: Polity Press, 2017.

———. *Growth Fetish.* Crow's Nest: Pluto Press, 2011.

———. "The Anthropocene as Rupture." *The Anthropocene Review* 3, no. 2 (2016): 93–106. DOI: 10.1177/2053019616634741.

Haraway, Donna J. "A Cyborg Manifesto: Science, Technology, and Socialist-Feminism in the Late Twentieth Century." In *Simians, Cyborgs and Women: The Reinvention of Nature,* 149–81. New York: Routledge, 1991.

———. "Staying with the Trouble: Anthropocene, Capitalocene, Chthulucene." In *Anthropocene or Capitalocene? Nature, History, and the Crisis of Capitalism,* edited by Jason W. Moore, 34–76. Oakland: PM Press, 2016.

———. "Tentacular Thinking: Anthropocene, Capitalocene, Chthulucene." *e-flux* 75 (2016). http://www.e-flux.com/journal/75/67125/tentacular-thinking-anthropocene-capitalocene-chthulucene/.

———. "Tentacular Thinking: Anthropocene, Capitalocene, Chthulucene." In *Staying with the Trouble: Making Kin in the Chthulucene,* 30–57. Durham: Duke University Press, 2016.

———. "When We Have Never Been Human, What Is to Be Done?" *Theory, Culture & Society* 23, nos. 7–8 (2006): 135–58. DOI: 10.1177/0263276406069228.

Hardin, Garrett. "The Tragedy of the Commons." *Science* 162 (December 13, 1968): 1243–48. DOI: 10.1126/science.162.3859.1243.

Hardt, Michael, and Antonio Negri. *Commonwealth.* Cambridge: Belknap Press of Harvard University Press, 2011.

———. *Multitude: War and Democracy in the Age of Empire.* New York: Penguin Books, 2005.

Hartzog, Paul B. "Panarchy: Governance in the Network Age." 2005. https://www.academia.edu/210378/Panarchy_Governance_in_the_Network_Age.

———. "Panarchy Is What We Make of It: Why a World State Is Not Inevitable." 2004. https://www.academia.edu/2409728/Panarchy_Is_What_We_Make_of_It_Why_a_World_State_Is_Not_Inevitable.

———. "The Future of Economics: From Complexity to Commons." 2017. OECD *Insights*. http://oecdinsights.org/2017/01/09/the-future-of-economics-from-complexity-to-commons.

———. "Winning by Playing: A Political Economy of Networks." 2004. https://www.academia.edu/2409729/Winning_By_Playing_A_Political_Economy_of_Networks.

Harvey, David. *A Short History of Neoliberalism*. Oxford: Oxford University Press, 2005.

———. *The New Imperialism*. Oxford; New York: Oxford University Press, 2003.

Hassan, Samer, and Primavera De Filippi, "The Expansion of Algorithmic Governance: From Code Is Law to Law Is Code." *Field Actions Science Reports* 17 (2017): 88–90. https://journals.openedition.org/factsreports/4518.

Havelock, Erik. *The Greek Concept of Justice: From Its Shadow in Homer to Its Substance in Plato*. Cambridge: Harvard University Press, 1978.

Hayek, Friedrich A. von. "Economics and Knowledge." *Economica* 4, no. 13 (1937): 33–54. DOI: 10.2307/2548786.

———. *Law, Legislation and Liberty, Volume 2: The Mirage of Social Justice*. Chicago: University of Chicago Press, 2012.

———. *The Road to Serfdom*. Abingdon: Routledge, 1997.

Hecker, Frank. "Setting Up Shop: The Business of Open-Source Software." *IEEE Software* (January–February 1998): 45–51.

Held, David. "Cosmopolitanism." In *Governing Globalization: Power, Authority, and Global Governance*, edited by David Held and Anthony G. McGrew, 305–24. Cambridge: Polity Press, 2002.

Helfand, Ira. "Nuclear Famine: Two Billion People at Risk: Global Impacts of Limited Nuclear War on Agriculture, Food Supplies, and Human Nutrition." *Physicians for Social Responsibility,* December 10, 2013. https://www.psr.org/blog/resource/nuclear-famine-two-billion-people-at-risk/.

Heidegger, Martin. "Letter on 'Humanism.'" In *Pathmarks,* edited by W. McNeill, 239–76. Cambridge: Cambridge University Press, 1998.

Helfrich, Silke, and Jorg Haas. *The Commons: A New Narrative for Our Times.* Heinrich Böll Stiftung, 2008. http://commonstrust.global-negotiations.org/resources/Helfrich%20and%20Haas%20The_Commons_A_New_Narrative_for_Our_Times.pdf.

Hesiod. *Works and Days.* London: Penguin Classics, 2018.

Hicks, David. "Teaching about Global Issues, the Need for Holistic Learning." In *Lessons for the Future, the Missing Dimension in Education,* edited by David Hicks, 98–108. London: Routledge Falmer, 2002.

Hippel, Eric von, and Georg von Krogh. "Open Source Software and the 'Private-Collective' Innovation Model: Issues for Organization Science." *Organization Science* 14, no. 2 (2003): 209–23. DOI: 10.1287/orsc.14.1.209.14992.

Hobbes, Thomas. *Leviathan.* London: Penguin, 1985.

Holland, John H. *Hidden Order: How Adaptation Builds Complexity.* Reading: Addison-Wesley, 1995.

Homer-Dixon, Thomas. *The Upside of Down: Catastrophe, Creativity, and the Renewal of Civilization.* Washington, DC: Island Press, 2010.

Hopkins, Rob. *The Transition Handbook: From Oil Dependency to Local Resilience.* Cambridge: UIT Cambridge Ltd., 2014.

Horkheimer, Max. *Dawn and Decline: Notes 1926–1931 and 1950–1969.* New York: Seabury, 1978.

———. *Eclipse of Reason.* New York: Columbia University Press, 1947.

Horkheimer, Max, and Theodor W. Adorno. *Dialectic of Enlightenment.* Stanford: Stanford University Press, 2007.

Hornborg, Alf. "The Political Ecology of the Technocene: Uncovering Ecologically Unequal Exchange in the World-System." In *The Anthropocene and the Global Environmental Crisis: Rethinking Modernity in a New Epoch,* edited by Clive Hamilton, Christophe Bonneuil, and François Gemenne, 1–13. Abingdon: Routledge, 2015.

———. *The Power of the Machine. Global Inequalities of Economy, Technology, and Environment.* Walnut Creek: Altamira Press, 2001.

———. "Zero-Sum World: Challenges in Conceptualizing Environmental Load Displacement and Ecologically Unequal Exchange in the World-System." *International Journal of Comparative Sociology* 50, nos. 3–4 (2009): 237–62. DOI: 10.1177/0020715209105141.

Horsman, Mathew, and Andrew Marshall. *After the Nation State: Citizens, Tribalism, and the New World Disorder.* London: HarperCollins, 1994.

Howard, Philip H. *Concentration and Power in the Food System: Who Controls What We Eat?* New York: Bloomsbury, 2016.

———. "Intellectual Property and Consolidation in the Seed Industry." *Crop Science* 55, no. 6 (2015): 2489–95. DOI: 10.2135/cropsci2014.09.1669.

———. "Visualizing Consolidation in the Global Seed Industry: 1996–2008." *Sustainability* 1, no. 4 (December 8, 2009): 1266–87. DOI: 10.3390/su1041266.

Huggan, Graham, and Helen Tiffin. "Green Postcolonialism." *Interventions: International Journal of Postcolonial Studies* 9, no. 1 (2007): 1–11. DOI: 10.1080/13698010601173783.

Huntington, Samuel. *Clash of Civilizations and the Making of World Order.* New York: Simon and Schuster, 1997.

Huron, Amanda. *Carving Out the Commons: Tenant Organizing and Housing Cooperatives in Washington, D.C.* Minneapolis: University of Minnesota Press, 2018.

Iaione, Christian. "The CO-City: Sharing, Collaborating, Cooperating, and Commoning in the City." *American*

Journal of Economics and Sociology 75, no. 2 (2016): 415–55. DOI: 10.1111/ajes.12145.

Ibn Khaldun, *The Muqaddimah: An Introduction to History.* Translated by Franz Rosenthal and N.J. Dawood. Princeton: Princeton University Press, 1967.

Illich, Ivan. *Deschooling Society.* 1971; rpt. London: Marion Boyars Publishers, 2000.

———. *Medical Nemesis: The Expropriation of Health.* New York: Pantheon, 1976.

———. *Shadow Work.* Boston and London: M. Boyars, 1981.

———. *Tools for Conviviality.* 1971; London: Marion Boyars Publishers, 2001.

Inayatullah, Sohail. "Six Pillars: Futures Thinking for Transforming." *Foresight* 10, no. 1 (2008): 4–21. DOI: 10.1108/14636680810855991.

IPCC. *Special Report: Global Warming of 1.5 ºC. Summary for Policymakers.* 2018. https://www.ipcc.ch/sr15/chapter/spm/.

Jameson, Fredric. "Notes on Globalization as a Philosophical Issue." In *The Cultures of Globalization,* edited by Fredric Jameson and Masao Miyoshi, 54–77. London: Duke University Press, 1998.

J.E.M. Ag Supply v. Pioneer Hi-Bred International, Inc., 122 S. Ct. 593 (2001), rehearing denied, 122 S. Ct. 1600 (2002).

Jo, Arrah-Marie. "The Effect of Competition Intensity on Software Security: An Empirical Analysis of Security Patch Release on the Web Browser Market." *The Economics of Digitalization: Proceedings of the 16th Annual Workshop on the Economics of Information Security.* 2017.

Kaldor, Mary. *Global Civil Society: An Answer to War.* Cambridge: Polity Press, 2003.

———. *New and Old Wars.* 3rd edition. Cambridge: Cambridge University Press, 2012.

Kaplan, Robert D. *Coming Anarchy: Shattering the Dreams of the Post Cold War.* New York: Random House, 2000.

Karatani, Kojin. *The Structure of World History: From Modes of Production to Modes of Exchange.* Translated by Michael K. Bourdaghs. Durham: Duke University Press, 2014.

Karitzis, Andreas. *The European Left in Times of Crises: Lessons from Greece.* Amsterdam, Quito, and Buenos Aires: Transnational Institute (TNI), Instituto de Altos Estudios Nacionales (IAEN), Consejo Latinoamericano de Ciencias Sociales (CLACSO), 2017.

———. "Unleash the Kraken!" In *Supramarkt,* edited by Cecilia Wee and Olaf Arnt, 425–39. Nössemark: Irene Publishing, 2015.

Karkkainen, Bradley. "Post-Sovereign Environmental Governance," *Global Environmental Politics* 4, no. 1 (2004): 72–96. DOI: 10.1162/152638004773730220.

Kauffman, Stuart A. *At Home in the Universe: The Search for Laws of Self-Organization and Complexity.* New York: Oxford University Press, 1995.

———. *The Origins of Order: Self Organization and Selection in Evolution.* New York: Oxford University Press, 1993.

Kaul, Inge, Isabelle Grunberg, and Marc A. Stern, eds. *Global Public Goods: International Cooperation in the 21st Century.* Oxford: Oxford University Press, 1999.

Kaul, Inge, Pedro Conceiçao, Katell Le Goulven, and Ronald U. Mendoza, eds., *Providing Global Public Goods: Managing Globalization.* Oxford: Oxford University Press, 2003.

Karlstrøm, Henrik. "Do Libertarians Dream of Electric Coins? The Material Embeddedness of Bitcoin." *Distinktion: Scandinavian Journal of Social Theory* 15, no. 1 (2014): 23–36. DOI: 10.1080/1600910X.2013.870083.

Keane, John. "Cosmocracy and Global Civil Society." In *Global Civil Society: Contested Futures,* edited by Gideon Baker and David Chandler, 149–70. New York: Routledge, 2005.

Khoo, Su-ming, Lisa K. Taylor, and Vanessa Andreotti. "Ethical Internationalization, Neo-Liberal Restructuring and 'Beating the Bounds' of Higher Education." In *Assembling and Governing the Higher Education Institution,* edited by Lynette Shultz and Melody Viczko, 85–110. London: Palgrave Macmillan, 2016.

KIASualberta. "Donna Haraway - SF: String Figures, Multispecies Muddles, Staying with the Trouble."

YouTube, June 27, 2014. https://www.youtube.com/watch?v=Z1uTVnhIHS8.

Kloppenburg, Jack. "Re-Purposing the Master's Tools: The Open Source Seed Initiative and the Struggle for Seed Sovereignty." *The Journal of Peasant Studies* 41, no. 6 (November 2, 2014): 1225–46. DOI: 10.1080/03066150.2013.875897.

Koch, Max. *Capitalism and Climate Change: Theoretical Discussion, Historical Development and Policy Responses.* Basingstoke: Palgrave Macmillan, 2012.

Kontopoulos, Kyriakos M. *The Logics of Social Structure.* Cambridge: Cambridge University Press, 1992.

Kostakis, Vasilis, et al. "Design Global, Manufacture Local: Exploring the Contours of an Emerging Productive Model." *Futures* 73 (2015): 126–35. DOI: https://dx.doi.org/10.1016/j.futures.2015.09.001.

Kostakis, Vasilis, and Michel Bauwens. *Network Society and Future Scenarios for a Collaborative Economy.* Basingstoke: Palgrave Macmillan, 2014.

Krasner, Stephen. *Sovereignty: Organized Hypocrisy: Change and Persistence in International Relations.* Princeton: Princeton University Press, 1999.

Krisch, Nico. "*Pouvoir Constituant* and *Pouvoir Irritant* in the Postnational Order." *International Journal of Constitutional Law* 14, no. 3 (2016): 657–79. DOI: 10.1093/icon/mow039.

Laat, Paul B. de. "Governance of Open Source Software: State of the Art." *Journal of Management & Governance* 11, no. 2 (2007): 165–77. DOI: 10.1007/s10997-007-9022-9.

Laclau, Ernesto, and Chantal Mouffe. *Hegemony and Socialist Strategy: Towards a Radical Democratic Politics.* New York: Verso, 1985.

Lakhani, Karim R., and Robert G. Wolf. "Why Hackers Do What They Do: Understanding Motivation and Effort in Free/Open Source Software Projects." In *Perspectives on Free and Open Source Software,* edited by J. Feller, B. Fitzgerald, S. Hissam, and Karim R. Lakhani, 3–22. Cambridge: MIT Press, 2005.

Larrain, Jorge. *Theories of Development: Capitalism, Colonialism and Dependency*. Malden: Polity Press, 2013.

Lasch, Christopher. *The Revolt of the Elites and the Betrayal of Democracy*. London and New York: Norton Paperback, 1995.

Latham, Alan, and Derek P. McCormick. "Moving Cities: Rethinking the Materialities of Urban Geographies." *Progress in Human Geography* 28, no. 6 (2004): 701–24. DOI: 10.1191/0309132504ph515oa.

La Torre, Massimo. *Law as Institution*. London and New York: Springer, 2010.

Latour, Bruno. "An Attempt at a 'Compositionist Manifesto.'" *New Literary History* 41 (2010): 471–90. DOI: 10.1353/nlh.2010.0022.

———. *An Inquiry into Modes of Existence: An Anthropology of the Moderns*. Cambridge: Harvard University Press, 2013.

———. "Facing Gaia: Six Lectures on the Political Theology of Nature." Gifford Lectures on Natural Religion, 2013. http://www.bruno-latour.fr/sites/default/files/downloads/GIFFORD-BROCHURE-1.pdf.

———. "Fifty Shades of Green." *Environmental Humanities* 7, no. 1 (2015): 219–25. DOI: 10.1215/22011919-3616416.

———. *Politics of Nature: How to Bring the Sciences into Democracy*. Translated by Catherine Porter. Cambridge: Harvard University Press, 2009.

———. *Science in Action: How to Follow Scientists and Engineers through Society*. Cambridge: Harvard University Press 1987.

———. *We Have Never Been Modern*. Translated by Catherine Porter. Cambridge: Harvard University Press, 1993.

La Vía Campesina. "Declaration at the II International Symposium on Agroecology, April, 2018 – Via Campesina English," April 8, 2018. https://viacampesina.org/en/declaration-at-the-ii-international-symposium-on-agroecology/.

Le Roy, Étienne. "How I Have Been Conducting Research on the Commons for Thirty Years Without Knowing It." In *Patterns of Commoning*, edited by David Bollier and Silke Helfrich, 277–96. Amherst: Off the Common Books, 2014. http://patternsofcommoning.org/how-i-have-been-conducting-research-on-the-commons-for-thirty-years-without-knowing-it

Lessig, Lawrence. *Free Culture: How Big Media Uses Technology and the Law to Lock Down Culture and Control Creativity*. New York: Penguin Press, 2004.

Li, Chenxing, Peilun Li, Dong Zhou, Wei Xu, Fan Long, Andrew Yao, "Scaling Nakamoto Consensus to Thousands of Transactions per Second." arXiv preprint arXiv:1805.03870 (2018).

Lifton, Robert J., and Richard Falk. *Indefensible Weapons: The Political and Psychological Case against Nuclearism*. Revised 3rd edition. New York: Basic Books, 1991.

Linebaugh, Peter. *Stop, Thief! The Commons, Enclosures and Resistance*. Oakland: PM Press, 2014.

———. *The Magna Carta Manifesto: Liberties and Commons for All*. Berkeley: University of California Press, 2008.

Linera, Alvaro Garcia. *Plebeian Power*. Chicago: Haymarket Books, 2014.

Ljungberg, Jan. "Open Source Movements as a Model for Organising." *European Journal of Information Systems* 9, no. 4 (2000): 208–16. DOI: 10.1057/palgrave.ejis.3000373.

Lobrano, Giovanni. *Res Publica Res Populi. La Legge e la Limitazione del Potere*. Turin: Giappichelli, 1997.

Locke, John. *Two Treatises of Government*. Cambridge: Cambridge University Press, 1988.

Lofthouse, Joseph. "Adaptivar Landraces," 2017. http://garden.lofthouse.com/seed-list.phtml.

———. "For Sale: Genetically-Diverse Promiscuously-Pollinated Landrace Seeds Grown by Joseph Lofthouse in Cache Valley in the Rocky Mountains," 2017. http://garden.lofthouse.com/seed-list.phtml.

————. "Landrace Gardening: Do It for the Taste." *Mother Earth News,* April 27, 2016.

Louafi, Selim, Ida Westphal, Maywa Montenegro, Daniele Manzella, Gloria Otieno, Sophie Steigerwald, and Jack Kloppenburg. "Open Source for Seeds and Genetic Sequence Data: Practical Experience and Future Strategies." CIRAD Policy Brief: Agricultural Research for Development, December 2018.

Lowenhaupt Tsing, Anna. *Mushroom at the End of the World: On the Possibility of Life in Capitalist Ruins.* Princeton: Princeton University Press, 2015.

Luby, Claire, and Irwin Goldman. "Improving Freedom to Operate in Carrot Breeding through the Development of Eight Open Source Composite Populations of Carrot (*Daucus carota* L. Var. *sativus*)." *Sustainability* 8, no. 5 (May 14, 2016): 479. DOI: 10.3390/su8050479.

————. "Release of Eight Open Source Carrot (*Daucus Carota* Var. *Sativa*) Composite Populations Developed under Organic Conditions." *Horticultural Science* 51, no. 4 (2016): 448–50.

Luby, Claire H., Jack Kloppenburg, Thomas E. Michaels, and Irwin L. Goldman. "Enhancing Freedom to Operate for Plant Breeders and Farmers through Open Source Plant Breeding." *Crop Science* 55, no. 6 (2015): 2481–88. DOI: 10.2135/cropsci2014.10.0708.

Luhmann, Niklas. *Social Systems, Writing Science.* Stanford: Stanford University Press, 1995.

Luke, Timothy. "Eco-Managerialism: Environmental Studies as a Power/Knowledge Formation." In *Living with Nature: Environmental Politics as Cultural Discourse,* edited by Frank Fischer and Maarten A. Hajer, 103–20. Oxford: Oxford University Press, 1999.

————. "On Environmentality: Geo-Power and Eco-Knowledge in the Discourses of Contemporary Environmentalism." *Cultural Critique (The Politics of Systems and Environments, Part II)* 31 (1995): 57–81.

Lyotard, Jean-François. *The Postmodern Condition: A Report on Knowledge*. Translated by Geoff Bennington. Minneapolis: University of Minnesota Press, 1984.

Machiavelli, Niccolo. *Discourses on Livy*. Chicago: University of Chicago Press, 1998.

———. *The Prince*. Edited by M. Viroli. Oxford: Oxford University Press, 2008.

Madison, Michael J., Brett M. Frischmann, and Katherine J. Strandburg. "Constructing Commons in the Cultural Environment." *Cornell Law Review* 95 (2009): 657–710.

Mair, Peter. *Ruling the Void*. London and New York: Verso, 2013.

Malm, Andreas. *Fossil Capital: The Rise of Steam Power and the Roots of Global Warming*. London: Verso, 2016.

Malm, Andreas, and Alf Hornborg. "The Geology of Mankind? A Critique of the Anthropocene Narrative." *The Anthropocene Review* 1, no. 1 (2014): 62–69. DOI: 10.1177/2053019613516291.

Mandelbaum, Michael. *The Case for Goliath: How America Acts as a World's Government in the Twenty-First Century*. New York: Public Affairs, 2005.

Marella, Maria Rosaria, ed. *Oltre il Pubblico e il Privato. Per un Diritto dei Beni Comuni*. Bologna: Ombre Corte, 2012.

Margulis, Lynn, and Dorion Sagan. *Microcosmos: Four Billion Years of Microbial Evolution*. Berkeley: University of California Press, 1997.

Martin, Chris J. "The Sharing Economy: A Pathway to Sustainability or a Nightmarish Form of Neoliberal Capitalism?" *Ecological Economics* 121 (2016): 149–59. DOI: 10.1016/j.ecolecon.2015.11.027.

Marx, Karl. *A Contribution to the Critique of Political Economy*. Translated by N.I. Stone. Chicago: Kerr, 1904.

———. *Capital Volume 1*. Moscow: Progress Publishers, 1887.

———. *The Eighteenth Brumaire of Louis Bonaparte*. Moscow: Progress Publishers 1972.

Marx, Karl, and Friedrich Engels. *Collected Works*, Volume 3. London: Lawrence & Wishart, 2010.

Mason, Colin M., and Richard T. Harrison. "Barriers to Investment in the Informal Venture Capital Sector." *Entrepreneurship & Regional Development* 14, no. 3 (2002): 271–87. DOI: 10.1080/08985620210142011.

Mason, Paul. *Postcapitalism*. London: Penguin, 2016.

Masri, Mazen. *The Dynamics of Exclusionary Constitutionalism: Israel as a Jewish and Democratic State.* Oxford: Hart, 2017.

Massumi, Brian. *Parables for the Virtual: Movement, Affect, Sensation*. London and Durham: Duke University Press, 2002.

Mathews, Freya. *For Love of Matter: A Contemporary Panpsychism*. Albany: State University of New York, 2003.

Mattei, Ugo. *Beni Comuni. Un Manifesto*. Bari: Laterza, 2011.

———. "Future Generations Now! A Commons-based Analysis." In *Protecting Future Generations through Commons*, edited by Saki Bailey, Gilda Farrell and Ugo Mattei, 9–26. Trends in Social Cohesion 26. Council of Europe, 2014.

McCarthy, James. "Commons as Counterhegemonic Projects." *Capitalism Nature Socialism* 16, no. 1 (2005): 9–24. DOI: 10.1080/1045575052000335348.

McGuire, S., and Louise Sperling. "Seed Systems Smallholder Farmers Use. Food Security." *Food Security* 8, no. 1 (2016): 179–95. DOI: 10.1007/s12571-015-0528-8.

Meadows, Donella H., et al. *The Limits to Growth*. New York: Pan Books, 1972.

Mehar, Muhammad, Charlie Shier, Alana Giambattista, Elgar Gong, Gabrielle Fletcher, Ryan Sanayhie, Henry Kim and Marek Laskowski. "Understanding a Revolutionary and Flawed Grand Experiment in Blockchain: The DAO Attack." *Journal of Cases on Information Technology* 21, no. 1 (2017): 19–32. DOI: 10.2139/ssrn.3014782.

Mehra, Salil K. "Paradise Is a Walled Garden? Trust, Antitrust and User Dynamism." *George Mason Law Review* 18 (2011): 889–952.

Merchant, Carolyn. *The Death of Nature: Women, Ecology, and the Scientific Revolution*. San Francisco: Harper & Row, 1980.

Mill, John Stuart. *Considerations on Representative Government*. 1861; rpt. Lahore: Serenity Publishers, 2008.

Millennium Ecosystem Assessment. *Ecosystems and Human Well-being: Synthesis*. Washington, DC: Island Press, 2005.

Mitman, Greg. *The State of Nature: Ecology, Community, and American Social Thought, 1900–1950*. Chicago: University of Chicago Press, 1992.

Mockus, Audris, Roy T. Fielding, and James D. Herbsleb. "Two Case Studies of Open Source Software Development: Apache and Mozilla." ACM *Transactions on Software Engineering and Methodology (TOSEM)* 11, no. 3 (2003): 309–46. DOI: 10.1145/567793.567795.

Moor, Tine de. *Homo cooperans. Instituties voor collectieve actie en de solidaire samenleving*. Utrecht: Universiteit Utrecht, Faculteit Geesteswetenschappen, 2013.

Moore, Jason W., ed. *Anthropocene or Capitalocene? Nature, History, and the Crisis of Capitalism and the Crisis of Capitalism*. Oakland: PM Press, 2016.

———. "The Capitalocene, Part I: On the Nature and Origins of Our Ecological Crisis." *The Journal of Peasant Studies* 44, no. 3 (2017): 594–630. DOI: 10.1080/03066150.2016.1235036.

Montenegro de Wit, Maywa. "Beating the Bounds: How Does 'Open Source' Become a Commons for Seed?" *The Journal of Peasant Studies* 46, no. 1 (2019): 44–79. DOI: 10.1080/03066150.2017.1383395.

———. "Stealing into the Wild: Conservation Science, Plant Breeding and the Makings of New Seed Enclosures." *Journal of Peasant Studies* 44, no. 1 (2017): 169–212. DOI: 10.1080/03066150.2016.1168405.

Morton, Frank. "Open Source Seed: A Farmer-Breeder's Perspective." In *Organic Seed Growers Conference Proceedings,* edited by Kristina Hubbard, 147–49. Corvallis: Organic Seed Alliance, 2014.

Mouffe, Chantal. *The Democratic Paradox.* London and New York: Verso, 2000.

Mousis, O., et al. "Instrumental Methods for Professional and Amateur Collaborations in Planetary Astronomy." *Experimental Astronomy* 38, nos. 1–2 (2014): 91–191. DOI: 10.1007/s10686-014-9379-0.

Mueller, Tadzio. "Diversity Is Strength, the German Energiewende as a Resilient Alternative." *Source Network,* 2017. http://thesourcenetwork.eu/wp-content/themes/showcase-pro/images/Diversity%20is%20Strength%20-%20FINAL.pdf.

Mulgan, Geoff. *Big Mind.* Princeton: Princeton University Press, 2018.

Naim, Moises. *The End of Power.* New York: Basic Books, 2013.

Nakamoto, Satoshi. *Bitcoin: A Peer-to-Peer Electronic Cash System* (2008). http://www.bitcoin.org/bitcoin.pdf.

Negri, Antonio. "Il Comune come Modo di Produzione." *EuroNomade,* June 10, 2016. http://www.euronomade.info/?p=7331.

Nightingale, Andrea J. "Commons and Alternative Rationalities: Subjectivity, Emotion and the (Non)rational Commons." In *Patterns of Commoning,* edited by David Bollier and Silke Helfrich, 297–308. Amherst: Off the Common Books, 2014. http://patternsofcommoning.org/uncategorized/commons-and-alternative-rationalities-subjectivity-emotion-and-the-nonrational-commons.

Norgaard, Richard. *Development Betrayed: The End of Progress and a Co-evolutionary Revisioning of the Future.* Abingdon: Routledge, 1994.

Nowak, Martin A. *Super Cooperators: Altruism, Evolution and Why We Need Each Other to Succeed.* New York: Free Press, 2011.

Noy, Fleur, and Dirk Holemans. "Burgercollectieven in kaart gebracht." *Oikos* 78, no. 3 (2016) 69–81.

Olson, Mancur. *The Logic of Collective Action, Public Goods, and the Theory of Groups.* Cambridge: Harvard University Press, 1971.

Olsson, Per, Michele-Lee Moore, Frances R. Westley, and Daniel D.P. McCarthy. "The Concept of the Anthropocene as a Game-Changer: A New Context for Social Innovation and Transformations to Sustainability." *Ecology & Society* 22, no. 2 (2017): art. 31. https://www.ecologyandsociety.org/vol22/iss2/art31/.

Ong, Walter. *Orality and Literacy.* 2nd edition. London: Routledge, 2002.

Orsi, Janelle. "Legal Structures for Social Transformation." *Sustainable Economies Law Center,* January 18, 2019. https://www.theselc.org/transformativestructures

———. *Practicing Law in the Sharing Economy: Helping Build Cooperatives, Social Enterprise, and Local Sustainable Economies.* Chicago: ABA Publishing, 2012.

Ost, François. *La nature hors la loi. L'écologie à l'épreuve du droit.* Paris: La Découverte, 2003.

Ostrom, Elinor. *Governing the Commons: The Evolution of Institutions for Collective Action.* Cambridge: Cambridge University Press, 1990.

———. "Green from The Grassroots." *Project Syndicate,* June 12, 2012. https://www.project-syndicate.org/commentary/green-from-the-grassroots.

Ostrom, Elinor, Joanna Burger, Christopher B. Field, Richard B. Norgaard, and David Policansky. "Revisiting the Commons: Local Lessons, Global Challenges." *Science* 283, no. 5412 (1999): 278–82. DOI: 10.1126/science.284.5412.278.

Page, Scott. *Diversity and Complexity.* Princeton: Princeton University Press, 2010.

———. *The Difference: How the Power of Diversity Creates Better Groups, Firms, Schools, and Societies.* Princeton: Princeton University Press, 2008.

———. *The Diversity Bonus: How Great Teams Pay Off in the Knowledge Economy.* Princeton: Princeton University Press, 2017.

Pasquale, Frank. "Two Narratives of Platform Capitalism." *Yale Law and Policy Review* 35 (2016): 309–19. https://digitalcommons.law.yale.edu/ylpr.

Pazaitis, Alex, Primavera De Filippi, and Vasilis Kostakis. "Blockchain and Value Systems in the Sharing Economy: The Illustrative Case of Backfeed." *Technological Forecasting and Social Change* 125 (2017): 105–15. DOI: 10.1016/j.techfore.2017.05.025.

Pearce, Fred. *Common Ground: Securing Land Rights and Safeguarding the Earth.* Land Rights Now, International Land Coalition, Oxfam, Rights + Resources, 2016. http://www.landcoalition.org/sites/default/files/documents/resources/bp-common-ground-land-rights-020316-en.pdf

Peet, Richard, and Elaine Hartwick. *Theories of Development: Contentions, Arguments, Alternatives.* London: Guilford Publications, 2015.

Perelman, Michael. *The Invention of Capitalism: Classical Political Economy and the Secret History of Primitive Accumulation.* Durham: Duke University Press, 2000.

Philippopoulos-Mihalopoulos, Andreas. "The Triveneto Transhumance: Law, Land, Movement." *Politica and Societa* 3 (2012): 447–68. DOI: 10.4476/38032.

———. "Actors or Spectators? Vulnerability and Critical Environmental Law." In *Thought, Law, Rights and Action in the Age of Environmental Crisis,* edited by Anna Grear and Evadne Grant, 46–75. Cheltenham: Edward Elgar, 2015.

Pieraccini, Margherita. "Beyond Legal Facts and Discourses: towards a Social-ecological Production of the Legal." In *Contributions to Law, Philosophy, Ecology. Exploring Re-embodiments,* edited by Ruth Thomas-Pellicer, Vito De Lucia, and Sian Sullivan, 227–43. Abingdon: Routledge, 2016.

———. "Property Pluralism and the Partial Reflexivity of Conservation Law: The Case of Upland Commons in England and Wales." *Journal of Human Rights and the Environment* 3, no. 2 (2012): 273–87. DOI: 10.4337/jhre.2012.03.05.

Pignarre, Philippe, and Isabelle Stengers. *La sorcellerie capitaliste: Pratiques de désenvoûtement.* Paris: La Découverte, 2005.

Piques, Celine, and Xavier Rizos. "Peer to Peer and the Commons: A Path towards Transition: A Matter, Energy and Thermodynamic Perspective." P2P Foundation Report, 2017. http://commonstransition.org/wp-content/uploads/2017/10/Report-P2P-Thermodynamics-VOL_1-web_2.0.pdf.

Plant, Raymond. "Hayek on Social Justice: A Critique." In *Hayek, Co-ordination and Evolution: His Legacy in Philosophy, Politics, Economics and the History of Ideas,* edited by Jack Birner and Rudy van Zijp, 164–77. Abingdon: Routledge, 1994.

Plumwood, Val. *Feminism and the Mastery of Nature.* Abingdon: Routledge, 1993.

Podoll, David. "Prairie Road Organic Seed." *Open Source Seed Initiative: Plant Breeders,* November 5, 2014. http://osseeds.org/people/.

Polak, Fred L. *The Image of the Future: Enlightening the Past, Orientating the Present, Forecasting the Future.* New York: Sythoff, 1961.

Polanyi, Karl. *The Great Transformation.* Boston: Beacon Press, 1944.

Potts, Annie. "Deleuze on Viagra (or, What Can a Viagra-body Do?)." *Body and Society* 10 (2004): 17–36. DOI: 10.1177/1357034X0401759.

Prigogine, Ilya, and Isabelle Stengers. *Order out of Chaos: Man's New Dialogue with Nature.* Toronto: Bantam Books, 1984.

Raftery, Adrian E., Alec Zimmer, Dargan M.W. Frierson, Richard Startz, and Peiran Liu. "Less than 2 C warming by 2100 unlikely." *Nature Climate Change* 7, no. 9 (2017): 637–41. DOI: 10.1038/nclimate3352.

Ramos, Jose. "Liquid Democracy and the Futures of Governance." In *The Future Internet, Public Adminstration and The Futures of Governance,* edited by Jenifer Winter and Ryota Ono, 173–91. Dordrecht: Springer, 2016.

———. "Cosmo-localization and Leadership for the Future." *Journal of Futures Studies* 21, no. 4 (2017): 65–84. DOI: 10.6531/JFS.2017.21(4).A65.

Ramos, Jose, Michel Bauwens, and Vasilis Kostakis. "P2P and Planetary Futures." In *Critical Posthumanism and Planetary Futures,* edited by Debashish Banerji and Makarand R. Paranjape. New Delhi: Springer India, 2016.

Raymond, Eric S. "The Cathedral and the Bazaar." *Philosophy & Technology* 12, no. 3 (1999): 23–32. DOI: 10.1007.s12130–999–1026–0.

————. *The New Hacker's Dictionary.* 3rd edition. Cambridge: MIT Press, 1996.

Read, Jason. "A Genealogy of Homo-Economicus: Neoliberalism and the Production of Subjectivity." *Foucault Studies* (2009): 25–36. DOI: 10.22439/fs.v0i0.2465.

Read, Rupert, and Molly Scott-Cato. "A Price for Everything? The Natural Capital Controversy." *Journal of Human Rights and the Environment* 5, no. 2 (2014): 153–67. DOI: 10.4337/jhre.2014.03.03.

Reijers, Wessel, Iris Wuisman, Morshed Mannan, Primavera De Filippi, Christopher Wray, Vienna Rae-Looi, Angela Cubillos Vélez, and Liav Orgad, "Now the Code Runs Itself: On-Chain and Off-Chain Governance of Blockchain Technologies." *Topoi* (2018): 1–11. DOI: 10.2139/ssrn.3340056.

Rheingold, Howard. *Smart Mobs: The Next Social Revolution.* Cambridge: Perseus Publishing, 2002.

Robbins, Paul. *Political Ecology: A Critical Introduction.* 2nd edition. Malden: J. Wiley & Sons, 2012.

Roberts, Alasdair. *The Logic of Discipline.* Oxford: Oxford University Press, 2010.

Robinson, William I. *A Theory of Global Capitalism.* Baltimore: John Hopkins University Press, 2004.

————. "What Is Critical Globalization Studies? Intellectual Labor and Global Society." In *Critical Globalisation Studies,* edited by Richard P. Applebaum and William I. Robinson, 2–18. New York: Routledge, 2005.

Rockström, Johan, et al. "Planetary Boundaries: Exploring the Safe Operating Space for Humanity." *Ecology and Society*

14, no. 2 (2009): 32–65. http://www.ecologyandsociety.org/vol14/iss2/art32/.

Rodney, Walter. *How Europe Underdeveloped Africa.* London: Bogle-L'Ouverture Publications, 1972.

Romano, Santi. *L'Ordinamento Giuridico.* 2nd edition. Florence: Sansoni, 1946.

Root, Al. "DowDuPont Is Splitting into 3 Companies. Here's Everything You Need to Know." *Barron's,* April 29, 2019. https://www.barrons.com/articles/dowdupont-spinoff-dow-dupont-corteva-51556552428.

Rosenau, James N. *Distant Proximities: Dynamics beyond Globalization.* Princeton: Princeton University Press, 2003.

Ross, Alec. *The Industries of the Future.* New York: Simon & Schuster, 2016.

Rowell, Lonnie L., and Eunsook Hong. "Knowledge Democracy and Action Research: Pathways for the Twenty-First Century." In *The Palgrave International Handbook of Action Research,* 63–68, edited by Lonnie L. Rowell, Catherine D. Bruce, Joseph M. Shosh, and Margaret M. Riel. New York: Palgrave Macmillan, 2017.

Rutherford, Paul. "The Entry of Life in History." In *Discourse of the Environment,* edited by Eric Darier, 37–62. London: Blackwell, 1999.

Samieifar, Shadi, and Dirk G. Baur. "Read Me If You Can! An Analysis of ICO White Papers." *Finance Research Letters* (2020): 101427. DOI: 10.1016/j.frl.2020.101427.

Sacks, Danielle. "The Sharing Economy." *Fast Company* 155 (May 2011): 88–93. https://www.fastcompany.com/1747551/sharing-economy.

Salleh, Ariel. "Neoliberalism, Scientism and Earth System Governance." In *The International Handbook of Political Ecology,* edited by Raymond L. Bryant, 432–46. Cheltenham: Edward Elgar, 2015.

Salmond, Anne. "The Fountain of Fish: Ontological Collisions at Sea." In *Patterns of Commoning,* edited by David Bollier and Silke Helfrich, 309–29. Amherst: Off the Common

Books, 2014. http://patternsofcommoning.org/the-fountain-of-fish-ontological-collisions-at-sea.

Sánchez-Bayoa, Francìsco, and Kris Wyckhuys. "Worldwide Decline of the Entomofauna: A Review of its Drivers." *Biological Conservation* 232 (2019): 8–27. DOI: 10.1016/j. biocon.2019.01.020.

Saxonhouse, Arlene. *Fear of Diversity: The Birth of Political Science in Ancient Greek Thought.* Chicago: University of Chicago Press, 1992.

Schillmoller, Anne Louise, and Alessandro Pelizzon. "Mapping the Terrain of Earth Jurisprudence: Landscape, Thresholds and Horizons." *Environmental and Earth Law Journal* 3, no. 1 (2013): 1–32. https://lawpublications.barry.edu/ejejj/vol3/iss1/1.

Schmitt, Carl. *The Concept of the Political.* Chicago: University of Chicago Press, 2007.

———. *The Nomos of the Earth in the International Law of the Jus Publicum Europaeum.* New York: Telos Press, 2006.

Scholz, Trebor. *Platform Cooperativism: Challenging the Corporate Sharing Economy.* New York: Rosa Luxemburg Stiftung, 2016.

Scholz, Trebor, and Nathan Schneider. *Ours to Hack and to Own: The Rise of Platform Cooperativism, A New Vision for the Future of Work and a Fairer Internet.* New York and London: OR Books, 2017.

Schor, Juliet B. "Does the Sharing Economy Increase Inequality within the Eighty Percent? Findings from a Qualitative Study of Platform Providers." *Cambridge Journal Of Regions, Economy and Society* 10 (2017): 263–79. DOI: 10.1093/cjres/rsw047.

Schultz, Thomas. *Transnational Legality: Stateless Law and International Arbitration.* Oxford: Oxford University Press, 2014.

Scott, James C. *Seeing Like a State: How Certain Schemes to Improve the Human Condition Have Failed.* New Haven: Yale University Press, 1998.

Securities and Exchange Commission v. Telegram Group Inc. et al, 19-cv-09439-PKC (S.D.N.Y. Oct 11, 2019).

Seegert, Alfred. *Ontology Recapitulates Ecology: The Relational Real in Evolution and Ecophilosophy.* Master's Thesis, University of Utah, 1998.

Semal, Luc. "Anthropocene, Catastrophism and Green Political Theory." In *The Anthropocene and the Global Environmental Crisis: Rethinking Modernity in a New Epoch,* edited by Clive Hamilton, Christophe Bonneuil, and François Gemenne, 87–99. Abingdon: Routledge, 2015.

Shareable. *Sharing Cities: Activating Urban Commons.* San Francisco: Tides Center/Shareable, 2018. https://www.shareable.net/sharing-cities.

Shellenberger, Michael, and Ted Nordhaus. "An Ecomodernist Manifesto: From the Death of Environmentalism to the Birth of Ecomodernism." *The Breakthrough Institute,* April 15, 2015. https://thebreakthrough.org/articles/an-ecomodernist-manifesto.

Shrader-Frechette, Kristen. "Methodological Rules for Four Classes of Scientific Uncertainty." In *Scientific Uncertainty and Environmental Problem Solving,* edited by John Lemons, 12–39. Oxford: Blackwell, 1996.

———. *Risk and Rationality. Philosophical Foundations for Populist Reforms.* Berkeley: University of California Press, 1991.

Shue, Henry. "Climate Dreaming: Negative Emissions, Risk Transfer, and Irreversibility." *Journal of Human Rights and the Environment* 8, no. 2 (2017): 203–16. DOI: 10.4337/jhre.2017.02.02.

Slaughter, Anne-Marie. *The New World Order.* Princeton: Princeton University Press, 2004.

Smith, Cyril S. *A History of Metallography.* Chicago: University of Chicago Press, 1960.

Song, Sonia Y., and Steven. S. Wildman. "Evolution of Strategy and Commercial Relationships for Social Media Platforms: The Case of YouTube." In *Handbook of Social Media Management,* edited by Mike Friedrichsen and Wolfgang

Muhl-Benninghaus, 619–32. Berlin and Heidelberg: Springer, 2013.

Srnicek, Nick. "The Challenges of Platform Capitalism: Understanding the Logic of a New Business Model." *Juncture* 23, no. 4 (2017): 254–57. DOI: 10.1111/newe.12023.

Steffen, W., A. Sanderdon, P.D. Tyson, J. Jäger, P.A. Matson, B. Moore III, F. Oldfield, K. Richardson, H.J. Schellhuber, B.L. Turner II, and R.J. Wasson. *Global Change and the Earth System: A Planet under Pressure.* Berlin: Springer 2005.

———. "Welcome to the Anthropocene." *Australasian Science* 37, no. 2 (2016): 28–29.

Steffen, Will, Wendy Broadgate, Lisa Deutsch, Owen Gaffney, and Cornelia Ludwig. "The Trajectory of the Anthropocene: The Great Acceleration." *The Anthropocene Review* 2, no. 1 (2015): 81–98. DOI: 10.1177/2053019614564785.

Stengers, Isabelle. *Catastrophic Times: Resisting the Coming Barbarism.* Luneburg: Open Humanities Press/meson press, 2015.

Stigler, Georg J. *The Organization of Industry.* Homewood: Irwin, 1968.

Stout, Margaret. "Competing Ontologies: A Primer for Public Administration." *Public Administration Review* 72, no. 3 (May–June 2012): 388–98. DOI: 10.1111/J.1540-6210.2011.02530.X.

Støvring, Kasper. "The Conservative Critique of the Enlightenment: The Limits of Social Engineering." *The European Legacy* 19, no. 3 (2014): 335–46. DOI: 10.1080/10848770.2014.898959.

Streeck, Wolfgang. *Buying Time.* London and New York: Verso, 2014.

Strogatz, Steven H. *Sync: The Emerging Science of Spontaneous Order.* New York: Theia, 2003.

Sullivan, Sian. "Green Capitalism, and the Cultural Poverty of Constructing Nature as Service-provider." *Radical Anthropology* 3 (2009): 18–27.

Sundararajan, Arun. *The Sharing Economy: The End of Employment and the Rise of Crowd-based Capitalism.* Cambridge: MIT Press, 2016.

Swyngedouw, Erik. "CO2 as Neoliberal Fetish: The love of Crisis and the Depoliticized Immuno-Biopolitics of Climate Change Governance." In *The SAGE Handbook of Neoliberalism,* edited by Damien Cahill, Melinda Cooper, Martijn Konings, and David Primrose, 295–307. London: Sage, 2018.

Tallacchini, MariaChiara. *Diritto per la Natura. Ecologia e Filosofia del Diritto.* Turin: Giappichelli Editore, 1996.

———. "A Legal Framework from Ecology." *Biodiversity and Conservation* 9, no. 8 (2000): 1085–98. DOI: 10.1023/A:1008926819.

Taylor, Mark C. *The Moment of Complexity: Emerging Network Culture.* Chicago: University of Chicago Press, 2001.

Teubner, Gunther. *Constitutional Fragments: Societal Constitutionalism and Globalization.* Oxford: Oxford University Press, 2012.

"The Philippines: Supreme Court Decision in *Minors Oposa V. Secretary of the Department of Environment and Natural Resources (DENR)* (Deforestation; Environmental Damage; Intergenerational Equity)." *International Legal Materials* 33, no. 1 (1994): 173–206. https://www.jstor.org/stable/20693894.

Thierer, Adam. *Permissionless Innovation: The Continuing Case for Comprehensive Technological Freedom.* Macon: Mercatus Center at George Mason University, 2016.

Thompson, E.P. "The Moral Economy of the English Crowd in the Eighteenth Century." *Past and Present* 50, no. 1 (1971): 76–136.

———. *Whigs and Hunters: The Origin of the Black Act.* 1st edition, reprinted with a new postscript. Harmondsworth: Penguin, 1975.

Thompson, William I. *Pacific Shift.* New York: Random House, 1986.

———, ed. *Gaia, A Way of Knowing: Political Implications of the New Biology.* Barrington: Lindisfarne Press, 1987.

"Tokyo Declaration on Global Commons." *Environmental Policy and Law* 29, no. 5 (1999): 249–50.

Tremmel, Joeng, ed. *Handbook of Intergenerational Justice.* Cheltenham: Edward Elgar, 2006.

Ummenhofer, Caroline C., and Gerald A. Meehl. "Extreme Weather and Climate Events with Ecological Relevance: A Review." *Philosophical Transactions of the Royal Society B: Biological Sciences* (2017): 1–13. DOI: 10.1098/rstb.2016.0135.

UNEP. *The Fifth Global Environment Outlook, GEO-5: Environment for the Future We Want.* DEW/1417/NA, 2012.

"User-driven Discontent." *MetaFilter,* August 26, 2010. http://www.metafilter.com/95152/Userdriven-discontent#3256046.

Vayrynen, Raimo. "Reforming the World Order: Multi- and Plurilateral Approaches." In *Global Governance in the 21st Century: Alternative Perspectives on World Order,* edited by Bjorn Hettne and Bertil Oden, 110–11. Gothenburg: Almqvist and Wiksell International, 2002.

Vera-Herrera, Ramon. "Ejercer Nuestros Saberes Es Su Mejor Protección." *Biodiversidad,* August 2016. http://www.biodiversidadla.org/index.php/layout/set/print/layout/set/print/Principal/Secciones/Documentos/Ejercer_nuestros_saberes_es_su_mejor_proteccion.

Villey, Michel. *La formation de la pensée juridique moderne.* Paris: PUF, 2003.

Vogler, John. "Global Commons Revisited: Global Commons Revisited." *Global Policy* 3, no. 1 (February 2012): 61–71. DOI: 10.1111/j.1758–5899.2011.00156.x.

Voigt, Christina. "The Principle of Sustainable Development. Integration and Ecological Integrity." In *Rule of Law for Nature: New Dimensions and Ideas in Environmental Law,* edited by Christina Voigt, 146–57. Cambridge: Cambridge University Press, 2013.

Wackernagel, Mathis, and William Rees. *Our Ecological Footprint: Reducing Human Impact on the Earth.* Philadelphia: New Society Publishers, 1998.

Wall, Derek. *Elinor Ostrom's Rules for Radicals: Cooperative Alternatives beyond Markets and States*. London: Pluto Press, 2017.

Wallach, Lori, and Michelle Sforza. *Whose Trade Organization? Corporate Globalization and the Erosion of Democracy*. Washington: Public Citizen, 1999.

Wallerstein, Immanuel. *Utopistics: Or, Historical Choices of the Twenty-first Century*. New York: The New Press, 1998.

Wapner, Paul, "Politics Beyond the State: Environmental Activism and World Civic Politics." *World Politics* 47, no. 3 (April 1995): 311–40. DOI: 10.1017/S0043887100016415.

Watts, Michael. "Political Ecology." In *A Companion to Economic Geography*, edited by Eric S. Sheppard and Trevor J. Barnes, 257–74. Blackwell Companions to Geography 2. Oxford: Blackwell, 2000.

Weber, Andreas. *Enlivenment: Towards a Fundamental Shift in the Concepts of Nature, Culture and Politics*. Berlin: Heinrich Boll Stiftung, 2013.

———. "Reality as Commons: A Poetics of Participation for the Anthropocene." In *Patterns of Commoning*, edited by David Bollier and Silke Helfrich, 369–91. Amherst: Off the Common Books, 2014.

———. *The Biology of Wonder: Aliveness, Feeling and the Metamorphosis of Science*. Gabriola Island: New Society Publishers, 2016.

Weinberger, David. *Small Pieces Loosely Joined: A Unified Theory of The Web*. Cambridge: Perseus Publishing, 2002.

Wendt, Alexander, "Why a World State Is Inevitable." *European Journal of International Relations* 9, no. 4 (2003): 491–542. DOI: 10.1177/135406610394001.

Weston, Burns, and David Bollier. *Green Governance: Ecological Survival, Human Rights and the Law of the Commons*. Cambridge: Cambridge University Press, 2013.

Whitaker, Mark D. *Ecological Revolution: The Political Origins of Environmental Degradation and the Environmental*

Origins of Axial Religions; China, Japan, Europe. Cologne: Lambert Academic Publishing, 2010.

White, Damian, Alan Rudy, and Brian Gareau. *Environments, Natures and Social Theory: Towards a Critical Hybridity.* London: Palgrave Macmillan, 2015.

Widlok, Thomas. *Anthropology and the Economy of Sharing.* New York: Routledge, 2017.

Wilson, David Sloan. *Does Altruism Exist? Culture, Genes and the Welfare of Others.* New Haven: Yale University Press, 2015.

Winters, Jeffrey A. *Oligarchy.* Cambridge: Wiley Online Library, 2011.

Wood, Ellen Meiksins. "Modernity, Postmodernity or Capitalism?" *Review of International Political Economy* 4, no. 3 (1997): 539–60. DOI: 10.1080/096922997347742.

Wong, Janis, and Tristan Henderson. "The Right to Data Portability in Practice: Exploring the Implications of the Technologically Neutral GDPR." *International Data Privacy Law* 9, no. 3 (2019): 173–91

World Ocean Review. *The Future of Fish: The Fisheries of the Future.* Maribus, 2013.

Worster, Donald. *Nature's Economy: The Roots of Ecology.* 2nd edition. Cambridge: Cambridge University Press, 1994.

Wright, Angus Lindsay. *To Inherit the Earth: The Landless Movement and the Struggle for a New Brazil.* Oakland: Food First Books, 2003.

Youatt, Rafi. "Anthropocentrism and the Politics of the Living." In *Reflections on the Posthuman in International Relations: The Anthropocene, Security and Ecology,* edited by Clara Eroukhmanoff and Matt Harker, 39–49. Bristol, England: E-International Relations, 2017.

Young, Oran. *The Institutional Dimensions of Environmental Change.* Cambridge: MIT Press, 2002.

Zhang, Xiaoquan, and Fen Zhu. "Intrinsic Motivation of Open Content Contributors: The Case of Wikipedia." *Workshop on Information Systems and Economics* 10 (January 2006): 4.

Made in the USA
Middletown, DE
23 October 2020